UNDERDEVELOPED EUROPE:

Studies in Core-Periphery Relations

HARVESTER STUDIES IN DEVELOPMENT
*in association with the Institute of Development Studies,
University of Sussex*

1. UNDERDEVELOPED EUROPE: STUDIES IN CORE-PERIPHERY RELATIONS
Dudley Seers, Bernard Schaffer and Marja-Liisa Kiljunen (eds.)

2. TRANSNATIONAL CAPITALISM AND NATIONAL DEVELOPMENT
José Villamil (ed.)

UNDERDEVELOPED EUROPE:

Studies in Core-Periphery Relations

EDITED BY
DUDLEY SEERS,
BERNARD SCHAFFER,
MARJA-LIISA KILJUNEN

Institute of Development Studies
at the University of Sussex

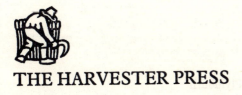

THE HARVESTER PRESS

First published in 1979 by
THE HARVESTER PRESS LIMITED
Publisher: John Spiers
2 Stanford Terrace, Hassocks, Sussex

© 1979 The Institute of Development Studies

British Library Cataloguing in Publication Data
Underdeveloped Europe.
  1. Europe – Foreign economic relations
I. Seers, Dudley II. Schaffer, Bernard
III. Kiljunen, Marja-Liisa IV. Institute
of Development Studies
382.1'094   HF1531

ISBN 0–85527–524–3

Printed in Great Britain by
Latimer Trend & Company Ltd Plymouth

CONTENTS

LIST OF TABLES

PREFACE

This collection was originally prepared for a workshop at IDS, planned in collaboration with François Duchêne, Director of the Centre for Contemporary European Studies at the University of Sussex. Jointly sponsored by the two institutions, it was partially financed by the Nuffield Foundation and the EEC. The workshop is envisaged as forming the basis of a research group within the European Association of Development Institutes. After discussion at the workshop (24–6 November 1977), the papers were revised for this publication.

We must also thank those who took part in the Sussex workshop, but did not contribute papers to this volume. In particular, Ivo Baučić (Centre for Migration Studies, Yugoslavia) and Osvaldo Sunkel (IDS) contributed background papers; Richard Batley, Manfred Bienefeld, Robin Murray and Percy Selwyn (IDS) wrote reports on the discussions which were useful to those revising and editing the papers, and also listed topics for further research. The following also took part: Stelios Arghyros (Adviser to the National Bank of Greece), David Bell (Centre for Contemporary European Studies, University of Sussex), Christian Heimpel (German Development Institute, West Berlin), Richard Herd (Economists Department, Foreign and Commonwealth Office, London), Peter Holmes (Arts and Social Studies Division, University of Sussex), José Molero (Estructura Econômica de España, Universidad Complutense de Madrid), Pedro Nuñez (Department of Economics, ICADE, Madrid), Sungur Savran (University of Istanbul, Turkey), Eduardo Suarez (Department of Economics, ICADE, Madrid), Franco Viciani (FAO, Rome).

We are particularly indebted to Madeline Rowe for what she did both in the period before the workshop and subsequently, when the typescripts had to be got ready for the printers, and to Jenny Lythell who handled all the administrative arrangements for the workshop. We are also in the debt of a number of secretaries at IDS and elsewhere who collaborated in the rapid and efficient preparation of the final typescript, especially Angela Kent and Angela Lee, as well as Audrey Blaker, Betty Rider and Joan Thomas. We would also like to express our appreciation of the contributions of Charles Zuber who drew the maps, and Ann Segrave for her editorial help throughout.

DS   BBS   LMK

NOTES ON CONTRIBUTORS

Editors

DUDLEY SEERS, Professorial Fellow and former Director of IDS, President of the European Association of Development Institutes (EADI). In the past he has worked *inter alia* in the Economic Commissions for Latin America and Africa. He has widely published on development issues.

BERNARD SCHAFFER, Professorial Fellow of IDS. He has worked formerly in the United Kingdom Treasury, Australia and Papua, New Guinea. He is currently working on housing and employment in the mid-West of Ireland as part of an international comparative project.

MARJA-LIISA KILJUNEN, Research Officer, IDS. Previous research on Southern Africa, particularly Namibia.

Contributors

JEREMY BOISSEVAIN, Professor of Social Anthropology, University of Amsterdam and a Visiting Fellow, Mediterranean Institute of Social Studies, Malta. He has published on local level politics, clientilism and tourism especially in connection with Malta and the Mediterranean.

JOHN BRYDEN, Head of Land Division, Highland and Islands Development Board. Previously he has done advisory and research work in the Caribbean.

RAYMOND CROTTY, one-time farmer, is now Research Fellow of IDS. Works also as an economic consultant with special interest in the economics of cattle in LDCs. Current research on social and economic history of Ireland.

MARY EVANGELINIDES, D. Phil. student, University of Sussex.

STUART HOLLAND, Lecturer in Economics, University of Sussex. In 1974-5 he was special adviser to the Minister of Overseas Development.

KIMMO KILJUNEN, D. Phil. student, University of Sussex. Published a book on the problems of LDCs in Finnish.

JUAN MUÑOZ, Professor of Economics at the University of Madrid, and Technical Adviser at the Centre for Latin-American Co-operation.

SUZANNE PAINE, Lecturer, Faculty of Economics, University of Cambridge and Fellow of Clare College, Cambridge.

SANTIAGO ROLDÁN, Professor of Economics and Dean of the Faculty of Economic Science and Enterprises at the University of Barcelona.

PERCY SELWYN, Fellow of IDS. Worked as Senior economic adviser in Colonial and Commonwealth Relations Offices and to the Lesotho and Mauritius Governments.

ANGEL SERRANO, Professor of Economics at the University of Madrid and Director of the Department of Economics, ICADE, Madrid. Research and publications on the Spanish economy.

RICHARD STANTON, Research Officer, IDS. He has worked for some years in IDS on international aspects of development before carrying out research in Ireland.

CONSTANTINE VAITSOS, Professorial Fellow of IDS. Long-time economic adviser to the Centre on TNCs of the UN. Worked also for the Secretariat of the Andean Pact.

JOSÉ J. VILLAMIL, Associate Professor, Graduate School of Planning, University of Puerto Rico and Visiting Fellow at IDS (1976 and 1977).

ROBERT WADE, Fellow of IDS. Research and publications on irrigation and rural development in India and Italy.

ABBREVIATIONS AND SYMBOLS

CMEA	Council for Mutual Economic Assistance
EEC, EC	European Economic Community or associated organs
EFTA	European Free Trade Association
FRG	Federal Republic of Germany (West Germany)
GATT	General Agreement on Tariffs and Trade
GDP	Gross Domestic Product
GDR	German Democratic Republic (East Germany)
GNP	Gross National Product
IBRD	International Bank for Reconstruction and Development (World Bank)
ILO	International Labour Organisation
IMF	International Monetary Fund
LDC	Less Developed Country
NATO	North Atlantic Treaty Organisation
OECD	Organisation for Economic Co-operation and Development
OEEC	Organisation for European Economic Co-operation
OPEC	Organisation of Petroleum Exporting Countries
R. & D.	Research and Development
TNC	Transnational Corporation
UN	United Nations
UNCTAD	United Nations Conference on Trade and Development
..	not available
—	zero or negligible
N	not applicable

INTRODUCTION

Dudley Seers

This book marks a new departure by enquiring whether one can apply in Europe some of the theoretical insights obtained from work in the field conventionally called 'development studies'.

This field is of course a wide one in terms of theoretical schools as well as continents. Those who work in it range from the Chicago School to Marxists.[1] Most use, however, some hierarchy of countries. At the top are the 'rich' or 'developed' or 'imperialist' or 'industrialised' – the countries of North America, Western Europe, Japan and Australasia. A convenient metaphor has been to describe these as the 'core' of the world system (some would say the 'centre'), the remainder as the 'periphery'. Between the two groups of countries are big differences in levels of income, structures of employment, rates of fertility and social conditions. In the hands of some, especially dependency theorists, this is not just a metaphor; it is shorthand for a set of structural relationships, in which the core countries are dominant. But the use of the terminology 'core and periphery' does not necessarily imply this: it covers a range of theoretical positions.

This perception of the world structure needs amending in two fundamental ways. In the first place, many of the countries of Europe normally classed as 'developed' and part of the core have in significant respects much in common with the world's periphery, especially with countries like Mexico. (To describe European countries as 'Underdeveloped' is certainly controversial if only because the epithet carries associations with the old-fashioned argument that those so described need to model themselves on the 'developed' countries: still, it puts the basic point with brutal clarity.)

Secondly, there are geographical patterns. The core-periphery metaphor for the world as a whole is non-geographical: the countries usually considered the core of the world system are mostly to be found on both sides of the North Atlantic, but theoretically they could be scattered among the various continents. In Western Europe, however, the countries which are the more advanced (economically, politically, socially) are grouped together in the centre, and the others lie to the South and West, forming a partial ring, a periphery in a much more literal sense (Clark, *et al.*, 1969). Are there other geographical areas in which similar patterns can be found? One that immediately springs to mind is the northern part of the Western hemisphere – where the core, the US, is surrounded by a ring of countries with close economic, political and cultural ties – see the paper by José Villamil.

When we look at these two core-periphery systems (and they can be called systems), we notice some common and special features. One is that in both of them much labour has migrated towards the core. Another is that tourists tend to flow in the opposite direction, in great and growing numbers. As this book brings out, these two flows together have become for many countries on the periphery of an importance comparable to merchandise trade as a source of foreign exchange (though very much less studied by economists). This is not to say that they are the most important or fundamental linkages: after all, they only emerge after big differences in income levels have appeared, and to explain these we have to examine commercial, financial, technological, military and cultural asymmetries, such as can be found influencing countries further out from a core.

We can talk of a regional system in East Asia, centred on Japan, in which these human movements are not so significant. Japan exports technology, capital and industrial products all over the world in its attempt to make good deficiencies in natural resources, and – more recently – to find space for its pollutant industries. But there is clearly a concentration on the Western Pacific and South-East Asia. However, this is conspicuously different from the other two in that migration into Japan (which is culturally self-contained) is almost non-existent, and Japanese tourism tends to skip over its periphery in favour of Western Europe and the United States. So migration and tourism are clearly not essential parts of regional systems.

In Southern Africa on the other hand the migration aspect is the most striking symptom of economic dependence. Large fractions of the labour force of Mozambique, Botswana, Swaziland and especially Lesotho (earlier Tanzania, Zambia and Malawi) have been employed in the Republic of South Africa or Zimbabwe, which supply little capital or technology (see Wilson, 1976).

In the Middle East, migration is the central feature of the local system. Large proportions of the populations of countries lacking oil (such as North Yemen and Jordan) work in those possessing it, notably Saudi Arabia, Kuwait and Abu Dhabi (see Halliday, 1977). There is a certain flow of capital from the latter countries to the former through official channels, such as the Kuwait Fund for Arab Economic Development, and also to Egypt and Sudan. It is true that the desert oil producers cannot provide much technology, or tourism, or even capital equipment to be bought with their loans. They are not usually classed as developed countries, yet it might be useful to consider this a regional core-periphery model, too.[2]

We can see geographical core-periphery systems in the past as well as in other continents. All empires before the seventeenth century were also geographically compact and could be classed as such systems – such as the Persian, Greek and Roman Empires, based in part on captured slaves. Then after a phase of mostly worldwide, geographically fragmented, empires (Spanish, Portuguese, British, French, Dutch, etc.)[3] the original pattern has re-emerged, heralded by the transient German 'New Order in Europe' and Japanese 'Co-prosperity sphere' in Asia.

The Effects of Proximity

What are the special consequences of proximity that draw countries which are weaker in technological and other ways into hierarchical relationship with neighbours? One can only speculate tentatively on the reasons for this. Many of the most important linkages, especially in technology, are not greatly affected by location. If a government relies on imported equipment (including arms) and is politically dependent on the source, then this very largely determines its room to manoeuvre, however long the equipment's journey. Yet proximity to a core country transforms economic, political and cultural links. The closer a country is to those more industrialised, the lower the costs of transportation, the easier therefore for its exports to compete in neighbouring markets, but also the greater the danger that its industrialisation will be inhibited, especially if there are overland freight routes. Industries to make intermediate products, capital goods and arms are not easy to establish anyway, especially in a small country, and the difficulty is all the greater where distance does not provide a natural tariff barrier.

But there are also other, less well-known, effects of proximity in the modern world, which help bind a regional system. The dimensions of migration and tourism have been mentioned above as characteristic of many core-periphery systems. This is because passenger fares depend on the length of the journey. The cheapness of moving people a few hundred miles today opens up possibilities of labour migration to countries nearby. Though for many of the individuals concerned the migration is temporary, it can become for their country a permanent source of foreign exchange and employment. Emigrants not only regularly remit a fraction of their wages homewards, and spend them at home on regular visits, they bring capital back with them when they give up their work overseas. Thus migration relieves social pressures and provides valuable foreign exchange, but the foreign payments structure becomes adapted to it, and in time vulnerable to the labour and immigration policies of the government of the recipient country and to the level of economic activity there. Moreover, productive sectors are inhibited by the scarcity and cost of labour and the economy becomes dependent on foreign sources, even for necessities (especially food), financed in part by emigrants' remittances. Migration is also debilitating: it deprives the country from which it comes of skills and initiative, especially since a substantial fraction of migrants settle overseas. The greater expertise and capital of the returning migrant may help local industrialisation. But on balance he may raise dependence on imports by spreading foreign consumption styles. Moreover, he acts as vector for foreign attitudes to work, political perceptions, etc., which may in various senses be locally inappropriate.[4]

Another way in which the cheapness of passenger transport makes employment and foreign exchange dependent on economic activity and policies in other countries is to open them to mass tourism. This too has side effects on the local economy. Work in hotels may attract labour from other sectors, especially agriculture, thus affecting production. The policies of the tourist sector, including employment practices, are – like its organisation and architecture – in a degree based on foreign models, since many of its establishments, especially the bigger hotels, are usually foreign-controlled. The pace and type of hotel construction are determined largely outside the country. And as with migration, not only is economic dependence increased directly, but also indirectly through cultural effects on consumption styles and political attitudes.[5] The life-style of tourists reminds the natives of that of the core.

A country heavily dependent on migration and tourism finds other and more permanent constraints on its freedom of action; especially far-reaching political change. It cannot exercise effective control on the outflow of foreign exchange or the inflow of foreign agents. Policy is also affected by fear of alarming or offending tourists or losing the goodwill of governments of countries receiving migrant workers. Economic activity is especially sensitive to fluctuations in 'confidence' i.e. the extent to which foreign bankers, investors and traders approve of the policies of the government concerned, which in turn reflects in part the way the media report those policies. A decline in 'confidence' need not be due to the conscious decision of any government elsewhere to punish the country concerned: through thousands of private decisions, receipts of foreign exchange are automatically held up and payments expedited. Emigrants withhold remittances and remain abroad; tourists stay away and retired people leave; hotel construction ceases. These responses are more rapid and greater than any decline in merchandise exports in a similar political situation, unless there is an international embargo. Other more customary responses occur. Suppliers' credit becomes more difficult to obtain, foreign investment falls, domestic capital is exported and banks withhold loans. In the case of aided countries, aid agencies cut off help. So exchange reserves tend to fall, leading to devaluation of the currency and import restrictions, aggravating price rises, shortages and unemployment, and justifying and reinforcing the deterioration in 'confidence'. Deflationary policies are required by the IMF, as a condition of financial rescue. The political strains generated can then be used by forces inside and outside a government to press for the abandonment of social change.[6]

As I pointed out above, in the long term, no doubt, migration and tourism are less important basically than dependence on trade and investment which are more customarily studied, but in the short term, they can be a more powerful influence on policy, especially in checking egalitarian change.

There are also non-economic consequences of proximity. A traditional one is military vulnerability. Although the general military importance of distance may have been declining in the long term as the loads and range of aircraft have increased, and as missiles have displaced them, limits to the feasibility of invasion are still set by factors such as aircraft range and the time taken by aircraft carriers and other ships to reach a target area.

Military staffs are still very interested in whether hostile governments could establish bases in a neighbouring territory, especially one with a common land frontier. This would raise the cost of a given level of military security. It would diminish the warning time of the approach of bombers or missiles; and it would increase dangers of a surprise invasion, infiltration by guerillas or the illegal importation of arms. Even not being able to make military use of the country next door may raise serious strategic problems.[7] Economically powerful states have therefore the incentive as well as the means to keep neighbours at least neutral.

They can also exert cultural pressures. If neighbouring countries do not actually share the same language, at least they are likely to belong to the same linguistic group (e.g. Latin-based) so that communication is easy. It is also frequent. Regular face-to-face contacts, work and social relations may be customary near a common frontier, especially if this cuts across an ethnic or linguistic group, with frequent intermarriage. In various professions (including politics), meetings and conferences with people from nearby countries are commonplace. Techniques, attitudes and values are easily diffused to weaker neighbours.

In the world of today, diffusion is especially easy. Telephone conversations between neighbours are inexpensive. Newspapers are cheaper and more up to date, if bought close to the printing works.

Moreover, distance determines the effectiveness of radio broadcasts. There are limits of a few hundred kilometres to FM and medium-wave transmissions, the types normally received by domestic sets. The range is even less for television transmitters (though this depends very much on the terrain): there are also now often links between TV systems of neighbouring countries. (It is true that foreign broadcasts can be 'jammed' but if this is on an effective scale, it is costly and difficult to conceal). Economic strength provides the resources for developing cultural industries, such as film and book production, that have export markets in neighbours with a common culture and, especially, a common language.

Does a small, relatively unindustrialised country on the 'periphery' gain from belonging to a system, the 'core' of which consists of countries technically more advanced? It may do so in the narrow sense that its income is likely to be higher than it would otherwise be, but at the cost of structural dependence; proximity brings dangers of subjection to economic, military and cultural hegemony.

Dualism

There is a possible application of another part of core-periphery theory. One feature of this is that part of each peripheral country is closely linked to core. In the case of Europe, as my paper brings out, the advanced parts are those nearest to, in some cases touching, the core. So one could describe the periphery not as a group of countries but as a geographical space, stretching across frontiers. This not only raises fascinating questions – e.g. about the significance of state power. It also suggests another dimension for development studies. 'Dualism' of course is a well-known concept in this field, but it is usually also treated as a metaphor, in this case for what is seen as primarily urban-rural or industrial-agricultural or modern-traditional contrasts, and the spatial arrangement itself is tacitly considered irrelevant.[8]

Inside all countries there is in a sense a national core, an area which is more dynamic economically and exercises political and cultural sway over the more backward areas, primarily rural, linked to it of course even more closely than proximate countries. It receives internal migrants and generates much of the internal tourism.

If a country is itself peripheral, this dualism is aggravated by the links which develop between the continental and national cores. TNCs from core countries tend to establish their subsidiaries in the most developed areas, because of infrastructure, access to markets, etc. The subsidiaries may well displace small-scale industries of the national periphery. Governments of the leading core countries tend to support politically congenial national parties (and to try to stop drastic change). The national core relays to the national periphery ideologies, tastes and fashions imported from abroad – most obviously when its transmitters send out imported television programmes, or its newspapers carry agency material. It can also act as a stage in the emigration process, with migrants coming to the national core and later proceeding (or releasing others to proceed) abroad.

Peripheral governments may be particularly concerned about regional problems. This is partly because of the tendency to dualism, but it is also because citizens of peripheral countries feel immediate understanding of the problems of peripheral regions.

Development Studies and Europe

This way of looking at Western Europe opens the door to the application of 'development' studies. What parallels can we see between the problems of the countries and areas in the periphery of Western Europe and those to be found in the periphery, considered worldwide? And what similarities between the relations linking the core and periphery of Western Europe and those linking the core and periphery of the world as a whole?

If there are significant parallels and similarities, this approach to Western Europe carries important implications. There would be a presumption that the social sciences of Western Europe would gain from an infusion of theories developed in the 'Third World', again especially Latin America. The economics taught in Western Europe, for example, even in its periphery, ignores hierarchical relationships between countries, or within them. Further, the experience of the 'Third World' could well be relevant in some respects to some problems of the European periphery – for example in dealing with the governments and corporations of the core – if we are prepared to study them.[9]

There happens to be a particular reason in the late 1970s for applying this approach in Europe. The discussion of the possible further enlargement of the European Economic Community will come to a head in the near future. All three governments which have applied for membership (those of Greece, Portugal and Spain) lie on the periphery of Europe; so do possible future applicants such as Turkey and Cyprus. The incorporation of these countries into a predominantly core organisation raises structural issues that are familiar in the development field. If unemployment in them were not so great and so chronic, if they had no severely depressed regions, if wages were as high in the candidates as in the core of Europe, if their economies were diversified and political systems stable, enlargement would not raise the profound difficulties it does for the existing members of EEC. In various chapters of this book – especially the one on Portugal candidates – the issue of the relation between 'underdevelopment' and enlargement recurs.

There will naturally be resistance to various consequences of applying the concept of 'periphery' to countries in Europe.[10] 'Third World' strategists will deplore the blurring of the distinction between 'developed' and 'developing' countries. Bureaucrats in international organisations and aid agencies whose practices reflect this distinction will find it hard to adjust to a more complex world model. Academics, especially conventional economists, will want to ignore an approach that requires them to reshape their lectures and textbooks. Some ideologists of the Left will resist the implication that social revolution is not a sufficient condition for solving all inequalities, either international or national. A number of liberals will also, for different reasons, find the emphasis on geographical and cultural determinants unsympathetic, and more particularly the implicit endorsement of nationalism. Many Europeans will, for historical reasons, bridle at being classed for any purpose with Africans, Asians and Latin Americans.

All this need not dissuade us from trying to construct maps that would help those exploring new territory in Europe.

Notes

1 Since Marxists and the Chicago School have a great deal in common, perhaps a more appropriate way of describing the range is from neo-classical economists of various schools to structuralists, including *dependencia* theorists.
2 There are also other systems. Eastern Europe is described in my chapter. And there are many smaller ones. For example, Paraguay and Bolivia are in a sense in a peripheral relation with Argentina, Mali with Senegal.
3 In the Austrian and Russian Empires, however, the colonies adjoined the metropolis, or core.
4 Returning migrants often enter service occupations, e.g. using their capital to buy shops, rather than manufacturing. For a full analysis of the social implications of migration and extensive references see Böhning (1976).
5 I shall not go into the social costs of migration or tourism. Both disrupt local, in particular rural, culture, and both, especially migration, damage family life.
6 This whole chain of events is well illustrated by what happened in Portugal following the quasi-revolution of April 1974. See the chapter by Stuart Holland.
7 Experienced by the British Government when it could not make use of Irish ports during the 1939–45 war, to defend the Western approaches.
8 Economic geography, of course, does not ignore space, but this has remained a subject somewhat apart – symptomised by lack of communication between 'physical' and 'macro-economic' planning offices.
9 One such study is *IDS Communication 121* (1977).
10 These implications are discussed in Seers (1977).

References

Böhning, W. R. (1976), 'Future Demand for Migrant Workers in Western Europe', *World Employment Programme Research, Migration for Employment Project*, Working Paper No. 4, ILO, Geneva.

Clark, C., Wilson, Fiona, Bradley, J. (1969), 'Industrial Location and Economic Potential in Western Europe', *Regional Studies*, Vol. 3.

Halliday, F. (1977), 'Migration and the Labour Force in the Oil Producing States of the Middle East', *Economic Development and Cultural Change*, July 1977.

M.Phil. Faculty and Students (1977), 'North Sea Oil: The Application of Development Theories', *IDS Communication 121*.

Seers, D. (1977), 'Back to the Ivory Tower?' The Professionalisation of Development Studies and Their Extension to Europe, *IDS Bulletin*, 9, 2.

Wilson, F. (1976), 'International Migration in Southern Africa', *World Employment Programme Research, Migration for Employment Project*, Working Paper No. 3, ILO, Geneva.

I: GENERAL ISSUES

I

THE PERIPHERY OF EUROPE*

Dudley Seers

In this paper, I shall discuss the core-periphery system in Europe, both in terms of countries and as a spatial pattern.

Members of the Periphery

The first step is to seek a useful classification of countries that would give body to the core-periphery approach. What can be called 'Under-developed Europe'? There are two obvious candidates in Southern Europe: Portugal and Greece. They are both countries which are short of technological capacity and capital goods industries, and much of local manufacturing is foreign-owned. Militarily they are weak, and their governments have to cope with considerable political pressures from outside. The same is true of Spain and Yugoslavia, except that their industrial structures are relatively larger, better integrated and more nationally owned. But as Table 57 shows, even Spain's exports to West Germany consist in large part of food and raw materials, whereas she imports mostly manufactures and semis.

It is of course well known that these countries all demonstrate problems of dualism, that have both historical and international roots.[1] Salaried staff, some in modern industries, together with many in the bureaucracies, as well as self-employed professionals, enjoy living conditions comparable to those of their counterparts in richer countries (with the additional advantage of cheap domestic service). Some of the wage-earners are also relatively well off. On the other hand, the rural population (the majority) live at quite different levels, as can be seen from data on water and electricity connections (Table 49). Some regions show declining employment, depopulation and acute poverty. In housing qualities, as in birth-rates and life expectancy, however, their national averages are closer to those of the US and the big, industrialised centres of Europe than to even the more economically advanced countries of the Third World (see Table 50). On the other hand, their *per capita* income is distinctly nearer to many of the latter.

* I have benefitted from comments by a number of colleagues at IDS, and from research by Nezhat Sedaghat and Marja-Liisa Kiljunen.

Diagram One

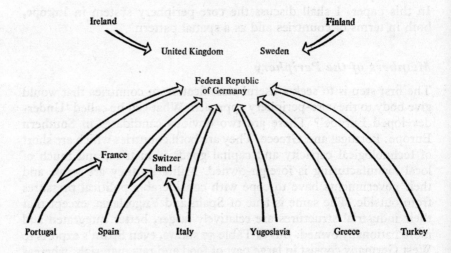

MAIN INTERNATIONAL FLOWS OF MIGRANT WORKERS WITHIN EUROPE
(1970)

Diagram Two

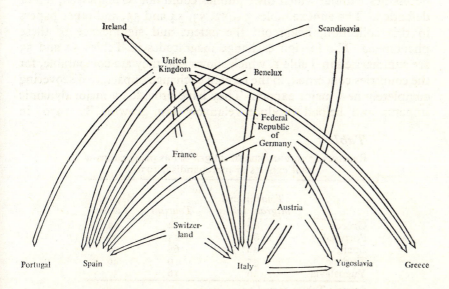

MAIN TOURIST FLOWS BETWEEN CORE AND PERIPHERY COUNTRIES WITHIN EUROPE (1970)

By the 1920s, Southern Europe had already fallen some way behind in economic and social terms. Social structures remained partially pre-industrial, and parliamentary institutions were weak and precarious. The area was the target for heavy political pressures from more powerful countries to the North, shown most conspicuously by Italo-German intervention in the Spanish Civil War and the subsequent German invasion of Yugoslavia and Greece.

During the last two decades, all of these countries have become heavily dependent on migration and/or tourism to purchase the basic necessities without which their publics could not be employed, fed or defended.[2] The annexe tables 51, 52, 53, 54 and 55, and other papers in this collection, bring out the extent and significance of these phenomena. The foreign exchange magnitudes in Tables 52 and 53 are summarised in Table 1, which shows that they are comparable, for the countries concerned, in the foreign exchange impact, to discovering completely new major exports. They have provided a major dynamic impetus and helped produce relatively fast growth. By 1970, in

Table 1

Receipts from tourism and migration as proportions of
total exports of merchandise, 1970

	(%)		
	Tourism and migrant labour	*Tourism*	*Migrant labour*
Greece	86	32	54
Portugal	80	25	55
Spain	88	68	20
Turkey	55	9	46
Yugoslavia	46	16	30

Source: Tables 52 and 53.

Greece and Spain, as in Portugal, the combined total of emigrants' remittances and tourist receipts was comparable to the value of merchandise exports, and this total was equivalent to about half of the exports of Turkey and Yugoslavia (see Diagrams I and II).

It is true that, compared to many tropical countries, nationalism in Southern Europe has deeper cultural and political roots and (except for Yugoslavia and perhaps Spain), they enjoy greater ethnic and linguistic unity. But they too are politically and economically dependent on bigger and more industrialised countries – in their case on countries nearby. They are also subjected to strong cultural influences, such as imports of films and TV programmes (see Tables 4 and 5).

Lack of diversification and factor mobility, and the inability of governments to impose sacrifices on any class, are – as in 'developing' economics – revealed by price inflation, especially in response to shocks such as the oil price rise of 1973–4. In all these countries, prices more than doubled between 1970 and 1976 – see Table 2.[3] In all of them the big rise in foreign indebtedness since 1973 has brought about a situation in which debt service absorbed more than one-quarter of export receipts. In Spain the disbursed debt rose from $1·6 billion in 1973 to $4·8 billion in 1976. By 1975, debt service accounted for two-thirds the merchandise exports of Greece, and more than the whole of Turkish exports (IBRD, 1977).

There are two other somewhat similar cases to the west and north of Europe respectively: the Republic of Ireland, and Finland. Judging from housing quality and demographic data they are quite comparable (Tables 49 and 50). They are also each dependent on one neighbour closer to the continental landmass, Britain and Sweden respectively, by which they were for centuries ruled, and which provided land-owning aristocracies, whose remnants still remain. Both countries obtain from their big neighbours not merely the usual imports of equipment and technology, but also jobs and tourists (though tourism in Ireland has been affected by political troubles), and in addition they both demonstrate dualism (e.g. in housing quality) and cultural (including linguistic) dependence.

However, in most respects, Ireland is less autonomous. In Finland the main industries are nationally owned and there is a small but significant technological capacity. The currency is more independent (the Irish pound has closely followed the pound sterling) and price inflation has been faster (Table 2). Finland has never been a big net receiver on tourist account (Table 52). It also enjoys a higher *per capita* income (Table 50). Ireland's exports are mainly primary products (especially livestock products) and they go largely to Britain, whereas Finland's are more diversified in both commodity and destination (Table 57). It seems best to class Ireland with the countries of the Mediterranean periphery. It has proved similarly unable to cope with the oil price rise, external debt rising from $0·8 billion in 1973 to $2·3 billion in 1976 (IBRD, 1977).

Yet Finland, despite its high income is, as Kimmo Kiljunen's chapter shows, nevertheless structurally dependent on the core. Let us call it a semi-peripheral country.

There are other countries, neither geographically nor culturally strictly part of Europe, but showing the same pattern, depending on it for tourism and migration, as well as trade and technology, because of the cheapness of fares over what are still relatively short distances. I refer to Turkey, Cyprus, Tunisia, Algeria and Morocco.[4] These countries can be considered an outer periphery. It is true that they are less accessible to either military invasion or propaganda, and that Islamic culture and their languages protect them in some degree from foreign influences on patterns of consumption and on attitudes and

Table 2

European consumer price indices, 1970, 1973 and 1976, in order of price rises 1970–6

(1970 = 100)		
	1973	1976
Portugal	140	245
Turkey	149	242
Ireland	132	220
Britain	128	215
Spain	131	208
Greece	124	202
Italy	123	200
Finland	126	198
Denmark	123	170
France	120	167
Netherlands	125	165
Belgium	118	163
Norway	122	163
Sweden	122	162
Austria	120	153
Switzerland	124	147
West Germany	119	147
USA	114	147

Source: *International Financial Statistics*, Vol. XXX, No. 10, October 1977, IMF.

perceptions. But they rely more heavily than Spain does on trading primary products for manufactures (see Table 57 for Turkey's trade with West Germany). They are all dependent in some degree on migration and tourism. Indeed emigrants' remittances are even more important to Turkey's economy than they are to the other countries covered by Table 53. There is in each of them a modern sector where foreign economic and cultural influences, including the use of French or English are common, and social conditions much better than in the hinterland. Social and economic indicators (Tables 49 and 50) suggest that they have characteristics in common with some countries of Latin America.[5]

Members of the Core

There are two 'cores' to the European periphery – in the sense of suppliers of capital and technology; centres of political, military and cultural dominance; providers of tourists and absorbers of migration. These are the US and Central Europe. Although the latter is itself partly dependent on the former, in recent decades it has become in most of these dimensions the more important in relation to the European periphery. One exception is the military dimension. Western Europe still relies heavily on US armed forces and arms supplies (Table 3.) Another is the cultural area, the US being the predominant source of films and TV – Tables 4 and 5. I shall concentrate on Central Europe in this essay, which is about the European system, but we should not forget the United States connection.

West Germany, France, the Netherlands, Belgium, Switzerland,[6] Austria, Denmark, Norway and Sweden provide most of the tourists[7] and nearly all the jobs for migrants. They tend to draw workers from nearby countries – France from Portugal, Spain and Algeria; West Germany from the Balkans and Turkey; both from Italy (see Table 54). Tourism shows the same pattern (Table 51). These countries are also major exporters of capital, technology and equipment, and – some – of cultural artefacts (films, television programmes, newspapers, magazines, etc.). In all these respects, as the tables show, West Germany is the leading member of the core.

Culturally, the core is fairly homogeneous, sharing similar life styles, especially almost universal ownership of cars and the main household durables. Much the same consumer brands and architectural fashions can be found everywhere: a parachutist landing among the concrete blocks of an urban area in the core would probably take some time to recognise which city it was. There is a dense network of railways and motorways, and the horse is used only for sport.

Social and economic indicators (Tables 49 and 50) suggest social conditions like those of the US. In none of these countries are foreign exchange transactions controlled; they have single exchange rates which have appreciated against all other non-communist currencies (except the Japanese yen) since the Smithsonian Agreement of 1971. As Table 2 shows, in all of them the price inflation has been distinctly slower than for any countries of the periphery.

It is true that these countries too show regional inequalities – for example, Brittany and Corsica are somewhat less developed in most respects than Alsace-Lorraine or the Paris region (Table 6). But the contrasts are mild in comparison with those in the periphery.[8]

It is not so easy to classify Italy. It suffers from a well-known dualism between the North on the one hand and, on the other, the South, Sicily and Sardinia (see Table 6 again). The development of transportation and mass communications has brought these areas increasingly under the economic, political and cultural influence of the North, one symptom being the heavy migration of labour northwards (the resulting remittances covering their trade deficit – and very possibly an outflow of private capital, too).[9] Social conditions are on the whole worse than in most members of the core, as Tables 49 and 50 show: *per capita* income and birth-rates are closer to those of Greece. And foreign bankers' 'confidence' is by no means unimportant to Italian governments. This country also depends on tourism and is a net supplier of migrant labour to the core.

Table 3

Arms transfers of major suppliers from 1965–74, by recipient country
(millions current $US)

Recipient	Total	US	USSR	France	UK	Canada	FRG	Poland	All others
US	1,454	N	—	79	391	766	96	—	122
Austria	76	23	—	8	2	—	1	—	42
Belgium	383	181	—	34	10	—	151	—	6
Denmark	201	111	—	1	—	5	—	—	84
France	226	225	—	N	—	—	—	—	1
FRG	2,440	2,079	—	252	36	—	N	—	73
Luxembourg		1	—	—	—	—	—	—	—
Netherlands	537	233	—	94	18	102	69	—	21
Norway	350	237	—	7	22	19	35	—	30
Sweden	130	80	—	—	18	—	14	—	18
Switzerland	239	138	—	10	61	—	14	—	16
Finland	138	1	120	116	1	—	—	—	16
Italy	848	676	—	2	N	—	55	—	26
UK	1,278	1,231	—	—	—	—	19	—	—
Cyprus	20	—	18	—	—	—	—	—	2
Greece	1,230	1,082	—	42	—	—	97	—	9
Ireland	5	1	—	3	—	—	—	—	1
Malta		—	—	—	1	—	—	—	—
Portugal	248	31	—	136	1	—	35	—	45
Spain	609	464	—	99	2	15	11	—	18
Turkey	2,219	1,959	—	—	1	—	167	—	93
Yugoslavia	514	2	477	4	1	—	7	—	11

TABLE 3—cont.

Recipient \ Supplier	Total	US	USSR	France	UK	Canada	FRG	Poland	All others
USSR	1,725	—	N	—	—	—	—	995	730[1]
GDR	1,798	—	1,718	—	—	—	—	80	—
Czechoslovakia	1,127	—	1,087	—	—	—	—	40	—
Hungary	511	—	490	—	—	—	—	21	—
Poland	1,533	—	1,502	—	—	—	—	N	31[2]
Bulgaria	435	—	409	—	—	—	—	21	5[2]
Romania	473	—	468	—	—	—	—	—	5[3]
NATO	11,854	8,447	—	770	505	893	724	—	515
Warsaw Pact	7,602	—	5,674	—	—	—	—	1,157	771
OPEC	6,825	2,374	2,152	668	662	89	154	8	698

Source: US Arms Control and Disarmament Agency. World Military Expenditure and Arms Transfers. 1965-74 Publication 84. (1976).

Notes: none or negligible.
1 Czechoslovakia, 695 million.
2 Czechoslovakia.
3 People's Republic of China.

B

Table 4   Number of locally produced and origin of imported full-length feature films, 1972*

	Number locally produced	Number imported	Country of origin†					Next largest
			US	UK	France	FRG	Italy	
Austria	7	432	132	30	37	128	56	7 (USSR)
Denmark	18	270	130	40	20	15	25	..
FRG	85	290	102	35	46¹	N	52	8 (Japan)
Netherlands	5	358	113	61	51	43	57	7 (Sweden)
Norway	9	336	130	44	38	14	5	26 (Sweden)
Sweden²	19	290	119	40	19³	..	13	15 (Spain/Italy)
Switzerland	8	453	154	35	73	66	91	..
Finland	8	309	126	24	..	18	25	25 (USSR)
Italy	294	261	139	27	24	20	N	7 (Japan)
UK⁴	89	297	155	N	31	10	29	5 (Spain, Sweden, Switzerland)
Cyprus	1⁵	681	127	142	22	18	70	170 (Turkey)⁶
Greece	142	847	207	60	50	54	223	20 (USSR and Turkey)
Ireland	6	331	199	66	21	10	20	2 (Canada and USSR)
Portugal⁷	3	347	147	46	28	5	64	9 (Spain)
Spain	103	398	120	45	46	5	87	23 (Mexico)
Yugoslavia	24	244	57	18	33	8	51	18 (USSR)

TABLE 4—cont

	Number locally produced	Number imported	Country of origin†					Next largest
			US	UK	France	FRG	Italy	
USSR[8]	134	92	..	..	6	..	5	11 (N. Korea)
Czechoslovakia	35	142	13	..	14	..	10	28 (USSR)
Hungary	19	150	25	..	16	..	10	31 (USSR)
Poland	21	154	21	13	18	4	7	28 (USSR)
Bulgaria	17	150	..	..	..	..	..	46 (USSR)

Source: Compiled from UNESCO (1975) *World Communications*, a 200 country survey of press, radio, television, film, The UNESCO Press, Paris.

Notes:

* Detailed information for the rest of the European countries is not available in the source.
† In the case of co-productions country of origin is difficult to identify.

1 Out of these 25 French/Italian co-productions.
2 1971.
3 Out of these 10 French/Italian co-productions.
4 Over half of the features produced in recent years have been either fully or partly financed from US sources.
5 1973.
6 104 from Greece.
7 1970.
8 The socialist countries imported significant amounts of features from other socialist countries as well.

Table 5

Origin of TV series imported in selected countries, 1970

	Series as % of programme time	Imports as % of programme hours of series	(% of total imports) from US	UK	largest of remainder
Netherlands	21	72	56	38	6 (Belgium)
France	6	54	..	..	
FRG[1]	7	41	90	2	5 (France)
Sweden	2	96	55	34	7 (Denmark)
Switzerland[2]	9	97	26	12	20 (FRG)
Finland[3]	17	92	47	32	4 (FRG)
Italy[4]	4	49	60	20	10 (FRG)
UK[5] BBC	7	56	95	N	4 (Canada)
ITV	26	40	..	N	
Portugal	8	100	..	..	
Yugoslavia[6]	2	100	58	25	17 (France)

Source: Compiled from: Tapio Varis (1973), *International Inventory of Television Programme Structure and the Flow of TV Programmes between Nations.* Research Institute, University of Tampere. B research Reports.

Notes
1 1971. In the first two columns ARD (Deutsches Fernsehen) and ZDF (Zweites Deutsches Fernsehen) are combined. Breakdown figures are for ARD.
2 German language programme of SBC.
3 Finnish Broadcasting Company and commercial television are combined.
4 1968–9.
5 1971–2.
6 Television Beograd.

But in Italy these activities are less important to the balance of payments than in the other countries of Southern Europe. A much smaller proportion of its industrial structure is foreign-controlled, and it is a substantial manufacturer of equipment, steel, chemicals, etc. Its trade unions have reduced the gap between wages in the North and elsewhere, and have put pressure on public corporations (e.g. Alfa-Romeo) to locate new factories in the South. There are bodies (such as the *Cassa per il Mezzogiorno*) with special responsibilities for the underdeveloped regions. So social conditions are much better in Southern Italy than (say) Southern Portugal. Moreover, it is not intuitively obvious that Italy is as dependent in other economic respects, or in the cultural and political dimensions.

A question-mark also hangs over the classification of Britain. This is a country increasingly penetrated by foreign capital which has gained a big fraction of North Sea oil concessions, and by foreign goods, which have captured a large share of important domestic markets, especially for products with dynamic demand, such as electronic equipment. While Britain has been an importer of labour from the Caribbean and South Asia, as well as the Irish Republic and (though

Table 6

Regional *per capita* product differences in relation to national average[1] in some EEC members

Country	Year	(National average = 100) Poorest region or state		Richest region or state		Mini/Max ratio
West Germany	1974	Schleswig-Holstein	84	Hamburg	149	1·8
France	1970	Bretagne	81	Paris	139	1·7
Italy	1973	Calabria	55	Liguria	137	2·5
United Kingdom	1974	N. Ireland	74	South-east	117	1·6

Source: EC, 1977.

1 GDP at factor cost for Germany, market prices for other countries.

on a smaller scale) Southern Europe, it has been an exporter to the
United States and the 'old' Commonwealth. In the last few years
immigration has dried up, making it on balance a marginal exporter
(see Table 56). It is also now a net receiver of tourists (see Table 52).
Social conditions in Scotland, Wales and the South West are worse
than in most core countries. There are areas which live partly off
tourism and suffer from above-average unemployment and partial
depopulation. (From 1951 to 1975, the net emigration from Scotland
was 666 thousand, an annual average of 28 thousand, or rather over $\frac{1}{2}$
per cent of the population: about half have gone overseas, half to the
rest of the UK, predominantly Southern England). In both Scotland
and Wales political nationalism is powerful. But, even more than in
Italy, the fiscal system is strong enough (as in the countries of the
core) to prevent great social contrasts emerging between different
areas (see Tables 6, 49 and 50). Its average social conditions are not
noticeably different from those of a core country (despite a distinctly
lower average income).

However, Britain and Italy are both weak in government R. & D.
compared to other members of the core (see Table 7), and it is interesting that they both have shown more clearly than the remainder of
the EEC (with the exception of the Republic of Ireland) the characteristic symptoms of 'under-development' – chronic inflation and periodic
foreign exchange problems – especially since the shock of the price
rises in 1973–4 in oil and other commodities (see Tables 2 and 8). Of
the two, Britain is more similar to a country of the core. It is going to
seem increasingly similar, because the revenues from oil will – as in all
major oil producers – permit the symptoms of structural problems,
such as a weak exchange rate, to be suppressed. However, most indicators suggest, that for the present they should both be considered
'semi-peripheral', with Finland.

The Spatial Pattern

Map A shows the countries of the core and the periphery. The core
countries are not only so in the sense of being the centres of economic,
political and cultural power, but also in a strictly geographical sense.
Broadly speaking, they lie in the spatial centre, whereas the 'peripheral'
and 'semi-peripheral' countries (among which we include Finland)
jut out into the Mediterranean, the Atlantic and the Arctic. Norway,
which has only recently joined the core is an apparent exception, but
it is effectively a North Sea country, only a small fraction of the
population living on the Atlantic coast (small enough to be supported
by the remainder, especially since the exploitation of North Sea oil
started).

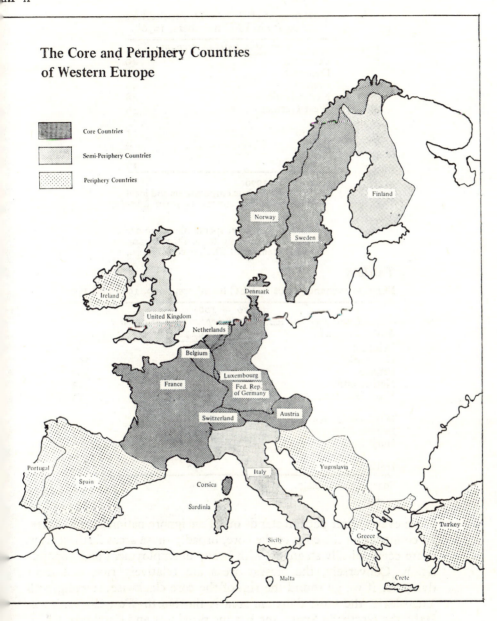

The Core and Periphery Countries of Western Europe

Core Countries

Semi-Periphery Countries

Periphery Countries

Finland

Norway

Sweden

Denmark

Ireland

United Kingdom

Netherlands

Belgium

Luxembourg

France

Fed. Rep. of Germany

Switzerland

Austria

Portugal

Spain

Italy

Yugoslavia

Corsica

Sardinia

Turkey

Sicily

Greece

Malta

Crete

Table 7

Government civil R. & D. expenditure *per capita* in EEC members, 1976[1]

European units of account	
Belgium	40
Denmark	38
France	40
Netherlands	48
West Germany	58
Britain*	21
Italy	9
Ireland	10

Source: EC, 1976.
1 Excludes public corporations and local authorities (except the German Länder).

* Britain, however, spends far more *per capita* on military R. & D. than any other member of EEC, except France.

Table 8

Relative exchange rates in EEC members, 1970, 1973 and 1976

	(1970 = 100) Local currency units per European unit of account	
Stable currencies	1973	1976*
Belgium	97	87
Denmark	101	101
France	100	103
Netherlands	96	93
West Germany	91	88
Weak currencies		
Britain	123	153
Italy	117	163
Ireland	123	153

Source: See Table 7.
* March.

An even clearer pattern stands out if we ignore national boundaries. In countries on the edge of the core, broadly those areas farthest from it are economically stagnant, with heavy unemployment and depopulation. Conversely, the closest areas are relatively rich and most dynamic. If we go round the rim of the core clockwise, starting with Yugoslavia, the most dynamic area is the North-West, Slovenia; in Italy, the North; in Spain, the Basque provinces and Catalonia, which lie to the North and North-East; in Britain, the South-East; in Finland, the South-West.

The pattern is brought out strikingly by Map B. The core areas form an incomplete egg, partially upside-down, with its centre just north of

Kassel in West Germany. (The missing segment is part of Eastern Europe which I shall discuss later.) The length of the longest axis is 2,700 km and its breadth 1,500. Such a strong pattern could hardly arise from a purely random process, and it is mute evidence of the influence of proximity.[10] It also casts some doubt on climatic theories of development, which would imply horizontal bands. Of course, too much attention should not be paid to the exact path of the boundary. Dynamic cities like Aberdeen are comparable to some that are inside the egg, which, on the other hand, contains several slums. (These consist, however, partly of migrants from the periphery.)

Broadly speaking, those living inside the egg are less likely to be working in agriculture or tourism, to be unemployed, to see their families broken by migration, or to receive a very low income, than those outside. Nearly all the big European transnational companies (including banks) have their headquarters inside, as well as most of the television studios, newspaper offices, book publishers, etc.

And generally, the closer to the centre of the egg, the greater the concentration of power. One could imagine a 'yolk', which would include Denmark, West Germany, the Benelux countries, Paris, the Lyon area, Switzerland and Lombardy.

Outside the egg, the pattern still broadly holds. In Ireland, the east coast is the more dynamic; in Turkey, the western provinces.[11] The picture is less clear in Greece and Portugal, perhaps because people and goods mostly move to the core by sea and air through Athens and Lisbon respectively (rather than overland via northern frontiers). But here too many of the poorest regions lie to the South, or in islands off to the South-east and South-west respectively. The same pattern also can be found farther afield: the poorest areas in North Africa are those nearest the Sahara.

In fact, as a generalisation the farther from the core a place is, the poorer it is likely to be,[12] the more dependent technologically and more likely to be catering for tourists and relying on the core to provide employment for its surplus labour. This pattern is so marked that we can describe it as systemic. A region which is remote may, however, still preserve more political and cultural autonomy than those closer to the cultural core of Europe.

The possibility of describing this European system in spatial terms raises the question: 'Do countries matter?' However, for many purposes – e.g. in discussing future membership of the EEC – it is necessary to conduct analysis at the national level. The nation-state remains a major factor, especially in rich countries with a considerable measure of homogeneity. In fact the European system can be analysed in both spatial and national terms, and they are not by any means mutually exclusive.

Eastern Europe

The egg in the metaphor of the European system is incomplete (see Map B again). What about the countries to the East of West Germany? Can one see a somewhat analogous system?

The economically most powerful is East Germany, which lies in fact very close to the Western European core. Not only does it export equipment and technology, as is typical for a core country; it employs migrant labour (though not in great quantities) from countries further east and is a net exporter of tourists to them. Its social conditions and average income are not much inferior to those of West Germany, at about the Austrian level (see Tables 49 and 50).

As within the Western European system, broadly the further a country is from Germany, the worse the social conditions of an East European country. The tables show strikingly that Czechoslovakia, Hungary and Poland can be considered (like Britain, Finland and Italy) intermediate between core and periphery, though the social conditions and income levels in Hungary and Poland are more similar to those of the periphery of Western Europe. Bulgaria and Romania are more clearly peripheral in economic structure, income levels and social conditions, as well as being more dependent on imported technology (mainly from East Germany),[13] though able to show greater cultural and political independence (especially Romania).

The same geographical pattern can be seen, with the western regions more highly developed than those further east – i.e. further from the German core. One could in fact complete the egg of Map B, which would bring into the core Bohemia, Silesia and what was formerly East Prussia as well as Estonia, Latvia and Lithuania.

So one can again see a system. Of course it is also part of the periphery of Russia,[14] which has common land frontiers with the countries concerned, and stands in somewhat the same relation to Eastern Europe as the US does to Western Europe. In particular it is overwhelmingly the chief supplier of arms (Table 3). The military and economic links are strong (through the Warsaw Pact and CMEA), and Russia has twice intervened militarily in the semi-periphery of Eastern Europe (Hungary, 1956 and Czechoslovakia, 1968). Russia exports energy and technology, but sends relatively few tourists and accepts very few migrants. Its cultural influence is also weak – indeed the more developed countries of Eastern Europe show clear signs of US cultural influences. Russian income levels and consumer technology are inferior to those of the US. So it is not fully able to act as a major core, though its population size alone, together with its resource base, and the fear in Eastern Europe of German expansion, enable it still to exert a dominant influence.

MAP B

The Regional Core of Europe

Note:
The 'semiperipheral' countries of Map A are those where very roughly half the population live inside the 'regional core',

Long-term Trends

A core-periphery system is of course no novelty in Europe, though earlier systems had different types of linkage and not always geographically the same core. For several centuries, the centre was somewhat similar to today, consisting of what is now France and Austria and German principalities. But then the pattern started to change in the sixteenth century. Spain and Portugal, later Britain, France and the Netherlands, became increasingly important as the various overseas empires were formed and the centre of gravity of Europe was displaced to the Atlantic coast. It returned to the European heartland in the last two decades with the growing industrial leadership of Germany, the collapse of the colonial empires and the contraction of European influence overseas. The economic (though not of course the political) precursor of the present system was Continental Europe in 1939–45. Germany was able to control effectively all of Southern Europe (except Portugal). The German government and its corporations harnessed the occupied and allied countries to the German war economy. Labour was imported from the periphery on a large scale: German armed forces also lived in it rather like tourists, making use of hotels. But the military importance of proximity, especially common land frontiers, was shown by the lack of success of the attempt to incorporate North Africa as well.

This system collapsed with the defeat of Germany, but something formally similar reappeared in the 1960s, with the revival of industrial output and a new phase of technological advance. The proximate causes of the recent explosion of migration and tourism have been a number of simultaneous trends. The core's fast growth had its origins in national efforts, with US aid, to make good wartime destruction (in what was in fact the cockpit of the war). This growth then became self-sustaining, with the pace of advance itself creating capital investment needs and also the resources for financing R. & D. expenditures and advertising campaigns, which stimulated further needs for investment and consumption.

In the quarter-century 1948–73, not merely did the core economies of Western Europe grow at more than 5 per cent a year, raising both wage rates and the demand for labour: the natural growth of their population of working age was only about ½ per cent, so they were able not only to absorb their own labour reserves (and a considerable number of refugees from Eastern Europe), but also much foreign labour.[15] In addition, while wage rates were rising, fares remained stable or fell, due to technical progress in both airplane design (including size) and ticket marketing.[16] 'Charter inclusive tours' became especially cheap and their volume rose many times. The very influx of foreign workers (especially those accompanied by families) increased investment requirements for housing and other social infrastructure.

Within the core, this cumulative economic expansion since the war, together with strong fiscal systems, has brought a great improvement in social conditions. Virtually the whole population of the core has incomes of over $1,000 *per capita*, i.e. well in the top half of the world income distribution.

The very rise in the consumption of the dense population of the core has in various ways stimulated the centrifugal tourism. The formidable pollution has damaged the natural environment of the core. Secondly, the cost of services has become very high. Thirdly, the modernisation of the cities of the core has partially destroyed their character, making the cities of the periphery more interesting. Moreover, the rising expectations of the labour force of the core, not only with respect to wages but also working conditions and job security, turned the attention of employers to migrant labour. European movements of tourists and labour accelerated to greater total volumes than ever before.[17]

In both France and West Germany, migrant labour in the 1970s has accounted for more than 10 per cent of the number of employed. This helped stimulate expansion in the periphery, where growth rates were in general slightly faster than in the core (see Table 50), though they appear to have been of limited benefit to the poorest areas and classes.

Still, in a sense, this system worked – until 1973. There were defects but they were not conspicuous. Few recognised that its continued expansion required infinite supplies of metals and energy. Nor were the environmental costs widely perceived. However, the resource problem has become increasingly apparent, with a fundamental decline in the bargaining strength of European governments, especially due to their dependence on imported oil, and pollution controls have also been increasing. The secular rate of economic growth could well be slow henceforward, even after the recovery from the recession that started in 1974. Attempts to accelerate to the previous pace might generate inflation at rates politically intolerable, especially in West Germany.

In addition, the post-war decline in passenger fares relative to wages was temporarily reversed, following the sharp increase in fuel costs, and the tourist boom has faltered.

Moreover, the recruitment of foreign workers has become both less necessary and dearer to organise. Immigration is being resisted more strongly by trade unions. The social infrastructure needed by immigrants is appearing expensive to governments which find financial resources chronically inadequate, especially since migrant labour is obtaining more 'rights', including the right to be joined by families.

Recipient governments had in fact, already, before the oil crisis, taken steps to check immigration, such as the Franco-Portugese *protocole* of 1971 which limited migration to 65,000 a year, but guaranteed these better welfare and training facilities. In 1972, regulation of immigrant workers in France was tightened and the *Gastarbeiterstop* was announced in West Germany in 1973.

The effects of these measures were reinforced by the recent recession, which caused many migrant workers (often the most vulnerable) to lose their jobs,[18] and led to further migration controls. In 1974, a 'temporary halt' was announced in France to all immigration (and continues to operate, with exceptions for badly-needed workers), and in 1977, unemployed workers on public assistance were offered 10,000 francs (with extra payments for dependants eligible for work) if they gave up rights to social benefits and left France. In Switzerland, a policy of reducing the immigrant labour force was adopted in 1975, following a referendum.

Table 54 shows the dramatic decline in the rates of immigration between 1970 and 1975 (though less so in the case of Italians, who could not be excluded from other countries of the EEC). Several countries of the periphery have experienced a net immigration of labour, and unemployment rates have risen to over 10 per cent. Yet migration on the old scale is unlikely to be resumed,[19] especially in view of the long-term weakness of the labour-intensive industries in which migrants tend to congregate (Hiemenz and Schatz, 1976).

However, the *stock* of migrant workers in the core has not fallen greatly – thus in 1975 it was still at or above the 1970 level (Table 55). Core economies have become partly dependent on them, especially to do jobs which few native workers would take on. So emigrant remittances have remained at a high level, though they have been affected by the growing tendency for family dependants to arrive.

The Relevance of Development Studies

Enough has been said, perhaps, to indicate that core-periphery analysis yields insights into the problems which now face Europe with the slowing down of growth and the halt to net migration.

Whether the peripheral countries of this continent can usefully be called 'developing' is a moot point. In terms of *per capita* income, or even the extent and nature of poverty, they are clearly far distant from, say, Bangladesh (though not from Argentina).[20] Their fiscal systems, though not as strong as those of the core, are capable of providing more or less comprehensive welfare services, even if the volume of job opportunities is not adequate. Their economic structures are more diversified and their administrative systems arguably less incompetent. They have cultures rooted in long national histories without significant foreign settlement, importation of slaves, etc. – in contrast to Africa and Latin America, especially. But in terms of technology and political power, they are clearly qualitatively different from the United States – or from Japan or West Germany.

However, 'developing countries' is hardly a useful category now, anyway. A more pertinent question is whether the body of theory on development is more relevant to European countries, especially in the periphery, than conventional social science theory (e.g. naïve forms of neo-classical economics) developed in and for dominant countries, taking for granted their structural characteristics and interest in free trade.[21]

We can also expect the rich experience of governments of Latin America, Africa and Asia, especially Latin America, to be relevant to the crisis the periphery now faces. One conclusion which can be drawn from this experience is that economic growth *per se* may do little to relieve social problems, which it can in fact aggravate. The criterion for judging policy is not therefore whether it will accelerate growth, but rather structural change, especially reduction of regional inequalities.

Another lesson is that it is dangerous to treat symptoms as if they were basic problems. Thus, it is clear that inflation in the periphery is due to structural causes; it would be too much of a coincidence to believe that all the finance ministers of the periphery were irresponsible, but none of their counterparts of the core (see Table 2). It follows that purely financial policies are not likely to be effective even in the short term.

Thirdly, almost any social scientist of the Third World recognises that nationalism, is, on the whole, a constructive force for peripheral countries, indeed necessary for the preservation of a degree of economic, political and cultural autonomy (not necessarily autarchy). Some governments have learned to use, in political negotiations, whatever bargaining instruments were available and to be selective in welcoming foreign capital and technology, as Japan did in the period 1900–60. The government of Venezuela has been more successful than that of Britain in getting a grip on the pace and pattern of oil development.[22]

Perhaps the national interests of members of the periphery lie, on many issues, especially *vis à vis* the TNCs, rather with 'Group of 77' than with the core of Europe. If their delegations nearly always vote with the latter (in Group B at UNCTAD, for example), this must be attributed partly to a cultural lag and partly perhaps to feelings of ethnic solidarity. (The analogy at the national level is the reluctance of many professional associations in Britain and other 'developed' countries to join trade union federations – a reluctance which has gradually disappeared as the distinction between manual and non-manual workers has partially lost its significance in terms of both income and political power.)

The field of development studies carries also implications for future national strategy in dealing with the TNCs. This may raise important issues in the European periphery. Instead of labour moving to where capital is available, capital may increasingly flow to where labour is less organised and less dear (especially when fringe benefits are taken into account).[23] Often parts of a manufacturing process can be carried out abroad, reducing congestion and pollution in the core. This provides the receiving country with the foreign exchange to import from the core more skill- and capital-intensive products. The trade unions of the core can and do oppose the immigration of labour: they cannot stop the emigration of capital.

The European periphery offers an export base that may appear to corporations better than one further afield. Although wages are higher, the labour force is more highly skilled. And while this area is politically less stable than the core, it may well seem safer than much of the rest of the world.

However, the paper by Suzanne Paine, based on a careful analysis of trends and surveys of managerial motivation, throws doubt on this possibility, which as experience elsewhere shows, may anyway not add greatly (on balance) to foreign exchange earnings, local technical capacity, employment or local incomes.

The government of a peripheral country that depends on foreign investment also loses some of its control of its own economy. It has to rely on the companies concerned for marketing the output. The destination of their exports (like the origin of their imports) is therefore partially outside state influence: so are their levels of investment, output and employment. And since a threat to foreign companies would become a threat to the jobs of their local employees, trade union officials lobby ministers on their behalf. Foreign capital also often reinforces internal dualism, flowing into cities, especially ports, rather than into the rural areas where it is most needed. *Internal* migration is then stimulated.

In any case, even if it accelerates economic growth, foreign investment is hardly likely to make as significant an impact on local labour markets as international migration did in the 1960s, especially since capital movements are highly sensitive to political changes. Yet the population of working age in the periphery continues to increase steadily.

There is no space here to analyse the political developments in other continents but the same combination – fast growth, growing dependence, dualism and heavy unemployment – has contributed to the spread of authoritarian regimes, especially in South America. The same danger exists throughout the European periphery (including, for this purpose, Italy).

The analysis above implies that the social sciences of Europe, especially in the periphery and semi-periphery, would benefit from drawing on those of the 'Third World', especially Latin America (which experiences somewhat similar problems): these would be more useful than the social sciences of the 'core' countries (e.g. US functionalism and neo-classical economics, or the variety of Marxism taught in Russia).

Enlargement of the EEC?

There is now much discussion of another possible solution to the problems of the periphery: membership of the EEC. Formal applications by the governments of Greece, Portugal and Spain are being considered. This would guarantee the right of migration into recipient countries (no doubt after a long transitional period) as well as providing a degree of political support for the *status quo* in the periphery, and opening up new sources of official and private capital. There is therefore an *a priori* expectation that it would benefit capitalists and workers who are linked with TNCs, and the professional class, including the state bureaucracy.[24]

However, against greater access to the markets of the core must be set the further opening up of their own markets to competition that would destroy many small businesses. It would be (eventually) impossible to close national markets again by tariffs, import quotas or exchange controls. (If a monetary union is achieved, devaluation will also be ruled out.) The loss of these policy instruments is potentially costly for countries with chronic payments problems – it has weighed heavily on Ireland and the quasi-peripheral members, Italy and Britain. In Portugal, which in this respect is not atypical of the group, a large fraction of the manufacturing labour force (notably in textiles and clothing) is employed in small firms which could hardly face the full competitive power of the giant corporations of the core, despite the difference in wage levels. EEC membership might lock a country like this into dependence on exporting labour. Moreover, it would involve increased reliance on European TNCs, with the associated problems previously discussed. Foreign political and cultural penetration[25] would increase, mainly into the national cores, reinforcing dualism.

Further polarisation of Europe could in principle be mitigated by a European Fiscal System – just as national dualism is restrained by redistributive taxation. In the EEC, however, fiscal arrangements are very weak and far from egalitarian. Expenditure by all Community Institutions in 1977 was 0·7 per cent of the aggregate gross produce of

EEC members, or less than 2 per cent of their total public expenditures (EC 1977). The effect was only about 1 per cent of what would be needed to eliminate regional and state disparities.[26] Its one clearly peripheral member, Ireland, does not seem to have benefitted greatly from membership.[27] Nor has Southern Italy.[28] A successful enlargement would involve at least much bigger resources for the Regional Fund, the Social Fund and the European Investment Bank (and lending policies by the Bank that took more account of social needs). But perhaps more fundamental fiscal arrangements are needed to institutionalise the transfer of incomes from the richer areas of the Community to the poorer – including Ireland and Italy.

Enlargement would also require a transformation of the Common Agricultural Policy (which in the view of many, is needed anyway) so that French and Italian farmers would move out of products – such as wine and olive oil – in which the new candidates for membership have considerable productive capacity. (The difficulties are demonstrated by the reservations by the EEC in respect of agricultural products in Association agreements, with many products subjected to quota.[29]) It would necessitate structural changes in the manufacturing sectors of the core to accommodate supplies of steel (from Spain), or textiles (from all three) etc. And it would imply enlarged capacity in equipment industries in the area to meet the consequential investment needs in both the existing nine and the three. In brief, what would be involved would be not merely a shift away from the EEC's *laissez-faire* ideology, but the planned creation of a new European system to replace one that had major flaws and anyway has largely ceased to operate. This means a European Development Plan covering the restructuring of all members, old and new. Otherwise, indeed, labour migration, which would eventually be both permitted and stimulated by the enlargement would be on a scale very hard for the core to accommodate. More important, the polarisation of Europe would not be corrected and might be increased. Capital might flow increasingly *to* the core.

The total population of Greece, Portugal and Spain was 51 million in 1970, about the same as France, or one-sixth of the total enlarged EEC of 1975. Their average income was $2,300, about 40 per cent of the French. So the cost of, in effect converting a group of welfare states into a welfare continent, especially over a long period, would not be implausible.[30] It would provide employment for the unemployed labour and factories in the core. Moreover, capital could be diverted to the task. Transfers of some $20 to $30 billion a year, or two to three per cent of the GDP of the core members of EEC, would have a dramatic effect.[31] This, moreover, could be built up to gradually. Much finance flows from Europe to Africa, Asia and Latin America in the form of investment. Indeed, policy in these respects might switch its emphasis to the periphery. Aid has been stimulated in part by humanitarian motives, including guilt feelings over colonial exploitation: in Britain and France especially, its geographical pattern suggests a lingering colonial influence. But the resources for continuing to play this role are more difficult to extract from economies which are strained by internal demands (especially for investment in new sources of energy). So the justification for aid has increasingly stressed the importance to the core of long-term world economic progress and therefore political stability. This line of argument would, however, point to a greater priority for using the limited resources available on the ramparts of Europe itself.

However, the necessary redistribution of income would be resisted as would the removal of immigration controls, especially if the rate of growth of the core did not pick up. From the point of view of the 'periphery', it would mean little if governmental obstacles to migration were replaced by fierce trade union and neighbourhood resistance. And even if the transfers on a scale adequate to eliminate poverty were guaranteed, would the permanent opening of the doors to foreign competition produce permanent economic and cultural dependence, involving in the end the alteration of national identity? Is that price too high? But would there be sufficient political basis for alternative strategies looking rather to the Soviet Union and other 'developing' areas, especially the Middle East, perhaps in a Mediterranean Alliance? Would the governments of the core tolerate such a development? Would the bureaucracies of the periphery be capable (or become capable) of implementing the radical internal strategies that would be the counterpart of more independent external policies?

A further enlargement of the EEC would mean a profound change in its nature. It started as essentially a core organisation, dominated by West Germany and France, small enough for an eventual federation to be conceivable. The entry of Britain, Denmark and the Irish Republic, i.e. the western extension, modified it, but not beyond recognition. A southward extension, by incorporating Portugal, Spain and Greece – and perhaps eventually Cyprus and Turkey – would transform it. It would be much less closely-knit and would include a number of governments with strong interests in correcting continental imbalances – and with the power to compel attention to these interests (e.g. by blocking the Commission's business – if the national power of veto survives further enlargement).

An immensely important choice is emerging for the core governments of Europe. Enlargement seems impossible: yet it simultaneously appears inevitable. The possible continental rationalisation of industrial and agricultural production, and the stability of an enlarged EEC would be attractive for core business. A policy of 'collective self-reliance' would strengthen European bargaining power, reduce dependence on the US and other outside powers, and lessen the risk of Europe being drawn into war.

Moreover, if the new candidates were blackballed, or admitted into an unreformed organisation, without the resources to develop the periphery, the tensions could lead to the emergence of highly national-ist governments led by Euro-communists. The same interaction of declining 'confidence' and economic activity that normally discourages radical policies could produce the opposite effect in some circum-stances.[32] It is true that the resultant governments may well stress social reform rather than revolution and national interest rather than international proletarian solidarity, but they might nonetheless lead to a partial detachment from the European system. They could well de-velop links with countries suffering from similar structural problems in the Third World (to use a terminology of diminishing relevance). Besides, core governments must be well aware that another result could well be closer political links between such governments and the Soviet Union, involving a partial encirclement of the core. Con-ceivably, one or two political shocks to the governments of the core countries will be needed before the continent is consolidated in a reformed EEC.

Where would the expansion of the EEC stop? Cyprus and Turkey are obviously potential candidates. Eastern Europe might also be co-opted in time. There are already signs of its penetration, by West German TNCs, especially through joint ventures,[33] and also by West German tourists. Many Eastern Europeans, especially Poles, work in West Germany as temporary migrants.

A further shift eastwards in the core in the future is not incon-ceivable, involving the consolidation of Europe as a whole, with the Rhine-Ruhr at its heart, under the leadership of an economically re-united Germany – i.e. the peaceful achievement of the German government's political and economic aims in the 1939–45 war, the 'new order in Europe'.

But the complete integration of Europe would put greater strain on the fiscal resources of the core, and could hardly take place until after Southern Europe had been digested. It is also likely to be inhibited by the dependence of Eastern and Western Europe on the Soviet Union and the US, respectively. Institutions such as the Warsaw Pact and NATO are not easily eliminated – they become centres of political power in their own right. The Soviet government, in particular, would perceive such a development as a serious threat. Yet neither the Soviet Union nor East Germany appear to have the capacity to keep Eastern Europe dependent indefinitely.

Any expansion of the EEC would have major political consequences in the world as a whole. Presumably, an enlarged EEC would not be very outward-looking. Redistributive systems inside European nations have been developed to some extent at the expense of international redistribution, and this might well also be true of the continent of Europe, if it set up its own fiscal system. As has been pointed out above, there is to some extent a choice. The more concessions that are made to Southern Europe, the fewer can be made to other continents (though in the long run one could imagine an enlarged Community stretching down to the Sahara, its natural and historical boundary). The effect of greater self-reliance in Europe could be to stimulate national and continental self-reliance elsewhere.[34]

Notes

1   Malta could be included in this analysis, except that it is too small to have problems of dualism (though even here, Gozo is conspicuously poorer than the main island and heavily dependent on it).
2   However, it would be borne in mind that there is a fairly high foreign exchange content to tourism, because of imported inputs (e.g. furnishings and even foodstuffs) and profit remittances.
3   It is interesting to note that before the oil crisis as well as after, price inflation tended to be faster in the periphery.
4   Cyprus (like Malta) is not discussed here, for lack of time and space, and is omitted from the text tables.
5   Senegal and the Ivory Coast also depend on European employment and tourism, though to a much lesser extent. Libya would no doubt belong to the group of North African dependencies but for its oil.
6   Switzerland is a net recipient of tourists, as is Austria, but it is the banking centre of the core.
7   There are also significant tourist expenditures by peripheral countries (see Table 52), mostly in the core. This, however, is qualitatively and quantitatively different: it is not mass tourism, but tourism of the élite.
8   Many of them have 'development' areas, which are given special government help of some kind, but their backwardness is relative – such an area in the core may well be richer than a modern district in (say) Portugal.
9   A dependent region cannot of course apply trade or exchange controls against other parts of the same country, or stop the outflow of capital.
10 If distance were all-important, one might expect a circle rather than an egg. Indeed, the precise shape is a matter of personal judgment – I could easily broaden the egg into a circle by extending it to cover the whole of the British Isles to the north-west and almost the whole of Italy to the south-east. This would produce anomalies, however. Ireland, the Highlands and islands of Scotland and central Wales hardly seem to be core areas; nor do Sardinia or Southern Italy (or parts of Albania). I am unable to rationalise the egg shape.
11 In Turkey the population per physician was less than 800 in the European provinces, including Istanbul; more than 10,000 in the group of provinces on the eastern border (Turkey, 1972).
12 A regression diagram shows that the income per head in provinces of the original six EEC members tends to be lower the further a province is from

Düsseldorf (which is close to the centre of the egg) with a fairly high degree of correlation (Biel *et al.*, 1972).

13   Albania shows figures comparable to a moderately prosperous Latin American country of about the same size, such as Costa Rica. However, it is not a member of the East European system. Nor is Yugoslavia, in most respects, except for arms supply (Table 3).

14   This periphery extends eastwards to the Pacific, encompassing the former Tsarist colonies. A distinctive feature of the Tsarist Empire, that all its colonies were geographically adjacent, explains the retention of the colonies in the Soviet Union.

15   In the nineteenth century, of course, the industrialisation of Britain was accompanied not by immigration but *emigration* on a large scale. The basic reasons were that the industrial and agricultural revolutions displaced many artisans, tenant farmers and smallholders, but the labour needs of industrial expansion were relatively small (as has been confirmed by recent experience in many other countries, industrial growth is usually matched by an almost comparable growth in productivity, and unless the industrial sector is large, little impact is made on the employment needs of a population growing at 2 per cent to 3 per cent a year). Moreover, there were still 'empty' colonies overseas then, so a British citizen could expect to raise his income by emigration.

16   Scheduled air fares fell (absolutely, not merely relatively) from 1950 to 1968 for nearly all journeys (Peters, 1969). Indeed, as late as 1973, they were still generally below 1950 levels.

17   The phenomena are also linked. The migrant labour requirements of *internal* tourism in the core is especially high. 18 per cent of the employees in West German hotels and restaurants in 1972 were migrants.

18   In France, unemployed migrants receiving public assistance rose from 34,000 in 1973 to over 100,000 in 1977 (Scharffenberger, 1977). This would amount to about 5 per cent, but fewer than half of unemployed migrant workers are eligible for public assistance.

19   See Böhning (1976). Böhning estimates that, between 1973 and 1976, employment of migrants in the original six members of the EEC (excluding Italy), plus Austria, Denmark and Switzerland, fell by 1·3 million, or nearly 25 per cent. It is expected to decline slowly henceforward.

20   It is however not really possible – although people do so – to estimate *per capita* incomes in most of Africa or Asia, because of the lack of data on many types of rural income in such countries, especially from non-agricultural activities. (Seers and Lipton, 1977.) Moreover, exchange rates are inappropriate deflators because of the lack of information on non-tradables such as services and rent, which are relatively dear in Europe. So published data convey a highly exaggerated impression of the gap between incomes in the Third World and those in Southern Europe.

21   See (IDS *Communication* 121, 1977) for a case study, which includes a discussion of what one means by 'development theory'.

22   (IDS *Communication* 121, 1977) Chapters IV and V.

23   The large potential for this is estimated in Hiemenz and Schatz (1977).

24   Similar alignments could be seen in discussions about regional integration in Latin America – and also in the British debate about entry into the EEC.

25   On the other hand, some regional separatists consider European integration a way of preserving local culture from national domination, and a nationalist, especially in a core country, might consider it a form of protection from domination by the United States – or the Soviet Union.

26 (EC 1977) Vol II, Chapter 14. This is because the bulk of expenditure is agricultural (not social or regional) with benefits mainly for relatively rich members (Belgium, Denmark and the Netherlands). One poor country (Ireland) has also gained somewhat, but there is only a very limited impact on the other countries needing aid (Britain and Italy). The loan operations (mainly through the European Investment Bank) have little grant element and small redistributive effect.

27 Unemployment there has grown to more than 10 per cent of the labour force as in some countries of the Southern periphery. This is partly due to the recession, of course, and to a decline in 'confidence' affecting tourism.

28 Robert Wade points out that capital grants to Southern farmers have been small; there has been no intervention to change the structure of land ownership; and price supports are of little help (Wade, 1977). See also his chapter in this book.

29 An additional problem would be the effects on other Mediterranean countries (see Heimpel, 1977).

30 The demographic balance in Europe between core and peripheral countries and the economic inequality are very different from the corresponding figures for the world core and world periphery.

31 Commission of the European Communities (1977). It would not be unreasonable to expect Switzerland, Austria, Norway and Sweden to contribute to this task.

32 The resultant strains may make political repression unavoidable, whatever the motives of the political leadership.

33 Michael Shanks cites as one of the reasons why the reunification of West and East Germany was becoming a possibility that 'at considerable cost, West German industry has bought its way back into the traditional economic hinterland of Eastern Europe and the Balkans. Anybody who has travelled recently in these countries can testify to the extent to which German businessmen have seized the opportunity.' (*The Times*, 9 August 1976.)

34 For a discussion of the world hierarchy of dependence, see Seers, 1976, a new version of which will appear as 'Patterns of Dependence' in José J. Villamil, *Transnational Capitalism and National Development*, Harvester, 1978. Most Western European countries are there described as 'semi-dependent'.

References

Biehl, D., Hussman, D., and Schnyder, S. (1972), 'Dur regionalen Einkommenverteilung in der Europäischen Wirtschaftsgemeinschaft', *Die Weltwirtschaft*, pp. 64–8.

Böhning, W. R. (1976), 'Future Demand for Migrant Workers in Western Europe', *World Employment Programme Research, Migration for Employment Project*, Working Paper No. 4, ILO.

Commission of the European Communities (1977), Report of the Study Group on the Role of Public Finance in European Integration, vols I–II.

Heimpel, C. (1977), 'The Co-operation of the EEC with Southern Europe', in German Marshall Fund of the United States and Fundaçao Calouste Gulbenkian, *Conferencia Internacional sobre Economia Portuguesa*.

Hiemenz, U. and Schatz, K-W. (1976), 'Transfer of Employment Opportunities as an Alternative to the International Migration of Workers: the Case of the

Federal Republic of Germany (I)', *World Employment Programme Research, Migration for Employment Project*, Working Paper No. 4, ILO, Geneva.

Hiemenz, U. and Schatz, K-W. (1977), 'Transfer of Employment Opportunities as an Alternative to the International Migration of Workers: The Case of Spain and Turkey vis-à-vis the Federal Republic of Germany' (II), *World Employment Programme Research, Migration for Employment Project*, Working Paper No. 9, ILO, Geneva.

IBRD (1977), *World Debt Tables*, External Public Debt of Developing Countries, Vols I-II and Supplements 1-6.

M. Phil. Faculty and Students (1977), 'North Sea Oil; The Application of Development Theories', *IDS Communication 121*.

Peters, M. (1969), *International Tourism*, Hutchinson, London.

Scharffenberger, G. (1977), 'International Labour Migration and Development: The case of Senegalese Workers in France', M.Phil. dissertation, Sussex University, (unpublished).

Seers, D. (1976), 'A New Look at the Three World Classification', *IDS Bulletin*, 7, 4.

Seers, D. (1977), 'Urban bias – Seers versus Lipton', *IDS Discussion paper*, 116.

Statistical Office of the European Communities (1976), *Public Expenditure on Research and Development 1974-1976*.

Turkey (1972), *Statistical Pocketbook*.

Wade, R. (1977), 'Policies and Politics of Dualism: The Italian Case', *IDS Discussion Paper*, 106.

2

SOME THOUGHTS ON CORES AND PERIPHERIES*

Percy Selwyn

In this note, I raise a number of general issues. First, how do core-periphery relations start or persist? Secondly, what are the characteristics of the periphery? And lastly, what is the future of core-periphery relations – and in particular, what is the possible scope of government action in the periphery? Is this affected by whether or not the peripheral area constitutes a separate country?

How do Core–periphery Relations Start or Persist?

Uneven development is a virtually universal feature of all societies, other than the poorest. This is confirmed by a great deal of empirical data. As far as uneven development within countries is concerned (leading to what is frequently referred to as regional inequality) possibly the best known study is that by Williamson (1965). The uneven polarisation of development between countries or internationally defined regions is the subject matter of much of the development literature of the past thirty years.

We see core-periphery relations inside country borders or transcending them. Moreover, as several of the papers point out, all these core-periphery relations form part of a world core-periphery system, with greater or lesser degrees of polarisation around the American, West European and Japanese economies.

But these systems of *spatial* inequality must be seen in context. They coexist with systems of *social* inequality which may be defined in terms of class, occupation or ethnic group. Thus in Southern Africa there is spatial inequality – that is, development is polarised around the Witwatersrand region. But there are also extremes of social inequality, which exist irrespective of location. South Africa is indeed an extreme case, but serves to illustrate far more general situations.

I have summarised elsewhere various views on the significance of these core-periphery systems, especially in so far as small mainly peripheral countries are concerned (Selwyn 1975, Chapter 1). But how do they come about? There are several possible interpretations.

* My thanks to Bernard Schaffer for helpful comment on an earlier draft.

The level of costs may be seen as the central factor in the polarisation of development. The argument, which derives from Weber (1929) and later writers, suggests that economic activity will be located at the point of least cost. If there is a concentrated market for any reason, those activities where there is a locational advantage in proximity to markets will be encouraged. With economies of scale, such activities will become competitive over a wider area. The growth of a body of economic activity will create external economies – the economies of aggregation – which will lead to a cumulative process of localised growth. Places where such polarisation occurs will also be favourable to innovation (Friedmann, 1972) whereas the forces making for innovation in non-core or peripheral areas will be weak.

It has been argued from this (Murray, 1972) that such uneven development is a reflection of the capitalist system, since 'least cost' as a criterion for location is characteristic of a market economy. Moreover, in a system dominated by large multi-national enterprises, such enterprises will have the power both to control the surpluses arising from activities in the periphery and to limit the sources of supply and market for the products of such activities. There will be a concentration of power and decision-making on a world-scale – at least as far as the non-socialist countries are concerned.

This identification of polarised development with capitalism is not, however, adequate. Thus, in the Soviet Union, Ministries planning new investments are reluctant to locate them in small towns or in new and remote areas, because they see economies of scale, and economies also in social overhead capital, in erecting new plant in already highly developed areas (Nove, 1977; p. 76). In other words, whatever the system of ownership of resources, polarisation may occur if those who make the principal investment decisions are concerned to minimise certain types of cost. Indeed, Schaffer (1977) argues that organisational process inevitably tends towards a strengthening of the centre. This would be so in a capitalist or a socialist society.

In his review of the literature on polarised growth, Brookfield (1975) argues: '. . . one inescapable conclusion . . . is that a considerable number of theoretical strands of great value have not yet been incorporated into any synthesis . . . the conditions governing development and weakening of regional inequalities – or of inequalities in any dimension – vary greatly from place to place, have varied greatly through historical time, but include forces that are present in all places at all times. Even in the simplest most egalitarian societies there are inequalities between persons, and between groups on the basis of resources they command and can use, and the locations that they occupy. And although the reduction or elimination of inequalities is perhaps the most fundamental of social goals, it is also opposed to the self-interest and group self-interest of those with power, ambition and wealth . . . unequal advantage is an inevitable concomitant of any system of organisation, viewed in whatever dimension; the dimension of geographical space is merely one in which unequal advantage is most obvious' (pp. 122–3).

In the context of the discussion of the European periphery, one point is worth making. Core-periphery systems, while not unchanging, are very persistent. Several of the papers in this book refer to core-periphery relations going back a century or more (e.g. Scotland, Ireland, Southern Italy). This very persistence suggests that policies designed to reduce spatial inequalities need to deal with very deep rooted economic, social and political structures.

The Characteristics of Peripheries

How do peripheries differ from cores? Anybody who has lived for any time in a peripheral region or country will recognise their main characteristics. I will briefly summarise them:

(i)   The lack of effective local control over the use of resources. The major economic decisions – what to produce, where and how to produce it, the origin of inputs, the marketing of outputs, what to consume, what to invest, where to invest it – all these will either be entirely taken in the core or will be profoundly influenced by decisions in the core. This, indeed, is what we mean by dependence. One of the interesting questions is how far this situation is changed by the existence of separate centres of political decision-making – e.g. the difference between Ireland and Portugal on one hand, and Scotland and Southern Italy on the other. Does political independence in the periphery make any difference? I shall return to this question later.

(ii)   Following from (i), and indeed part of it, the comparative lack of local innovation. New products, new technologies, new ideas, are imported. This does not mean that articles incorporating the latest technology will not be produced in the periphery. Pocket calculators, which perform functions for which a small computer would have been required twenty years ago, are now made in Singapore. But Singapore does not have the capacity to have developed such a machine; the technology was imported ready-made. Occasionally part of the periphery will produce its own technology either as a spin-off from some local specialisation (e.g. sugar industry technology in Mauritius) or in response to a local demand where the gap between the products specified by the core and those required (or indeed affordable) at the periphery is unbridgeable. But by and large the forces making innovation are weak.

(iii)   The weakness of internal linkages. This has been noted for small poor countries (e.g. Demas, 1965) but it will be true of peripheral areas generally. The weakness of regional multiplier effects is characteristic of the periphery. Whereas the creation of an economic activity in the core will probably encourage other activities in the core, the creation of such activities in the periphery will have a comparatively limited impact in the periphery. Thus material flows will tend to be between the core and the periphery rather than within the periphery.

(iv)   Information flows within the periphery and from the periphery to the core will be weaker than such flows from the core to the periphery. Thus people in Scotland are probably better informed about events and ideas in London than about events and ideas in Ireland. Similarly people in London will be poorly informed about events in either Scotland or Ireland. It would be interesting to compare the reports in the English press of debates in the Dail with reports in the Irish press of debates in the House of Commons. In Mauritian villages, virtually everybody could tell you who was top of the English football first division, or what was the latest French pop song or the latest European fashion in shoes. How many people in England or France would be able to identify a Mauritian sega if they heard or saw one?

(v)   As virtually all the papers point out, migration flows will normally be from the periphery to the core, and such flows will reflect cyclical fluctuations in the core economy. This is one of the principal means by which fluctuations in the core are transmitted to the periphery. There are of course exceptions. Thus, Villamil points to the reduction in Mexican emigration to the United States – apparently reflecting restrictive policies in the States themselves. There will be some movement in the reverse direction – managers, technicians, occasionally skilled workers. But typically *mass* migration in the twentieth century is from peripheral to central areas. But, as several papers point out, such migration consists of various elements – from the more peripheral to the core areas inside the periphery, and from the core areas of the periphery to the core areas of the region. The effects are debateable: on one hand, it may lead to the decay of peripheral farming, or the draining off of potential enterprise or skills; on the other hand, there is the income from remittances (although this may be exaggerated). Where (as in Lesotho or Sicily) farming becomes an activity of old men, women and children, and anybody with any enterprise leaves (unless he has political influence and can gain local advancement) the possibilities for peripheral development must be lessened. But in the short run it is mainly through migration if at all that the periphery gains any benefits from development at the core.

(vi)   Government may be required to play a greater role in promoting economic development in the periphery than in the core. Since there are so many centres of decision-making in the core, of which government is only one, government's relative importance is far less. (I am excluding the socialist countries with command economies on the Russian model.) It is possibly a sign of the growing peripherality of the British economy that government is compelled to take a far more active role in economic decision-making (e.g. Leylands). I am not suggesting that state industries are a mark of peripherality; this is clearly not so. But the failure of private decision-making systems may well force a larger role on government than it would otherwise take. We have seen examples of this in Ireland, Scotland, Italy, Puerto Rico and elsewhere. This involves government agencies in making decisions about direct aids, concessions, privileges, jobs and so on – in other words, all the problems of access which are referred to in Bernard Schaffer's and Robert Wade's papers.

The Future of Core/Periphery Systems

Although periphery systems are very persistent, they can and do change. We can distinguish two kinds of change – those brought about by the operations of the market or through technical change, and those brought about by deliberate government actions.

There are various autonomous factors making for the decay of old cores and the creation of new ones. There may come a point when the diseconomies of agglomeration outweigh the economies. Cores become congested; transport becomes more difficult; the cores themselves decay and prove unattractive to managers; the agglomeration breeds crime; social costs of other kinds increase; local taxation rises steeply. We can see all this in the decay of old city centres in Britain. The move to the west and south in the United States may reflect similar processes. One factor which may be of importance is the desire of managers and decision makers generally to live in pleasant climates, California rather than New York or Chicago. This may have future parallels in Europe.

Technical change can work both ways. As is pointed out in Crotty's paper, reductions in transport costs increase polarisation – at least in the short run. They enable a particular core to dominate a wider periphery. But as transfer costs become less important as an element of total costs, so does the pull of markets become less important in location. More industries become foot-loose. All this is seen in the growth of the activities of multi-national companies in the periphery. As long as economies of agglomeration outweigh the lower costs which may exist in the periphery, polarisation will continue. But the forces for polarisation may well be weakened. As far as government action is concerned, in principle policies to diminish spatial inequalities can take two forms – moving people to jobs, or moving jobs to people. Italian policies for the South, for example, include elements of both. As I have already suggested, moving people to jobs involves social costs, and can indeed be part of the process whereby the backwardness of the peripheral areas is reinforced. Moreover, if this movement crosses national boundaries (e.g. from Greece or Turkey to Germany) any benefit which may accrue to the peripheral region is severely at risk. Moving jobs to people – either across or within national boundaries – is the main business of regional development. Policies to this end take two main forms.

First, there are policies for encouraging the multi-national corporations to establish activities by means of infrastructure investment, tax concessions, financial aid, and other concessions. This is Shannon, Puerto Rico, and many other places. The situation in Southern Italy appears different because the companies concerned are mainly state enterprises, but the approach is broadly similar. Such policies are popular among administrators, because they give them power – to select, to refuse. The ability to give access to jobs, to housing, to finance – all these are a valuable resource. Such policies are normally associated with the virtual ignoring of or active discrimination against local small and medium enterprise. The gain in investment by the multinationals is balanced by the loss of indigenous activities. Such policies clearly increase dependence. But in the short run, in regions with massive and growing unemployment and a weak local capitalist sector, they are an option which cannot be dismissed out of hand, however little they may do to reduce peripherality.

The other approach is the nationalist one – drawing on foreign information and technology as required, but essentially trying to build up a national economy with national decision-making. This is the Japanese pattern, the Soviet pattern and the Chinese pattern. It is the policy pursued by Bismarck's Germany or by Ireland before 1958. Various policy instruments may be used – protection, the positive encouragement of local enterprise, going into the market to buy technology, the encouragement of local technical innovation, national planning, and so on. But there are limitations on such policies in small peripheral countries. The costs may be greater than are politically acceptable. Both the local market and local resources may be inadequate. Moreover – and possibly this is the greatest difficulty – the governments of peripheral countries may lack the knowledge and ability needed to make good judgements. They will be at the mercy of international crooks and their own inexperience.

Possibly the answer lies in a mixture between a selective admission of foreign enterprise while bargaining for the best terms which may be obtainable, and a movement towards more 'national' types of policy. Such a mix will not produce instant results; after all, we have no reason to suppose that 'development', however defined, is part of the natural order of things. Policies in the peripheries are often directed towards the creation of mini-centres. But such hopes may turn out to be illusory. Governments may consider that they are creating 'growth poles', and that these will effectively counteract the existing forces making for polarisation. Thus we have Shannon. But, as Schaffer shows, there is the at least equal probability that such places, far from becoming new 'cores', remain foreign enclaves subject to major decisions in the existing cores.

Finally, I should like to raise a question which is of major concern for those involved in regional development policy. As we have seen, some areas which are generally regarded as peripheral are parts of larger countries including areas regarded as core; others are separate countries. What difference does it make if the peripheral area is a separate country? What options are open to the country which are not open to the region within a country?

Various answers are implied in the contributions to this volume. Thus Robert Wade points out that, being part of Italy, the South cannot protect its own industries. Indeed, it has often been said that the unification of Italy reinforced the backwardness of the South. This view implies that, if the South had been a separate country for the past century, it would in some sense be less backward. But the independent countries of Southern Europe (Spain, Portugal and Greece) have not been able to counter the forces of polarisation much more successfully than the Italian south. On the other hand, peripherality within a large country with central elements does allow for fiscal and other transfers from the rich to the poor. Thus Brown (1972) argues that the 'mis-match' between regional rates of natural increase of population and regional rates of growth of employment opportunity in the UK is mitigated, quite powerfully, by the extremely close commercial relations of the regions – far beyond anything yet demonstrated by State members of common markets – and by the powerful pooling and stabilising effects of public expenditure. It has been mitigated also, powerfully since the beginning of the 1960s, by deliberate regional policy, despite a tendency in the last twenty years for the structural elements in the underlying mis-match to get stronger (p. 346).

Fiscal transfers and regional development policies are the more likely if the peripheral area has political importance. Transfers or other forms of aid are of course possible between neighbouring countries if the rich country wishes to buy good neighbours, and many international economic associations (such as the EEC) have regional development policies. But such international transfers or regional policies may well be less far-reaching than those within countries; it is politically easier to raise taxes and provide privileges for the benefit of a country's own nationals than it is for foreigners – unless those foreigners appear to bring substantial benefits to the country. The main policy instrument which is not open to the peripheral area of a rich country is protection. But there is widespread use of discriminatory subsidies, which have much the same effect.

On a more general level, there are three types of question which must be considered if we are to assess the impact of statehood on peripheral areas: (a) What policy instruments are available to help the peripheral areas either as separate countries or as parts of larger countries? (b) What in each event is the likelihood that specific policy instruments will in fact be used? (c) How effective will such policy instruments be either in reducing regional inequalities or in promoting regional development?

The answer to these questions will differ in different situations. A peripheral region with substantial potential local resources (such as an independent Scotland with oil) will have a wider variety of policy instruments available and likely to be used than a region without such resources (although it is also possible that such resources could go less to reduce peripherality than to build up an expensive bureaucracy). Thus there can be no general answer to the question whether regional independence will make much difference. It is, however, an issue which arouses a good deal of concern in peripheral areas with any form of regional consciousness.

The questions which I have listed do not pretend to provide a comprehensive statement of issues which those concerned in such claims might consider; they are, however, the relevant questions in the context of unequal development.

References

Brookfield, Harold (1975), *Interdependent Development*, Methuen.

Brown, A. J. (1972), *The Framework of Regional Economics in the United Kingdom*, Cambridge University Press.

Demas, W. (1965), *The Economics of Development of Small Countries with Special Reference to the Caribbean*, McGill.

Friedmann, John (1972), *A General Theory of Polarized Development*, in Nils M. Hansen (ed.), *Growth Centers in Regional Economic Development*, The Free Press (New York).

Murray, Robin (1972), 'Underdevelopment, the International Firm and the International Division of Labour', in Society for International Development, *Towards a New World Economy*, Rotterdam University Press.

North, Douglass C. (1955), 'Location Theory and Regional Economic Growth', *Journal of Political Economy*, 43.

Nove, Alec (1977), *The Soviet Economic System*, George Allen & Unwin, London.

Schaffer, B. B. (1977), 'Spatial Dimensions and Institutional Factors', *IDS Discussion Paper* 119.

Selwyn, Percy (1975), *Industries in the Southern African Periphery*, Croom Helm.

Weber, A. (1929), *Alfred Weber's Theory of the Location of Industries*, Chicago University Press.

Williamson, J. G., 'Regional Inequality and the Process of National Development: A Description of the Patterns', *Economic Development and Cultural Change*, 13: supplement.

3

CORE AND PERIPHERY IN THE WESTERN HEMISPHERE

José J. Villamil

Introduction

This paper considers the core-periphery system as it is reflected in a set of relationships between the US and various countries in the western hemisphere. The experience of three countries – Canada, Mexico and Puerto Rico – will be presented, with some brief remarks on the Dominican Republic and the rest of the Caribbean.

It is hoped that the material presented will provide evidence of the existence of a core-periphery system as defined, as well as the means to refine the concept. Much additional work remains to be done in clarifying the nature of core-periphery relationships and their impacts, in analysing changes in the core through time and in determining the effects of these changes on core-periphery linkages.

This paper does not consider changes in the regional structure of the US economy in great detail. In fact it assumes, in the main, that the US as a whole is the core. Undoubtedly this is an oversimplification, for there have been important changes in the regional structure of that country's economy and there are fairly well defined periphery areas. New centres have developed such as Houston; others have been re-vitalised such as Chicago, and still others, New York, for example, have confronted problems in recent years which may indicate a weakening of their previously dominant position. Obviously these changes have an impact on the linkages between the US and its periphery. However, this is a subject which must be left for further work. There are many impacts from linkages in any core-periphery system. Depending on whether investment in manufacturing by the 'core' country is aimed at core or periphery markets one obtains a particular pattern of industrial location with industry concentrated on the ports or frontier in the former and in the large metropolitan areas in the latter. The impacts are not only of this type. The decision-making capability of the dependent country may be weakened by various means. Special arrangements may exist between the two countries which dictate how the armed forces of one of them are deployed. One can identify similar impacts in general dependence relationships. A core-periphery system

may introduce new ones (defence arrangements) or make others more intense (easier access to core lending agencies). In view of the experiences of Canada, Mexico and Puerto Rico some of these impacts will be discussed.[1]

Canada

From the latter part of the nineteenth century it became apparent that the US would substitute the UK as Canada's dominant economic partner. Thus in the early years of the twentieth century, US investment poured into Canada, particularly in those sectors requiring cheap power. This was particularly true in the period 1914–17, and in sectors such as pulp and paper abrasives. US automobile manufacturers, including Ford, were already dominant by 1920 (Wilkins, 1974).

Although a high percentage of investment was in raw materials and was oriented to the US market, by the late 1920s roughly 50 per cent of total US investment in Canada (excluding utilities) was for the Canadian market (Wilkins, p. 61). By 1928, General Electric (a US company) controlled the biggest electrical appliance manufacturer in Canada and by 1932, 68 per cent of electrical appliances were produced by US firms (Wilkins, p. 72).

But it was in 1922 that the incorporation of Canada into the US economy was assured. In that year, US investment exceeded that of the UK. This process of expulsion or substitution of UK capitalism by the US also extended to Mexico, Cuba and parts of Central America (Wilkins, p. 155).

After the Second World War, US investment in Canada increased rapidly in two areas, manufacturing for the Canadian market and in the exploitation of mineral resources to supply US industry.[2] By the mid-1940s it was becoming increasingly clear that Canada was looked upon in many ways as a part of the United States and that the risks of investing there were minimal. A quote from a recent publication provides an example (Wilkins, p. 311):

> Personally, I am afraid of foreign investments, wrote the treasurer of a large US company in 1946. He continued the internal memorandum, the record does not show that our foreign investments to date have been very profitable, except for those in Canada, which I do not regard as a foreign country.

The increase in US investment in Canada was explained thus (Wilkins, p. 61):

> The governments of the Dominion, provinces and municipalities were stable and friendly. In the United States and Canada, people, institutions, values and customs were similar . . . the risks for United States enterprise in crossing the northern border proved minimal.

Over the past two decades, US investment in Canada has extended to services and, to a lesser extent, the financial sector, in addition to automobiles and mining.[3] It is interesting to note, however, that by 1960 US investment in mining in Canada exceeded that in all of Latin America. This growth in US investment in Canada meant that by 1963, US firms controlled 46 per cent of manufacturing, 52 per cent of mining and smelting and 62 per cent of the petroleum and natural gas industry. Everything indicates that since 1963 the percentages have risen (Levitt, 1970, p. 122).

This is not to imply that the core-periphery relationship between Canada and the US is to be seen only with respect to foreign investment. Many of the variables mentioned with respect to the European periphery are also present in the Canadian case. Thus, in 1975, of a total number of 13·6 million tourist arrivals, 12·5 million came from the United States, and were responsible for 80 per cent of total receipts from tourism ($1·2 billion out of total $1·5 billion tourism receipts). Although these are hardly insignificant amounts, they are a relatively small proportion (4 per cent) of GNP for that year ($181·9 billion), or even exports ($37·5 billion). Similarly, migration flows exist between the US and Canada, but these are not significant. For 1976, 68 per cent of Canada's foreign trade was with the US.[4]

In effect, then, Canada exhibits many of the characteristics of a periphery: tourism from the dominant core, predominance of investment from the core country and high trade concentration.

However, it seems that the core-periphery relationship in Canada is somewhat different in that, at least, tourism and migration are not significant factors. What is very clear, however, is that the relationship to the US has entailed a major curtailment of Canada's room for manouvre in decision-making, and that the special relationship, with its undoubted benefits to sectors of both Canada and the US, has entailed significant costs for Canada.

The special status of Canada vis-à-vis the US is reflected in the fact that it is with respect to Canada that the US has been most willing to make exceptions in its regulations (Wilkins, p. 346–8). One example was the imposition in 1968 of mandatory controls on the outflow of US investment and on reinvestment of profits abroad (Wilkins, p. 347). Six months later, Canada was exempted. This special treatment for Canada has been repeated on other occasions. In 1965, Canada was exempted from a Federal Reserve Board regulation on capital outflow, and a similar exemption was granted in 1963. In all of these cases, there was a quid pro quo; changing Canadian reserves to non-convertible US securities or a reduction in Canadian reserves. The 1965 guidelines on foreign investment would have required massive repatriation of funds from US firms' Canadian subsidiaries. Again, the door was left open to exempt Canada. This was due to the 'conviction of at least some of the officials on both sides . . . that the spending programs of subsidiaries in Canada were so integrally connected with those of the parent companies that strict application of the direct investment guideline would have been practically inconceivable' (Wright and Molot, 1974). There have been exceptions to this pattern as when President Nixon imposed an import surcharge in 1971 (Stevenson, 1974).

A second dimension of the core-periphery relationship between Canada and the US is that related to the institutional and other links which develop at non-national government levels. Although these have been amply documented elsewhere, it is relevant to mention two here. One is the alliance between oil producing provinces (Alberta) and the oil companies against the Canadian Government. This had to do with the intention of Alberta, for example, to serve the US market and how this contradicted the Canadian Government's plans to build a cross Canada pipeline. Similarly, Toronto and a private gas company allied with an American company to bring in US gas to Ontario, creating a serious impediment to the trans-Canada pipeline (Freewood, 1974). Other instances of linkages between Canadian provinces and corporations or national entities have been documented (Stevenson, 1974). The end result is a weakening of the Canadian nation state, and an increasing disintegration of its unity (Stevenson, 1974).

These examples should make clear the nature of the relationship between Canada and the US. Obviously it has not always been a conflict free relationship, but these conflicts have, most of the time, been resolved in such a way that the incorporation of Canada into the US has been furthered. This was certainly the case when after increasing concern at the dominance of *Time* and *Reader's Digest* (receiving together 60 per cent of all advertising revenues in Canada) a Commission recommended the elimination of tax deductibility for advertising in foreign media. The legislation was approved but, after some pressure from the US, both magazines were exempted (Levitt, 1970, p. 8).

Mexico

Pobrecito Mexico, tan lejos de Dios y tan cerca de los Estados Unidos. This Mexican popular saying perhaps sums up the core-periphery problem as well as anything said here. It includes the proximity factor and the absence of any alternative source of support against the dominant neighbour.

The role of Mexico as a periphery of the US extends, of course, to the nineteenth century when, after the Mexican-American war,

Mexico lost all of what is now Texas, California, Nevada, Utah, and parts of Colorado, New Mexico and Arizona. This was not a minor loss, encompassing more than half of the country's territory (Fagen, 1977).

But the peripheralisation of Mexico in terms more related to the discussion in this paper can be said to have started with Porfirio Diaz, the dictator of Mexico from 1880 until 1910. His modernising zeal in effect opened up the country to US and other foreign investment and technology. Although these were years of relatively rapid growth, 2·7 per cent per annum in *per capita* income, by 1910 close to 80 per cent of the total capital in mining, railroads, utilities, export agriculture, industry, banking and commerce was foreign. Of this, half belonged to the US. External debt also grew rapidly, having increased ten-fold in twenty-five years, and trade, which also increased, was more tightly linked with the US. By 1909 75·7 per cent of exports were to the US and 57·9 per cent of imports were from that country. Foreign investment by 1910 was divided between France (26·7 per cent), England (27·9 per cent) and the US (38·0 per cent) and was concentrated in railroads, mining and agriculture. Seventy per cent of all investment was foreign and one-seventh of all the territory, 29 million hectares, was foreign owned (Carmona, 1977).

With the revolution which followed, US economic involvement began a period of contraction which continued until 1940. A number of factors explain the diminishing importance of US investment: unrest in Mexico during the period, the depression of the 1930s and, in the latter part of the 1930s, the expropriations carried out by the Cárdenas government. The 1917 Constitution included a number of restrictions on foreign investment.

From the early 1940s onwards, US investment in Mexico rose rapidly again. From 1943 to 1972, it increased from $286 million to approximately $2,000 million. This increase was at twice the rate at which US investment increased in the rest of Latin America. However, it is interesting to point out that it was only about a tenth of US investment in Canada, which by 1972 was over $24 billion, twice that in all of Latin America.

This increase in US investment in Mexico was stimulated by the governments which followed that of Cárdenas, particularly that of Miguel Alemán and, more recently, the Echeverría administration. It is interesting to note that roughly 53 per cent of total US investment in Mexico in the period 1941–76 took place between 1971–5, despite the fact that Echeverría's presidency was characterised by nationalist rhetoric. Not only did direct foreign investment increase but its composition changed. Whereas in 1939 it was concentrated in public services (63 per cent) and mining and agriculture (27 per cent), manufacturing accounting for only 6 per cent, in 1970 manufacturing was responsible for 75 per cent and commerce for 16 per cent (Wionczek, 1974; Carmona, 1977; Sepùlveda and Chumacero, 1973).

Unlike Canada, Mexico has had restrictive legislation concerned with foreign investment for many years. Mention has been made of the 1917 Constitution, but more recently, in 1972, legislation was approved with the purpose of stimulating Mexican investment and regulating foreign investment. In fact this legislation merely collected many of the regulations which existed previously, concerned with the need for Mexican control in enterprises and the exclusion of foreign investment from certain sectors and areas.

This legislation, however, made little difference in the amount of foreign investment. This is so for a number of reasons: there are no restrictions on repatriation of profits, there are loopholes which permit 'business as usual' and the restrictions, such as that 51 per cent of stocks must be Mexican owned, were not really restrictive. In fact, what this legislation did was to strengthen the links between Mexican and foreign, primarily US capital (Chapoy, 1977; Sepùlveda and Chumacero, 1973).

The core-periphery nexus between Mexico and the US manifested itself in two other areas: migration and tourism. Although the figures on illegal migration are difficult to obtain, the estimates made by the US government provide an idea of the magnitude. It appears that *legal* migrant workers between 1955 and 1970 totalled approximately 750,000. Illegal Mexican migrants in the US are presumed to be at least 4 million (Fagen, 1977). However, it is not only in the migration figures that one gets an idea of Mexican manpower movements to the US. The *braceros*, agricultural workers from Mexico who go to the South-west US to work in mostly agricultural jobs, were a very significant factor, providing abundant and cheap labour. The number of agricultural workers going to the US from Mexico reached a maximum of 450,000 in 1957, and declined slowly (in part due to restrictive US legislation) until 1970 in which fewer than 10,000 were admitted (Gonzalez Navarro, 1974). Mexico has been undoubtedly the most important supplier of migrant workers. The remittances from Mexican agricultural workers was, in the 1940s and early 1950s, an important factor but it became increasingly less so. In the mid-1940s *bracero* remittances ($43,6 million) exceeded tourism receipts ($34 million) and together almost made up the deficit in the balance of trade. By 1970, tourism receipts had exceeded $1 billion while recorded *bracero* remittances were negligible. It is, however, very difficult to gauge the importance of remittances from illegal migrants, and these could be significant. Undoubtedly, the Mexican government has every intention of making tourism a priority development area with massive investments in various states. By 1974 total tourism receipts (including border travel) was $2,056 million (US), about 32·3 per cent of Mexico's exports of merchandise. The US is the traditional tourist market, providing roughly 80 to 85 per cent of tourist receipts.[5]

As with Canada, the core-periphery relations have not been entirely free of conflict. Perhaps the most serious conflicts (aside from those which occurred during the Revolution, and which included the occupation of the Port of Veracruz), have arisen with respect to the nationalisation of the petroleum industry in the 1930s and with respect to the flow of migrants to the US. Since the early years of the century the US government has taken a very active participation in protecting the interests of US firms in Mexico (Wilkins, 1974).

In most cases the conflicts were resolved to a significant extent without any lasting rupture in the relationship. With respect to migration, which has been a sore point, it appears that the recently started programme of industrialisation in Mexico's frontier is aimed at bringing work to Mexicans rather than the other way around. This programme has benefitted from US legislation which permits the export of raw materials and intermediate goods for processing and re-exporting back to the US, tariff free.[6] The Mexican government, for its part, provides a number of incentives. Although this programme has become quite important, foreign manufacture in Mexico is still primarily for the Mexican market.

In general, then, the core-periphery links in Mexico's case are through direct foreign investment (where US investment is 80 per cent of the total), increasing external debt,[7] labour migration, trade,[8] and tourism, in which the links are almost exclusively with the US. The future of the relationship will, apparently, take on a new meaning with the discovery of massive petroleum reserves in Mexico. All indications are that Mexico will become an important supplier of both gas and petroleum to the US, with pipelines built by Mexico and financed mostly from the US.[9] As with Canada, Mexico will almost certainly become not only a market for US firms, but also an increasingly important supplier of raw materials. There are differences in how the core-periphery relationships have developed and in their impacts. This has to do with many factors: the revolution and its aftermath, the fact that Mexico's borders are with a region of the US which is still peripheral (although this may change), a number of factors related to the ideology of the ruling party and to the highly centralised nature of government. However, everything appears to indicate that the process will accelerate in tourism, direct foreign investment in manufacturing, the purchase of energy, in financial relationships and in the continuing flow of illegal emigrants from Mexico.

Puerto Rico

Puerto Rico has been a territory of the United States since 1898 and is perhaps the most extreme example of a dependent country or periphery. It certainly exhibits all the traits which have been mentioned in this respect: high levels of investment by one country, the US; trade is mostly with that country (75 per cent); there are important migration flows with the US and tourism is geared to a US clientele (83·5 per cent come from that country). Politically, and in terms of its capacity for decision-making, it is more a region of the US than a nation-state. Just to mention some aspects: there are no tariff barriers between the two countries; Puerto Rico has no foreign relations whatever; decisions of the Puerto Rican courts can be appealed in the US Supreme Court, and so on.[10]

The history of Puerto Rico since 1898 mirrors, to some extent, that of Mexico and Canada with respect to its peripheralisation. After 1898 and until the mid-1940s, US investments in the island were primarily, and almost exclusively, in export agriculture (sugar cane). In fact, it was US investment which developed sugar cane into the major sector, for until the 1920s, it had run a poor third to tobacco and coffee. This shift brought about very important changes in many aspects of Puerto Rican life: movement of population from the mountains to the coastal plains, a shift from the previously *hacienda* type of social organisation to the 'plantation'; and the substitution of the local class of *hacendados* by American plantation owners. In part, the process of absorption of agriculture by US capital was a result of two things: a substitution of the local currency by the US dollar at very favourable rates for the US, and legislation in the US which granted sugar a protected market at preferential prices.

In most respects, Puerto Rico was the typical Caribbean plantation island through the 1930s, exhibiting very low levels of income, dependence on the one crop, and a very skewed income distribution. In 1940, the Popular party was elected on a platform of social reform, independence and modernisation. During the war a number of transformations took place, despite the fact that the government was controlled by the US; new government structures were created such as the Budget Bureau and Planning Board; a land reform was initiated and the government established its own industrial plants for producing concrete, glass, paperboard and a number of other products. A number of public services, among them, mass transportation and electricity, were nationalised.

Thus, at the end of the Second World War, Puerto Rico found itself with a nationalist pro-independence government (although less firm than in 1940), a substantial industrial sector which was, except for the sugar refineries, government owned and a strong, and highly centralised government. With the end of the war it again became possible for the US to take a renewed interest in its colony in the Caribbean and pressures were exerted for the government of the island to soft pedal its 'socialism'. Partly as a result of this and partly as a result of internal factors, the government decided to sell the state industrial enterprises and adopt a radically different industrial development strategy, based on foreign investment and exports.

The government's role became a very different one, more of a catalyst than a direct producer. A number of incentives were offered to industry in the form of tax holidays and subsidies. The government invested in infrastructure and became responsible for maintaining the appropriate conditions for attracting foreign investment. It is interesting to note that the discussions in Puerto Rico after the Second World War on the subject of maintaining an appropriate 'industrial climate' are closely paralleled in Mexico and Canada.

This change in strategy was accompanied by substantial changes in social policy. Although there had been some migration to the US from the early years of the American occupation, and labour was imported from Puerto Rico to work in US farms, the very heavy migration flows began in the late 1940s supported and stimulated by the government. This led to an annual average of 60,000 Puertoricans leaving the island for the next ten years. It is estimated that close to one third of the island's population emigrated (Domínguez, 1975).

The last thirty years have been years of high income growth, although the process slowed down drastically after 1973. *Per capita* personal income increased from approximately $300 in 1950 to $2,500 in 1976 and the economy experienced the transformations which one expects from a process of modernisation, agriculture's relative importance declined, industry and services increased. Thus, employment in agriculture fell from 214,000 in 1950 to 46,000 in 1976, while in manufacturing it increased from 55,000 to over 130,000 in the same period. However, despite the massive out-migration, unemployment never fell below 10 per cent of the labour force (whose definition excludes those not actively looking for work) and is now 23 per cent, on the basis of official, Labour Department survey figures. Throughout the period 1950–76, the net increase in employment was only 122,000, between roughly 596,000 and 718,000.[11]

United States' investment in Puerto Rico in the post-war years, has been primarily in the manufacturing industry, although recently it has extended to services, tourism and commerce. In the industrial sector close to 80 per cent of production is in firms owned by US capital, and in tourism the control is again almost total (70 per cent or more of hotel beds are controlled by US companies). In banking, the two large American banks (Chase and National City) are very significant but still control a minority of total assets.

The process of industrialisation which began in 1948 was successful to a significant extent in raising incomes. The cost, however, was high. As mentioned, unemployment was not reduced, but more important was the cost in terms of political and economic dependence. Although this is not the place to go into a detailed exposition of the Puerto Rican experience a few aspects of it can be mentioned. Industrialisation, as already mentioned, was based on the provision of substantial incentives and on the government's provision of infrastructure. This meant, in fact, that the most dynamic sector in the economy was not paying taxes while, at the same time, the government had to provide the infrastructure. This generated serious problems for the government which was faced with a situation whereby, on the one hand, it needed to generate employment and on the other had to continue to finance the construction of infrastructure. Two things resulted. One was the increasing external public debt, particularly from the early 1960s; another, the heavy dependence on United States funds for financing welfare services.

The public debt increased from $600 million in 1962 to roughly $6 billion in 1976. This debt is concentrated in the public corporations responsible for the provision of infrastructure, with the electricity generating utility being perhaps the most important one in this respect. The rapid increase in the government's external debt led to a very serious crisis in 1973 due to the slowdown in the world economy and to the fact that the proportion of Puerto Rico debt issues in the New York financial markets was increasing too rapidly. This led to the creation of a committee to study Puerto Rico's finances, with heavy representation from the US lending syndicates. This committee made a number of recommendations aimed primarily at providing a higher degree of safety to the creditors by assuring that the government had the capacity to pay. In many respects the committee's recommendations were similar to those imposed on Mexico by the IMF or on New York City by its creditors (Tobin, 1976).

Transfer payments to the island have increased substantially and by 1976 reached approximately $1,000 *per capita*, close to 40 per cent of personal *per capita* income. This meant, of course, that US government intervention in determining social policy became very much greater. These transfer payments went almost exclusively to individuals in the form of food coupons, pensions, unemployment compensation, medical assistance and other forms of welfare payments.

This situation was made much worse by the fact that the industrialisation process, emphasising light industry, reached its limits by the mid-1960s. The new US investments were in heavy industry, particularly petrochemicals. These, in addition to being highly polluting, were also consumers of energy and space, and generated very few jobs. This feature meant that while fewer jobs were created, infrastructure requirements were increasing. To a significant extent it was this which generated the financial crisis in Puerto Rico over the past four years.

Tourism, meanwhile, had grown significantly in Puerto Rico, but still remained marginal. Thus, in 1976, the total number of visitors to the island was 1·3 million and the contribution of tourism ($393 million) was a small proportion of total GNP ($7·5 billion) or even exports ($4·5 billion). Employment in tourist activities was also rather limited, being less than 5 per cent of total employment. However, the tourist industry became even more tightly linked to the US market and controlled by US capital.

Some Brief Remarks on the Caribbean

It is interesting to consider briefly the Dominican Republic and the rest of the Caribbean. In many ways the Dominican Republic is becoming the new Puerto Rico. Tourism is becoming increasingly important and it is mostly (80 per cent) US tourism; large US multinationals are investing heavily (Gulf and Western, for example, in addition to owning a number of hotels and other enterprises, also owns 270,000 acres of farmland); light manufacturing is growing rapidly, trade is heavily concentrated with the US (70 per cent), and finally, it has experienced massive outflows of migration to the US (approximately 200,000 Dominicans reside in New York).[12] In many ways, the US intervention in 1965 against a moderately left-of-centre revolution, can be interpreted as the starting point for this new phase of peripheralisation. The trajectory is similar to that in Puerto Rico, from sugar to light industry and tourism and eventually heavy industry.

The rest of the Caribbean also reflects many of the conditions of a periphery area. Its economies have always been externally dependent on a metropolitan country; France, Great Britain, the Netherlands, Spain and the US. During this century, and particularly after the Second World War, the United States has become predominant with perhaps the exception of Martinique and Guadeloupe, which have become departments of France.

Two areas are particularly important in defining the Caribbean's role as a periphery; emigration and tourism. Migration from Puerto Rico and the Dominican Republic has already been mentioned, but it is also an important factor in Haiti and the other islands (Domínguez,

1975; Palmer, 1974). Caribbean migration to the United States (other than Puertorican) grew in the early 1960s due to restrictions on immigration placed by Britain at the same time that the US eliminated the quota system for western hemisphere countries (although maintaining an overall ceiling). Not only did this stimulate migration from the Caribbean but it also changed its character, as under US immigration policy professionals and skilled workers were given preference (Palmer, 1974). Over the past fifteen years, close to one million have migrated to the US from the Caribbean, excluding Dominicans and Puertoricans. Many have done so illegally. By 1973, there were over 300,000 Dominicans in the US and close to 230,000 Haitians (Domínguez, 1975).

Mass tourism in the Caribbean is largely a post Second World War phenomenon, particularly after the early 1960s, as a result of cheaper and faster air travel. Over the past fifteen years tourism to the Caribbean grew quite rapidly. Between 1962 and 1968 tourist arrivals to the Commonwealth Caribbean numbered 4·7 million, while between 1965 and 1974 the number doubled. In the past two years the growth has levelled off and the future prospects are for slower growth (Villamil, 1978).

Tourism in the Caribbean originates mostly in the US, with Jamaica, Puerto Rico and the US Virgin Islands receiving close to 80 per cent of their tourists from the United States. Others receive a smaller proportion from that country but it still accounts for a significant and growing proportion. This reflects, in part, the proximity of the US but it is also related to the importance of US investment in the tourism industry. Most major tourism facilities are owned by foreign, mostly US, capital, and in many cases the tourism industry is vertically integrated, with the same corporation operating tour companies, airlines and hotels. Unfortunately, little work has been done on who controls the tourism industry and on its operations.

The Caribbean has experienced many of the impacts associated with mass tourism, perhaps made worse by the fact that many of the countries are quite small and all have very high population densities. Socially, the Caribbean has experienced serious outbreaks of violence and racial antagonisms to which tourism has undoubtedly contributed. With respect to resource allocation, the requirements of tourism frequently lead to substantial investments in infrastructure. Jamaica, for example, has two airports, one in Kingston, the capital, and one in Montego Bay, the tourist centre. In effect, one finds that tourism begins to determine government investment priorities. With very high import coefficients, and thus low multiplier effects, the overall economic impact of tourism has been overstated, at least for the Caribbean (Bryden, 1973).

Culturally, tourism had led in many cases to distortions which respond to what the tourist industry believes is desired by the (mainly US) tourists. Thus, the popularity of pseudo-Spanish restaurants in Puerto Rico, limbo dancing in various other places, colourful attire for hotel workers which has nothing to do with local customs, the creation of a new 'native' cuisine, development of a tourist-oriented handicraft industry, whose products, because they have to be taken home by the tourist, are miniatures of the original production. But, perhaps worst of all has been the fact that mass tourism has meant the imposition of an image on the Caribbean people, an image which responds to what the tourist expects. Thus, the many campaigns to greet tourists with a smile, to be *simpatico* and so on. Although some have argued that tourism has led to a cultural revival in places, this has certainly not been the case in the Caribbean. What has developed is a bastardised cultural production with little relation to indigenous traditions.

Conclusions

The three countries examined exhibit a number of similarities and differences. Canada shares, to some extent, the characteristics of the core. Although there are obvious regional inequalities in Canadian income distribution (Maritime provinces versus Ontario, for example) these tend to be less serious than in Mexico or even Puerto Rico. Canadian unemployment levels are similar to those of the US. Mexico has, until now, been able to resist wholesale incorporation, or peripheralisation, owing in part to the factors mentioned. However, it shares many of the characteristics of those countries in the European periphery, particularly the importance of tourism and migration flows. Its income level is much below that of the core, and unemployment and concentration of income much worse.

One could argue that both Canada and Mexico are the primary periphery, with the Caribbean and Central America as a secondary periphery. This is supported by the importance which the two countries have for US foreign investment, but perhaps even more so in terms of their importance as suppliers of critical raw materials. As already mentioned, one can detect an increasing tendency to develop sources for these materials in the western hemisphere.

The process of peripheralisation is a dynamic one which is affected by many factors. Thus, in the US, one senses that very dramatic changes are taking place in its spatial and economic organisation. The recent closing down of a large share of the Youngstown steel industry, the financial collapse of New York, the surge in the South and in Texas are all examples of this. In fact, this movement away from the traditional core in the North-east to the South and South-west will have very significant implications for the core-periphery relationship both with Canada and with Mexico. The frontier industrialisation programme in Mexico is perhaps a first manifestation. The development of Toronto in Canada, as an important economic centre, another. The point to emphasise is that the core-periphery system is a dynamic one, experiencing changes all the time.

One process which is, to some extent, similar in the three countries is the export of the heavily polluting industries from the core to the periphery. Petrochemicals were established in Puerto Rico and the Maritime provinces of Canada and, to a lesser extent, some heavy industry has also been located in Mexico. Again, this is a manifestation of the changing core-periphery system: as resistance to certain activities develops in the core, they get shifted to the periphery. This is also true with respect to some of the factors defining the core-periphery links. Thus, Puerto Rico during the war and in the decade after, was an important defence outpost of the US. This is no longer so in the case of Puerto Rico, although perhaps the defence aspect is still critical with respect to Canada.

The future of the core-periphery system in the western hemisphere is related to the changes in the world situation and how they affect the security of the US. This is particularly true with respect to energy and some critical mineral resources. In this sense Puerto Rico, with substantial copper (and possibly petroleum) deposits, may become a reserve of this mineral. The Dominican Republic already plays an important role in the provision of nickel.

Finally, it is interesting to consider the role which the dominant classes have played in this process. It is clear that in some instances one sees a segment or fraction of a ruling elite which has been victimised by the process of peripheralisation become a beneficiary and align itself closely with foreign capital. This was certainly the case in Mexico (Fagen, 1977) and Puerto Rico (Villamil, 1976) where a previous agricultural oligarchy became closely linked with foreign industrial capital. In the Mexican case these links were aided considerably by legislation on foreign investment requiring Mexican participation. In the case of Puerto Rico, the previous landed oligarchy shifted to finance, services and the import sector. A complementary relationship was achieved with foreign capital which minimised conflict. In Canada a similar process has been observed (Stevenson, 1974).

Many items have been left out of this discussion. One which is central in understanding the core-periphery system in the western hemisphere is the experience of Cuba, before and after the Revolution, both in terms of itself and its impact on the rest of the Caribbean and Latin America. A second item which might be looked at more closely is the changing world capitalist economy and the way it affects the regional core-periphery systems. A third item not discussed in any detail is that of changes within the US and how these may have affected the periphery countries.[13] In this way we have simplified the analysis by assuming that the core is the US and the periphery also a number of countries. The problem, of course, is not that simple.

Notes

1   The core-periphery idea was first suggested by the Economic Commission for Latin America. For a recent discussion of this concept see the article by Pinto and Kñakal, 1973. Core-periphery relationships have also received much attention from regional economists such as Walter Christaller, as well as from others concerned with regional inequality. Pablo González Casanova, the Mexican sociologist, has developed the idea of 'internal colonialism' and Gunnar Myrdal has analysed regional inequalities within countries utilising the core-periphery framework.

2   US direct foreign investment for the period 1935–70 grew as follows (US dollars): 1935, $1·7 billion; 1950, $3·6; 1960, $11.1; 1970, $22·8 (Wilkins, p. 330, Levitt, p. 160). In manufacturing, US investment increased from $1·9 billion in 1950 to $10·1 billion in 1970.

3   With respect to a number of minerals the US relies on Mexico and Canada. The following table (Bosson and Varon, 1977) provides an idea.

Percentage of 1973 US Imports Supplied
by Canada and Mexico

Mineral	Canada	Mexico
Nickel	82	—
Fluorspar	—	77
Tungsten	61	9
Zinc	60	24
Mercury	59	17
Iron Ore	50	—
Copper	31	—
Lead	29	17

In this respect it is interesting to note that in 1972, total US foreign investment in mining and smelting was $7·1 billion. The authors point out that, although economies in transportation have been a major factor in shaping the pattern described in the table, the political stability of the two suppliers and the history of horizontal and vertical integration of the multinational corporation have also been influential (p. 92).

4   Helleiner, in his presentation to the Conference on Intra-Firm transactions, IDS, November 7–11 1977, indicated that 58 per cent of US imports from Canada were intra-firm transactions.

5   World Tourism Organisation Figures on Mexican tourism reflect receipts from tourism (gross) of $782 million for 1965, $1,171 for 1970 and $1,710 for 1975. Net tourism receipts for the three years were $368 million, $416 and $750 and whereas in 1965 net tourism receipts were 92·7 per cent of the current deficit in the Balance of Payments, by 1974 they made up only 31·4 per cent.

6   This programme of 'international sub-contracting' was made possible by US legislation which added items 806·30 and 807 to the tariff lists, as items

which could enter the US free of tariffs. In effect, this permitted US companies to subcontract operations which were labour intensive to countries in which labour costs are low, such as Mexico. These plants, which are located in the frontier with the US were responsible for exports of $1,021 million (US), of which $485 was value added in Mexico. Mexico was responsible for 50 per cent of total imports into the US under these regulations, according to Helleiner. (For a detailed description of the programme see Rubin, 1977.)

7   According to the UN, ECLA, Mexico's external debt increased as follows: 1969, 3·8 billion (US); 1970, $4·3; 1971, $4·8; 1972, $5·7; 1973, $7·4; 1974, $10·4; 1975, $14·6. By 1975 it is estimated that debt service plus net payments of profit and interest abroad came to 50 per cent of exports (UN, ECLA, 1974, 1976). By 1976 external debt to US banks alone amounted to $11·5 billion, about one-third of the debt to the US banks by all other Third World countries (Fagen, 1977).

8   Exports were $3·8 billion (US) and imports $6 billion in 1976. 62 per cent of exports went to the US and 62 per cent of imports likewise (US Central Intelligence Agency, July 1977). Approximately 82 per cent of Mexico's manufacturing exports are intra-firm transactions. ECLA estimates that these are undervalued by 40 to 45 per cent (UN, ECLA, 1976).

9   *International Herald Tribune*, October, 1977. To cover the construction cost of the natural gas pipeline 'the Export-Import Bank of the US has provided $590 million a month of credit, while a consortium of six US gas distribution companies – the Texas Eastern Transmission Co., the Transcontinental Gas Pipeline Co., the Florida Gas Co., the Southern National Resources Co., the El Paso Natural Gas Co., and Tenneco Inc. – are providing additional financing . . .' (p. 1). In effect it appears that Mexico has exchanged its potential bargaining power from petroleum for assistance – mostly financial – from the US aimed at permitting the exploitation of its resources.

10 A more detailed exposition of the Puerto Rican case can be found in Villamil (1976). The figures utilised are all from the Puerto Rico Planning Board.

11 There are some parallels with the Mexican experience where income grew rapidly, at roughly 3 per cent per annum per capita (GDP) between 1950 and 1973, but unemployment remained very high. Although the concepts are not strictly comparable, it is estimated by ECLA that Mexico's unemployment and underemployment (what they call underutilisation of labour) was 29·2 per cent in 1970. Also in Puerto Rico and Mexico income was highly concentrated. For 1968 in Mexico, the 50 per cent poorest families received 15·7 per cent of income, while the richest 10 per cent received 42·1 per cent. In Puerto Rico, the poorest 40 per cent received 8 per cent of total income and the richest 10 per cent, 35 per cent of income in 1970.

12 There is little information published on the Dominican Republic and yet it is a most interesting – and tragic – case for it appears to be adopting the Puerto Rican model with even fewer controls than existed in Puerto Rico. Already the effects are being felt of adopting this strategy. As former President Juan Bosch recently stated, it is not so much that the Dominican Republic is pro-American as that it belongs to them! (Héctor and Mártinez, 1975; Baez, 1975).

13 The case of Hawaii, before and after becoming a State, is a most interesting one in this context. Unfortunately, little work has been done on this topic.

Before becoming a State in the 1950s, Hawaii had two main economic sectors: the military and pineapple exports, both tightly linked to the US. Although both remain important, others have increased their contribution to the island's economy, principally tourism. There is one aspect of Hawaii's experience which is important, particularly for Puerto Rico, that of the emigration of a large proportion of the original population to the US and other parts of the Pacific, and its substitution by US mainlanders. Prior to the Second World War there had been a large Japanese population, but the changes in population composition over the past two decades have overshadowed any previous changes. It has been argued that statehood for Hawaii represented a guarantee for the United States that it would be able to keep its military base there. It is useful to remember that when statehood was granted conditions were such in the Pacific that a strong US military presence was deemed important. In any case, the experience of Hawaii should be of great interest to Puerto Rico, where the issue of statehood vs. independence is being debated (Villamil, 1967).

References

Baez, F. F. (1975), 'Azucar y Dependencia', *Ciencia*, 2, 2, Santo Domingo.

Bosson, R. and Varon, B. (1977), *The Mining Industry and the Developing Countries*, Oxford University Press, Oxford.

Bryden, J. (1973), *Tourism and Development: A Case Study of the Commonwealth Caribbean*, Cambridge University Press, Cambridge, UK.

Carmona, F. (1977), 'El Capitalismo Monopolista de Estado y la Política de Inversión Extranjera', in Aguilar, A., *et al.*, 1977, *Política Mexicana Sobre Inversiones Extranjeras*, Universidad Nacional Autonoma de México, México.

Chapoy, A. (1977), 'La Ley Sobre Inversiones Extranjeras y sus Repercusiones', in Aguilar, A., *et al. Política Mexicana Sobre Inversiones Extranjeras*.

Domínguez, V. R. (1975), *From Neighbor to Stranger: the Dilemma of Caribbean Peoples in the United States*, Antilles Research Program, Occasional Paper No. 5, Yale University, New Haven.

Fagen, R. (1977), 'The Realities of US–Mexican Relations', *Foreign Affairs*, 55, 4.

González, N. M. (1974), *Población y Sociedad en México (1900–1970)*, Tomo II, Universidad Nacional Autonoma de México, México.

Greenwood, T. (1974) 'Canadian-American Trade in Energy Resources', *International Organisation*, 28, 4.

Héctor, C. and Martínez, L. (1975), 'Turismo y Dependencia', *Ciencia*, 2, 3, Santo Domingo.

International Herald Tribune (1977), Special Report on Mexico, October.

Levitt, K. (1970), *Silent Surrender: the Multinational Corporation in Canada*, MacMillan, Toronto.

Palmer, R. W. (1974), 'A Decade of West Indian Migration to the United States, 1962–1972: An Economic Analysis', *Social and Economic Studies*, 23, 4.

Pinto, A. and Kñakal, J. (1973), 'The Centre-Periphery System Twenty Years Later', *Social and Economic Studies*, 22, 1.

Rubin, A. L. (1977), 'Foreign Production for the US Market in Apparel Goods: a Critique of "Interdependence" between the United States and Mexico', M. Phil. dissertation, Institute of Development Studies, University of Sussex.

Sepúlveda, B., and Chumacero, A. (1973), *La Inversión Extranjera en México*, Fondo de Cultura Económica, México.

Stevenson, G. (1974), 'Continental Integration and Canadian Unity', in Axline, A. *et al*. (eds.), *Continental Community? Independence and Integration in North America*, McClelland and Stewart Ltd., Toronto.

Sunkel, O. (1973), 'Transnational Capitalism and National Disintegration in Latin America', *Social and Economic Studies*, 22, 1.

Tobin, J. *et al*. (1976), Informe al Gobernador del Comité para el Estudio de las Finanzas de Puerto Rico, Editorial Universitaria, Río Piedras.

United Nations, Economic Commission for Latin America (1977), *The Economic and Social Development and External Relations of Latin America*, Santiago.

United Nations, Economic Commission for Latin America (1975), *Economic Survey of Latin America*, 1974, Santiago.

United States, Central Intelligence Agency (1977), *National Basic Intelligence Factbook*, Washington, July.

Villamil, J. (1967), 'Puerto Rico y Hawaii', Graduate School of Planning, University of Puerto Rico, San Juan.

Villamil, J. (1976), 'El Modelo Puertorriqueno: Los Limites del Crecimiento Dependiente', *Revista Puertorriquena de Investigaciones Sociales*, 1, 1, June–December. Forthcoming in English in the volume, Villamil, J. (ed.), *Transnational Capitalism and National Development: New Perspectives on Dependence*, Harvester Press.

Villamil, J. (1978), 'Tourism in the Caribbean', The World Bank, forthcoming.

Wilkins, M. (1974), *The Maturing of Multinational Enterprise: American Business Abroad from 1914 to 1970*, Harvard University Press, Cambridge, USA.

Wionczek, M. (1974), 'La Inversion Extranjera Privada: Problemas y Perspectivas' in Wionczek, M. (ed.) (1974), *La Sociedad Mexicana: Presente y Futuro*, Fondo de Cultura Económica, México.

Wright, G. and Molot, M. A. (1974), 'Capital Movements and Government Control', *International Organisation*, 28, 4, Autumn.

II: MOVEMENTS OF PEOPLE AND CAPITAL

4

REPLACEMENT OF THE WEST EUROPEAN MIGRANT LABOUR SYSTEM BY INVESTMENT IN THE EUROPEAN PERIPHERY

Suzanne Paine

Introduction

The key role of access to reserve supplies of labour in the rapid post-war economic development of the advanced capitalist countries of Western Europe has for some time been well established. An increasingly important aspect of this was access to reserve supplies of migrant labour from the countries of the European periphery, especially those located in the Mediterranean basin, and, over time, this became the most important factor conditioning economic relations between the two groups of countries. In the aftermath of the energy crisis, this ceased as a result of host country policy. There are good reasons – many of which were beginning to manifest themselves before 1973 – to expect that the system will not be revived either on the scale of or in the particular form which it took in the past. This obviously raises the question of what kind of transformation in the economic relations of the advanced central countries with their periphery can be expected. One possibility which has been widely discussed is whether or not European firms would, particularly in the light of high fuel and domestic labour costs, attempt to keep down total production costs by locating new plants in the peripheral countries where local workers would have to be paid even less than was the case under the foreign labour import system, and where the substantial and rising social costs of the labour import system could be avoided. This chapter attempts to evaluate this proposition, primarily from an analytical perspective, but with certain relevant empirical evidence also being reviewed briefly. Of course, much more rigorous investigation based on very much more detailed data is necessary before any conclusive results can be reached: here only a preliminary discussion is attempted based on certain immediately available published data.

The chapter is arranged as follows. It first explains and evaluates the origins of the proposition that termination of the temporarily recruited migrant labour system from the European periphery may lead to location of new plants there. It then examines at a very general level some of the relevant empirical evidence, focussing mainly on the W. German and Swiss cases. Finally, it summarises the extremely tentative results obtained: obviously no firm conclusions can be reached without the detailed disaggregated research which proved impossible to carry out at this stage.

The limited scope of the issue raised here should be emphasised. In particular, the paper is not concerned with Western European investment in sectors in which labour factors play only a minor role (e.g. raw materials – see the chapter by Vaitsos in this volume), with the impact of any kind of Western European investment on peripheral economies, with the role of Western European based TNCs in particular in peripheral economies, or with any attempts by West European firms with plant in the periphery to recruit returned migrant workers. Rather it is concerned with whether or not the remoulding of one key link between the 'centre' Western European economies and the European periphery (i.e. the migrant labour system) is likely to forge on a major scale another kind of link (i.e. labour-orientated direct investment in the latter). It should perhaps also be noted that although the standpoint of the present analysis is that of certain 'centre' economies in general and firms in particular, it is to periphery country governments and their populations that the issue is probably of most concern.

Investment in the Periphery?

The proposition that the end of the temporarily recruited migrant labour system from the European periphery may lead to location of new plants there emerged as a result of the following considerations: (1) Migrant labour utilisation in the Western European host countries played a key role not only in labour intensive industries, but also in more capital intensive dynamically expanding ones. (2) It appears unlikely that within the host countries, the migrant labour system will be revived in the same form or on the same scale as existed prior to the energy crisis. (3) High fuel costs plus inflationary wage pressures in advanced European economies would make cheap labour especially attractive to entrepreneurs. (4) Such labour could most easily be obtained in neighbouring countries of the European periphery. These considerations are now examined in turn.

The Pattern of Migrant Labour Use

The significance of the contribution made by net immigration to the increase in the non-agricultural labour force in the main Western

European host countries is clear from the data presented in Table 9. As is well known, the majority of migrants from countries of the periphery were recruited explicitly for industrial manual employment, and, in terms of absolute numbers tended to be more highly concentrated in the less human capital intensive areas (see Hiemenz and Schatz, 1976, for an analysis of this for the case of the Federal Republic of Germany). However, within industry the available data on migrant labour utilisation in the Federal Republic of Germany before 1973 bring out clearly the fact that it played its most important role by expanding employment in more rapidly growing branches. Table 10 shows that between 1961 and 1970, the 4 industries in which migrant employment rose most sharply were electrical engineering, mechanical engineering, road vehicles and aircraft, and iron, steel, sheet and metal goods, with it

Table 9

Increase in non-agricultural civilian labour force, selected core countries, 1950–73

	Time period covered by data	Average annual increase	Percentage points attributable to:			
			(1) Change in national population of working age	*(2)* Change in participation rates	*(3)* Migration from agriculture	*(4)* Net migration from abroad
FRG	1960–73	0·7	−0·3	−0·3	0·5	0·8
France	1954–73	1·7	0·5	−0·3	0·9	0·6
Switzerland	1950–73	1·8	0·5	0·3	0·3	0·7
Netherlands	1950–73	1·6	−1·5	−0·3	0·4	0·0
Sweden	1950–73	1·7	0·5	0·5	0·4	0·3

Source: OECD McCracken Committee Report, Chapter 4, Table 5.
Note: Because column (4) does not distinguish between net migration from the periphery and that to/from other locations, the significance of the former is disguised for countries (e.g. Netherlands) where the latter was substantially negative.

Table 10

Changes in numbers of manual workers in West German industries between 1961 and 1970,[1] German and foreigners

	(thousands) German	Foreign	Total
Road vehicles and aircraft	+62	+108	+170
Mechanical engineering	−71	+109	+38
Electrical engineering	−31	+147	+115
Iron, steel, metal goods	−101	+96	−3
Total of above	−141	+460	+320
Chemicals	−15	+44	+29
Textiles	−181	+74	−107
Clothing	−32	+35	+3
Food beverages and tobacco	−78	+48	−30
Other industries	−674	+304	+371
Total	−1,121	+965	−156

Source: Compiled from data presented in Böhning, 1975.
1 September

exceeding by 44 per cent the total increase in manual employment in these industries, and by 14 per cent total manual employment in the first three (manual employment in iron, steel, etc., fell very slightly over the period). In chemicals, foreign workers not only accounted for all of the actual increase in employment, but also replaced a substantial number of German manual workers. In textiles, clothing, and food processing, beverages and tobacco, foreign workers mainly played a replacement role: the increase in their numbers here was less than one third than in the 4 industries discussed initially, and only 16 per cent of the increase in migrant employment in all branches of industry covered in the table.

However, it is important to note that there were two types of migrant labour utilisation from the standpoint of employers.[1] First, for all employers, there were various ways in which migrant labour was *absolutely* cheaper than domestic labour, for instance, because lower wage grades could be created for them, because they were less resistant to methods which reorganised the labour process more profitably, etc. Second, foreign workers constituted a reserve supply of labour at the going wage rate, irrespective of whether or not they could be obtained more cheaply than domestic labour in an absolute sense. In open economies with the sort of fixed or limited exchange rate flexibility which prevailed in Western Europe during the two and a half postwar decades, this presented certain potential competitive advantages, depending primarily on the possibilities for expanding export markets, for instance (i) preventing production bottlenecks arising from labour shortages, (ii) permitting realisation of Kaldorian-type scale economies, (iii) increasing investment in new capacity above the level which would otherwise have been attained (because of higher profitability or of the ability to meet rising demand), (iv) contributing to export-led growth by depressing the growth in export prices (via some depressant effect on wage increases or via (ii) above, etc.), and (v) containing inflationary pressures and so potential deflationary policies. Of these potential effects, only the first two necessarily require actual utilisation of migrant labour, rather than mere *access* to it (or to other reserve supplies) for their realisation. Furthermore, individual employers could benefit indirectly from almost all these effects through utilisation of migrant labour by others. Here it is the *relative* cheapness of labour arising from the labour market flexibility created by access to or utilisation of reserve supplies which is important throughout. However, the central point to note here is that only *access* to some source of reserve labour supply is required for realisation of the relative cost advantages: termination of sources of migrant supply would lead only to the loss of the special absolute cost advantages peculiar to it if other sources of reserve supply were available. And since by the early 1970s,

many of these absolute cost advantages were being eroded (on account, for instance, of stricter controls on illegal immigration, higher
recruitment and social security costs to be paid by the employer,
greater organisation of the migrant workers themselves, etc.[2]) it is
clear that the benefits from migrant labour utilisation in the growing
economies of the time arose increasingly from labour market flexibility.
However, from the standpoint of international competitiveness, reduction in the absolute cost advantages represented an ever more serious
loss as domestic currencies appreciated in value and as the challenge
facing certain labour intensive industries from cheap imports intensi-
fied (see below).

The Future Prospects for the Migrant Labour System

The energy crisis and subsequent recession led to stricter or absolute
limitations by the host countries on new immigration and, as the
recession persisted, repatriation (often backed up by government
schemes) of a significant proportion of those migrants already there.[3]
It is now fairly widely recognised that because of the operation of certain factors which have come into play comparatively recently, the
situation likely to emerge when the host country economies have recovered will not simply be more or less of that of the pre-crisis years;
this particular recession would probably mark a turning point in the
system's operation. These factors are of two kinds: those arising from
the evolving character of the migration system itself, and those arising
from important changes in domestic and international economic
conditions.

Consider initially the first kind. The erosion of certain absolute cost
advantages from employing migrants has already been mentioned.
Other developments included (from the standpoint of employers) the
need to take migrants from increasingly distant geographical origins
(so tending to delay their integration into the labour force), and (from
the standpoint of the state), the much higher social costs of the system.
The latter arose partly as a result of the 'ageing' of the migrant
worker stock and the consequently increased family immigration, and
partly as a result of previous neglect of social infrastructural investment. Indeed even before the migrant recruitment moratoria, the
'social cost' issue had led to local controls on immigration which were
imposed irrespective of the state of employers' demand. And the social
problems which increasingly emerged, together with the fact that host
country populations were not in a position to perceive directly the net
benefits accruing to the national economy from the migration system,
led to rising social resistance to it – resistance which inevitably
hardened substantially during the recession itself.[4]

Other factors were also changing. First, in contrast to the 'tight' domestic labour supply situation of the later 1950s and the 1960s, the population of working age has recently been growing more rapidly in certain countries (notably West Germany) as the children born during the 'baby boom' of the early 1950s join the workforce.[5] Although only a comparatively short-term phenomenon, since at the latest, a shift back to slow domestic labour force growth can be expected from the early 1980s onwards, its effect may well be very substantial on account of the consequent much greater 'slack' to be taken up as the recession comes to an end, and on account of certain other factors explained below. Second, it is uncertain whether productive investment will be sufficient to generate the increase in capacity required to permit progressive return to full employment. In 1977, the OECD McCracken report suggested that:

> ... there are arguments which point to the possibility of an investment problem arising in a number of countries from various combinations of the following changes: – increased capital requirements because of recent underinvestment and an accelerated increase in the capital intensity of production in the future, – reduced willingness to invest in productive assets, reflecting uncertainty about future growth and lower profit expectations, – reduced ability to invest because of lower profits and/or difficulties in ensuring the appropriate flow of funds from lenders to borrowers. The common factor underlying each of these possible changes affecting investment is an increase in the real cost of certain key inputs relative to the value of output (and relative to each other). Basic input prices which have increased relatively are the real cost of energy, the cost of environmental protection and in some countries the relative real cost of labour ... during the adjustment period of some years, at least, they stimulate an accelerated shift towards more capital intensive production, requiring that a larger share of current output be devoted to investment, while at the same time they tend to reduce the profits which would normally, *ceteris paribus*, be required to induce that investment ... unless this lower incentive to invest is offset by a reduction in the cost of raising capital, there will be insufficient investment, and in any case what there is will be biased towards labour-saving equipment. The available capital stock will be inadequate to employ fully all the potential labour force. (ch. 5, pp. 225–6)

In fact, the McCracken Committee's arguments on all these points are not entirely convincing. To be sure, a serious recession means that considerable 'catching up' of investment is required; however, it is less clear whether there are more long-term causes which necessitate more capital intensive investment that in turn will not be completely effected owing to lower incentives and reduced profitability. The first part of the argument, i.e. the postulate of an accelerated increase in

REPLACEMENT OF WEST EUROPEAN MIGRANT LABOUR SYSTEM   71

the capital intensity of production, rests on the view that changes in
input prices will prevent the cheapening of the price of fixed capital
relative to output – a cheapening which during the 1960s, meant that
increases in the physical quantity of equipment per worker were accompanied by no rise in the value of fixed capital per worker, so that
incremental capital-output ratios actually declined.[6] This may well
apply to the transitional period, though there seems to be little reason
to expect it to persist once output growth and capacity utilisation have
recovered. Rather the point is surely that the transitional period may
be long, particularly if profit depressant forces persist on account of
non-shiftable increases in input costs, if there is insufficient availability
of external finance, and/or too high a degree of uncertainty. (The high
current ratio of saving to personal disposable income in Europe's advanced industrial economies would seem to preclude an overall
shortage of savings.)

However, although the McCracken Committee may overemphasise
the longer term possibility of a rise in the capital-output ratio, their
arguments seem to suggest that during the transitional period, there
will be difficulties in ensuring that domestic investment will rise
sufficiently for full employment to be reattained in the near future.
This is particularly so given the increasing importance attached by
governments to the goal of reducing inflation, as compared with
achieving high output growth rates.

Furthermore, certain changes in the international economic environment have had very important effects. First, the collapse of the
de facto US role in preserving international economic order ended the
expansionary bias in world output. It also led to many conflicts and
uncertainties concerning international monetary arrangements, resulting, inter alia, in the end of the old exchange rate system and its
replacement by floating rates. In principle, this may reduce the significance of any competitive advantage to an economy from access to reserve supplies of labour, but in practice, unions may well be strong
enough to achieve a sufficiently favourable new wage bargain to offset
much of the adverse effect of exchange depreciation on real wages.
Second, the increasing liberalisation of capital movements during
the postwar period made it easier to relocate production abroad. It also
led to the strengthening of certain West European currencies, which in
turn stimulated foreign investment in general. Third, the comparative
attractiveness of markets in the newly rich oil countries and in certain
rapidly expanding LDCs (e.g. Brazil) at a time of recession in the west
has provided further stimulus to growth in investment abroad relative
to that at home. Indeed, the increased importance of export markets at
a time of domestic recession, together with keener international export
competitiveness, has probably encouraged investment in other ad-

vanced industrial economies, if only for the defensive motive of maintaining market shares. (See below for evidence on this in the West German case.)

Given the character of the migration system by the 1970s, the net impact of all these factors had undoubtedly tended to reduce the general importance to West European economies of access to reserve supplies of migrant labour, most especially during the high unemployment of the recession, but also more generally in the longer term. On the other hand, in a few labour intensive industries, this may to some extent have been offset by adjustment pressures arising from growing imports from LDCs. Between 1970 and 1974, West German imports of manufactures from LDCs rose by an average annual rate of 13·2 per cent as compared with 8·7 per cent for manufactures from all sources; however, the impact was very much sharper in the case of certain consumer goods industries where labour constitutes the dominant element in costs (Walter, 1975).

Fröbel *et al.* (1977) examined the case of the German textile and garment industry. This faced competition from producers with wage costs between one-fifth and one-twelfth of those at home, with average working hours from 25 per cent to over 50 per cent of those in the FRG, and with approximately the same, or even higher, labour productivity. These factors were sufficient to induce relocation of production abroad (particularly in South East Asia) even during the heyday of the migrant labour system. But such labour intensive industries do not constitute the core of domestic growth in or export expansion by advanced industrial economies, so that it would be misleading to overqualify the reduced general importance to the economy as a whole of access to reserve supplies of migrant labour on the basis of these industries.

The Impact of Changing Input Costs on the Demand for Cheap Labour

This is a complex subject which can only be touched on here. Essentially in competitive markets with constraints on the viability of output price increases, the main consequence of a rise in input prices is a search for all means which enable cost increases relative to value added to be kept down as much as possible. In the West German case, the possibility of access to absolutely cheap labour in the European periphery is obviously a potentially important factor since, in 1976, manufacturing labour had on average become more expensive (though still less productive) than that in the US, and twice as expensive as that in Britain or Japan (Table 11), despite the high unemployment rate (around 4·6 per cent). In fact, although the larger increase in direct

Table 11

Average hourly labour costs in manufacturing, selected industrial economies 1975 and 1976.

	Average hourly total labour cost		Average hourly wage cost			Hourly 'additional labour costs'		Of which as % hourly wage cost			
				Index (1970 = 100)				Payment for time off	Manda-tory	Agreed + collective	Other social costs‡
	(DM) 1976	(DM) 1975	(DM) 1975	(DM) 1975	(national currency) 1975	Average amount (DM) 1975	As % wage cost 1975	1975	1975	1975	1975
FRG	17	15·7	9·8	158	158	5·9	60	17	25	5	13
France	10·5	11·4	6·8	175	203	4·5*	66*	14*	32*	7*	13*
Italy	9·5	11·0	5·9	155	244	5·1*	87*	19*	48*	1*	20*
Netherlands	—	16·1	9·7	200	208	6·4*	66*	20*	23*	10*	13*
Belgium	17·5	15·9	9·7	199	218	6·3*	65*	20*	32*	2*	10*
Great Britain	7·5	8·5	6·9	143	229	1·6†	24†	11†	7†	4†	3†
Ireland	8·5	7·3	6·0	162	260	1·3	22	9	10	2	1
Denmark	18	16·8	14·0	188	214	2·9	20	13	4	1	3
Sweden	20·5	17·8	12·7	149	176	5·1	40	11	24	4	—
Switzerland	15·5	15·2	10·8	194	172	4·4	34–49	10–13	8–10	8–16	8–10
Austria	11·8	10·1	5·6	191	191	4·5	79	13	30	23	13
USA	16	16·1	11·8	97	143	4·3	36	14	9	12	2
Japan	8·5	8·3	7·2	210	258	1·1	15	3	6	1	5

Sources: Salowsky 1976, 1977a, 1977b, Institut der Deutschen Wirtschaft.

Notes:
'Additional labour costs' include all the categories listed in columns 8–11.
* = 1972.
† = 1973.
‡ = Other social expenditure plus taxation of a social nature (excluding the mandatory social contributions listed in column 9).

wage costs between 1975 and 1976 in the FRG than in the US was immediately responsible for giving Germany this absolute lead, the high social cost element in total German manufacturing labour costs has played a key role – if hourly wage costs alone are considered, US labour was the more expensive. Column 7 of Table 11 shows that in 1975, as compared with the US and Japan (or even with Britain and Ireland), 'additional labour costs' (measured as a percentage of hourly manufacturing wage costs alone) were much higher in West Germany (at 60 per cent), and even higher still in France and Italy.

The table also shows that even when measured in terms of national currencies, total industrial labour costs rose more in West Germany than in the US between 1970 and 1975. Indeed, if costs are measured in DM, those in the US actually declined slightly – as compared with a 58 per cent increase in German industry. These figures clearly suggest that German firms will, *ceteris paribus* – a very important assumption here – be extremely interested in utilising supplies of labour which are cheaper in the absolute sense, though as explained above, the erosion of much of this 'cheapness' in the case of migrant workers means that such supplies are difficult to obtain in the domestic economy, and the operation of various international factors means that they are much more likely to be sought elsewhere. Furthermore, explicit recognition of the problems caused by high and rising labour costs are borne out by surveys of German business (and also of Swiss firms). However, obtaining cheaper labour is only one aspect of improving international competitiveness: reducing unit costs by introducing higher productivity technologies and/or by expanding market size to achieve greater scale economies, or locating production within new or existing markets may well be more important, depending on the industry concerned – and, on the basis of the evidence reviewed below, appears to have been so.

The Location of New Sources of Cheap Labour

The countries of the European periphery can obviously provide cheaper sources of labour to European firms who locate plants there. However, even cheaper sources – often very much so – are available elsewhere (e.g. in Asia), and utilisation of cheap labour when explicitly sought (i.e. assuming that the nature of the technology to be used has been decided) will be weighed against the differences in factor productivities, in other industrial and transport costs, and in tax liabilities (or possibly subsidies), etc., which varying plant locations entail, and against other objectives of plant location policy (e.g. maintaining or expanding markets and/or overcoming trade barriers). Furthermore, the particular controls on foreign investment enforced by prospective host countries, and the risk or stability expected in different environments may play an overriding role.

In other words, for those manufacturing industries where production can be transferred elsewhere but would not be done so on account of market or raw material factors alone, it is comparative marginal returns and the certainty with which they can be expected to be realised which ultimately determine plant location. And of these, only industries where 'other costs' (including skilled labour, technicians and managers) vary little between alternative locations, and which do not need to produce either close to material input sources or to final markets, can be expected to focus predominantly on locating plants in cheap labour countries with liberal foreign investment laws and stable political climates.

Thus, the fact that migrant labour in its role of relatively and absolutely cheaper labour was important throughout the whole spectrum of manufacturing industries, most especially in the more rapidly expanding ones, and the fact that for economic and national policy reasons, its benefits to host country employers can no longer be reaped on the same scale, do suggest that one possible strategy which employers might adopt would be to locate new plants abroad. However, various other factors in the international economy (some of much greater importance than the changes in the migrant labour situation) have tended to stimulate West European foreign investment. And although supplies of cheaper labour are readily available in the European periphery, other key factors in the investment decision process mean that such new plants may well be located elsewhere. Note, however, that these latter factors are not explicitly taken into practical consideration by the McCracken Committee, who write on the subject of investment relocation in peripheral countries:

> To the extent, however, that lower rates of migration are likely to continue then this places pressure on the former labour-exporting countries to create more jobs at home. This would in turn require a higher rate of investment for which the most logical source would be increased capital flows from the countries which previously accepted the immigrants. In principle, at least, this should be possible, because if those countries are now importing less labour, they might also be expected to export the capital which would normally be required to employ that labour. Their own capital and investment requirements appropriate to a lower rate of job creation at home should be less, so that savings to finance the capital flows should be available for export, while national income (although not necessarily national output) continues to rise at past rates. (p. 187)

Clearly the facts that available savings permit foreign investment, and that unemployed cheaper labour exists nearby do not imply that

D

investment will take place there in practice, not principle, unless firms are planning to increase their investment overseas and face greater prospective gains nearby than elsewhere.[7] Indeed, it could be argued that foreign investment geared primarily to production with cheap labour for export elsewhere would be located in even cheaper host countries than those of the European periphery, while that geared to production for internal markets would gravitate either towards cheaper advanced industrial economies with large markets, or towards rapidly growing LDCs – not to periphery countries which, partly on account of migrant repatriation, have been particularly hard hit by the post-1973 recession.

Some Evidence on the Patterns of Core Investment

Although the existing published data cannot constitute a sufficient basis for providing a conclusive answer to the issue under examination of this paper, this section attempts to piece together from the available material such insights as can be obtained. The main focus, as previously, is on the West German case, with two kinds of data being examined: overall data on patterns of German direct foreign investment over time, and survey data on firms' foreign investment motivations. This is supplemented by a discussion of the results from a survey of Swiss firms' foreign investment policies in reaction to the tighter labour market situation created by national changes in migrant employment policy, and also by a brief discussion of patterns of French foreign investment.

Table 12 presents data on the growth in and countrywise pattern of German direct foreign investment between 1952 and 1975, with particular emphasis on the major recipients. By June 1977, it amounted to DM 49,600 million, exceeding slightly the figure for foreign direct investment in the Federal Republic of Germany (DM 47,000 million), though both of these are underestimates, and also do not take into account either investments financed by subsidiaries in the country of their operation or the successive revaluations of the Deutschmark – for which, in the German case, an upward adjustment factor of at least 20–30 per cent has been proposed.[8] The data clearly show that such German investment has grown rapidly. Indeed, according to estimates based on $US figures,[9] between 1960 and 1973 it grew by an annual average of 23·6 per cent, as compared with 9·8 per cent for the US and 7·1 per cent for the UK, but less than the 31·8 per cent estimated for Japan.[10] During the sub-periods 1962–6, 1967–71 and 1972–6, its annual average rates of change were 20·6 per cent, 12·0 per cent and 19·6 per cent respectively (measurement here being in Deutschmarks), though there were for instance very substantial variations during the

TABLE 12

West German direct investment abroad by host country 1952–77

	D.M. million					Percentage distribution				
	1952–June 1977*	1962–66†	1967–71†	1972–76†	Jan.–June 1977*	1952–June 1977*	1962–66†	1967–71†	1972–76†	Jan.–June 1977*
Total	49,620	1,177	2,757	4,654	2,572					
EUROPE Incl.	n.a.	792	1,622	2,625	n.a.	n.a.	67·3	58·8	56·4	n.a.
EC‡ of which	n.a.	517	1,009	1,632	n.a.	n.a.	43·9	36·6	35·1	n.a.
Belgium	4,976	232	282	404	279	10·0	19·7	10·2	8·7	10·8
France	4,813	135	321	438	138	9·7	11·5	11·6	9·4	5·4
Netherlands	3,205	47	199	355	116	6·5	4·0	7·2	7·6	4·5
G.B.	2,103	36	96	250	138	4·2	3·1	3·5	5·4	5·4
Italy	1,680	53	94	156	n.a.	3·4	4·5	3·4	3·4	n.a.
EFTA§	n.a.	196	440	574	114	n.a.	16·7	16·0	12·3	4·4
Switzerland	4,694	158	270	394	31	9·5	13·4	9·8	8·5	1·2
Austria	1,635	18	126	76	n.a.	3·3	1·5	4·6	1·6	n.a.
Spain	2,880	58	144	358	n.a.	5·8	4·9	5·2	7·7	n.a.
AMERICA	n.a.	256	876	1,496	976	n.a.	21·8	31·8	32·1	38·0
N. America	9,522	129	522	906	778	19·2	11·0	18·9	19·5	30·3
US	6,114	48	303	654	198	12·3	4·1	11·0	14·1	7·7
Canada	3,408	80	219	252	n.e.	6·9	6·8	7·9	5·4	n.a.
Latin America	n.a.	127	353	590	n.a.	n.a.	10·8	12·8	12·7	n.a.
Including S. America	n.a.	103	211	411	295	n.a.	8·8	7·7	8·8	11·5
of which Brazil	3,747	49	153	361	n.a.	7·6	4·2	5·6	7·8	n.a.
AFRICA	n.a.	75	175	272	n.a.	n.a.	6·4	6·3	5·8	n.a.
ASIA Incl.	n.a.	40	68	255	40	n.a.	3·4	2·5	5·5	1·6
Iran	n.a.	n.a.	n.a.	n.a.	n.a.	n.a.	n.a.	n.a.	n.a.	n.a.
AUSTRALIA Incl.	n.a.	13	16	5	n.a.	n.a.	1·1	0·6	0·1	n.a.
Not specified by country	10,023	0	0	0	442	20·2	0	0	0	17·2

Sources: Federal Ministry of Economic Affairs, Bonn; Krägenau 1971; Klanner 1977; Author's calculations.

Notes

* Data for top 10 countries only accessible to the author.
† 5-year averages.

‡ Including Denmark, GB and Ireland.
§ Excluding Denmark and GB.

Figures may not add precisely because of rounding.
n.a. = data not accessible to the author, though no such individual country among top 10 recipients.

last period. However, the total stock is still quite small relative to the size of the German economy.[11] Also, partly because of the difficulties encountered in the interpretation of differences in growth rates of which some (here those for the early 1960s) are measured from an initially very small base, and partly because of those arising on account of exchange rate changes, comparisons between German investment growth for particular sub-periods are not very helpful indicators of its recent dynamic.[12] None the less, most experts on the subject[13] agree that during the 1970s its growth has not just been substantial, but remarkable. To cite the view of two specialists:

> Foreign investments of German business enterprises have soared in the past ten years by leaps and bounds. In 1975, the output abroad of the German manufacturing industry probably reached a value of between DM 65 and 70 billion or 7 to 8 per cent of its total turnover. The parent companies of German MNCs are estimated to account for more than a third of the industry's sales. (Jungnickel and Krägenau, 1977, p. 35)

Whither has this investment been directed? Table 12 includes data on its distribution between geographical areas and between major individual recipient countries. Over the period as a whole, two-thirds was accounted for by investment in the US, Belgium and Luxemburg, France, Switzerland, Canada, the Netherlands, the UK, Italy, and Austria; two other major but less developed recipients were Brazil with 8 per cent, and Spain with 6 per cent. However, important trends were occurring, the most striking being the rising share of North America in general (and the USA in particular) and a corresponding decline in those of Europe and the EC. Whereas the US had an average share of only 4 per cent between 1962–6, this had reached 14 per cent by 1972–6 (and was over 30 per cent during the first half of 1977 – a percentage similar to that for the whole of the enlarged EC). Examination of recent annual data shows that although in 1975 the level of new investment which took place in Europe recovered slightly, this was followed by a 24 per cent decline in 1976 (by 16 per cent for countries of the enlarged EC and by 27 per cent for those of EFTA).[14] These data also show the rising amount directed to Latin America in general (the increase between 1973 and 1976 being 164 per cent), and of Brazil in particular (which in the first half of 1977 became the second largest recipient after the US).

Classification of recipient countries as developed or developing brings out particularly sharply how much German foreign investment has been concentrated within advanced industrial economies. Table 12 shows that their average share did fall slightly (from three-quarters to two-thirds) between 1962/6 and 1972/6, but this was on account of the rising share of rapidly industrialising countries, notably Brazil and

Iran (which entered the ranks of the top 10 recipient countries in the first half of 1977). The proportion directed to the European periphery countries of Greece, Malta, Spain, Turkey and Yugoslavia rose somewhat from an average of 6·3 per cent for 1962–6 and 6·2 per cent for 1967–71 to 9·5 per cent for 1972–6, but this was largely accounted for by Spain. Subtracting this leaves residuals of 1·3 per cent, 1·0 per cent and 1·8 per cent for these three sub-periods respectively, and clearly indicates the very minor role from the standpoint of the German economy played by investment in these locations over this 15 year period.[15]

Examination of the composition by economic sector of new West German investment (shown in Table 13) reveals a very high concentration in industry which (excluding petroleum) accounted for an average of 85 per cent in 1962–71, declining somewhat to 70 per cent from 1972–6, when it was matched by a rise in the share of services.[16] During this latter period, the most important industrial branches were chemicals, electrical engineering and electronics, mechanical engineering, iron and steel and automobiles.[17] Columns 7–10 show that the sectoral distribution was somewhat similar in both the industrialised and developing country sub-groups, though with service sector investment (particularly banking and insurance) rising more sharply in the latter. Of industrial investment alone the share of iron and steel in advanced economies and of petroleum in developing ones both rose substantially. In both years the share of automobile investment in developing countries was almost twice that in advanced ones. At the same time, consumer goods' investment in developing countries rose twice as fast as in industrialised countries.[18] Consequently the high degree of rank correlation observable between the structure of industrial assets in advanced and developing countries (Spearman coefficient 0·73 for the overall 1952–75 period) is not matched when the rates of change of new industrial investment in the two country groups are correlated.[19] In both groups, however, petroleum, chemicals, electrical industries, iron and steel, automobiles and mechanical engineering amounted to about three-quarters or more of industrial investment in 1971 and 1976.

In general, the above data do not seem to suggest that labour costs have been a dominant factor in German investment location. Rather (excluding the case of obviously resource-based industries such as petroleum), they seem to support the hypothesis that it has been motivated mainly by expanding markets, or by attempts to maintain or expand, by means of local production, existing market shares in large but less rapidly growing ones. Latin America would be an obvious instance of the former type, and the US of the latter. In other words, substantially lower average wage costs even in semi-industrialised LDCs (and, since the end of 1975, the slightly lower ones in the

Table 13

Percentage distribution of West German foreign investment by economic sector, industry, branch and region of location 1971 and 1976

	Between regions of location						Within regions of location			
	1971			1976			1971		1976	
	Total	ICs	DCs	Total	ICs	DCs	ICs	DCs	ICs	DCs
Agriculture	0·6	0·6	—	0·7	0·5	0·2	0·8	—	0·7	0·7
Industry	83·8	60·6	23·2	76·8	55·9	20·9	84·3	82·6	80·1	69·2
Including Crude oil	4·2	3·0	1·2	6·4	3·7	2·6	5·0	5·2	6·6	12·4
Chemicals	23·1	17·2	5·8	18·7	13·5	5·2	28·4	24·9	24·1	24·9
Electrical industries	11·6	8·7	2·9	10·5	7·5	3·1	14·4	12·5	13·4	14·9
Iron and steel	6·1	4·4	1·7	8·0	6·7	1·3	7·2	7·4	12·0	6·2
Automobiles	9·1	5·5	3·6	6·2	3·7	2·5	9·0	15·5	6·6	12·0
Mechanical engineering	7·2	5·1	2·1	8·0	6·0	2·0	8·4	9·1	10·7	9·5
Services	13·4	8·9	4·5	20·9	12·0	8·9	12·4	16·0	17·2	29·5
Private households	2·2	1·9	0·3	1·5	1·3	0·2	2·6	1·1	1·9	0·7
TOTAL	100	71·9	28·1	100	69·8	30·2	100	100	100	100

Source: F.R.G. Ministry of the Economy; data cited in Krägenau (1977).
IC = Industrialised countries.
DC = Developing countries.

US) would appear to be more of a subsidiary attraction than a major determinant. Rather, in the face of overt and hidden barriers to trade and of marketing advantages from local production, overseas investment would appear simultaneously to be a substitute for, complement to, and catalyst for overseas sales.

The hypothesis that markets have been the key explanatory variable is also supported by micro-surveys of the motivations of German investing entrepreneurs. Jungnickel *et al.* (1977) obtained information from 119 subsidiaries of 20 German transnationals (including the 10 biggest). Their results (reproduced in Table 14) suggest that

> ... direct investments are predominantly determined by marketing considerations: the competitive struggle between the large MNCs is for market shares rather than for short-term profits ... Market orientated direct investments very frequently follow successful export sales, being only rarely the first step to gain access to a market. Nor are they exclusively intended to secure positions already gained. What German MNCs are mainly interested in is the expansion of existing markets ... their direct investments are still of a remarkably aggressive character (p. 36)

Note however, that this emphasis on market rather than on immediate profitability considerations is not necessarily inconsistent with long term profit maximisation, and may well be the best strategy to attain it.

The survey found that: (i) Overt or hidden barriers to trade were a very important factor – slightly more so for investment in developing countries than in industrialised ones. (ii) Investments to by-pass such trade barriers also promoted German exports (particularly electrical goods), so that there appeared to be a positive, not an inverse link, between overseas production and exports. (iii) Investments to *start* international investment bases abroad were of comparatively small importance and occurred mainly within the EC. Usually subsidiaries established in the first instance for export purposes supplied the German domestic market, moving only subsequently into selling elsewhere. This was true even when activities transferred abroad were labour intensive. (iv) Both export orientation in general and re-export to Germany in particular were mainly characteristics of what the study calls 'resource-based' investments, including both raw materials and labour in this category. Such investments amounted to quite a small share of the total (about 15 per cent), appeared to be more influenced by availability considerations rather than by those of lower production costs, and were *not* particularly attracted to LDCs. Thus even the absolutely quite small relocation of labour-orientated electrical engineering activities had been directed more to the EC and EFTA than to

Table 14

Motives for foreign investments of West German multinationals by regions and branches[1]

Motives	Regions					Branches			
	Original EEC	Original Efta	Other industrialised countries	LDCs	Total	Chemicals	Electrical engineering	Metal industry (incl. automobiles)	Other firms
(a) Basic motives									
Marketing motives									
1. Opening up markets abroad	1.1	0.9	2.4	1.6	1.4	1.6	1.2	1.4	1.6
2. Expansion of existing market positions abroad	1.8	1.5	2.2	2.3	2.0	2.1	2.0	1.7	1.9
3. Securing of existing markets abroad	1.3	1.1	1.5	1.8	1.4	1.6	1.0	1.8	0.9
Resource-oriented motives									
4. Availability of labour or raw materials	0.7	0.6	0.5	0.8	0.7	0.7	0.7	0.7	0.7
5. Lower production costs	0.3	0.3	0.3	0.8	0.5	0.4	0.4	0.5	0.8
(b) Other influencing factors									
1. Higher profits than in Germany	0.1	0.1	0.7	0.8	0.4	0.6	0	0.6	0.4
2. Surmounting of trade barriers	0.4	0.7	1.9	1.8	1.3	1.5	1.0	1.3	0.6
3. Adjustment to measures of competitors	0.8	0.5	0.8	1.1	0.9	1.1	0.4	1.0	0.4
4. Political pressure of country of investment	0.1	0	0.3	0.4	0.2	0.2	0	0.4	0.3
5. Promotion of exports of parent company	0.9	0.9	1.1	1.1	1.0	0.9	1.3	1.0	0.5
6. Establishment of an export base for neighbouring countries	0.6	0.9	0.6	0.7	0.8	0.9	0.6	0.9	0.5
7. Securing of the German market	0.6	0.4	0	0.2	0.3	0.2	0.5	0.3	0.2
8. Financial incentives of the host country	0.5	0.5	0	0.3	0.4	0.4	0.4	0.3	0.5
9. Other motives	0.5	0.3	0.1	0.1	0.3	0.6	0.3	0.3	0
Number of subsidiaries included	33	22	14	50	119	51	26	22	20

[1] The data contained in the tables are the result of two different weightings: in the first instance the firms estimated the strength of their motivation for investments abroad against a four-tier scale (from 'o' = no importance to '3' = decisive importance): in addition, a five-tier weighting according to the size of the subsidiaries was applied in tabulating the data. As the foreign MNCs do not vary so much in size, they were weighted by three classes only.

Source: Juergichel et al Export

LDCs. There was, however, a very small (in relative terms) group of labour orientated investments which had been established in South Europe, Belgium, France, Austria and Ireland for the purpose of supplying the German market, but this was of minor importance. The survey also found that German TNCs were more concerned with sales promotion of their subsidiaries than were TNCs based in other countries, possibly because they were somewhat less well-established.

What are the implications of this survey for the proposition under discussion in this chapter? First, that as compared with product market factors, only in a small sub-group of cases has the labour market situation significantly affected German TNCs' investment location, and even then, other advanced industrial countries were often preferred. Second, that in such cases, labour availability was frequently a more important consideration than labour cost.[20] Thus, since other factors have been primarily responsible for recent labour cost increases, these results suggest that the changed migrant labour situation may contribute only slightly to production relocation. Furthermore, demographic factors plus recession-induced unemployment mean that it may not have any impact until the 1980s.

However, any inferences based on the above survey results must be qualified very carefully. First, it covered only TNCs – yet results from the Swiss survey described below suggest that these may have been less concerned with labour cost and availability than were domestic firms which at that time lacked substantial established production facilities abroad.

Second, the motives recorded were those of TNCs at, and immediately prior to, the time of the survey, i.e. as German labour's increasing lack of cost competitiveness was still only in the process of being appreciated. Third, it relied exclusively on motives reported by the TNCs themselves, so that, as in all surveys of this kind, the precise accuracy of the replies must be questioned since they may well also have been conditioned by such factors as a desire to create a favourable impression from the standpoint of public relations, etc.

That the first, and possibly the second, of the above qualifications may be important is suggested by a survey in 1976 by the IFO Institute of Munich, which covered other firms as well as TNCs proper. This found that the need for market proximity (either to respond quickly to changing demands or to avoid import restrictions) was the most important motivating factor cited concerning foreign investment decisions, although cutting labour costs often played an important supplementary role. Indeed, just under half of the firms which had actually invested abroad or definitely planned to do so indicated that the latter was one element in their decision, and a significant number intended to export at least some of their output back to Germany and

Table 15

Survey of Swiss firms, 1976

(a) Reactions to labour shortage (%)

Industry	Suffering from immigration restrictions	Immediate response to immigration restrictions (1)					Medium-term planned reaction			
		Sub-contracting in Switzerland	Sub-contracting abroad	Rationalisation investments	Producing abroad	Limiting production growth	Sub-contracting abroad	Rationalisation investments	Producing abroad	Limiting production growth
Food	60	—	—	100	—	—	—	100	—	—
Textiles and clothing	82	12	22	22	22	22	13	33	44	23
Chemicals	54	—	—	50	40	10	18	60	27	—
Metallurgy	67	—	29	57	14	—	14	64	18	—
Engineering	67	15	18	27	31	9	13	41	39	7
Watch-making	67	17	8	58	17	9	—	67	33	—
Other	57	—	—	50	25	25	—	72	14	14
TOTAL	66	10	14	41	26	9	9	54	31	6
Total employment size	No significant differences						Not related to enterprise size			
Under 100		20	25	25	15	15				
100–999		6	17	44	25	8				
1,000 or over		10	—	50	35	5				
Size of employment in foreign plant	No significant differences									
0		17	17	58	—	8		⋮		
1–19		—	12	53	23	12				
20–59		13	10	37	33	7				
60 +		11	21	26	32	10				
TNCs		12	18	41	47	—	17	38	42	3
Others		10	18	41	20	11	6	60	28	6

Note

1 Some firms adopted more than one response to the immigration restrictions.

TABLE 15—cont.

(b) Geographical location of plants and distribution of investments

Industry	% of enterprises with plant abroad			% geographical distribution of direct investment by firms with plant abroad		
	Periphery	ICs	3rd World	Periphery	ICs	3rd World
Food	67	100	67	29	43	28
Textiles and clothing	44	44	12	44	45	11
Chemicals	58	92	33	32	50	18
Metallurgy	44	89	—	33	67	—
Engineering	43	83	23	29	56	15
Watch-making	46	46	46	33	33	34
Other	20	80	20	17	66	17
TOTAL	45	76	26	32	53	15

Total employment size, Size of employment in foreign plant, TNCs and Others: figures not available.

Source: Jeanrenaud et al., 1977.

neighbouring European markets. This represents a change from previous experience, since previously the industrial composition of German foreign investment in LDCs had, like that in industrialised economies, clearly been orientated towards local sales. After the advanced industrial and oil countries, the preferred locations reported were Latin America and the Mediterranean periphery. However, within the latter, prospective market expansion and political stability were obviously considerations attributed at least as great an importance as cutting labour costs through transferring production.

Further light is shed on both the question of European investment in the periphery and on that of the differential response of domestic and transnational companies to labour shortage difficulties by the results of a survey of 250 Swiss firms (of which 103 sent comprehensive replies) by Jeanrenaud et al. (1977).[21] In general, this supported the trends in and motivation described above for the case of German investment. The international product, not the domestic labour market situation was the key determining variable, with the latter having only a marginal effect on both choice of technique[22] and production location. This was so despite the facts that when selecting firms to be surveyed, emphasis had been placed (amongst other things) on those in branches of industry which could be expected to gain from transferring production to labour surplus countries (textiles and clothing, metallurgy, engineering and clock-making), and that 66 per cent of the firms had either felt their expansion constrained by the immigration restrictions or had had to take some adjustment measures. The proportions for individual industries are shown in Table 15. This also shows the distribution of firms' immediate reactions: as their first priority, two-fifths were making rationalisation investments, one quarter were transferring production abroad, and another quarter were using subcontractors either abroad or in Switzerland. There was no significant difference between large and small firms in whether or not they were affected by the immigration restrictions, nor between those with and those without existing production facilities abroad. However, large firms and those a large proportion of whose labour force was already abroad were *more* likely to be relocating domestic production activities as their first priority (Table 15). Indeed 47 per cent of transnational corporations proper (as defined in the study) compared with 20 per cent for others were doing so. As concerns future medium-term policy, over half of all firms envisaged as their main priority rationalisation investment, while almost a third planned production transfer.[23] TNCs were still more likely than other firms to have the latter strategy in mind (though the proportion of other firms reporting this planned option rose as compared with those reporting this as a current strategy); however, the percentage of TNCs indicating this declined slightly –

subcontracting abroad being a quite highly favoured alternative. Whereas chemical firms had been the most likely to have given immediate priority to transferring production, textiles were the most likely to be giving it medium-term priority (twice as many envisaging this as actually implementing it at the time of the survey). The percentage for watch-making also virtually doubled, those for engineering and metallurgy also rose somewhat, while those for chemicals and for other industrial branches declined substantially, rationalisation investment being much preferred. Indeed, in the medium term, the latter was still the dominant priority for all branches except textiles.

In most industries, four-fifths or more of all firms had plant in other industrialised economies, although in textiles and watch-making less than half did so. The industries most likely to have invested in the traditionally labour-supplying periphery were food (67 per cent) and chemicals (58 per cent), though 45 per cent of all firms had some plant there (as compared with 26 per cent in the Third World and 76 per cent in industrialised countries). No industries *preferred* investment in the periphery as compared with industrialised economies, but watch-making firms were equally likely to have plant in either location (or indeed in the Third World) and textile firms almost so. But, excluding textiles, the propensity to have plant in the periphery as compared with other areas varied little, and was not correlated significantly with labour intensity of production. Furthermore, although three-quarters of all firms which made little use of skilled labour had some investment in the periphery, over three-quarters had some investment in other advanced economies, while just under a third had some in the Third World. Advanced economies were also the preferred priority location for future investment, excluding the watch-making industry which much preferred the Third World. However, an average of almost a quarter of all firms planned to give first priority to peripheral investment (almost half for textiles and 30 per cent clothing) 25 per cent for food, 22 per cent for engineering, 20 per cent for watch-making, and 14 per cent for chemicals). As the second priority location, the Third World was most highly preferred, especially by chemical, textile and engineering firms.

Perhaps the most interesting results of the survey for our purposes here are contained in the analysis shown in Table 16 of the priority reason for investment in the periphery. For this sub-group of firms, just over half attached greater importance to labour market than to product market considerations, though inter-industry variations in this were substantial. Over four-fifths of textile and watch-making firms accorded priority to the labour situation, with availability being more important for textiles, and cost factors (notably wage levels, given the possibilities for using an electronic technology with unskilled

Table 16

Main reason for production in the periphery (Swiss firms) %

Industry	Lower wage levels	Plentiful labour force	Lower production	Labour shortage in Switz.	Markets	Trade barriers	Product market	Labour market
Food	—	—	33	33	—	34	34	66
Textiles and clothing	17	17	17	32	—	17	17	83
Chemicals	—	—	17	—	50	33	83	17
Metallurgy	—	—	—	34	33	33	66	34
Engineering	14	9	9	9	45	14	60	40
Clock-making	27	18	18	18	10	9	18	82
TOTAL	14	10	14	15	29	18	47	53
TNCs	5	5	8	10	48	24	72	28
Other	20	13	17	20	17	13	30	70

Source: Jeanrenaud *et al.*, 1977.

labour) for watch-making. Chemicals and, to a somewhat lesser extent, metallurgy and engineering were predominantly concerned about product market factors, with chemicals and engineering giving greater, and metallurgy equal weight to developing markets as to by-passing trade barriers. The food industry gave equal weight to production costs, labour shortage problems, and trade barriers. Furthermore, the picture remains relatively unchanged when the second priority motivation for investment in the periphery is also taken into account, except that in watch-making, market factors were attributed as great a role as more favourable labour market conditions.

The data do indicate a very marked difference between the first priority motives of transnational and other companies. 72 per cent of TNCs accorded priority to product market considerations as compared with only 30 per cent of other firms. Amongst the labour market considerations emphasised by the latter, cost factors had a slight edge over availability ones, though again with substantial inter-industry variations. In so far as TNCs were concerned with labour factors, availability was more important than cost. This differential reaction pattern towards labour factors in general, arising from the much greater flexibility possessed by transnationals, is of considerable importance since it suggests that had other firms as well as TNCs been included in the Jungnickel survey for Germany, labour market factors would have been accorded greater significance in the foreign investment decision.

Two further interesting results from the Swiss survey are that of those firms with investment abroad, almost 80 per cent adapted their technology somewhat to labour availability conditions in their foreign production centres, and that inter-industry differentials in this were small. This contrasts with the low technological response to Swiss labour availability conditions described above.

To sum up, therefore, these Swiss data suggest that production re-location arising from domestic labour market factors may over time become a somewhat more important policy response than it would appear if only the actual reactions of firms up to the time of the survey are considered. Further, whereas both those firms which had already given priority to relocating production activities and those planning to do so in the future were those – especially transnationals – most easily able to do so, such firms were somewhat *more* likely to be doing the former than planning the latter. Non-TNCs were keener to transfer production in the future than they had been in the past, but even then, were still less so than transnationals. And, in any case, other in-dustrialised countries would still remain the first choice of location. Even among firms in highly labour intensive production lines, non-labour market factors played an important role in the geographical location decision. Indeed, of all firms with investment in the periphery already, product market considerations had been of slightly greater importance. But the latter arose from the greater weight of TNCs in this particular subgroup of firms than in the sample as a whole. Non-TNCs were more than twice as likely to have invested there because of labour cost and labour availability advantages.

But, as in the case of the German surveys, inferences from this evidence require careful qualification. Switzerland has been atypically highly dependent on migrant labour (which, before the restrictions, amounted to about one-third of the labour force, as compared with around one-tenth for West Germany and France), has rather different economic and industrial structures, and is not a member of the EC. The first two points mean that firms were probably more seriously affected there than in France and Germany by the changed migration situation *per se* (although, as in Germany, currency appreciation played a very important absolute role in changing domestic labour market conditions as a whole); the third means that in the future, the Swiss economy cannot expect to benefit, as can the EC ones, from the elimination or reduction of periphery countries' trade barriers as their transition to full or associate membership of the Community proceeds. Furthermore, it is also necessary to draw attention to possible biases in the survey results themselves, given the low sample response rate and the small numbers covered by some of the categories discussed.

It did not prove possible to obtain comparable published survey results for French firms. None the less, trends in French foreign in-vestment during recent years seem to have been somewhat similar in nature though not in magnitude to those described for Germany, pre-sumably because it faced the same major developments in the international economy but had a somewhat weaker currency. French foreign investment plus loans abroad increased by 105 per cent between 1970 and 1975, accelerating subsequently – though here oil-related projects played an increasingly important role. As in Germany, the share of that directed to the US rose substantially, from 4 per cent during 1968–70 to 12 per cent during 1971–2 and to 17 per cent between 1973 and 1975. Again, in comparative terms, investment in periphery countries has played very much of a subsidiary role.

Finally, it is worth noting that the results of this section as concerns the primary motivational behaviour of TNCs on the whole conform with the weight of international research on this subject. Lall and Streeten (1977) summarise the findings obtained when the survey method is used to investigate such behaviour:

> The survey approach seems to suggest that the most important considerations affecting investment decisions are the host government's attitudes, political stability in the host country, the prospects of market growth and the threat to established markets. Different surveys attach different weights to these factors ... but they all agree that such factors as cost considerations, threat of local competition, tax incentives or short-term strategic gains are of relatively minor significance. (p. 37)

Results from the econometric method of investigation (which tests the significance of various potential explanatory variables in the investment decision) were less clear because different variables appeared to perform well in different tests:

> ... the general impression conveyed is that the foreign-investment decision is governed by a variety of factors, of which the most important are growth of sales and some measure of profitability (perhaps adjusted for risk and tax differentials) or of maximization of the firm's market value. (*Ibid*, p. 37)

Overall, both methods of investigation implied that TNCs' investment in LDCs in particular was primarily motivated by the existence of a large, politically stable and growing market, a conclusion largely supported by the German and Swiss evidence reviewed above.

Summary

In recent years, developments in the international economy stimulated the growth of foreign investment by firms in the advanced industrial economies of Western Europe. Further stimulus was provided by domestic economic developments, including the difficulty of expanding in domestic markets during a severe and internationally synchronised recession, and the problems arising from high and rising labour costs – to which the reduced impact of the migration system on the wage and social costs of employing labour played an important contributory role. Partly (and in some countries, predominantly), because the currencies of the major labour-import economies appreciated, in some cases very substantially, and partly because certain of the absolute cost advantages of employing newly recruited migrant labour (although declining over time) could not be realised in the same way from utilisation of unemployed domestic labour, the reconstitution of the domestic reserve army of labour which occurred as a result of the post-1973 recession has not, at least in the German case, been sufficient to restore the previously highly favourable ratio of labour costs to productivity, and so maintain as keen an internationally competitive edge. This led to the suggestion that transfer of production to cheaper labour countries might become an important additional factor to those already stimulating expansion in direct foreign investment. However, in recent years, other motives seem to have dominated the pattern of Western European foreign investment in general (and West German in particular): West German investment has gone predominantly to other advanced industrial economies, particularly those with absolutely large markets, and to rapidly expanding LDCs which, incidentally, have cheap labour costs, particularly in Latin America. On the other hand, production transfer *combined* with product market expansion factors seems to have led to a sub-pattern (as yet small in magnitude) of foreign investment in peripheral countries. Thus, to date, location of new plants in the European periphery seems to have been a relatively minor response to termination of the old-style temporarily recruited, migrant labour system, and has occurred in a way complementary or subsidiary to other factors within a particular international environment. On the basis of this evidence, the firms most likely in the future to transfer production to the periphery for labour market reasons would appear to be those large ones for which output produced abroad does not yet play a major role.

The labour intensity of production seems to be of some importance, but is complexly inter-related with other factors in the decision of whether – and if so where – to relocate productive activities. Furthermore, in so far as labour market considerations do stimulate such relocation, the changed migrant labour situation may contribute in a minor way only, and one of possibly declining importance – though this will depend on the extent and character of economic recovery in Western Europe. Of course the elapse of time from the implementation of migration restrictions has been insufficient for any confident appraisal of their impact, and the restrictions' coincidence with severe economic recession means that the period over which reactions are being examined may be dominated by special factors. The pattern of effects can be expected to be rather different as recovery proceeds – directly so on account of an expansionary bias to investment and to labour demand, and indirectly so on account of the changes in the international economy and so in factors influencing foreign investment decisions to which higher economic growth in the west will lead. (Note here that economic recovery in peripheral economies may also be a factor of considerable importance.) And as labour markets tighten further in certain West European countries as a result of demographic factors coming into operation during the 1980s (assuming these are not offset by the persistence of recession, or a major increase in the capital intensity of investment), yet more changes can be expected. The piecemeal evidence reviewed here gives a limited picture of adjustments taking place during a period of migration restrictions, economic recession, and for the West German case at least, a surplus of new entrants to the labour market because of demographic trends *per se*. It obviously cannot be used to predict effects during a period of restrictions, recovery, and a surplus of new job-seekers, or during one of restrictions, recovery and possible tightness in the supply of new entrants – quite apart from new international economic developments which may by that time have occurred.

None the less, to end on a controversial note, the above analysis does appear to suggest that the increasing internationalisation of capital spells increasing irrelevance for the traditional core-periphery type of approach. Firms appeared to be interested in markets and exports, combined as much as possible with a favourable ratio of production costs to productivity. Even if these goals could be satisfied by investment in periphery economies, this would not be effected if there were better prospects elsewhere. It would be unfortunate if undue emphasis on the impact of relationships which peripheral countries have developed with their proximate 'centre', conventionally defined, distracted attention from those of possibly greater significance which they are developing with advanced economies located elsewhere.

Notes

1   These mechanisms are analysed in more depth in Paine (1977).
2   See further Paine (1974), chapter 5, and Paine (1977).
3   The borderline between 'voluntary' and 'compulsory' repatriation cannot be defined precisely, since where residence rights depend on job possession, recession-induced unemployment can ultimately force repatriation. The magnitude of the latter has been high (although somewhat delayed as compared with the 1966–8 recession, for reasons explained in Paine (1977)). For instance, in West Germany, the number of migrant workers fell from around 2·6 million in 1973 to under 1·9 million in 1976, and is estimated to

decline further to 1·5–1·6 million by 1980, afterwards remaining stable (OECD, 1977a). Between 1973 and 1976, foreign workers in Switzerland (including the border and seasonal categories) fell by 25 per cent from 897,000 to 670,000 (OECD, 1976). Despite such repatriation, in the EC as a whole, the unemployment rate for foreign workers in 1976 (around 5 per cent) was similar to that for all workers in the community as a whole.

4   Perhaps the most well known example of such hostility was the anti-Algerian riots in France in 1977.

5   Thus it is for instance estimated that during the next few years, about 80,000 more new jobs will be required in the FRG than was the case in the early 1970s. On the other hand, in most countries, the total population size is stagnant or (as in West Germany) declining.

6   For the relevant data, see UN, 1971, Part 2, and for a discussion of this process, Rowthorn, 1976, pp. 65–66.

7   The McCracken Committee's argument is clearly one of principle only, but the context in which it is presented, together with the absence of any theoretical or empirical counter-arguments, gives the impression that investment relocation to the periphery is in practice likely.

8   Droucopoulos (1977), citing, inter alia Mennis and Sauvant (1976).

9   The unit of measurement is of importance here owing to adjustments in currency parities.

10   Mennis and Sauvant (1976), p. 17.

11   Droucopoulos (1977) points out that whereas W. Germany's foreign production in relation to annual exports rose from 13 per cent to 35 per cent between 1960 and 1973, US foreign production was more than three times the level of its exports, and that of the UK as much as two times.

12   Klinner (1977) quotes the following annual average rates of change in West German investments abroad: 1962–6, 20·6 per cent; 1967–71, 12·0 per cent; 1972–6, 19·6 per cent.

13   For instance, Klinner (1977), Krägenau (1977), Jungnickel et al. (1977), Droucopoulos (1977).

14   Klinner (1977), p. 217.

15   Though not from the standpoint of the recipient countries themselves – see other chapters of this volume.

16   See Klinner (1977), p. 218.

17   Ibid., pp. 218–9.

18   Hiemenz and Schatz (1977), p. 22.

19   Ibid.

20   Note here that this survey – like most others – does not consider the important question of the degree of control over the labour process.

21   The response rate ranged from 5 per cent for the food industry to 43 per cent for engineering, yielding an industry-wise composition of returns of 5 per cent (food), 11 per cent (textiles and clothing), 13 per cent (chemicals), 9 per cent (metallurgy), 43 per cent (engineering), 15 per cent (clocks and watches), and 7 per cent (other branches). In terms of the total labour force employed (whether in Switzerland or abroad), the composition was as follows: less than 50, 10 per cent; 50–99, 15 per cent; 100–199, 18 per cent; 200–499, 21 per cent; 500–999, 13 per cent; 1,000–4,999, 15 per cent; 5,000 and over, 10 per cent.

22   An average of 81 per cent of firms stated that labour force availability was not an important element in the choice of production techniques. The figures by industry were food, 75 per cent; textiles and clothing, 70 per

cent; chemicals, 92 per cent; metallurgy, 56 per cent; engineering, 85 per cent; clocks and watches, 87 per cent.

23 TNCs were defined as those firms which (1) produced more than 40 per cent of their output abroad, (2) located production in at least two groups of countries (industrialised economies, peripheral economies traditionally supplying labour, oil economies, and the Third World), and (3) employed more than 500 workers.

References

Böhning, W. R. (1975), *Mediterranean workers in Western Europe: effects on home countries and countries of employment*, ILO World Employment Programme Working Paper, Geneva.

Droucopoulos, V. (1977), West German expansionism, *New Left Review*, 105, pp. 92–6.

Fröbel, F. Heinrichs, J. and Kreye, O. (1977), *Die Neue Internationale Arbeitsteilung – strukturelle Arbeitslösigkeit in den Industrieländern und die Industrializierung der Entwicklungsländer*, Rowohlt Taschenbuch Verlag, Hamburg.

Hiemenz, U. and Schatz, K.-W. (1976), *Transfer of employment opportunities as an alternative to the international migration of workers: the cost of the Federal Republic of Germany (I)*, ILO World Employment Programme Working Paper, Geneva.

Hiemenz, U. and Schatz, K.-W. (1977), *Transfer of Employment opportunities as an alternative to the international migration of workers: the case of Spain and Turkey vis à vis the Federal Republic of Germany (II)*, ILO World Employment Programme Working Paper, Geneva.

Jeanrenaud, C., Maillat, D., and Widmer, J. P. (1977), *Transfer d'emplois vers les pays qui disposent d'un surplus de main-d'oeuvre comme alternative aux migrations internationales: le cas de la Suisse III – le comportement de l'entrepeneur face à la penurie de main-d'oeuvre: résultats d'une enquête par questionnaire*, ILO World Employment Programme Working Paper, Geneva.

Jungnickel, R. and Krägenau, H. (1977), 'Motives of multis in Germany', *Intereconomics*, 1/2, pp. 35–9.

Jungnickel, R., Lefeldt, M., Krägenau, H. and Holthus, M. (1977), *Der Einfluss multinationaler Unternehmen auf Branchenstruktur und Aussenwirtschaft der Bundesrepublik Deutschland*.

Klinner, B. (1977), 'German investments abroad and foreign investments in the Federal Republic', *Intereconomics*, 7/8, pp. 217–21.

Krägenau, H. (1977), Deutsche Direktinvestitionen in den siebzigen Jahren, *Wirtschaftsdienst*, *VII*, July, pp. 360–5.

Lall, S. and Streeten, P. (1977), *Foreign investment, transnationals and developing countries*, Macmillan.

McCracken, P. *et al.* (1976), *Towards full employment and price stability*, OECD, Paris.

Mennis, B. and Sauvant, K. P. (1976), *Emerging forms of transnational community*, Lexington, Mass.

OECD (1977a), *Germany*, OECD, Paris.

OECD (1977b), *Switzerland*, OECD, Paris.

Paine, S. H. (1977), 'The changing rôle of migrant labour in the advanced capitalist economies of Western Europe', in R. T. Griffiths (ed.), *Government, business and labour in European capitalism*, Europotentials Press, London.

Paine, S. H. (1974), *Exporting workers: the Turkish case*, Cambridge University

Department of Applied Economics Occasional paper No. 41, Cambridge University Press.

Rowthorn, R. (1976), 'Late Capitalism', *New Left Review*, 98, July–August, pp. 59–83.

Salowsky, H. (1976), *Lohnentwicklung in Westlichen Industrieländern*, Beiträge zur Wirtschafts – und Sozialpolitik, Nos. 38/39, Institut der deutschen Wirtschaft, Cologne.

Salowsky, H. (1977a), *Personalzusatzkosten in Westlichen Industrieländern*, Beiträge zur Wirtschafts – und Sozialpolitik, Nos. 40/41 Institut der deutschen Wirtschaft, Cologne.

Salowsky (1977b), 'Wages and indirect labour costs in western industrialised countries', *Intereconomics*, 7/8, pp. 213–16.

UN (1971), *Economic Survey of Europe in 1971*, UN New York.

Wolter, F. (1975), 'Relocation of production in developing countries', *Intereconomics*, 12, pp. 366–8.

5

A NOTE ON TRANSNATIONAL CORPORATIONS (TNCs)[1] AND THE EUROPEAN PERIPHERY

Constantine Vaitsos

There exist five different broad sectoral areas where the operations of the TNCs will affect the internal development prospects of the European periphery, as well as its relations with both the European core and the rest of the world. Such operations of the TNCs concern not only their direct investment activities, but also trade patterns created by such firms and flows of different factors of production within the EEC. They also involve polarisation effects and concentration of strategic activities like the development of technological capabilities in the companies' headquarters. The five sectoral areas need to be treated separately and include: (1) import substituting manufacturing activities; (2) resource based export operations; (3) labour based manufacturing exports; (4) investments in 'subsidy-intensive' countries; (5) activities where the European periphery could serve as a go-between, for core European interests, with the rest of the world.

(1) IMPORT SUBSTITUTING FOREIGN DIRECT INVESTMENTS IN THE MANUFACTURING SECTOR.

A large part of existing TNC investment activities, particularly in countries like Spain, Greece, and to an extent Portugal after the revolution, concentrated in import substituting operations which have been induced by the high tariff and non-tariff barriers in selected product areas of the periphery.

The effects of such investments are not very different from those in Latin America. Namely, (a) there has been a very small foreign financial contribution as compared to the total funds used by such firms in view of their heavy local borrowing; (b) significant attention is paid to non-price competition based on product differentiation and heavy advertising; (c) several local firms were displaced directly through acquisitions or indirectly through non-price competition; and (d) the net income and balance of payments effects have been shown to be in various cases either small or even negative in view of high protection or government subsidies and the ability of firms to remit untaxed effective profits through transfer pricing.

The incorporation of the European periphery to the EEC would affect such import substituting foreign direct investments through various mechanisms. First, the abolition of intra-regional tariffs and some of the non-tariff barriers would reduce the attractiveness to the TNCs of developing such activities in the periphery, and would promote exports from the core countries. Such an outcome will reduce production inefficiency in the periphery, but it would also dismantle part of its industrial and technological infrastructure.

Second, the concentration of technological and overall institutional capabilities in the countries of the parent firms of the TNCs will be further strengthened. For the types of products which are of interest to the peripheral countries for their technological development, trade liberalisation and the limitations that this implies on industrial policy, would be of considerable importance. In contrast, technological development and industrial planning in the core countries could be maintained through particular non-tariff barriers, especially government procurement practices in sectors such as the aviation industry, computers and electronics. The latter types of industries are more susceptible to government procurement practices, while those in which the periphery has been specialising do not provide sufficient opportunities for such direct public policies, with the one possible serious exception, the pharmaceutical industry.

Third, free-flow of capital movements in an enlarged EEC would render unacceptable regulatory policies on foreign direct investments and technology, like those recently instituted by the government of Portugal. Furthermore, European subsidiaries of US and Japanese based transnationals would offer to their parent firms, in terms of foreign investment operations, equal access to the European market as those applicable for the European TNCs. Since subsidiaries of non-European TNCs can be legally constituted and incorporated as enterprises in Europe, they are – under existing rules – European firms.

Fourth, with respect to the free-flow of capital within the EEC, two very interesting evolutions might take place. The first concerns the possibility that the enlargement of the EEC could create or accentuate significant capital *out*flows from the periphery to the core countries, rather than vice versa. Such outflows would most likely take the form of portfolio investments or bank deposits, rather than foreign direct investments. The other issue concerns the grave preoccupation of the core countries on labour migration to them from the periphery. This process has caused significant social and economic problems, especially during the recent economic crisis. In view of the above and under the initiative of the West German government, discussions and informal pre-negotiation consultations have been taking place for a (transitory) re-structuring of the EEC rules, so as to introduce the following *quid pro quo* arrangement: the periphery countries could maintain (for a given period) certain types of control mechanisms on capital flows, as long as the core countries could also introduce controls on labour migration. Although this issue has been raised in connection to the more advanced negotiations for the entrance of Greece, it appears that despite its general applicability (particularly for the case of Portugal), they key concern for the German government involves Turkish labour. In the middle 1970s, hundreds of thousands of migrants' applications from Turkey were still pending to be approved by the German authorities.

Five, foreign investment from the core countries (especially from Germany) will continue to take place during the coming years in the periphery, both as a means for assuring or enhancing market shares in the latter countries during the transition period, or in order to provide marketing outlets and in order to overcome non-tariff barriers during the period of full membership of the European periphery countries. Furthermore, in specific activities (like the automobile sector) countries in the periphery with large internal markets and relatively developed productive capacities (e.g. Spain) could create as a spin-off of their import substituting activities a base for manufacturing exports to the rest of the EEC. The TNCs would use such possibilities to diversify their risks in the face of strong trade-union action in the core countries.

Six, a triangular relationship exists between the core countries, the European periphery and the outer periphery. According to this relationship, access to the markets of the outer periphery of products controlled by the TNCs could be compensated by exports from such countries to the EEC, including peripheral members, of products which are usually not manufactured by the transnationals (e.g. textiles). Yet, such exports through preferential treatment (Lomé Convention) could endanger locally controlled industry in the periphery.

(2) RESOURCE BASED EXPORT INDUSTRIES.
The transnational enterprises will continue to invest in the periphery's natural resources, like the Pechiney investment in Greece's bauxite. The decision to invest would depend basically on the availability of such resources in the periphery and not on the internal operations of the EEC. Yet, the negotiating terms of the investments will be affected by the community's rules on the freedom of movement of capital, technology and machinery. Such terms could potentially be of considerable significance (in a negative sense) for the development of the periphery's productive and technological capabilities in specific activities, such as in parts of the capital goods and engineering sectors. These capabilities could have been developed by a more selective import policy on inputs used for the resource based industries.

A specific possibility of foreign investment in the periphery, as a result of factor and product mobility within the EEC, could relate to the high pollution industries. Considering the environment as a resource and in view of stricter regulations in the core countries, some of the high pollution industries could progressively be relocated in the European periphery. In another geographic region, Japan – representing the East Asian core – has used similar relocation strategies in the East Asian periphery for activities which generate a high degree of environmental contamination, like primary and secondary petrochemical products.

(3) LABOUR-INTENSIVE MANUFACTURING EXPORTS.

The end and, in various cases, partial reversal of intra-European migration have been considered by some as the initiation of a more serious re-location of industrial activities, especially in sectors where internationally mobile TNCs operate. This argument is based on the premiss that instead of moving labour from the periphery to the industry of the European core – a process which carries significant social and economic costs for the overall interests of all countries concerned – industry could move to where labour is available. Transportation of the goods produced in the periphery and their export to the centre, could prove less costly than labour migration.

The possibilities, though for such a re-location of industrial activities appear to be quite limited. There are several reasons for it:

First, although there are obvious wage differentials between the European periphery and the core, they are not as significant as those between Europe and the outer periphery. The level of wages in Ireland is not all that lower than those in the United Kingdom. Industry has been attracted to Ireland for exports of manufactures, not so much because of its low wages, but in view of the highly generous government subsidies and tax exemptions. Such policies have been noted in some studies as leading to overall negative effects for Ireland. If it is a question of labour costs, European TNCs will invest – and have shown to do so – in the outer and not in the European periphery.

Second, structural rather than cyclical unemployment in the core European countries is recognised as a fundamental political, social and economic concern. Beginning in the early 1970s, the new phase into which the European economy has entered (as is also true for other industrialised countries) has brought powerful political and trade union pressures to curtail re-location plans by the TNCs.

Thirdly, technological change – as recently happened in the electronics industry through automated minuterised component production and assembly as well as in the textile and apparel industry through the application of laser technology – could abruptly set significant limits in the attractiveness of available labour supplies abroad.

As a result of the above reasons, TNC activities in the European periphery prompted by lower wage levels or labour availability are likely to be very limited. Location or re-location decisions to the European periphery are more likely to be undertaken on account of government subsidies or in certain cases for tax reasons.

(4) INVESTMENT IN SUBSIDY 'INTENSIVE' COUNTRIES.

The entrance of part of the European periphery in the EEC could reinforce, as a result of government policies in the periphery, existing trends to attract foreign investment through heavy subsidisation of the operations of foreign firms. The most notable case is that of Ireland which pursues quite comprehensive incentive strategies, including tax exemptions, grants, infra-structural support and other indirect subsidisation, tariff exemptions, etc. Other countries, like Greece and Portugal, have shown in the past their willingness to follow similar, even if more limited, strategies directed towards specific enterprises.

As a result of these government policies, which often tend to be biased in favour of large-scale capital, the periphery could become the locus of capital intensive rather than labour intensive activities. Furthermore, competition among the European periphery countries as to who will attract foreign investment, could lead to a race on incentives offered to the TNCs. Such a race, though, will be conditioned by the EEC rules and practices on policy harmonisation. (It is of interest to note that during a recent EEC negotiation on rules about subsidies, the Irish government pushed very strongly for the maintenance of the subsidies presently offered by that country).

It is also of interest to note that subsidies and tax exemptions offered by the European periphery could adversely affect the income, balance of payments, and industrial development of the outer periphery in view of transfer pricing practices and location decisions by TNCs in the processing of minerals or commodities originated in the outer periphery. Such triangular relationships (i.e. TNCs, European peripheral countries offering incentives on export oriented industries, and outer periphery with resource endowments) is exemplified in a recent case between an aluminium processing TNC in Ireland and a bauxite producing West African country.

(5) EUROPEAN PERIPHERY AS A GO-BETWEEN THE EUROPEAN CORE AND THE REST OF THE WORLD.

In view of historical, linguistic, as well as geographic contacts of the European periphery, the latter could, in specific sectors and for particular enterprises, serve as an intermediary for reinforcing the pres-

ence of European based TNCs in the rest of the world. Such is the
case of Spain with respect to Latin America as well as that of Greece
and Turkey with respect to the Middle East. In these cases, joint
ventures or sales of machinery, services and technology could take
place via the European periphery, with an eye in the markets of the
rest of the world.[2]

Notes

1 Strictly transnational *enterprises*, since they can only be incorporated as
   national enterprises.
2 A geographic area where the European periphery is not likely to play a significant role as an intermediary is that of Eastern Europe. In the latter case
   the European core governments and TNCs have already established very
   important and direct links of their own.

6

FOREIGN INVESTMENT AND HOST-COUNTRY POLITICS: THE IRISH CASE*

Richard Stanton

The transfer of metropolitan industry to peripheral havens offering cheap labour or financial privileges, from which to supply external markets, seems likely to remain a minor element in total international investment flows – possibly declining (cf. Suzanne Paine's contribution to this volume). This paper examines Ireland's exceptionally long experience as a site for foreign export-manufacture. It suggests that such activity, if a drop in the bucket of internationally-mobile capital, can make a large splash in a small peripheral country.

First it sketches the historical background to the decision to invite this investment, its contribution to the national economy, and the main types of corporate strategy involved. The consequent demands on Irish classes and society are then analysed. Finally two questions are addressed: Why has this society been a relatively congenial environment for foreign export-oriented investors? How has their presence helped to alter the lines of force in host-country class relations – to alter its politics?

Background

Big farmers, 'ranchers', working large holdings primarily for profit, had hegemony in Ireland after independence in 1922: in long perspective, state policy – beginning with a conservative, devolutionary separation from Britain – has expressed their priorities. But there was no immediate contradiction between their concerns and those of smaller farmers, working primarily for personal income. As shown elsewhere in this volume, pressures on land were stemmed by filial inheritance and sustained emigration; land tenure was effectively inviolate. These two rural classes formed an unequal condominium,

* This paper draws extensively on the ideas of Bernard Schaffer and Raymond Crotty (see their chapters in this volume.) A heavy debt to the latter will be most immediately obvious. Neither is to blame for my interpretations. For a partly contrasting view the reader is urged to consult McAleese (1977), published as this paper was undergoing final revision.

pursuing a predictable approach to external economic relations: dairy/cattle exports being the main source of foreign exchange, with tariff protection for the remaining domestically-oriented industry, much of it in traditional consumer-goods sectors (Meenan, 1970, p. 46).

The sluggish rate of accumulation and shrinking employment entailed by this approach became, as metropolitan Europe emerged from war, a matter for increasing concern in Dublin. As a condition – significantly – of receiving Marshall Aid, Irish authorities were obliged to make a projection of import requirements, which at OEEC's prompting they elaborated into a Long Term Recovery Programme (1949), the state's 'first exercise in economic planning' (Murphy, 1975, pp. 123–4). With it were introduced a Central Statistics Office, Export Board, and Industrial Development Authority. Though little effect was then given to the Recovery Programme, the process of reshaping national economic policy had begun. It gained urgency as the country sank into recession in the mid-1950s, marked by a resurgence of activity on the part of the IRA (Irish Republican Army), the residual nationalist guerilla force, and came to fruition in the 1958 Programme for Economic Expansion.

The year 1958 saw a 'turning towards the outside' in two distinct senses. First it was implicitly decided that Ireland would integrate with the European market at the first opportunity (see Ireland, 1958, p. 38). Embracing Europe was fundamental, the authentic choice of Ireland's dominant, agricultural exporting class.[1] The second, complementary decision was to start industrialisation-by-invitation. Ireland's employment needs, compounded soon by the effect of EEC membership on uncompetitive 'traditional' firms, would be tackled by attracting new industry to manufacture for export; it would be funded so far as necessary (though local capital was never excluded) by private foreign capital (loc cit., pp. 35–7). Keeping in mind the unity between these two decisions, we turn now to the implications of the latter.

An extraordinarily generous system of incentives to potential investors, Irish or foreign, was installed (see also the discussion by Schaffer below). Two were central: zero tax on profits attributable to export sales (currently guaranteed until 1990); and grants towards fixed assets. Of the stringent criteria to which such grants were subject in principle, only one seems to have been imposed uniformly: exportability of the product.

Another incentive, in effect, was the establishment in 1959 of a customs-free manufacturing zone adjoining Shannon Airport in the west of Ireland, where firms would be exempt from import duty on goods to be processed for export (and eligible for all the other incentives). Now a minor element in Ireland's industrial structure, the Shannon Free Zone was initially a focus for the new policy.

Among public institutions formed or adapted since 1958 to help implement the strategy, the most prominent has been the Industrial Development Authority (IDA). This organisation, responsible for all aspects of the export-oriented investment from promoting Ireland internationally as an industrial location to administering grants and providing 'after-care' to the investor,[2] has become a major component of the Irish state apparatus.

Foreign-controlled Export Manufacture (FCEM) and the Irish Economy[3]

The total of 510 'overseas companies in Ireland' by October 1976 (IDA 1976) may have implied an FCEM population above 450. Predominant sectors have been metal-working and engineering, electronics, and 'miscellaneous'. But clothing, textiles, and agriculture-based products have also been represented consistently, while more recent arrivals include several firms in the pharmaceutical and 'health-care' sectors.

At the level of aggregate national employment and output* (Table 17) the consequences of the post-1958 strategy seems less than dramatic.

In a decade and a half, industry increased its percentage contribution to GDP by less than three points, to national employment by five. The latter modest rise owes more to the decrease of 140 thousand in agricultural employment than to industry's increase of 60 thousand. Total jobs were 1·3 per cent fewer.

FCEM itself has at first sight had a limited impact on employment structure. Firms of this kind appear to have employed 1–1·5 per cent of the labour force in 1966, and 3–4 per cent in 1974 (IDA 1977, p. 4; possibly closer to 6 per cent in 1975, another survey would imply (AnCO 1975)). Otherwise, however, FCEM's dynamic effect is unmistakable.

Firstly, within an industrial sector undergoing relatively little expansion, changes in FCEM's employment share which are small on the national scale will correspond to a sharp contraction of domestically-oriented industry. Moreover, its employment instability means that its impact on the labour force goes far beyond the number of jobs it offers at one time.

Secondly, FCEM, which in 1966 comprised probably less than 1 per cent of the country's fixed asset stock, and not much above 1 per cent of its labour force, appears to have contributed at least one-fifth of the

* The severe analytic weaknesses of these measures are recognised of course. They provide a starting point. The effect of recession, reflected in the final column of Table 1, must be allowed for.

Table 17

Sectoral distribution of employment and gross domestic product, Republic of Ireland: 1960–75

	1960	1965	1970	1973	1974	1975
Employment: per cent						
Agriculture*	35	31	25	23	23	22
Industry	22	26	28	29	29	27
(o.w. manufacturing)	(15)	(18)	(19)	(19)	(20)	(19)
Other†	37	38	41	42	43	43
Out of work	6	5	6	6	6	8
	100	100	100	100	100	100
= Total labour force						
(000)	1,118	1,108	1,118	1,132	1,125	1,132
Gross domestic product:‡						
per cent						
Agriculture*	25	21	17	19	16	18
Industry	30	32	35	34	34	33
Other†	45	47	48	47	50	49
	100	100	100	100	100	100
= Total GDP‡						
(£m)	558	844	1,400	2,329	2,574	3,248

Sources: *Employment*: National Industrial Economic Council (1967: 15, Table 2). Central Bank of Ireland (1977: 70, Table 56).
   GDP: Central Statistics office (1977b: 11, 58, Tables A.3, B.3).
   * Includes forestry, fishing.
   † Distribution, transport and communication; public administration and defence, etc.
   ‡ At current factor cost.

growth in Irish GDP over the next 8 years. As a proportion of GDP, its output (all sectors) had expanded in this period from 3–4 per cent to about 15–16 per cent (McAleese 1977; IDA 1977, p. 4; Central Statistics Office 1977: Tables A.3, B.3).

Thirdly, its share in fixed capital formation has climbed abruptly in recent years. Over the decade 1960–69, fixed asset investment by IDA-grant-aided foreign firms (up to 10 per cent of FCEM omitted) was about 5 per cent of Ireland's gross domestic fixed capital formation. Fixed asset investment 'commitments' (projections) by new IDA-grant-aided foreign firms from 1972–5 amounted to 20 per cent of GDFCF in those four years.[4]

Fourthly, FCEM has helped propel visible exports steeply upwards. Around 10 per cent annually, 1961–68, their growth rate was near 30 per cent each year from 1972 to 1976. Manufactured exports (food, drink and tobacco excluded), only about one-fifth of visible exports in 1960, first exceeded half the total in 1974; by then, apparently, almost 60 per cent of their annual value – and just over 60 per cent of their increase since 1966 – was due to FCEM sales. (Coras Trachtala, various years; Kennedy and Bruton, 1975: 122, Central Statistics Office, 1977a, pp. 4–5; IDA 1977, p. 4; McAleese, 1977).

The main *sources* of Ireland's FCEM investment are indicated in Table 18. EEC capital constitutes most of the 'other' category. These limited data suggest that, particularly in terms of fixed capital per project, US investors have responded to Ireland's EEC accession much more vigorously than those in metropolitan Europe. True, 1973 and 1974 saw the highest ever rate of 'starts' by German companies (IDA *Annual Reports*, various years; IDA 1976): 11 and 15 respectively as against the average seven per annum of the 1960s. But this can hardly be reckoned a flood of new investment, especially as German establishments in Ireland are consistently on a smaller scale than those of other 'major' nationalities, except the UK. If Europe's integration has implied some migration of productive facilities to its periphery, the process has been governed by factors more gradual and more basic than the signature of accession instruments in Brussels, or the *Gastarbeiterstop*.

Table 18

Sources of new foreign export-manufacturing (IDA grant-assisted) investment: 1960–70, 1974–6

| | 1960–70 | | | |
	Projects no.	%	Total investment* £m	%
USA	98	25	42	34
UK	178	44	35	29
Germany	72	18	12	10
Other	53	13	33	27
Total foreign	401	100	122	100

| | 1974–76† | | | |
	Projects approved no.	%	Fixed-asset investment‡ £m	%
USA	56	38	192	74
UK	42	28	13	5
Germany	18	12	26	10
Other	33	22	27	11
Total foreign	149	100	258	100

Sources: McAleese (1972: 78). IDA, *Ann. Reports*.
* Includes working capital: expenditure incurred.
† Inclusive: 1974 April to December.
‡ Commitments only.

A recent study[5] of FCEM in the Shannon Free Zone and the surrounding region suggests that most of the substantial operations[6] would be accounted for by one of three alternative *strategies:*

E

(i)   Manufacture at high volumes where the benefit of Irish location lies in the combination of relatively low final-cost labour-power[7] with export profits tax relief (EPTR). Many earlier operations are instances (e.g. the processing of light high-value electronic components). European markets were often not of primary interest. Factories reflecting this strategy continue to be established (e.g. in textiles, consumer electronics). In several recent cases their output is high-bulk for the European market, so transport and tariff considerations justify an inner-peripheral location for a labour-cost-sensitive operation.

(ii)   Manufacture for a narrower market: European or global, it may be narrowed institutionally (intra-firm trade), by product differentiation, or by ability to meet individual specifications rapidly. Fixed assets are usually slight. The firm locates in Ireland to enjoy the EPTR benefit of a market niche; but this is often relatively insecure and labour cost remains a major concern. Operations in this category are numerous, and probably below FCEM's average employment size.

(iii)   Mass or flow manufacture by complex processes, using extensive fixed assets. These are the industries now most keenly promoted by the IDA, which are likely to account for most FCEM investment by value in the next few years: pharmaceuticals, synthetic textiles, automated electronics manufacture, petro-chemicals. Though basic labour cost may often be of marginal importance, management control is critical because of the need (technical or financial) for continuity of production, so potential control cost is significant. EPTR and capital grants are now both key benefits. A European sales focus is likely. Much of the recent heavy US investment (see Table 18) will fall within this category.

Political Requirements of FCEM

Recurring through these strategies are investors' two political demands. These are for: (i) comparatively low final cost of labour power (see note 7) and (ii) state commitment: both to help restrain labour cost, and to guarantee official benefits and services.

This is not to suggest that labour cost and host-state policies add up to a complete explanation of the metropolitan firm's decision to manufacture for export at the European periphery.[8] Fulfilment of these twin demands is not a sufficient but a necessary condition for attracting and retaining FCEM investment.

Their relative weight will vary over time. The FCEM strategy now in the ascendant ((iii) above)[9] involves fixed capital formation on a scale quite different from most earlier operations. Corporate concern may consequently be shifting towards state investment subsidies. But for most firms up to the recession, it is suggested, and for many firms still, the focus has been on labour cost – always *in conjunction with* EPTR.

The two requirements will now be considered more closely. Why are they important to firms; and how, if at all, has Irish society been able to meet them?

Labour Cost

Evidence gathered during the 1977 study,[10] together with comment from sources involved with establishing new industry, gives a tentative idea of the cost/earnings outlook for less capital-intensive FCEM (strategies (i) and (ii) above).

First, predictable but significant, its *raison d'être* is a handsome trading profit: not growth potential, but profit here and now. Historically, margins of 20 to 25 per cent appear to have been normal; often they have gone much higher. Secondly, profits from an FCEM enterprise in one year would thus quite often exceed the total capital grant disbursed by state agencies in the project's lifetime. So also, in some lucrative cases, would annual profit-tax saving. Even including its subventions towards buildings and rental costs, the state's direct support on capital account could at a suitable rate of depreciation usually explain only a minor part of the rich returns demanded of an FCEM operation.[11]

The extent to which they depend alternatively on indirect subsidies (e.g. state provision of cheap credit) cannot be assessed here. The impact of EPTR is evident but does not explain FCEM's trading profitability. Appropriate transfer pricing may well play an important part.

Finally, however, it is clear that advantageous labour cost has often made a vital contribution. For many FCEM firms during the 1970s, even in a relatively 'developed' part of Europe's periphery after several years when Irish earnings had risen rapidly by international standards (McCarthy *et al.* 1975, p. 19), sums of much the same order as profit margins may have arisen from the saving on payroll (mostly wage) costs relative to a major metropolitan economy.

In addition to payroll, there are at least three components of final labour cost which an Irish location may help the FCEM investor to reduce: (i) social security payments by the employer, which with payroll are part of basic labour cost; (ii) excess-hire cost: one Shannon firm, for example, during an adverse period in 1974–5, exploited labour flexibility with spasmodic sackings and a 'three-day week' for part of its workforce while at the same time introducing 24-hour shift working; (iii) control cost.

Firms themselves take the first step towards reducing final labour cost. FCEM operations investigated in this study rarely involved complex transformation: extended chemical processes, for instance, or production of many components in-house from raw materials. Characteristically they were built around a single procedure, or small set of procedures, circumscribed and changing little in the life of the business. The purpose of FCEM investment is typically to perform a particular manufacturing act on specified material(s): e.g. assembly, perhaps with limited machining, spinning, repetitive precision metalworking, etc.

In most production workers, therefore, only a semi-skill is needed, while the maintenance function is minimised.[12] This picture is not much altered by the trend towards 'advanced' product lines, such as electronic instruments.

Restriction of the operation's technical content would present opportunities for cutting final labour cost irrespective of location; moving to Ireland enables the manufacturer to take relatively full advantage[13] of them. This is essentially because of agriculture: its past preponderance and the continuous steep decline in its workforce, particularly on smaller farms.[14]

First, FCEM's wage levels may reflect rural incomes which are low by European standards, or did so at least in the 1960s; though the most obvious, this factor may be the least enduring. Secondly there is a sustained labour surplus of which, thirdly – in Ireland's case – a large proportion will be cheaper workers: youth and females. Among both these groups many will rely for part of their (short or medium-term) subsistence on other income in the household. Fourthly, they are joined in FCEM employment by farmers and others continuing to live partly by agriculture. A further source of auxiliary income, increasingly important in Ireland as elsewhere at the inner periphery, is the state transfer payment (cf. Wade's paper in this volume). The typical FCEM workforce, while drawing a wage from a single employer, will be marked by considerable heterogeneity in sources of supplementary income.

It tends also to be deeply fragmented: economically, by this diversity of incomes; physically, by its recruitment partly from a dispersed rural population, often from other regions of the country; temporally, by high rates of labour turnover. The migration 'option', or notional access to a metropolitan labour market, may tend (even when the flow is at a standstill) to discourage commitment either to the workplace or to politics. Meanwhile, political mobilisation may be inhibited by the ideological influences arising over a long period from class interests prominent within peripheralised agriculture.

In the technical context which most FCEM operations appear to provide, these factors can act cumulatively – not simultaneously or with equal force – upon basic labour cost, excess-hire and control costs. Acting with them, rooted also in agricultural interests, is a more visibly political factor: state commitment to FCEM.

State Commitment I: Restraining Labour Cost

Dublin authorities have had various reasons for trying to influence industrial incomes besides pressure from a foreign export-manufacturing constituency. None the less, it seems clear that adopting the export-manufacturing strategy made it obligatory within a few years to attempt state restraint. This could take the form of a relatively permissive national incomes policy, most basically because the lines of conflict over contractual incomes corresponded to no major class antagonism; but also, for example, because Ireland's trade union movement is large, well-established and to a considerable degree politically incorporated – though hampered as a political instrument by fragmentation and uneven balance of membership.[15]

A Department of Labour within the government was first set up in 1966. The influential National Industrial Economic Council, a state/employer/trade union advisory body reporting to the government, began vigorously to argue for an explicit incomes policy; rapid growth and full employment were conditional on

> ... improving the competitiveness of the Irish economy ... (i.e.) the rate of increase in money incomes relative to productivity must be somewhat slower here than in neighbouring countries. (National Industrial Economic Council 1967, p. 80)

Only at the end of 1970, however, after the government had threatened statutory pay controls, did the Irish Congress of Trade Unions (ICTU) agree to negotiate a set of formal pay constraints with employers. The 1970 settlement was the first in an unbroken series of National Wage Agreements putting comprehensive, specific limits on pay rises for a fixed term. Inevitably, wage drift away from the national guidelines has set in recently, but most FCEM managers interviewed in this study indicated that the process of wage determination has in a large measure been transposed from factory or sector to officially-constituted institutions. The two most important of these have been the bilateral Employer-Labour Conference, where each new National Agreement is drawn up; and the Labour Court, arbitrating in disputes over application of the Agreements.

Besides helping to establish these institutions and participating in the Conference as the country's largest employer, the government is making increasing use of its ability to influence labour's remuneration

and employment prospects by tax and subsidy, turning a nominally
bilateral into an avowedly tripartite process. This approach was apparently mooted first about 1972 – significantly, by the Federated
Union of Employers (their industrial relations body): wages could
best be restrained by treating them as one variable in an 'integrated
pay package', together with state interventions (personal taxation, public spending). It was commended warmly by several of the FCEM
managers. Their enthusiasm is understandable, since the state would
be making up the pay package from an exchequer to which their
firms contributed virtually nothing.

Labour cost has so far been considered mainly with respect to its
basic component, the wage bill. But incomes policy has acted also upon
another component: by pacifying industrial relations (IDA 1974, I,
p. 1) it relieves employers of part of their possible labour-control costs.

This aspect the proponents of incomes policy have been happy to
link publicly with the interests of FCEM investors. The advisory
council quoted earlier, observes in its 1967 'Report on Full Employment' that:

> Representatives of some foreign firms . . . in Ireland have expressed
> concern at the recent history of industrial relations, even though very
> few of them have had any actual or threatened stoppages . . . many (new
> firms) whose contributions will be needed if the 1970 (industrial sector)
> targets are to be reached are not committed irrevocably to an Irish
> location . . . the problem of industrial relations cannot be ignored in its
> effects on foreign industrialists who may be contemplating locating a new
> plant in Ireland, for many of our major disputes . . . have been inter-
> nationally newsworthy. (National Industrial Economic Council 1967,
> pp. 103–104)

Incomes policy has reduced the chances of industrial conflict, temporarily at least, in two main ways. First, within a centralized and
cross-sectoral negotiation process there is more likely to be prior con-
sensus as to the 'reasonable' area of settlement, while recourse to
industrial action as a bargaining weapon is more difficult. This labour
armistice is extended to the country's workplaces by the quasi-
contractual National Agreement and supporting institutions:

INDUSTRIAL PEACE
. . . Trade unions undertake not to enter into a strike or . . . encourage
any other form of industrial action calculated to bring pressure to bear on
an employer to concede an increase in pay in excess of the amount set
out in . . . this Agreement. Where employers or trade unions consider
that a dispute may arise . . . (contravening) . . . this Agreement, they will
advise the Steering Committee of the Employer-Labour Conference and
seek their advice . . . etc. (Employer-Labour Conference, 1977, p. 8)

There is a distinct secondary effect, however, on labour organisation at local level. Trade union officials in Ireland, at least in its more western parts, appear often to have been rather closer to members than their counterparts in many metropolitan countries (see Hyman and Fryer, 1977, pp. 161–70). With the advent of incomes policy, they may be largely confined to administering the local application of the national settlement. Formal opposition to workpeople may then take the place of formal solidarity. The most spectacular case is that of the Ferenka firm[16] near Limerick in the Mid-West Region, Ireland's biggest FCEM employer, where in autumn 1977 a mass resignation of general operatives from the hegemonic Irish Transport and General Workers' Union led to a work stoppage, precipitating close-down and the withdrawal of the investment. In the long run, more thorough incorporation of union officials due to incomes policy may call forth alternative, possibly 'disruptive' groupings as at Ferenka; but for a few years it has (with the recession) apparently helped to disarticulate and so neutralise labour organisation locally, with savings to firms accordingly under each of the headings that make up control cost.

State Commitment II: Official Benefits and Services

Most conspicuous among these are the incentives specifically for export-oriented manufacturing, such as grants, tax relief and subsidies. Discussion so far suggests that while, historically, these may not have outweighed labour pricing among Ireland's attractions, they are (especially EPTR) of major and probably rising importance to the FCEM investor. The zeal which host-state authorities must display in maintaining them is illustrated below.

In addition there is a wide range of state investments and activities to whose benefits the export-manufacturing firm has access jointly not exclusively: physical infrastructure; provision of productive inputs such as electricity, telecommunications; manpower assistance in the form of education 'relevant to industry's needs', recruitment services, industrial training schemes; and social services contributing to the subsistence of employee and dependants. Erosion of such benefits might affect foreign firms' willingness to start or continue an Irish operation – but less immediately and probably less severely than would a withdrawal of the specific export-manufacturing incentives.

Those types of commitment are looked at by Schaffer below. Of particular interest, however, in the present context is a third type of service required of the host state: external political (including diplomatic) representation. The exporter located in Ireland will normally be looking for representation in the European Community (though the

Irish government's cultivation of Third World links, *via* both the UN system and European development co-operation, is likely to be of increasing interest to such firms[17]). Its object will generally be one of the following:

(a) THE IMPROVEMENT OF EUROPEAN MARKET POSITIONS

In continental Europe the Irish diplomatic service was active from the early 1960s on behalf of foreign-owned export-manufacturers, for example in pressing the French government (unsuccessfully) during 1961 to open up an import quota, under the Irish-French Trade Agreement then in force, for a consumer product manufactured at Shannon by a non-European firm. Encouraging such investors was of course one motive for the protracted effort to join a European trade grouping (National Industrial Economic Council, 1967: 108).

Given EEC membership, the emphasis today is rather on protection. Ireland's textile manufacturers, for example, among whom FCEM now predominates, campaigned in 1977 for revision of EEC trade policy to limit penetration by Third World and East European textile goods. Speaking for 'the industry' just before a meeting with the Commissioner for Industrial Affairs, the chairman of the Irish Textile Federation – chief executive of Snia Viscosa, a large Italian-owned synthetic textile firm located in Ireland's north-west Region – insisted that new EEC restrictions were imperative. His call to action seemed implicitly to be addressed in part to Dublin authorities. The first priority

> ... is to secure our markets for the future by making our voice heard in the corridors of Brussels at both official and trade level ... The fact that many less privileged regions of the community such as Ireland still rely heavily on textile/based [sic] employment must be adduced in favour of tempering official trade policy ... (*Sunday Independent*, Dublin, 18 September 1977)

(b) SECURING A SHARE OF COMMUNITY FINANCIAL TRANSFERS

Locating in Ireland might seem to assure the metropolitan capitalist of getting maximum benefit from EEC programmes of redistributive transfers;[18] this is the only member state whose entire territory has been designated a regional development area. Recent applications of EEC Regional Fund payments in Ireland which could benefit FCEM include contributions to the capital cost of a few new industrial projects, and infrastructural investments. The European Social Fund assists in the manpower area, contributing 50 per cent of each Irish government grant to firms for in-house training; of these grants a disproportionately large number are likely to be taken up by FCEM enterprises.

Merely to be sited in Ireland is not enough. Taking advantage of

EEC redistributive policy depends on the Irish state's proficiency as intermediary. Not only must it, for specific projects, submit proposals, match the EEC contribution with expenditure of its own, and administer the eventual spending of funds. It has also to participate in Community decisions about the size of total budgetary allocations for these programmes. Here it engages fully with the European political system. Since Ireland's receipts will be proportionate to the global allocations, its EEC representatives will be required to press for these to be as high as possible. They did so for example, without success, in July 1977 when the German and other metropolitan governments insisted on heavy cuts in the Commission's 1978 Regional Fund allocation (*Irish Times*, 21 July 1977).

Overall though, transfers of this kind and the associated host-state functions are probably of limited significance. The aggregate size of the transfers – however energetically Irish and Italian missions may lobby in Brussels – is likely to remain simply too small to exert much influence on metropolitan corporate decisions. Ultimately, fiscal redistribution is not what the Community is about.

(c) DEFENDING IRELAND'S SYSTEM OF PRIVILEGES FOR EXPORTING INDUSTRY

'Harmonisation' of industrial and commercial conditions (to ease the expansionary passage of capital) is at the focus of the European Community's activity, as redistribution is not. For Ireland's representatives, therefore, the task of fending off EEC pressure to trim industrial incentives is critical, certainly more important than the attempt to win extra financial transfers.

This is exemplified by an important episode in 1977 when Irish-EEC relations were briefly filled with exceptional hostility.[19] Protocol 30 to the Treaty of Accession had recorded an understanding that in applying its 'competition' policy the EEC would deal leniently with Ireland's incentive schemes.[20] In mid-September 1977, however, word allegedly reached Dublin that in the interests of Community 'co-ordination' the Commission had decided to seek the early abolition of much of Ireland's incentive package, in particular of the export profit tax relief (EPTR) scheme.

We have one glimpse of the FCEM response:

Asked how he thought his members would react if (EPTR) was abolished, a spokesman for the US Chamber of Commerce in Ireland said he thought the first reaction would be surprise and the second horror. US firms investing in Ireland had a contract with the Irish Government which had assured them that (EPTR) would continue. Abolition of the relief 'would put the kibosh' on a lot of US firms coming here ... (*Irish Times*, 21 September 1977)

No evidence is available that foreign firms told the government it should resist. More to the point, it needed no telling. Mr. Desmond O'Malley, Minister for Industry and Commerce, immediately sought a meeting with the Commissioners for Industrial Affairs and for competition policy. The government indicated that if he did not get satisfaction there, the issue would be taken to the EEC Council of Ministers.

From the direction of Ireland's dominant social interests came unequivocal expressions of solidarity with Mr. O'Malley and the FCEM investor. Dr. Garrett Fitzgerald, leader of the opposition Fine Gael party, urged the government to stand firm and declared that the Community must permit peripheral countries like Ireland to maintain 'much more generous' incentives than those at the centre. The director-general of the Confederation of Irish Industry (representing employers on questions of broad economic policy) announced that it would be 'totally opposed' to any proposal to abolish EPTR, and indeed would reject the idea of limiting the relief to certain levels of profit (*Irish Times*, 21 September 1977). The 'serious' *Irish Times*, in one of the less vehement editorial statements of 21 September 1977, put the view widespread among Dublin officials that EPTR would be unnecessary 'if the European Community had a proper regional policy'. The *Irish Independent*, closest to the Fine Gael party, felt that industrial incentives were 'a matter of life and death to us' and that the EEC, if it seriously threatened the incentives system,

> ... will have to be told that over and above our obligation to uphold the terms of the Treaty of Rome is our obligation to ourselves.

Later on some commentators asked whether the Dublin authorities themselves might not have had an interest in staging the crisis. Scepticism was encouraged by the speed with which the breach was healed. Mr. O'Malley's Brussels visit immediately elicited a statement that the Commission would come to no decision about Irish industrial incentives without consulting Dublin; this he interpreted as an 'emphatic' assurance, meaning there would be no 'early' end to EPTR.

Whatever the urgency of the 'EEC threat' on this occasion, it is clear that a significant defensive function had been performed by Irish organs of state – by Irish administrators attached to the Commission who first alerted Dublin to the possible trend of its deliberations, for instance, as well as government departments which took up the issue officially. Irish state authorities made it plain that they recognised the longer-run danger of EEC intervention. Mr. O'Malley's claim to have been reassured by his Brussels meeting was hedged with equivocations; as to the precious Protocol 30, he had to acknowledge that – there might be 'a difference of opinion between the Commission and Dublin over (its) juridical value'. Besides, even were it true that the whole 'crisis' of September 1977 was a stage-managed exercise in public relations or bargaining, it would have been no less impressive a demonstration of the Irish state's concern to represent the interests of the FCEM investor.

We have identified external political representation as one of three types of benefit or service which the state must offer to FCEM firms. If not necessarily the most important, it has seemed worth examining in some detail. It has been largely overlooked so far in analysis of 'export platform' investment. It could conceivably play a part at the margin in locational decisions: in certain cases, for instance, could the advantages of being represented by a European 'power' draw investors to Southern Italy or Northern England in preference to say, Ireland or Greece? Above all, its performance might over time have effects on domestic political relations which are out of proportion to its immediate commercial value to the firms concerned: for instance, on relations between the state apparatus and large agricultural interests, or between these groupings and FCEM managements.

The state's FCEM commitment across the several areas discussed, finds its social basis in peripheralized agriculture. Opting for export-oriented industrialisation-by-invitation was the immediate counterpart to opting for integration with Europe. Ireland was led into this doubly integrationist course, we have suggested, by the larger-scale farmers. Their interest is hardly enough to explain the pursuit of 1958 industrialisation policy, little changed, over two decades. Such consistency probably reflects a convergence of the interests of almost all Ireland's dominant classes and class fractions.[21] All were concerned to maintain national import capacity, for consumption or investment needs; and to provide full employment, if only with a view to social peace. Besides, the years of promoting FCEM have enormously increased the state's political weight at the expense of the rancher class (see below) so that this must now be considered primarily a state policy. But it is important to recognise that its initial impetus was rural.

Conclusion

An agricultural history governed by external markets, rapid contraction in agricultural employment, together with proximity to a metropolitan area and political independence (statehood), were factors which interacted to give a politico-economic context where FCEM firms might expect downward pressures on relative final labour cost and sustained state support – a context reasonably likely to draw a protracted inflow of this investment.

There is a corollary. The absence of a dominant entrepreneurial class and of a proletariat, relatively highly (i.e. efficiently) exploited by international standards, is the essence of being peripheral to the capitalist system. It is also what justifies metropolitan capital's move to the periphery for export-manufacture. As well as labour that is at least partly new to wage-employment, this mobile, export-oriented capital is likely to seek a social context where it stands apparently alone as the means of dynamic accumulation, since this should guarantee it first call on state services and funds. The demands made by FCEM investors with respect to labour cost and state support, do not come together coincidentally. They are the two aspects of a single concern, to locate in a non-accumulatory environment. Ireland could pursue the FCEM strategy only because peripheralisation had left it without industrial classes – in particular an industrial bourgeoisie – of significant size.

When Ireland's dominant groups, headed by the 'ranchers', opted for FCEM, they called into being a novel social relationship. They offered foreign capital not a working class but a 'labour pool' (the standard IDA promotional phrase), a surplus population with which they had no functional relationship; they delegated to the state the task of promoting and servicing FCEM – which eventually meant dealing with labour cost. Relations of production would run between the Irish workforce and an overseas employer, often virtually invisible but obviously mobile. The long-term political relationship, the axis of possible mobilisation and conflict, would run between the 'labour pool' and the state.

Ranchers and small farmers with whose interests Irish politics had hitherto been largely occupied, are extraneous to this relationship. It is not merely that their products are gradually being overtaken by manufactures, in GDP and exports, or that sheer loss of numbers among small farmers (and assisting relatives) is reducing their major political presence. Neither rural class has a function within the FCEM-based social relationship. Small farmers encounter it only when they themselves enter the 'labour pool', seeking temporary FCEM employment. The interests of large farmers, who set the process in motion, could even collide soon with state efforts to service FCEM (possibly for example over taxation to help fund industrial subsidies, or the trading of agricultural for industrial advantages in negotiations with the EEC).

The pool of potential FCEM recruits, people who have either worked in this type of industry or consistently sought to do so, has steadily expanded. Rapid circulation through FCEM employment, due to voluntary turnover, dismissals, and plant closures, raises this total far above the number working in FCEM at any one time. By the late 1970s it must represent a large minority of the Irish labour force, latent and recorded, and may be a majority in certain localities and in younger age groups. The post-1958 strategy has at least succeeded in persuading Ireland's growing surplus population that employment, if it comes, is likely to be industrial.

Without FCEM, the ending of emigration would have meant an excess population composed of rural youngsters who, if they were to stay in Ireland, mostly still looked upon land as the primary source of livelihood. There would have been a real prospect by the early 1980s of a struggle over land tenure, even of agrarian guerrilla warfare. This is no longer conceivable. FCEM industrialisation has moved the locus of conflict away from the countryside – not necessarily to the factory but to the street.

At the same time it has elevated the state into a social-structural position more dominant than would have been likely under the earlier, agricultural-exporting policies. Not only have state authorities to provide for and administer the domestic benefits and services required by FCEM firms, which means a steep increase in the quantity of resources they are to allocate in a discretionary way (see Bernard Schaffer's analysis, below). They must also take on specialised and multiplying external tasks, promoting Ireland across the advanced capitalist world as an investment site and representing FCEM's interets, particularly in Brussels. As FCEM becomes a crucial element in Ireland's economy, and the most dynamic, the state's domestic and international role does not shrink but grows in importance.

The rate of new job creation in FCEM is extremely unlikely to come near to meeting Ireland's future employment needs, for three main reasons. First, Ireland has to be promoted, as investment location, in an increasingly competitive 'market'. Second, if the FCEM firms survive in Ireland for more than a few years, their employment size tends to decline in the normal way as process technology is adjusted (often with IDA assistance), or the intensity of labour increased, to keep the plant internationally competitive. Thirdly, they are normally dependent to a high degree on a tightly defined market; established to perform a limited manufacturing operation on specified materials, they appear rarely to carry out a major change of product line. If the market in question begins to look uncertain, closure of the Irish plant will often ensue. The risk does not necessarily fade and may even increase with FCEM's shift, encouraged by the IDA, into technologically advanced sectors; this tends to raise investors' fixed-capital stake in the Irish operation, it is true, but may also mean that an output relatively inflexible in specification is destined for markets where the pace of product innovation is fastest. (But see McAleese, 1978, p. 65.)

There is no substantial local bourgeoisie awaiting its chance. Successive Dublin administrations have repudiated the idea that the state itself should become a major agent of industrial production and employment. So the difficulty of generating new 'foreign-sponsored' jobs is critical. It brings into focus the antagonism in the relationship between state and FCEM's 'labour pool'. Though the former may seek to accelerate foreign investment by larger and larger pump-priming payments, based on growing national debt, these are only likely to raise the capital-intensity of new plants; if there is to be any chance of getting extra employment from FCEM, the labour-cost requirement cannot be evaded.

The state thus presents to labour in FCEM's 'pool' the prospect both of growing unemployment and of increasingly systematic official restraints on final labour cost (assuming it is not much depressed by excess supply). Heterogeneous and deeply fragmented, this quasi-proletariat seems to be some way from the common conception of its relationship (actual and potential) to the country's productive resources which would enable it to generate an alternative to the FCEM strategy. Resistance to the strategy's consequences offered by its members, employed or unemployed, is likely to increase but to lack political articulation. To this situation the state may well respond first by making maximum use of nationalism;[22] and subsequently with the forthright repression it has managed to avoid for most of the FCEM period. That the road to integration with the 'Western European democracies' might have this terminus, is an irony that needs no emphasis.

Notes

1   The immediate EEC effect on sales revenues apart, those financially involved in local agricultural processing (especially through dairy co-operative shareholdings) may more recently have been interested in ensuring an open door for foreign – usually British – food concerns offering export marketing knowhow and/or guaranteed market outlets.

2   The Shannon Free Zone has been managed throughout by the Shannon Free Airport Development Company (SFADCo), which has also since 1969 been responsible for industrial development strategy and administration in the Mid-West Region around Shannon.

3   An exact picture of FCEM in Ireland is difficult to arrive at. Naturally, the IDA endeavours to fudge the distinction between foreign and national beneficiaries of its assistance. For the purposes of the following rough estimates, it is assumed where necessary that (a) FCEM firms which are not GA (of these there have always been several substantial examples) would add no more than 10 per cent to employment and output figures for those which are GA; (b) foreign-owned firms not manufacturing primarily for export, would again add less than 10 per cent (employment/

output) to totals for FCEM firms (GA & non GA) (Cf. McAleese 1972, pp. 75, 78–9) (GA = grant aided).

4   IDA *Annual Reports*, various years. Firms' 1972 investments figure adjusted to calendar year basis. Since firms' projected expenditure is normally to be realised over several years, this percentage might be expected to exaggerate its current contribution to capital formation. A staggered comparison, firms' investment in 1972–4 against GDFCF 1973–5, actually gives the same ratio, however (20 per cent).

5   The following remarks draw on material gathered in a research project on labour organisation and state policy in FCEM carried out mainly in Shannon and the Mid-West, April–Oct. 1977. Sources included interviews with management in 21 firms, and with trade union officials, some factory workers, and administrators; plus documents. For details see Stanton (1978a).

6   A large minority of FCEM projects, but a marginal part of FCEM employment, assets and output, are due to investments representing a fourth strategy: manufacture of a specialist product, based on a patent or other exclusive knowledge, low-volume, usually low-bulk, for a very restricted market.

7   The final or real cost of labour to the employer, it is suggested, should be reckoned as the sum of (1) basic cost: approximately, the wage plus social security charges, employer's subsidies and training expenses; (2) excess-hire cost: the increment of basic cost due to 'carrying' labour not needed in a production period, inversely related to the degree of capacity utilisation and of labour flexibility; (3) control cost: expenditure necessary to ensure that the worker performs at full intensity, both all day and over a long production period (this concept owes much to Brighton Labour Process Group (1977)).

8   Nor is it implied that, because cheap labour and government assistance are on offer in many peripheral countries, export-manufacturing establishments must come to account for the greater part of external direct investment by metropolitan firms. In the process of internationalisation of production since the 1950s, improved market penetration has always been the leading motive. As Suzanne Paine shows, elsewhere in this volume, this 'market expansion' is likely to remain the basis of most international direct investment in manufacturing.

9   Just this phasing of types of FCEM ('world-wide sourcing') was anticipated by Adam (1975, pp. 91–2).

10 As regards firms' finances – of which no full survey was conducted in the present study – this evidence is limited and partly indirect: interviews with managers, trade union records, balance-sheet data in certain cases, etc.

11 This claim finds some corroboration in the ratio between fixed asset stock (plant/machinery) and turnover in a given year, which it was possible to compute for nine Mid-West FCEM firms only, the date varying from 1967 to 1977. The ratio was 3 per cent in three firms (two of them relatively large); between 11 per cent and 34 per cent in another five cases; and as high as 62 in just one case. Unweighted average was 22 per cent. Such proportions again imply that, even if the host state were to defray every penny of the capital expenditure which firms ever undertook, its contribution per annum could still hardly account for the majority of normal net earnings.

12 Maintenance requirements may of course rise where automation has been the means of 'simplifying' the Irish factory's operation. Such cases, rare so

far, are those which may now increase fastest under the fourth of the corporate strategies identified earlier.

13 Again, we are dealing with a sub-set of international investors – those who can usefully conduct a (geographically separate) part or all of their manufacture within narrow technical confines, and have special reasons, including incentives, for staying within the European system.

14 See Table 1. Reasons for this crucially important trend are indicated in Crotty's chapter below; see also Crotty (1966). The following two paragraphs are elaborated in Stanton (1978b).

15 The Republic has approximately 0·4 m trade unionists, just over half of all employees, of whom some 40 per cent are in the Irish Transport and General Workers' Union, more than four times the size of the next largest union; 33 per cent in another nine unions with more than 6,000 members each; and the remainder split among about 80 other unions, some of them minute. Explanation of this structure would start of course with the very long, contradictory history of Irish industrial development and peripheralisation – ancestors of several present unions were active in Cork and Dublin soon after the mid-eighteenth century.

16 Subsidiary of the Dutch-based MNC Akzo, manufacturing steel cord for tyres. For accounts of the onset of the dispute see for example *Limerick Leader*, 8 October 1977, *Irish Times*, 11 October 1977. Though many other factors were involved in the workers' repudiation of their union and Akzo's subsequent withdrawal from Ireland, a union-worker relationship following the pattern discussed here evidently made a key contribution.

17 The manager of a Shannon firm manufacturing a minor variety of political capital goods (on this concept see Stanton (1977)), said that the US parent had chosen Ireland partly because its image of international neutrality – blue helmets in the Congo, etc. – would be helpful in expanding sales to Third World governments.

18 This refers to 'unrequited transfer' payments made systematically by the EEC with redistributive intent. Other intra-EEC redistributive mechanisms (e.g. agricultural pricing) and public capital flows (e.g. *ad hoc* credit provision by European institutions) may indirectly affect the Irish industrial environment, but are excluded here because they would not call in the same way for regular official representation as an implicit service to the FCEM investor.

19 The following account is composed from what seem to be the more reliable parts of reports in these newspapers: *Irish Times* (21 and 22 September 1977), *Irish Independent*, and *Cork Examiner* (21 September), *Irish Press* (22 September). Specific references are given only where these may be of particular interest.

20 Article 92 of Treaty proscribes aids to industry tending to distort competition; but Protocol 30 attached to the Treaty affirms that in applying this rule the Commission would 'take into account' Ireland's economic development needs.

21 The only group clearly threatened by the turn towards the exterior, was the domestically-oriented Irish manufacturing bourgeoisie. Even within this small group, interests differed. A minority, in branches such as packaging or more specialised metal-working, might hope for increased business when FCEM arrived, especially if the IDA were diligent in demanding 'linkages' from new foreign investors.

22 There are sound historical reasons for questioning the motives of an English observer who comments sceptically on Irish nationalism. So clari-

fication may be in order. To say that (anti-British) nationalism is an instrument of potential value to the Irish state is not to defend policies, past or present, pursued by the British towards Ireland – in particular their retention of control over its six north-eastern counties.

References

Adam, G. (1975), 'World-wide sourcing' in H. Radice (ed.) *International Firms and Modern Imperialism*, Penguin, Harmondsworth.

ANCO (Industrial Training Authority) (1975), *An Investigation of Skill Shortages as Factors Influencing Industrial Development in Ireland*, mimeo, Dublin.

Brighton Labour Process Group (1977), 'The capitalist labour process', *Capital and Class*, 1.

Central Bank of Ireland (1977), *Annual Report 1977*, Dublin.

Central Statistics Office (1977a), *Trade Statistics of Ireland: December 1976*, Stationery Office, Dublin.

Central Statistics Office (1977b), *National Income and Expenditure 1975*, Stationery Office, Dublin.

Coras Trachtala (Irish Export Board) (various years 1964 to 1975), *Annual Report*, Dublin.

Crotty, R. (1966), *Irish Agricultural Production*, Cork University Press.

Employer-Labour Conference (1977), *Employer-Trade Union National Agreement 1977*, Dublin.

Hyman, R. and Fryer, R. H. (1977), 'Trade unions: sociology and political economy', in T. Clarke and L. Clements (eds.) *Trade Unions under Capitalism*, Fontana/Harvester, London and Hassocks.

IDA (Industrial Development Authority) (1974), *Annual Report 1973–74*, Dublin.

IDA (1976), 'Overseas Companies in Ireland' (publicity list), Dublin.

IDA (1977), *Annual Report 1976*, Dublin.

Ireland, Government of (1958), *Programme for Economic Expansion* (White Paper Pr. 4796), Stationery Office, Dublin.

Kennedy, K. A. and Bruton, R. (1975), *The Irish Economy*, Commission of the European Communities: Studies: Economic and Financial Series No. 10, Brussels.

McAleese, D. (1972), 'Capital inflow and direct foreign investment in Ireland 1952 to 1970', *Journal of the Statistical and Social Inquiry Society of Ireland*, 22, 4.

McAleese, D. (1977), *Profile of grant-aided industry in Ireland*, Industrial Development Authority, Dublin.

McCarthy, W. E. J., O'Brien, J. F., and Dowd, V. G. (1975), *Wage Inflation and Wage Leadership: a Study of the Role of Key Bargains in the Irish System of Collective Bargaining*, ESRI Paper No. 79, Economic and Social Research Institute, Dublin.

Meenan, J. (1970), *The Irish Economy since 1922*, Liverpool University Press.

Murphy, J. A. (1975), *Ireland in the Twentieth Century*, Gill and Macmillan, Dublin.

National Industrial Economic Council (1967), *Report on Full Employment*, N.I.E.C. Report No. 18 (Pr. 9188), Stationery Office, Dublin.

Stanton, R. (1977), 'Exports of political capital goods to peripheral countries: the case of broadcast TV equipment', mimeo, Institute of Development Studies, Brighton.

Stanton, R. (1978a), *Foreign-Controlled Export Manufacturing at the Periphery: Labour Organisation and State Policy: Case-Study of the Shannon Free Zone*, mimeo (forthcoming), Institute of Development Studies, Brighton.

Stanton, R. (1978b), 'The European periphery as export platform: metropolitan firms and local class relations in Ireland', mimeo, Institute of Development Studies, Brighton.

7

TOURISM AND THE EUROPEAN PERIPHERY: THE MEDITERRANEAN CASE*

Jeremy Boissevain

The mushrooming growth of the tourist industry has become prov-
erbial. Eight hundred million holidaymakers travelled in 1975. One
out of every four travelled across national frontiers and of these
roughly one third, upwards of some eighty million, were to be found
along the northern shore of the Mediterranean, where they spent
some US $11,291 million. Four out of every ten of these went to
Europe's underdeveloped Mediterranean periphery.[1] What is the
effect of this massive tourist connection between the metropolitan
core of Europe and its southern periphery? Is it in fact a form of
exploitation that is producing ever increasing dependency, as many development specialists maintain? Opinions are divided.

> The stimulation of tourism to poor countries on a commercial basis is not
> a positive contribution to the development of these countries with nega-
> tive effects, but is an extreme form of neo-colonial exploitation. (Dutch
> sociologist)
>
> Compared to my youth – ozu! The difference is like day to night. Every
> time I can help one I do it gladly. Isn't it thanks to them that this village
> is prosperous now? (Old goatherd, Costa del Sol)
>
> International tourism is like King Midas in reverse; a device for the
> systematic destruction of everything that is beautiful in the world.
> (British economic analyst and author)
>
> We are proud they have come so far to see our procession. They could
> have gone to other villages. They chose to come to Naxxar. (Maltese
> villager)

Numbers

The growth of tourism in the South European periphery has been
spectacular, increasing by an average of 13 per cent during the past
decade (Table 19). Following the oil crisis in 1974 the annual growth

* I am grateful to Ton Langendorff and Paul Galea for help with facts and
figures.

rate fell sharply, but not for long. A recent report from World Tourism Organisation (Reuters, 9 December 1977) indicated that everywhere tourism is rapidly reviving. In Europe arrivals for 1977 were eleven per cent higher than in 1976. Tourism appears to have withstood the world economic recession better than most other sectors.

Table 19

Rate of growth of tourism in South European periphery, 1965-75

	From Europe		From all countries	
	Total (thousands)	Annual growth %	Total (thousands)	Annual growth %
1965	13,545		18,529	
1970	22,764	13·6	34,348	17·1
1975	28,196	4·8	42,640	3·9

Sources: Table 51 and OECD, 1976.

In 1975 tourists made 149 million visits to European countries. Of these, almost 92 million, or 62 per cent, were to the European Mediterranean: 49 million to Italy and France and the rest, 43 million, to the peripheral countries of southern Europe.

Table 20

International tourist arrivals and expenditure in Europe by region: 1975

	Arrivals Total (thousands)	%	Receipts Total (US $ millions)	%	Average expenditure per arrival (US $)
France and Italy	49,130	33	6,031	23·7	123
Southern periphery	42,687	29	5,260	20·7	123
Other W. Europe	57,236	38	14,172	55·6	248
TOTALS:	149,053	100	25,463	100	182

Source: Table 51 and OECD, 1976.

During their visits to the poorer countries of the northern Mediterranean, tourists spent some US $5,260 million (Table 20). In more human terms, tourists in the South European periphery spent an average per visit of US $123. (The corresponding figure for Northwest Europe was US $248.) This represented a very rough average expenditure of US $50 for each of the 106 million inhabitants of the peripheral countries of the European Mediterranean. The country by country figures vary enormously, however. They ranged from a low in Turkey of US $5·60 to a high in Malta of US $241, more than double that of Spain (US $113), the second highest average tourist expenditure per head of population.

It is important to note that these figures refer to *international* tourism. In most north European countries, domestic tourism is considerably more important than international tourism and its volume grows apace. While in 1975, 6·5 million visits from France were recorded in the eight countries of the southern periphery, this was but a very small percentage of the French who went on holiday. In 1971, for example, almost half of all Frenchmen took an average of 29 days holiday. They spent 24 days in France and only five days abroad (84 per cent and 16 per cent respectively) (Bartje, 1975, p. 23). A detailed study of a seaside resort in Tuscany also showed that 60 per cent of the hotel guests were Italian (van der Werff, 1976). In Western Germany domestic tourists accounted for no less than 92 per cent of the total overnight stays in 1975, while in Yugoslavia and Spain they accounted for only 55 and 36 per cent respectively (OECD, 1976, p. 64, cf. Langendorff, 1977: Table 14).

Growth

Why has tourism grown so spectacularly? This has to do with the increase in paid holidays, earlier retirement, rising welfare, reduced costs for transport, increasing car ownership and the improvement of the European highway network. It is also a consequence of the pressure of and pollution engendered by the rapid growth of the industrial base of the core area of western Europe. Tourism is in a very real sense a flight from everyday working conditions and pressures in industrial society. This need to escape is of course also promoted by the sophisticated marketing technology at the disposal of this giant industry, including millions if not billions spent on advertising and assiduous cultivation of travel agents and 'writers'. Tourism has thus also become consumerism, and people are prepared to pay handsomely for their momentary escape. Studies of income elasticity have shown that for every extra pound available, Europeans are willing to spend an additional £1·70 on their holidays (Artus, 1970, and Frentrup, 1969).

South Europe is popular precisely because it offers the greatest contrast to the everyday environment of the north European, and can be reached by road or a short flight. In the Mediterranean the north European finds sun, warm weather, a rural setting, exuberant feelings, and a relaxed attitude to work and time. These contrast sharply with the cool wet climate, the industrial urbanisation, the controlled emotions and the tension filled attitude to work, productivity and time that are characteristic of his own environment. If, in the 1960s, travel abroad was still an elite leisure activity, it certainly no longer is so. The modern tourist is increasingly working class. For example, research by the Malta Tourist Board showed that 37 per cent of British holiday visitors to Malta during the summer of 1975 were skilled and unskilled industrial and agricultural workers, while only seven per cent held high administrative posts. The other visitors were intermediate administrative workers (30 per cent), shopkeepers and assistants (14 per cent) and housewives and pensioners (12 per cent). As tourism continues to be democratised it will keep growing. Considering that in 1971 only one per cent of the world's population had flown; that 95 per cent of the world's population did not cross an international boundary and that only 15 per cent of the British planned a foreign holiday in 1973, the growth potential of international tourism is truly enormous (Turner and Ash, 1975, p. 13). Consequently, experts predict that by 1985 from two and a half to three and a half times as many tourists will visit Yugoslavia, Greece, Malta and, especially, Turkey, as in 1975. By 1995 tourist arrivals in the Mediterranean will have risen to five or six times the 1975 figures (Schulmeister, 1976, p. 29 in Langendorff, 1977, pp. 16–17; Bartje and Thurot, 1976). This increase is premissed on reasonable political stability in the area and gradually rising workers' incomes in the core of Europe.

Developments in Tourism

The tourist industry at present is characterised by three major trends. A steady, though somewhat slower rate of growth, which has already been touched on; a concentration of major components in fewer hands; and a decrease in *per capita* expenditure. As in other sectors of the economy, tourism has seen increasing concentration of the means of production among fewer firms. Tour operators place smaller travel agencies, which operate on commissions from the hotel and transport industry, under increasing pressure by chartering entire planes and hotels. The recent successful move by major operators to market their tours through banks, department stores, supermarkets and even petrol stations has further wounded travel agencies. The larger the tour operator, the greater the economies of scale are for advertising, computer and telex facilities. The larger the firm, the greater is its bargaining leverage with airlines and hotels. The more favourable rates thus obtained mean more business, more growth. The same concentration is also discernible in the hotel industry. The large hotel capable of accommodating hundreds of arrivals at a time and of arranging for this via its own telex connection can service the growing mass tourist market in a way small family hotels cannot. Many smaller hotels in order to compete and to ensure winter bookings are obliged to become part of giant catering chains. Fortes Trust Houses, for example, recently bought up a number of declining Maltese hotels. Vertical integration is thus a logical development, as banks, breweries and oil companies expand into the lucrative tourist industry. TWA own

Hilton International and Pan Am own Inter-Continental Hotels. Holland International is another example of this development. Formed three years ago by a consortium composed of KLM, a major Dutch bank and a Dutch shipping company, it bought up over a dozen Dutch travel agencies and tour operators. From its new gleaming office tower in the Hague, it develops, often via its own hotels, package tours throughout the world. It markets these through hundreds of its own direct outlets all over Holland.

Parallel with this concentration has been the decline in *per capita* tourist spending. The average international tourist today is increasingly lower middle-class or even working-class and more price conscious than in the past. All tourist areas have also reported a decline in hotel bookings and an increase in the use of the less expensive self-catering flats and villas. For example, the hotel occupancy rate in Malta declined gradually from a high of 61 per cent in 1972 to its present low of 43 per cent. During the same period, however, tourist arrivals increased by 90 per cent, while the number of available beds rose only by 18 per cent (Malta Government Tourist Board and *Times of Malta*, 2 November 1977). The decline in the use of hotels is not merely a result of greater cost consciousness following the oil crisis or of increasing foreign travel by a poorer segment of the population. It is a long term development which also has to do with the professionalisation of the price conscious tourist. Increasingly he is acquiring the social skills that enable him to dispense with the mediating role of hotels. In a flat or house he not only can live more cheaply, he can also eat what he wants and live more privately, or in closer contact with the local population, should he wish to.

There is also another trend likely to become more pronounced as the Mediterranean coast becomes increasingly built up, and the countries along the littoral seek to diversify their economies. This is the conflict between industrial development and tourism. Obviously, many industries are incompatible with tourism. Many polluting industries are located in underdeveloped coastal regions. These are the areas also often favoured by tourists. In Spain there has been protest against the establishment of oil refineries and nuclear reactors (*International Tourism Quarterly*, 1975). In Malta there was (successful) agitation against the proposed location of a cement factory on Gozo; more recently there was (unsuccessful) protest against the location of a stone quarry overlooking a unique neolithic monument (Malta Press, April and May, 1977).

Tourism and Development

Many people concerned with development problems regard tourism as a typical manifestation of the abject dependency of an underdeveloped periphery on its metropolitan core. Tourism, it is argued, furthers modernisation[2] and is therefore detrimental to development. It leads to progressive economic, technological and cultural dependency (Schneider, Schneider and Hansen, 1972). It is also seen as a form of neo-colonial imperialism (Wertheim, 1975) that systematically destroys everything that is beautiful (Turner and Ash, 1975). As one development economist remarked to me, 'Small islands like Malta that have no resources are destined to become nations of waiters and prostitutes'. To this indictment others have added that it destroys important traditional values by commercialising social relations and cultural manifestations. The result is 'culture by the pound' (Greenwood, 1976. See also Bryden, 1973; Greenwood, 1972; Pi-Sunyer, 1976; and the discussion and surveys in Young, 1973; Unesco, 1975, 1976; Noronha, 1975).

The economic dependency on tourism in most Mediterranean countries is high, though not as extreme as it is in Malta (see Table 21).[3] There it represents 43·2 per cent of the exports of merchandise, one-fifth of the Gross National Product and hotel employment alone accounts for almost 4 per cent of the labour force.

The heavy infrastructural costs, the technology and expertise required by the industry also generate heavy dependence on the advanced nations. The tourist industry, at least in the initial stages, depends heavily on outside expertise, whether foreign or metropolitan. A recent case study, one of the very few, indicated that 48 per cent of the 9,500 hotel beds in Malta were foreign owned and that these accounted for 55 per cent of the net profit on accommodation and board (Spiteri, 1977). In Pescaia, a town of 5,000 on the Tuscan coast, it was found that outsiders controlled 88 per cent of the 20,000 beds

Table 21

International tourist arrivals and gross expenditure as percentage of GNP: South European periphery, 1975

Country	Arrivals, including excursionists (thousand)	Receipts (US $ million)	GNP (US $ billion)	Receipts as % of GNP
Cyprus	79	15	1	1·5
Greece	3,173	621	22	2·8
Malta	384	76	0·4	19·0
Portugal	1,966	175	15·0	1·1
Spain	30,126	3,404	96	3·5
Turkey	1,540	201	35	0·6
Yugoslavia	24,149	768	32	2·4
Total of above	61,414	5,260	201,400	2·6

Source: Table 50 and World Tourism Organisation, *World Travel Statistics*, 1975.

(camping places and second houses as well as hotels) (v.d. Werff, 1976). Half the money spent by the 65,000 tourists and 300,000 day trippers there went to establishments owned by outsiders. These outsiders included foreign as well as metropolitan Italian magnates. Moreover, government subsidies by and large went to the large entrepreneurs, who generally were outsiders. This was not only because they were bigger. Local entrepreneurs and even their sons were generally not prepared to sacrifice their traditional way of life to the capitalistic work ethic embraced by these outside magnates (v.d. Werff, 1976. Also see Fraser, 1973).

In spite of these consequences of tourism, the pessimism of north European experts is generally not shared by many in the periphery. There, tourism is widely seen as contributing handsomely to such common development targets as employment, rising standard of living and foreign exchange (Boissevain, 1977). Some South European governments are beginning to adopt measures to reduce external dependence and internal tensions provoked by tourism. In Malta, one of the pioneers in this field, such measures have included mandatory joint ventures, restrictions on air travel via non-national carriers, and direct involvement of parastatal agencies in hotel and tour operations. It has also stopped grants and tax holidays to hotel developers. Moreover, it has limited foreign property ownership and built considerable public housing to ease the tourist induced housing shortage, which by 1971 had become an electoral issue. In addition, to reduce foreign exchange leakage and to increase its revenue from tourism it banned the importation of some foreign produced souvenirs, increased the airport tax and sharply raised taxes on the use of freshwater for hotels and swimming pools (Boissevain and Serracino Inglott, 1976, Boissevain, 1977). It seems likely that as competition for foreign tourists grows keener governments in the region will increasingly impose similar measures.

Local capital does in time become available, after foreigners have shown the way and arranged for much of the infrastructure. The increasing shift from hotel occupancy to villas and flats will also benefit locals, who generally exert greater control over this sector of the accommodation market. Moreover, while the technological requirements for designing and running first-class night clubs, restaurants and hotels are considerable, they are of a different order than the technological input of the multinational clothing, electronic and pharmaceutical industries that are also being established in Europe's periphery. Given the educational level in southern Europe, the technology of the tourist industry can be learned fairly rapidly. Training and research takes place on the job, in contact with the consumer, and not in multimillion-dollar laboratories and international fashion centres located in the north.

While many north European consumption patterns are certainly transplanted to the south, as Schneider, Schneider and Hansen point out, the reverse also takes place. There is a two-way traffic. Increasingly, elements of the Mediterranean *savoire vivre*, such as wine, olives, garlic and music, flow to the north via returning tourists and migrant labourers. These elements are not only symbolic; they provide an expanding market for Mediterranean products. They assist metropolitans and migrant labourers alike to bridge the gap until their next pilgrimage to the south.

Cultural Aspects

Does tourism also destroy important traditional values by commercialising social relations and cultural manifestations? Tourism has certainly affected the youth of the Mediterranean, who have seized upon the freer foreign life style of the visitors. Costa del Sol and Maltese young men with money in their pockets imitate the dress and some of the behaviour of the tourists. In particular they have found north European girls willing to help emancipate them from traditional Mediterranean sexual restrictions. This creates tension with their own girl friends, who are either obliged to follow suit or, as is more usual, to remain alone for most of the tourist high season (Fraser, 1973 and Boissevain, 1977). Thus tourism has contributed to the gradual erosion of such traditional Mediterranean moral values as modesty in dress, chastity and the separation of sexes. In this, tourism has joined television, foreign travel, expanding education and the impact of recent films and pulp literature as an agent of change.

To an extent tourism has also tended to supply 'culture by the pound' (Greenwood, 1976). Examples abound, from tinny suits of armour in Malta to false flaminco guitarists in Madrid. One of the most blatant cases of cultural pimping comes from the Basque country, where a few years ago the Spanish government ordered local authorities of Fuenterrabia to run a second showing of a traditional pageant so that more tourists could see it. The local participants, quite understandably, boycotted the procession (Greenwood, 1976).

Generally, however, the commercialisation-of-culture theme has been grossly overplayed by sympathetic outsiders. There is evidence that tourism helps to revitalise local culture, whether decaying monuments, local festivals, all but lost folk songs or forgotten local history. People in many tourist zones in the Mediterranean, their attention focussed by tourist interest, have become aware or have reappraised elements of their own culture. In Malta, for example, this newly discovered cultural heritage has provided an important dimension to the search for a new national identity of a recently independent people

(Boissevain and Serracino Inglott, 1976, pp. 19–22). Similarly, it is not unthinkable that the heightened self-awareness that tourism fosters, together with the feeling that the central government is manipulating local traditions for its own profit, have contributed to the upsurge of regional nationalism among Basques and Catalans as well as among Occitans and Corsicans.

Most people, even those inundated by tourists like the inhabitants of the Spanish coast, by and large seem to learn to live with tourists. There is little of the hatred of tourists reported in Tanzania or in the Caribbean.

> Tourists, like the weather, have become a fact of life. . . . If tourism commoditizes culture, natives categorize strangers as a resource or a nuisance rather than as people. (Pi Sunyer, 1976)

Interdependence

Wealthy locals, affluent tourists and foreign social scientists may lament the coming of mass tourism to the European south. The less well off, who constitute the overwhelming majority of the region, when they have experienced its impact, have welcomed it. Their attitude is vividly expressed by the Ibizan saying, 'If the tourists stop coming to Ibiza there are not enough pines in Sa Talaia [the highest local mountain] for the people to hang themselves from!' (Cooper, 1977). My own feeling about tourism is ambivalent. Personally I deplore what tourists have done to the Malta I knew. Yet they have benefitted the Maltese, and they are grateful for this.

It is quite possible that the tourist connection between the core of Europe and its Mediterranean periphery is asymmetrical in economic terms, although this has not yet been demonstrated by hard studies. But even if it were demonstrated that the north earns more than the south from the tourist connection, economic dependency is but one dimension of the interdependency. I am suggesting that there is a growing cultural if not psychological dependence of the western European worker, whether executive or manual, upon the possibility of a momentary escape to recharge his physical and mental batteries in order to be able to cope with his job. This need to flee to recover will increase as the pressure for higher productivity, which is so much a part of industrialised society, continues to mount. It is in this sense that north and south Europe are increasingly interdependent. Just as industrialised European man increasingly depends on psychiatric help to keep him working, so he also depends on his holiday escape to the periphery. Europe needs its periphery for its physical and mental well being. As long as that is so, the periphery will continue to make a great deal of money.

The progressive, debilitating dependence of a less developed periphery on its metropolitan core, predicted by so many development experts, does not seem to hold for the tourist connection between northern Europe and its less developed southern periphery. Tourism has established a relation of greater interdependence between north and south. Both have benefitted but in different ways. It is not possible to speak of the development of underdevelopment in this case. Access to the Mediterranean by means of an annual holiday is increasingly being viewed by metropolitans not as a luxury but as a necessity, not as a privilege of a wealthy few, but as the right of all workers. Like the automobile, the fridge and television, travel to the Mediterranean has become part of the European way of life.

Notes

1   Cyprus, Greece, Malta, Portugal, Spain, Turkey and Yugoslavia.
2   'Modernisation refers to the process by which an underdeveloped region changes in response to inputs (ideologies, behavioural codes, commodities and institutional models) from already established industrial centres, a process which is based on that region's continued dependence upon the urban-industrial metropolis. Development refers to the process by which an underdeveloped region attempts to acquire an autonomous and diversified industrial economy on its own terms' (Schneider, Schneider and Hansen, 1972, p. 340).
3   No studies of the Mediterranean yet exist of the calibre, for example, of Bryden's study of the economic impact of tourism in the Caribbean (1973). It is likely that when they are made they will find, as Bryden did, that foreign exchange leakage is far higher and the multiplier effect much lower than generally calculated by the rough and ready methods of the area's government statisticians.

References

Artus, J. R. (1970), 'The Effect of Revaluation on the Foreign Travel Balance of Germany,' *IMF Staff Papers*, 17.

Baretje, R. (1975), 'Le Tourism face a la crise', *Economie et Humanisme*, 226.

Baretje, R., and J. M. Thurot (1976), 'Touristes par Millions', *Mediterranee + 20*, Paris, La Documentation Francaise.

Boissevain, J. (1977), 'Tourism and Development in Malta', *Development and Change*, 18.

Boissevain, J., and Serracino-Inglott (1976), *Tourism in Malta*, A Report to the World Bank, Amsterdam.

Bryden, J. M. (1973), *Tourism and Development: A Case Study of the Commonwealth Caribbean*, Cambridge University Press.

Cooper, R. (1977), 'Images of Tourism', *New Society*, 25 August.

Economist Intelligence Unit Ltd. (1975), Spain: National Report No. 24, *International Tourism Quarterly*, 28–41.

Fraser, R. (1973), *Tajos: The Story of a Village on the Costa del Sol*, Pantheon Books, New York.

Frentrup, K. (1969), *Die okonomische Bedeutung des internationalen Tourismus fur die Entwickleungslander*, Hoffman und Campe, Hamburg.

Greenwood, D. J. (1976), 'Culture by the Pound: An Anthropological Perspective of Tourism as Cultural Commoditization', *in* Smith.

Greenwood, D. J. (1972), Tourism as an Agent of Change, *Ethnology*, 11.

Langendorff, T. (1977), 'Tourism in the Mediterranean: An Economic Review', Working Paper, Centre for European and Mediterranean Studies, University of Amsterdam.

Noronha, R. (1975), *Review of the Sociological Literature on Tourism*, A report for the World Bank, Washington, April 30.

OECD (1976), *Tourism Policy and International Tourism in OECD Member Countries*, Paris.

Pi-Sunyer, O. (1976), 'Through Native Eyes: Tourists and Tourism in a Catalan Maritime Community', *in* Smith, *op. cit.*

Schneider, P., Schneider, J., and Hansen, E. (1972), 'Modernisation and Development: the Role of Regional Elites and Noncorporate Groups in the European Mediterranean', *Comparative Studies in Society and History*, 14.

Schulmeister, S. (1976), 'Prospects of International Tourism Until 1985', Vienna: Austrian Institute of Economic Research.

Smith, V. L. (1976), *Hosts and Guests: The Anthropology of Tourism*, University of Pennsylvania Press, Philadelphia.

Spiteri, A. (1977), *The Hotel Industry in Malta: An Appraisal of Ownership and Risk*, B.A. (Hons.) Dissertation, Department of Economics, University of Malta.

Turner, L. and Ash, J. (1975), *The Golden Hordes: Internal Tourism and the Pleasure Periphery*, Constable, London.

UNESCO (1975), *Les Effets du Tourism sur les Valeurs Socio-Culturelles*, Paris, 20 September, SHC/OPS/TST/100.

UNESCO (1976), *Social and Cultural Impacts of Tourism: Main Conclusions of Literature Reviews*, CC/CH/23.4.76, Paris.

Van der Werff, P. (1976), *Pescaia: Splijtende werking van toeristen-industrie*, Docteraal Scriptie (M.A. thesis) European Mediterranean Study Group, University of Amsterdam.

Wertheim, W. F. (1975), *Spelevaren als Weldaad voor de Hongerende Mensheid*, Contribution to the Festschrift for R. F. Beerling.

Young, G. (1973), *Tourism: Blessing or Blight?* Penguin Books, Harmondsworth.

III: THE SOUTHERN PERIPHERY

8

DEPENDENT DEVELOPMENT: PORTUGAL AS PERIPHERY

Stuart Holland

From Core to Periphery

There was a period in recent memory when Portugal was considered by its ruling elite to be the metropolitan core of a colonial periphery. The loss of Brazil was only recently followed by the loss of Goa, Mozambique and Angola. Between the wars, fascism in Portugal was matched by the establishment of fascism in Spain, while two of the main European powers – Germany and Italy – also submitted to fascist régimes. If colonial history old style was repeating itself as both tragedy and farce in Abyssinia, Italy also was a colonial power, with France operating on the southern edge of the Mediterranean basin. Insulated by quasi-autarchy from the influence of foreign capital, Portugal's fall from the big power league and economic degeneration was masked until the eleventh hour from those who ruled her.

The revolution of April 1974 overthrew the fascist régime in Portugal and gave independence to the remaining colonies in Africa. In itself this revolved the axis of Portugal's international relations. From being the nominal centre to a major African periphery, she became a minor nation state on the periphery of Europe to which, by geography and culture, she had always belonged. The return of nearly 400,000 Portuguese from the former colonies – half of whom were still unemployed in December 1976 (see Table 23), and the loss of massive investment and infrastructure could in principle be offset by a parallel loss in military expenditure and administrative costs which had syphoned resources away from metropolitan Portugal and inhibited her modernisation during the previous forty years. None the less, the combined social, psychological, economic and political adjustment was fundamental.

Besides, even before the overthrow of the fascist régime, the Salazar and Caetano governments had been forced by events to change the previous degree of autarchy and independence from Western Europe. Institutionally, Salazar had joined EFTA under a hangover from the old time 'special alliance' with the British, sanctioned by a

F

Conservative government which itself had need of a sizeable European counterpart to the original six members of the EEC. Under successive British applications for EEC membership, and with the evident crisis of confidence in EFTA itself, the fascist régime was caused – however reluctantly – to consider joining the EEC, or at least gaining associate EEC status and access to the Community market for Portuguese exports. After April 1974, and especially following the establishment of a democratic – if minority – government, the way was opened for further integration with the EEC.

The Change in Dependence

Behind the institutional change and the trend to closer political links with Western Europe lay basic economic factors which the later fascist governments found it increasingly difficult to ignore. They amounted to nothing less than the failed modernisation of the Portuguese economy. Since the early nineteenth century the industrialisation of Portugal had been partial and hesitant. The exports of wine from Oporto so dear to the heart of Ricardo were from the start dominated by the English wine merchants rather than indigenous entrepreneurs (and in this sense a clearer forerunner of the later multinational division of labour between the same enterprise in different countries than an example of the international division of labour figuring in his own theory of trade). The textile trade which Ricardo warned would be hard put to compete successfully with Manchester found just that then, and the same more than a century later when faced with competition from lower wage production by multinational companies located in Hong Kong, Taiwan, Singapore, South Korea and other South East Asian countries.

In effect, neither of these classic industries provided the economic or social base for the emergence of a Portuguese bourgeoisie capable of diversifying and extending into other industries on a major scale. The very partial nature of the so-called Liberal Revolution in Portugal in 1820 was one factor of fundamental significance later. Unlike the French Revolution of 1789, which at least abolished share cropping or *métayage* in French agriculture, the 1820 Revolution in Portugal failed to change the land tenure in agriculture, which has remained neo-feudal throughout the following 150 years. In 1968, 1 per cent of the farms in Portugal, with an average size of 50 hectares or more, accounted for more than half of the total agricultural area in the country and were concentrated in large *latifundia* estates in the South, while the North was still dominated by peasant smallholdings (see Table 27).

The persistent backwardness of traditional agriculture was compounded by the undynamic and unsustained pattern of industrialisation. The 1820 Revolution had, if anything, reinforced the strength of the nobility as a mercantile and land-owning class, giving rise to a virtually physiocrat assumption that wealth essentially derived from land rather than industry, and from trade rather than either. It might well be claimed that real industrial development began only when the expectation of retrieving Brazil was totally lost. Even then, the most powerful social class in the country – the former mercantile traders and the nobility – invested mainly in finance and banking rather than industry.

By the 1950s, the Portuguese economy was failing to absorb much of the increasing population of working age, especially in rural areas.[1]

Foreign products predominated in the markets for manufactures, partly due to the ease with which they could be penetrated by the industries of France, West Germany, etc. New industrial investments were highly capital-intensive. So a big outflow of labour took place, first to Brazil, the United States and the African colonies, but in the 1960s mostly to Europe, especially France. More than 100,000 a year migrated in the 1960s, or some 3 per cent of the economically active population,[2] most of them illegally. The total working elsewhere in Europe in 1971 exceeded 700,000, or about a quarter of the potential Portuguese labour force. The economically active population of Portugal declined – even the total population, especially in the rural areas, where it fell by 18 per cent in this decade.[3]

While the combined impact of emigration and tourism was considerable and provided some stimulus to industry, wages and social conditions continued to lag far behind most of the rest of Europe. In 1971, the rate of infant mortality was 50 per thousand, more than twice as high as in France. This lag was specially severe in rural areas (including the offshore islands),[4] which show still worse values for social indicators and a curious demographic structure as a result of the emigration. By 1970, the proportion aged over 65 in the interior provinces was 11·6 per cent compared to 9·0 per cent for those along the coast. These areas also contain a high proportion of women, supported by remittances. Dualism is in fact as noticeable as in many countries of Latin America, and – as there – is among the causes and effects of dependency.

The economic structure also was very fragile. By 1970, emigrant remittances were by far the biggest source of foreign exchange: they accounted for 14 billion escudos. Tourism became the second main source, providing a further 6 billion. Together, migration and tourism approached the total value of merchandise exports of all kinds. Portugal was now dependent on these 'invisible' exports for imports not merely of materials, energy and equipment, but even food, about half of the nation's food being imported (see also tables 52 and 53).

Meanwhile, the Salazar régime responded to the lack of a modern industrial structure by what amounted to an example of State monopoly capitalism. By the *Lei de Conicionamento Industrial* or Control of Industry Act he paved the way for protectionist control of a handful of private monopolies, centred round a small group of families. As has been commented on the working of the act, 'other capitalist countries, despite often ruthless anti-trust legislation, have failed to resist the trend towards larger concentrations of industrial power. Portugal actually encouraged the process. Industries in which monopolies or oligopolies already existed, such as cement, beer, tyres and fertilisers, were protected from even the possibility of fresh competition. Salazar used the laws consistently and deliberately to encourage a few private empires, protecting them both from small businessmen and (until the 1960s) from the encroachment of foreign investment.'[5]

The result was a tremendous concentration of industrial power both in a few enterprises and in a few families of the haute bourgeoisie. The rise of an indigenous industrial bourgeoisie, and the expectations of the petty bourgeoisie were frustrated or diverted into the colonies. Yet by the same token, the protectionism prevented modernisation in what should have been modern industries. By the 1960s Salazar had become aware of the need for both new capital and new competitiveness to protect the economic base of the country following the agreement to join EFTA which he had made for fundamentally political reasons. He thus reversed his protectionist objection to foreign investment, and specifically encouraged its expansion. At first domestic large-scale capital linked with the newcomers rather than faced real competition. Later it faced more direct competition. But the result was reinforcement of the trend to concentration in Portuguese industry, with an increased dependence on foreign capital.

Thus, although Portugal became more dependent on external factors from the late 1950s – through joining EFTA, the increase in multinational penetration of the economy and labour migration and remittances, – the benefits appeared, to some, to outweigh the costs. The employment effects are corroborated by considering 'modern' versus 'traditional' industry. Table 24 shows that while employment in food, drink, tobacco, textiles, clothing and footwear declined between 1960 and 1973, employment in chemicals and related products, non-metallic minerals, metal industry, metal products and machinery, paper and printing and other modern industry increased substantially and in some cases dramatically – in the case of metal industries nearly five times from an almost derisory 9,000 to more than 46,000. Moreover, as illustrated in Table 25 this expansion was associated with positive and apparently healthy rates of growth of product in both 'modern' and 'traditional' industry. Even traditional export industries such as textiles, wines and processed food registered notable expansion (see Table 26) while the overall balance of payments was by and large positive.

Dependence and Crisis

The latter-day dynamism of Portuguese industry was short lived and two-sided. While permitting sizeable increases in economic performance in important areas of the economy, it at the same time revealed Portugal's dependence and vulnerability relative to centres of economic power and activity outside the economy. This included the demand for labour abroad and emigrants' remittances, a dependence on foreign exchange or tourism, the insecure reliance on foreign investment for dynamisation of the modern sectors of the economy, and the indirect income and employment generation at home dependent on investment and production momentum in manufacturing industry.

With the recession in the main Western European economies from 1974, the demand for migrant labour fell and the expulsion of emigrant labour began. It should be stressed that migration statistics are particularly unreliable in view of illegal employment secured without work permits by migrant labour abroad. None the less, gross migration abroad fell from 120,000 in 1973 to only 30,000 in 1975, or a level equivalent with the original low emigration levels of 1960 (see also Table 54).

The change of political régime reinforced the negative impact of economic recession. In the first three months of 1974, tourist arrivals had been running at almost exactly 1973 levels (in March they had in fact been higher). The decline was sharp after 25th April: in May, only 48 per cent as many tourists arrived as in May 1973, and the ratio continued at about that level during the summer. Tourist expenditures were down correspondingly and continued to sag throughout 1975. Migrants' remittances remained close to 1973 levels for some months, but started to fall as the crisis in 'confidence' deepened, especially after the departure of Spinola. In addition, outward remittances grew and private foreign investment dropped. So surpluses on 'invisible' and 'capital' accounts no longer covered the big deficit in merchandise trade, which in fact increased due to the world recession. Serious cuts in imports were avoided only because of the high foreign assets of the banking system.

Otherwise, Table 25 shows that the rate of growth of output in key sectors such as textiles, clothing and footwear fell by more than 17 per cent from 1974 to 1975; metal products, mechanical and electrical equipment and transportation equipment fell by 13 per cent in the same period, and basic metals by 18 per cent. Between 1974 and 1976, as illustrated in Table 22, employment fell in the main sectors of agriculture and forestry, fishing and manufacturing, while showing no increase in mining.

Table 24 indicates that employment was protected in specific sectors within manufacturing industry up to 1975, but mainly in those areas where the labour force was significantly urban and strongly unionised. Exports fell in the important traditional industries, as shown in Table 26. It also became increasingly clear that foreign multinational enterprise not only was responding to the recession in world demand in the more modern sectors of the economy, but also was implementing what amounted to a joint investment and export strike in reaction to the radical period of the provisional governments following the events of April 1974. The balance of payments deteriorated dramatically not only through loss of earnings from manufacturing exports, but also a major increase in the import of food products of nearly two-thirds in the one year 1973–4 (see Table 27(c)). The imbalance in agricultural imports relative to domestic production became dramatic, nearly 175 per cent in corn and nearly 60 per cent in wheat – products which the fertile estates of the southern *latifundia* should have been able to substitute effectively had they not been initially under so pernicious a form of exploitation, and in the throes of land reform (see Table 27(b)).

Political Periphery

At the same time, the post revolutionary governments found that the structural economic costs of increased dependence on the fate of the international economy was matched by an increased dependence on the politics and institutions of the international economy.

For one thing, the major deterioration in the trade balance meant an increased dependence on the International Monetary Fund and the World Bank. By 1978 it amounted to $1·2 billions. Salazar's cautious liberalisation of the Portuguese economy to foreign investment and trade had not damaged the balance of payments during a period of sustained international expansion. From a substantial reserve position, the national reserves were reduced within three years to gold alone, and a volume reputed to be equal to only a little more than one month's trade deficit.

By 1977 the International Monetary Fund was demanding the following terms for an international loan which would be funded mainly by West Germany and the US: (1) a reduction of the balance of payments deficit of 1977 by one-third in 1978 (from $1·2 billions to $800 millions); (2) a restriction of the rate of growth of domestic product to 3 per cent; (3) wage increases limited to 15 per cent, and reducing thereafter; (4) an adjustment of the trade deficit through export promotion (rather than import substitution) and a disguised devaluation of 30 per cent; (5) an interest rate increase; (6) a reduction of public expenditure through limits to social income support for the unemployed and limits to social spending.

In 1976 the World Bank had made similar recommendations to the Portuguese authorities, including reducing the growth of real consumption, reducing budgetary deficits, reducing food subsidies, decontrolling prices, and encouraging private savings. Against this it had admitted that a 'more active exchange rate policy' should be matched by an attempt at import substitution – especially in agriculture – and specific employment programmes.

Despite the cosmetics, both packages represented no less than a formula for the reduction of public intervention in the Portuguese economy and the restoration of the market mechanism, with its implicit conditions of dependence on foreign capital for the survival of modern industry. In short, an end to ventures in socialist economics and the re-establishment of capitalism in Portugal.

Essentially, acceptance of the IMF and World Bank terms would represent a continuation of dependent development, or in foreseeable circumstances, underdevelopment for Portugal. Whether it opted for further integration with the EEC, or an 'open sea' survival in the waters of world trade, they would condemn Portugal to the permanent periphery of lesser countries in the world league, rather than the pioneer of a new model of socialised development on the lines of the expectations raised by the events of April 1974.

Alternative Paths of Development

There are fundamental questions about what development path is really appropriate for Portugal, and in what way the country could escape the loss of sovereignty implied by peripheral dependence. As already indicated, one is the EEC and the open sea. This is basically a path of dependent development. It is the kind of path dependent on events outside Portugal and on centres of economic power abroad. The second main path is perhaps associate EEC status and more independent development. A third is autarchic or relatively more autarchic development which might well prove a path of independent underdevelopment.

The first of these paths would entail a capitalist or at most state capitalist path of development. The third by implication could embrace either a fascist cul-de-sac, as hitherto in Portugal, or a wholly centralised and planned model of a socialist or communist society. For various reasons, the middle path would be consistent both with a degree of internationalism and a strategy for socialist development in a substantially planned economy where the market was socialised both by planning itself and by new forms of public and co-operative enterprise in industry and agriculture, co-existing with private enterprise on a significant scale, especially in smaller enterprise. The middle path might be that most capable of offering the possibility of avoiding peripheral status in economic and political terms.

Associate EEC status would certainly guarantee formal economic sovereignty for Portugal, as against sovereignty-reducing supranationalism of the kind which might be established with economic and monetary union. But in one respect the sovereignty question is qualified on planning and the public sector in the present EEC because, whatever is said to the contrary by some enthusiasts in the competition directorate of the EEC Commission, any nation state inside the Community can actually do what it wants with its public sector, as far as their own treaty is concerned. It cannot of course necessarily do the same as far as its main creditor countries are concerned, for example, if they demand a reduction of the size of the public sector, whether they happen to be EEC members, the IMF or whatever, as a condition for granting a loan. In other words, the issue of formal sovereignty is different from effective sovereignty. Formal constraints on sovereignty need not mean effective contraints in the EEC case, while formal independence is no guarantee against dependent development outside the EEC framework.

In key respects, the question of what mix in a mixed economy is relevant to the issue of new roles for planning and the public sector in terms of an intermediate or middle path of development of the kind already described. And here one comes to two main factors. One is that, despite the fact that the Portuguese public sector in some respects represents a higher share of value added or capital formation than in some other EEC countries, it none the less remains concentrated significantly in basic service industries, infrastructural industries and finance rather than manufacturing industries (see Table 30).

These are not those industries which the French quite rightly call the 'transformation' industries. Transformation indicates that basic inputs are transformed into products with value, which then are marketable. It is a better French word than the English equivalent of manufacture, or 'made by hand', because it has a clear analytical context. It also has an important functional meaning in the economy as a whole. For instance, you cannot expand the Portuguese economy simply by expanding gas, electricity, water supply, railways, the post office, or the other basic infrastructural sectors. You cannot actually export any of these public utilities and services. You can export trains but not railway services. You might be able to export electronic equipment for automatic trunk dialling in the post office, but not your postal service, save for foreign mail; and so forth. In fact, the whole pattern of public ownership and its distribution throughout Western Europe, is concentrated in these basic service sectors, which are analytically distinct from the transformation industries in two senses: one, geologically, in the case of raw materials such as coal, where they are specifically tied down; and, secondly, with the same effect, geographically because they are concerned with basic services such as post, telecommunications, transport, etc.

Further, the existing public sector in most of the so-called mixed economies is itself growth dependent. It is substantially dependent on the expansion of the transformation industries, i.e. manufacturing industries, and some private services for its own expansion. In other words, however efficient the internal management of a state-owned company in basic industries, if you double steel capacity without a doubling of demand for steel you simply end up with considerable spare capacity; you do not end up with a transformed economy. And this becomes important if one looks at the breakdown of industries, since most public sector activities in industry are highly capital intensive.

TNCs and Wage Costs

It has been argued by some people that Portuguese private industry is capable of responding, on a world scale, to devaluation provided that wage costs are appropriately low and (implicitly) provided Portugal reverts to a capitalist mode of development. In this context one has to look at the share of manufacturing industry in Portugal commanded by multinational capital, where the decisions, whether or not to export from one country may be marginally influenced by changes in the exchange rate, and may be considerably influenced by wage levels. But not just in one country; in several countries at the time. Also, one has to look, for example, at the fact that in one of Portugal's ex-colonies, Brazil, wage costs utilised by multinational companies are about one-tenth of the wage costs in West Germany, which is something of which German private capital has become aware since this recent economic recession, which is why, over the last two years, German investment in Brazil has increased over four times, whereas there has not been anything like a comparable increase in Portugal.

These factors have to be taken into account in considering Bela Balassa's argument that since wage costs in Portugal are a third those of Germany, Portugal would have a comparative advantage in European trade and the attraction of foreign capital. His use of the case of Ireland's attraction of foreign capital is qualified by the common language for US direct investment; the increasing tendency to vertical integration of production and the location of its final stages abroad (e.g. the removal of meat processing and the substitution of export of cattle 'on the hoof'), plus his own admission that the scale of incentives offered to attract foreign capital are excessive (Balassa, 1977, p. 235). The implications of such excessive tax handouts (or non-taxation) of private enterprise for the fiscal and welfare policies of a country such as Portugal are argued later.

TNCs versus Labour

Further, one has to take into account the kind of political and social system prevailing in those economies which have succeeded in attracting foreign investment. Bela Balassa cites both Korea and Mexico. One could add not only Brazil but also Taiwan, the Philippines, Singapore, Indonesia and Hong Kong. Not only are the labour costs of these countries, on average, some third or less than those in Portugal, but all of them offer dramatic tax concessions which amount in some cases to no tax at all due from the enterprise for over ten years. This poses major fiscal problems for the states concerned on a major share of their productive capacity in modern industry. It means either low public expenditure on welfare, or regressive taxation on working people, or both.

As importantly, none of these countries has politically liberal labour relations. Several of them restrict not only the kind of rights for workers' committees, which Balassa criticises in the Portuguese case, but also basic trades union rights of the kind obtaining in the developed liberal capitalist societies and to which, at a minimum, Portugal could aspire. Some of them are effectively fascist, and similar to the kind of régime which was overthrown in Portugal by the April 1974 revolution. Further, several of them are clearly under the international hegemony of the US, or directly dependent on the US for their economic success. Their dependence, in key cases on both US foreign investment and US foreign policy, especially Korea, Taiwan and the Philippines, illustrates the kind of dependent capitalist development which lies behind liberalisation models.

Dependent Labour

In other words, the social and political costs of a model of dependent capitalist development of the kind recommended by Bela Balassa are considerable. This is implicit, in fact, in his own argument on the need for 'regulating labour relations ... to circumscribe the role of workers' commissions and to introduce compulsory arbitration with a view to avoid strikes and excessive increases in wages'. He adds that 'these measures would be further strengthened if illegal strikers were to lose certain privileges they enjoy in the form of seniority rights and fringe benefits' (Balassa, 1977, pp. 236–8).

Bela Balassa claims that 'the introduction of the proposed rules should not be considered to represent a loss of the rights the workers have acquired with the Revolution, but rather as measures necessary to normalise the situation'. He also calls for 're-establishing the possibility of firms dismissing workers under certain conditions' and for benefits to be provided for the unemployed.

But it is arguable that many Portuguese working people in fact would see his proposals very much as a loss of the rights gained by the Revolution. It is also crucial to see what kind of situation would be normalised by such controls of the labour force as he envisages. Basically, in capitalist economies, unemployment operates as the mechanism whereby capital maintains its capacity to determine not only the wage level but also the terms and conditions of work. It is crucial to its freedom to determine what shall be produced, where, for which market, in whose benefit, with whatever combination of capital and labour it chooses. In short it is crucial to restraint of labour and freedom to capital to allocate resources by its private criteria rather than planned public criteria for society as a whole. The norm which Balassa recommends for Portugal is capitalist development, regulated substantially by the mechanism of unemployment rather than a planned development.

Comparative Advantage and Disadvantage

In principle, by textbook international trade theorems of the old style, these lower foreign labour costs should be offset by higher unit costs: thus, higher Portuguese wages should be compensated by higher efficiency through more capital per worker, more modern capital, or both. But, for one thing, this argument works both ways. On the same unit cost argument, the more developed Western European economies could prove more efficient than Portugal. This is especially true if one adds the so called x efficiency factor, or the skill, training, experience and adaptability of management. It also becomes a bigger problem for Portugal if the oligopoly and minimum scale barriers to entry into modern markets in Western Europe are taken into account.

In other words, Portugal has yet to surmount the problems of developing independent, nationally based, large-scale, multi-product, multi-sectoral and multi-divisional companies of the kind which now dominate world trade. And it is not at all clear that she will be able to do so simply through weakening the bargaining power of the unions, establishing a low wage system, and relying on private enterprise. In fact, under such conditions low wages may simply reinforce the relatively archaic industrial structure of the economy during a critical period in which industrial and agricultural modernisation – by selective use of new public and co-operative enterprise, and strategic planning – should be taking place.

Multinational Capital versus National Exports

The comparative advantage model ignores the transformation in the dominant mode of world production, distribution and exchange which has occurred in the postwar period. For the large firms against which Portuguese business would have to compete on the world market are also multinational in operation. The rise of global production and trade between the same multinational firms in different countries has substantially undermined the textbook model of international trade between different firms in different countries.

It has recently been estimated by OECD that the total value of production by multinational companies in different countries now exceeds the total value of western world trade. What this means in practice is a trend for foreign production in different countries to offset and substitute for export trade from other countries. In terms even of neoclassical economic theory, this is only to be expected if one follows Ohlin's original argument that direct investment will tend to substitute for trade (Ohlin, 1967).

In Portugal it may well have proved the case that higher proportions of domestic production were exported in the 1960s and early 1970s by foreign multinationals. But several specific factors have to be taken into account. First, this was a period in which fascism offered clear advantages to capital versus labour in terms of repression of disputes and free market labour relations.

Second, for related reasons, this was a period in which the suppression of wage demands offered wage costs which were low in Portugal relative to other Western European economies which enjoyed genuine trades union rights. Thirdly, this was a period in which the main expansion of the Western European economies had not yet been checked by a combination of declining investment, falling growth and the commodity and oil price inflations with their increases to import costs.

During this period, productivity increases for the most part outstripped wage increases in key Western European economies. In other words, profits were not checked on a major scale, despite declining profit rates, and big business in the private sector was not notably wage rate sensitive.[6] But once the commodity and oil price inflations had pushed the leading Western European economies into deflationary policies in an attempt to reduce the increased import strain on their balance of payments, enterprise in economies such as West Germany became notably sensitive to wage costs. It was during this period that the dramatic increase in German foreign investment in Brazil occurred. In other words, German capital did not respond in some incremental rationalist way to the potential of labour costs in Brazil at a fraction of Portuguese costs until it was forced to take major account of the differential. When it did so, it by-passed the inter-mediate wage cost economy of Portugal and increased its attention to its ex-colony. Classically, it left Portugal on the new periphery.

Crisis in Capitalist Development

This argument can and should be generalised. Recommendations today for an economy such as Portugal cannot be seriously considered in isolation from the end of the postwar expansion of the Western European economies in general. France alone of the big league Western European economies actually managed to increase its average annual GNP growth through the 1950s, 1960s and early 1970s. The other economies, including, in particular, West Germany, underwent a relative decline. There are many reasons. One was the relative absorption of the labour reserves either from agriculture or specific sources of labour immigration such as East Germany, where the construction of the Berlin wall cut off one of the main sources which had sufficed to raise the indigenous full employment ceiling of the West Germany economy in the late 1940s and the 1950s. A second reason was the trend to over-investment relative to demand reflected in the de-clining rates of capital formation for economies such as West Germany. A third reason was a tendency for capital substitution of labour in the developed OECD economies associated with the major increase in capital accumulation of the 1950s. A fourth was a related disproportion in the supply of investment relative to private demand patterns. Put simply, the German and French consumer was happy to gain his first refrigerator, first automobile and first television, but did need three of each.

Each of these four factors in the end of the postwar expansion of the Western European economies can be related to Marxist theory of crisis. The first, on labour availability, concerns the drying up of the reserve army of labour which Marx, a century before Kindleberger,[7] had seen as a key lever in the process of capital accumulation, restrain-ing wage demands, and thereby increasing profitability during periods of expansion of capital. The second reflects the tendency to over production in capitalist economies, relating to the effects of an un-planned expansion of private investment capacity, as leading firms undertake that large-scale investment necessary for the minimally efficient utilisation of available technical progress under competitive conditions. The third relates to Marx's argument on a rising organic composition of capital, or relative capital intensity, with machinery displacing labour in the accumulation process. The third relates to the relative planlessness of disproportioned capitalist development, in which the demand for goods relates to which goods are demanded under a particular distribution of wealth and income by specific social classes; in other words, a system of resource allocation based on exchange value and profit rather than use value and social planning.

Whether from disposition or neglect, the IMF and World Bank hardly even address themselves to these problems. Yet the issue of capital displacement of labour, even taken in isolation, critically qualifies their recommendations for the Portuguese economy.

If Portugal is hoping to develop rather than stay in a no-mans land between the more developed and less developed economies favoured respectively for multinational capital companies in their more capital and more labour intensive production, it should look at the pattern of employment, dynamically, over time, in those economies ahead of it. It will find that while employment in metal products and chemical products increased by 3·6 per cent and 2·7 per cent per year in industrialised Western Europe in the period 1950–62, this fell to 1·1 per cent and 1·7 per cent respectively in the period 1962–9. For textiles in the same periods, the rate fell from 2·2 per cent to 0·1 per cent.[8] This was with relatively sustained rates of growth of demand. In other words, it is not simply the capital cost internal to the industry which counts, but whether one can count on anything like comparable future rates of growth of employment per industry through the rest of this century by such models of development.

The Meso-economic Sector

Table 28 shows that the structure of concentration in private enterprise which followed both the protectionist measures under Salazar and the penetration of foreign capital is very substantial in Portuguese industry. In leading 'modern' industries some half dozen firms or less account for between half and all of production. These enterprises are utterly different from the small-scale enterprise of the conventional micro-economic model. As already argued, both their size and their multinational character renders them insensitive to conventional macro-economic policies of indirect intervention. In practice, in Portugal, as elsewhere, they constitute a new *meso*-economic sector, in between the micro and macro orthodoxies and largely divorcing the orthodox micro-macro synthesis (Greek: *mesos* – intermediate).

The meso-economic character of enterprise in modern industry has also been indicated by the major command of agriculture through a minor number of farms. Table 27(a) indicates that 1 per cent of the farms in Portugal account for more than half of the agricultural surface area of the country. Similarly, Table 29 shows that nationalised industry in Portugal in 1975 was concentrated in large-scale enterprise, for the most part with 500 or more employees. A minor fraction of the total number of enterprises in sectors such as paper, chemicals and petroleum, around or less than 1 per cent – accounted for a third or more of total industry employment. With less than 1 per cent of enterprises, the nationalised sector accounted for nearly two-thirds of employment in transport and communications, and with 7·5 per cent of enterprises for 98 per cent of employment in banking and insurance (see Tables 29 and 30).

This is not to say that the re-mix of the Portuguese economy which followed the 1974 revolution was either equal or balanced. The public sector was notably under-represented in mining, food, drink and tobacco, mineral and metal products and metallurgy and engineering, quite apart from traditional sectors such as textiles and clothing or woodwork and furniture.

None the less, the concentration of industry, agriculture and finance capital in the Portuguese economy, jointly with the increased scale of the public sector following the events of April 1974, opens the possibility for new uses of public enterprise in a planning framework of a kind which should not yet be off the political agenda. If sufficient political awareness is created of the costs of continued peripheral underdevelopment, the gains from further extension of the public sector, and the purposive use of economic planning through leading meso-economic enterprise could provide the means to make feasible the ends of the new socialised mode of more autonomous development.

Towards a New Mode of Development*

It is here that one has to consider new modes of development. Multinational capital can now call on reserves of labour in less developed countries at a fraction of their cost in Portugal; technical progress and rising capital intensity give rise to technological unemployment and labour displacement; disproportion emerges in a major dualism between industry and agriculture on the one hand, and modern capitalist and primitive capitalist modes of operation within it on the other. In

* The author has elaborated his argument on a new mode of development for the Portuguese economy in German Marshall Fund of the United States and Fundacao Calouste Gulbenkian (1977), Conferencia Internacional sobre Economia Portuguesa, Vol. II, pp. 721–55.

such conditions, Portugal has to decide whether specialisation on the lines of old style comparative advantage has anything to recommend it other than dependent international development, low growth, low income, low public expenditure and high structural unemployment.

The Portuguese economy cannot avoid some key constraints so long as it remains open to external influence in foreign trade and foreign investment. But it can mitigate several of them through public enterprise and planning mechanisms which give the public authorities a greater strategic control over the allocation of resources.

Most importantly, on the strategic side, Portugal could develop a mode of development which did not simply import capitalist criteria of investment, growth and distribution. In other words, whatever the external economic climate, but certainly with associate EEC status, if negotiable, there is no reason why Portugal should not define both a social bill of goods for public expenditure and the domestic use of resources, and link this to the model of welfare state services achieved in Scandinavian countries and other European economies such as Britain.

That would not close the question of the ends and means of planning and its role in avoiding dependent, peripheral underdevelopment. For example, effective socialisation of public intervention and the public sector, in a wider sense, would involve both definition of feasible means for public intervention in the industrialised sectors of the economy, and a social bill of goods in terms of the right to equalised working hours, equalised social income, and an advance on conventional welfare state ends of a kind which now remains potentially within the grasp of the Portuguese people.

In general, the dimensions opened by such a social mode of development include national integration versus international disintegration. The 'two tier' Europe of inner Community countries and other peripheral countries has been well recognised – *inter alia* by ex-Chancellor Brandt and Chancellor Schmidt of West Germany, who have talked of the inner Community proceeding to economic and monetary union, while those less able outer countries do not. Irrespective of the path actually chosen by Portugal relative to the Common Market, whether full membership – if allowed, with its major implications for price support policy in agriculture – associate membership, or non-membership, the necessity for a planned social allocation of resources will remain central and acute to the issue of avoiding peripheral underdevelopment.

Notes

1 I owe a good deal of the following analysis in this section to Dudley Seers and Manfred Bienefeld of IDS.
2 The development plan of the Caetano government, published just before the 'revolution', envisaged that a growth rate of 7·5 per cent in 1973–9 would be accompanied by zero increase in employment, a 'target' which must be unique in the annals of planning, all the increase in the labour force being absorbed in other economies.
3 Actually only a minority of the international migrants come from these areas: the pattern is broadly that labour moves from the country to the town, many to work in the hotels, taking the place of urban workers who migrate. (This 'staging' process is typical.) There was also some immigration from Portuguese colonies in Africa, especially the Cape Verde islands, towards the end of the 1960s.
4 In predominantly rural provinces, the infant mortality rate was above 80 per thousand in 1965–6. ('Algumas consideracoes sobre a Mortalidade Portuguesa' by Dr. Oliveira Marques, INE 1970.) In 1960, only 14 per cent of dwellings in rural areas had piped water and 27 per cent electricity (*Statistical Yearbook*, United Nations, 1974).
5 The Sunday Times Insight Team, *Insight on Portugal* (1975), p. 57.
6 See the country studies and data in Kindleberger (1967).
7 Kindleberger seems scarcely aware of Marx's antecedent for his analysis of the role of 'labour availability' in high growth. See further Kindleberger (1967).
8 See further Holland (1976) Tables 6 and 7.

References

Balassa, B. (1977), 'Industrial and Trade Policy in Portugal', in German Marshall Fund of the United States and Fundacao Calouste Gulbenkian, *Conferencia Internacional sobre Economia Portuguesa*.
Holland, S. (1976), *Capital versus the Regions*, Macmillan, London.
Kindleberger, C. P. (1967), *Europe's Postwar Growth*, Oxford University Press.
Ohlin, B. (1967), *International and Intraregional Trade*, Harvard University Press.
The Sunday Times Insight Team (1975), *Insight on Portugal*, André Deutsch.

Table 22

Sectoral distribution of employment, 1960, 1965, 1970, 1975 and 1976

(Year-end figures for Continental Portugal in thousands)

Sector	1960	1965	1970	1975	1976(est.)
Agriculture, forestry, and hunting	1,363	1,153	958	814	802
Fishing	43	32	35	24	24
Mining	26	19	13	12	12
Manufacturing	701	722	740	751	753
Construction and public works	227	251	258	263	265
Electricity, gas, and water	16	19	19	20	20
Trade	247	271	287	286	287
Banking, insurance, and real estate	23	42	60	82	83
Transportation and communications	125	139	148	171	176
Other services	514	496	532	551	554
Poorly defined activities	10	81	104	60	58
Total (Job supply)	3,296	3,224	3,153	3,034	3,032
Index (1960 = 100)	100	97·8	95·7	92·1	92·0

Source: Central Planning Secretariat's estimates (Values corrected on the basis of the Electoral Census of December 1974).

Table 23

Unemployment estimates, 1970, 1974, 1975 and 1976
(Figures for Continental Portugal in thousands)

	Total unemployed	OF WHICH: Looking for first job	OF WHICH: Looking for new job	Repatriates
1970	85	65	21	..
1974	180	..	..	4
1975 December	456	141	135	180
1976 December	574	204	170	200

Source: Ministry of Labour.

Table 24   Employment in manufacturing industry, 1960, 1965, 1970 and 1975
(in thousands)

		1960	1965	1970	1975
	Total:	701.4	712.3	740.4	750.7
Traditional industry	Food, beverages, tobacco,	72	64	59	55
	Textiles, clothing, footwear,	258	251	248	228
	Wood, cork and products	102	110	109	110
Modern industry	Chemicals, related products	32	34	35	38
	Non-metallic mineral products	41	43	49	50
	Metal industries	5	21	38	47
	Metal products, machinery and transport equipment	137	134	130	147
	Paper and printing	28	36	33	33
	Other manufacturing industries	22	29	41	43

Source: Central Planning Secretariat and estimates.

Table 25

Manufacturing output-rates of growth, 1968–75
(At 1970 prices, in percentages)

	1968–73	1974	1975
Foodstuffs, beverages and tobacco	6·6	13·1	27·0
Textiles, Apparel and Footwear	11·6	5·8	−17·2
Wood, cork and furniture	4·8	−1·0	−6·9
Paper, printing and publishing	6·5	29·3	0·5
Chemicals and related activities	10·2	0	5·6
Non-metal minerals	10·5	2·8	1·9
Basic metals	11·9	−13·1	−18·2
Metal products, mechanical and electrical equipment, and transportation equipment	12·6	−1·0	−12·9
Miscellaneous manufacturing	2·2	−16·8	21·3
TOTAL Manufacturing	9·9	2·1	−4·9

Source: National Institute of Statistics: 1968–73, constant 1963 prices; converted by the Central Planning Secretariat into constant 1970 prices.
1974 – ibid., National Institute of Statistics estimates.
1975 – Central Planning Secretariat estimates.

Table 26

Exports of 'traditional' products
(At 1970 prices)

	Average rate of growth 1970–73	Annual change	
		1974	1975
Canned fish	3·3	−31·7	+21·0
Tomato pulp and paste	9·5	−48·7	−53·0
Port wines	11·2	−10·8	−13·2
Table wines	−0·1	−6·3	+4·6
Cellophane	6·8	+10·2	−55·2
Raw or sawn timber	8·0	+11·4	−47·8
Cork and cork products	·59	−5·0	−16·8
Pulp for paper	10·4	−21·8	−26·0
Cotton fibre	10·2	−30·1	−11·1
Synthetic textiles	26·6	−5·0	−0·2
Cotton cloth	5·6	−24·6	−33·5
Bed linens	23·2	−6·1	+26·8
Clothing	27·7	+12·0	−16·3
Footwear	3·1	+5·9	+16·3

Source: National Institute of Statistics.

Table 27

Agricultural structure and import dependence

(a) Dominance of large (mesoeconomic) farms (1968)

Percentage of farms	Average size	Percentage of total agricultural surface area
0·5	Over 100 hectares	45
0·5	50–100 hectares	6

(b) Imports of agricultural products relative to domestic production 1975 (thousand tons)

Products	Domestic production	Imports	Imports as percentage of domestic production
Cereals			
– Maize	684	1,188	173
– Wheat	600	345	57
Meat	198	30	15

(c) Food and total imports 1973 and 1974, and percentage increase (billions of contos)

Products	Jan./Sept. 1973	Jan./Sept. 1974	Percentage increase 1973–4
Food products	7,252	11,785	+61
Total imports	43,912	65,848	+50

Source: National Institute of Statistics.

Table 28

Concentration in 'Modern' industry
1973

Sectors	Number of leading (mesoeconomic) firms	Percentage of production in (mesoeconomic) control
Hardboard	6	100
Paper	6	100
Paper products	3	53
Tyres	4	100
Inorganic chemicals	3	73
Synthetic fibres	5	100
Synthetic resins	2	52
Oils	1	66
Paints	4	55
Phosphates	3	100
Pharmaceutical products	8	48
Petroleum	2	100
Bricks	3	100
Cement	7	100
Iron and steel products	4	100
Metal products	2	72
Motor vehicles and motors	3	93
Shipbuilding and repair	9	96
Stationery	2	56

Source: National Institute of Statistics.

Table 29

Public enterprises as share of total by size and sector*

%

Activity	Number of employees	0–100	101–500	501–1,000	1,000+	Total
Fishing		—	—	—	—	—
Mining		1·2	—	33·3	—	0·3
Manufacturing						
Food, drink and tobacco		1·2	—	14·3	—	0·1
Textiles and clothing		—	—	—	—	—
Woodwork and furniture		—	—	—	—	—
Paper		—	6·7	40·0	70·0	1·4
Chemicals and petroleum		0·9	1·5	28·6	42·9	0·3
Mineral and metal products		—	7·6	11·8	25·0	0·4
Metallurgy and engineering		—	—	—	27·3	0·0
Other manufacturing		—	—	—	—	—
Construction and public works		—	—	—	—	—
Gas, electricity and water		40·0	41·7	100·0	100·0	20·5
Wholesale-retail trade		—	—	—	—	—
Banking and insurance		15·6	84·6	81·8	100·0	7·5
Transport and communications		8·0	22·0	50·0	100·0	0·7
Services		—	—	—	—	—

* Provisional figures, September 1975.
Source: National Institute of Statistics.

Table 30

Employment in public enterprises as share of total by size and sector*

%

Activity	Number of employees	0–100	101–500	501–1,000	1,000+	Total
Fishing		—	—	—	—	—
Mining		1·9	—	35·2	—	4·1
Manufacturing						
Food, drink and tobacco		—	—	17·2	—	1·9
Textiles and clothing		—	—	—	—	—
Woodwork and furniture		—	—	—	—	—
Paper		—	14·9	39·2	98·0	33·9
Chemicals and petroleum		0·9	0·8	29·7	79·2	36·4
Mineral and metal products		—	9·7	11·8	23·3	7·9
Metallurgy and engineering		—	—	—	45·3	7·7
Other manufacturing		—	—	—	—	—
Construction and public works		—	—	—	—	—
Gas, electricity and water		47·7	30·2	100·0	100·0	57·7
Wholesale-retail trade		—	—	—	—	—
Banking and insurance		25·7	95·0	84·9	100·0	98·0
Transport and communications		8·7	32·6	53·2	100·0	61·0
Services		—	—	—	—	—

* Provisional figures, September 1975.
Source: National Institute of Statistics.

9

THE GROWING DEPENDENCE OF SPANISH INDUSTRIALIZATION ON FOREIGN INVESTMENT

Juan Muñoz, Santiago Roldán, Angel Serrano

General Considerations: Foreign Investment and the Working of the Spanish Economy (1959–75)

Foreign capital now holds a strong position in the distribution of economic power in modern Spanish society. Foreign investment was especially high between 1959 and 1975. Long-term foreign private resources received by the Spanish economy during that period reached nearly 800,000 million pesetas. This included various types of direct investment, portfolio investment, real estate investment, trade loans, financial loans and so on (see Figure 1).

The main role played by foreign investment has been that of a *compensating mechanism in the external balance* of the Spanish economy. It helps to reduce the growing trade deficit generated by the maintenance of high rates of GDP growth. Such growth requires a large quantity of imports. They are not easily replaced by local goods and services (Granell Trias, 1971, p. 20; de la Fuente, 1975, p. 889). As Table 31 shows, the growing visible trade deficit has been offset, mainly through the services and transfers, but also through the inflow of long-term foreign capital, except for the most recent period.

During a first stage, 1959–61, foreign investment was added to the surplus on current account (see Table 32), due partly to the stabilisation measures of 1959 which produced a severe deflation and a subsequent decline in the rate of growth of imports. In the next period, 1962–9, foreign investment improved 'our external credit standing although with growing difficulties' (Varela Parache, Rodriguez de Pablo, 1974, p. 14). The high deficit on current account[1] outweighed the positive balance on long-term private capital. In 1970–3, the balance on current account strengthened progressively despite the high rate of growth of GDP in 1972 and 1973, so the inflow of long-term foreign capital allowed an important growth in foreign exchange reserves. Due to the energy crisis at the end of 1973, the trade deficit doubled and the current account showed a big deficit again.[2] Once again, foreign long-term capital has come to the rescue of the Spanish economy, although

Figure 1

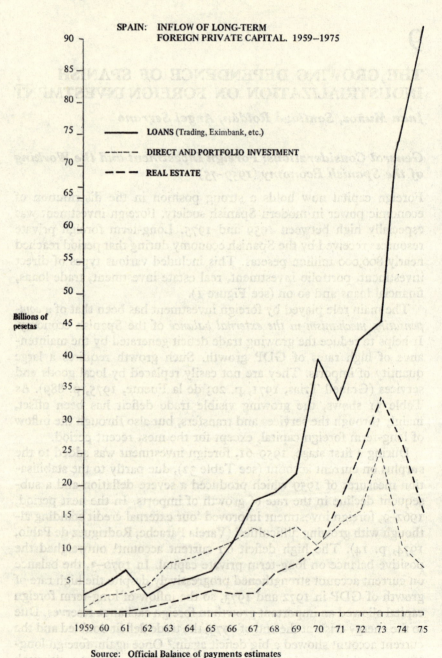

SPAIN: INFLOW OF LONG-TERM
FOREIGN PRIVATE CAPITAL. 1959–1975

LOANS (Trading, Eximbank, etc.)

DIRECT AND PORTFOLIO INVESTMENT

REAL ESTATE

Source: Official Balance of payments estimates

Table 31

Balance of payments 1960, 1970 and 1975

(billions of pesetas)

	1960	1970	1975
Exports	45	174	448
Imports	41	305	872
Trade account balance	3	−131	−424
Services and transfers	20	137	221
Current account balance	24	6	−203
Long-term capital	8	47	104
Basic balance	31	52	−100

Source: Balance of Payments, 1975 (Ministerio de Comercio, 1976).

Table 32

Current and capital account
(billions of pesetas)

Period	Current account (goods, services and transfers)	Long-term private capital account
1959 to 1961	+35	+21
1962 to 1969	−141	+168
1970 to 1973	+135	+198
1974 and 1975	−390	+196

Source: Own elaboration according to the Balance of Payments, 1975.

at a high cost, its balance showing a striking surplus in 1974 and 1975, offsetting more than half of the deficit on current account.

These high figures of the balance of long-term foreign capital in recent years are, for the most part, associated with a growing external indebtedness; direct investment and, above all, foreign investment in 'real estate' show important and sharp declines. These have been offset by the high amount of private and public loans which, in the first year of the economic crisis, represented more than 60 billion pesetas (see Figure 1), and rose further in 1975. This change in the composition of the capital balance during recent years has been analysed as follows:

> The situation has worsened, however, in compensatory transactions. These transactions appear as an inflow of foreign capital not directly connected with a material transaction – direct investment, real estate, long-term loans to finance the investment of Spanish firms – their main objective is the balancing of payments and revenues of the foreign accounts. They are called compensatory transactions to distinguish them from the autonomous inflow which is linked to real transactions. . . . An important compensatory transaction to obtain a formal equilibrium of the balance is justified if at the same time serious measures are adopted to attain a balance of payments and revenues on current account. But,

otherwise, it is dangerous to include compensation among the patterns of behaviour of a rather hazardous economic policy. (Alcaide, 1976, pp. 155–6)

The increase in external indebtedness was five times as much as direct investment in 1975, and the use of capital inflows also changed. The loans go towards the financing of consumption of energy-related goods or raw materials, while in previous years foreign capital went to boost the rate of investment. In this last phase, foreign long-term capital generated a growing financial cost of interest and debt redemption which even now can mean a short-term capital outflow much higher than the inflow of new foreign capital. We have a model of 'growing external indebtedness' as in most of the 'periphery'. But this model is not new to the Spanish economy: there was a similar development during the last decades of the nineteenth century.

A second role of foreign investment has been as a *supplement to domestic savings*. Between 1959 and 1975, total foreign investment in property – direct, portfolio and real estate – contributed an average of 6·2 per cent of gross domestic fixed capital formation. The corresponding figure was 8·7 during 1971–2 and 7·0 during 1973–5.[3] But long-term resources also include so-called financial investment – trade credit, company loans and so on – and foreign financing of all kinds represented about 20 per cent of the total.[4] 'Undoubtedly, domestic savings have received an important help from external financing and, if the latter had not been used, it is evident that the rates of growth attained during this period would not have been possible.' (Varela and Rodríguez de Pablo, 1974.)

The *financial cost* of foreign investments has not been excessive for the Spanish economy, considering the period as a whole. Table 33, which sums up the analysis of the Ministry of Trade, suggests that yields were moderate – smaller than in developed countries and, of course, than in the 'developing' countries – for direct investments. According to the latest estimates, there was apparently an increase in the years leading up to the crisis (1972–4).[5] 'The financial cost of loans is higher than that of direct investment' (Ministerio de Comercio, 1974, p. 27) and it is precisely since 1966–7 that loans to companies began to exceed direct investments.

But these conclusions need qualifying. As the Ministry of Trade points out, in the case of direct and portfolio investments, the yield refers to 'a net yield in which surpluses are not included' (Varela and Rodríguez de Pablo, 1974, p. 15). Secondly, there are many other mechanisms through which profit repatriations are carried out, such as transfer pricing, patents, technical services, etc. – which are not recorded as income from property in the balance of payments. An im-

Table 33

Profitability of foreign investments: 1963, 1967 and 1971[1]
(percentages)

Years	Yields on direct and portfolio investment	Yields on total investment and loans	Payments for technical services and royalties in relation to direct and portfolio investment
1963	7·9	5·9	22·2
1967	4·4	4·9	13·4
1971	5·4	6·3	10·7

[1] The calculation of profitability has been made dividing the payments of each year by the accumulated investment in the previous years, involving a time lag of one year.

Source: Balance of Payments, amounts paid for technical services and royalties 1963–9, SEME, November 1970 (Ministerio de Comercio, 1976).

portant part of the outflow is due either to technical services or trade marks, as well as patents and royalties (see Table 33);[6] this reflects the favourable fiscal treatment of such payments (UNCTAD, 1974, p. 13). Thus, the total financial costs – or, from a different point of view, the real yields – may be higher than the above analysis suggests.

Moreover, as can be seen in Table 34, the increase of outflow has been growing faster than the inflow, and has come to represent almost 50 per cent of the latter from 1966–7 onwards, a ratio which may well rise further in the next few years. The big direct investments made in the recent past will start the normal process of generation – and re-patriation – of profits after the usual delays. Moreover, interest will be high on the big loans negotiated in the years 1974–6.

Table 34

Net balance on long-term foreign private investment 1960–75
(billion pesetas)

	1960	1965	1970	1975	Total 1960–75
(a) Net inflow of long-term private capital	6·4	19·3	48·8	102·7	579·2
(b) Net profits on private capital	0·7	2·7	12·2	35·3	161·9
(c) Technical services and royalties (net)	0·6	4·5	8·2	14·4	112·8
(d) Total b and c	1·2	7·2	20·5	49·7	274·7
(e) a–d net balance of long-term foreign private investment	5·2	12·2	28·3	53·0	304·5
(f) d as % of a	19	37	44	52	47

Source: Based on the Balance of Payments, 1975 (Ministerio de Comercio).

The Sectoral Distribution of Foreign Investment

We cannot analyse the sectoral destination of loans, but it is possible to say something about direct and portfolio investment.[7] This was directed to industries and activities (chemical industry, cars, transportation equipment, mechanical and electrical engineering, etc.), where there were possibilities of introducing new technologies and maximising profits. It has also been important in some other activities like foodstuffs industries in which high yields are also assured, with minimum risks and increasing control of the diversification and modernisation of the industry. Foreign investment has been directed mainly – reflecting a clear international division of labour – to exploiting the *comparative advantages* provided by an abundant labour force with low wages and a certain level of skill, but above all submissive.

In 1962, the main sectors in which foreign direct and portfolio investment occurred were chemicals, 59 per cent, iron and steel, 15, private banking, 5, and food, 5: all other sectors accounted for only about 17 per cent. The 1973 pattern was more diversified. Chemicals accounted for 26 per cent, iron and steel 16, vehicles 9, real estate development 8, food 8, trade and similar services 5 and construction 4: the other sectors accounted for rather more than 22 per cent.

This pattern of investment has influenced the pattern of growth of the Spanish economy, inducing a strong process of '*industrial updating*' (Fanjul *et al.*, 1975). It has created an industrial structure dependent on TNCs. Although the strictly *financial* cost of foreign investment has not been high, the real cost of the process has been this progressive increase of dependence.

But these relationships have had a double-edged effect. Foreign capital, far from competing with Spanish capital – above all in banking and finance – has in many ways strengthened it, by contributing to the destruction of the traditional technologies which Spanish capitalism had used, though with slight success. But foreign capital has also spread new ways of extracting the economic surplus; introduced more up-to-date and complex technological advances; expanded the modern sector of production (into which banking and financial capital has been also introduced); developed more efficient forms of business organisation; increased the average size of industrial plants; stimulated the transfer of manpower from the country to the city, i.e. widened the market. *Foreign capital has lent new strength and vitality to Spanish capitalism: but this injection of new vitality has brought with it a new dependence, a new thraldom* (Muñoz, Roldán and Serrano, 1977, pp. 14 ff.). Without it, Spanish capitalism would have found itself in a *cul-de-sac*. That did indeed happen at the end of the 1950s. It was forced to look for more risky solutions. Given its obvious weakness, this system could only be upheld by increasingly strong doses of 'public order' and political authoritarianism. The State felt the need to compensate for the obvious weakness of the bourgeoisie and the limited success of industrialisation.

The 'collaboration' – or 'integration' – which has occurred between foreign and Spanish capital has continued to grow, both parties being aware of the considerable mutual advantages. In no way can one speak of opposing interests or use simplistic models which identify 'national banking and financial capital' with the 'comprador bourgeoisie' (Poulantzas, 1976, pp. 11 ff.; Acosta Sánchez, 1976, pp. 56 ff.). The interests of both are complementary and their contradictions are secondary.

Any resistance which certain factions of the national bourgeoisie might offer is vanishing at the same time as the old strongholds of economic power of these groups either disappear or lose their relative importance. The industries mentioned above have a growing importance in the functioning of the system of production (Gasoliba, 1975). They show the fastest growth rates. They superimpose their interests, when economic policy is being formed, on those of less dynamic sectors and industries.

During the period 1958–73, the chemical industry for example had an average annual compound growth rate of nearly 15 per cent, petroleum products more than 12, the car industry more than 20, electrical machinery and the heavy iron and steel industries 13 per cent.

At the end of the period we have studied, the industries where foreign capital had really made its presence felt accounted for more than 60 per cent of the profits of the industrial sector as a whole. Foreign capital is firmly established in all the eight industrial groups which grew fastest between 1959 and 1973, with the exception of shipbuilding. In the other 17 groups, there is little or no foreign capital.

Origin of Foreign Capital

Table 35 shows investments of foreign capital in majority shareholdings. North American and Swiss investment – which is mostly North American[8] – together formed more than 40 per cent of these majority investments accumulated to December 1972. In the following three years, the US reinforced its position and, by the end of 1975, these two countries accounted for nearly 60 per cent, whereas West Germany, France and Great Britain accounted for 26 per cent between them in 1975. Japanese investment, practically non-existent in the 1960s, has made its appearance recently, but in 1975 it still represented only 0·5 per cent of the total.

Indicators of Penetration

All these data need to be complemented by an analysis of the *degree of penetration* of foreign capital. Unfortunately, Spanish statistics are at their least reliable here, but we have chosen some indicators which allow a preliminary analysis:

(a) The sectoral indicator devised by the Technical Studies Department of the Spanish Ministry of Commerce relates the amount of capital subscribed by or acquired by foreigners to the nominal value of shares issued by Spanish companies between 1967 and 1971. Of special importance is the foreign penetration in chemical industries (48 per cent), food products (20), machinery and transport equipment (28), paper and printing (25), real estate and property development (18), building and allied activities, including glass manufacture (13), and mining (22 per cent).

(b) The Department of Foreign Transactions has made a study of the degrees of penetration by means of the analysis of the capital of the companies in each sector: viz, percentage of total capital of the sector subscribed to by foreigners: chemicals 31 per cent, glass 46, food products 23, paper 18 and printing also 18 per cent.

Only two studies by this Department show greater detail of behaviour in financial and in commercial terms, and information on individual companies. They refer to the two sectors where foreign capital has a special importance: chemicals and food products.[9] In the chemical sector, for example, the greater the total capital of a company, the more likely the participation of foreign capital. Of the 151 companies whose capital exceeds 100 million pesetas, 111 have foreign participation.[10]

The degree of penetration of foreign capital is especially important in the colouring and pigment industries (61 per cent); pneumatic tyres (60); bi-products of waxes and paraffins (54); detergents and soaps (51); acids, alkalis, salts, gases and electrochemical products (48); perfumes (48); photographic equipment (48); resins and synthetic fibres (47); pharmaceutical products (42); organic chemistry (42); insecticides (41 per cent), etc.

In food products, foreign capital is present in almost all branches. The levels of dependence were especially noteworthy at the end of 1974 in dairy products and non-alcoholic drinks (all colas, tonics and sodas are manufactured under foreign licence). If we add the production of fruit juices, one can say that foreign capital controls about 60 per cent of the soft drink market. (Participation defined in this way is much higher than in terms of the foreign share in company capital.) Foreign capital represents directly 20 per cent of the total capital of the brewing industry, and 60 per cent of all breweries have some foreign capital. In flour and its products, there is 53 per cent foreign participation in capital. Foreign capital can also be found in alcoholic beverages, chocolates and biscuits, chemical foodstuffs, etc.

(c) Another indicator refers to *the degree of control over production.* We refer to the study carried out for the year 1972 by the Ministry of Industry on the presence of foreign capital in the 600 largest industrial firms (in terms of the value of sales).[11]

From this study results can be deduced which are very similar to those given above. The 148 companies with a majority of foreign share-holders control 23 per cent of the production of the leading companies. But if one adds in the companies with an equal or minority participa-tion of foreign capital – which also figure in the report – 54 per cent of production is accounted for. This level of participation is even more significant from the point of view of industrial behaviour and policies in the respective industries.

(d) Also significant is the presence of foreign directors, which has in-creased substantially.[12] The capital of companies with foreign direc-tors grew sevenfold, going from 16 per cent of the total to 29 per cent between 1959 and 1970. Moreover, foreign directors are not, generally, 'mere decorative figures' on the boards, as many other directors are. The sectors where this foreign presence is most conspicuous are: cars (companies with foreign directors account for 76 per cent of the capital in the sector); plastics (73); glassware and optical goods (72); electrical material (69); paints, lacquer and enamel (59); pharmaceuticals, fertilisers, etc.

(e) Of the leading 154 TNCs (according to the world rankings for 1972 of the magazines *Fortune* (May and August 1972) and *Visión* (October 1972)), only 43 have no connection with Spanish companies (16 American and 10 Japanese). The other 111 have connections – to a lesser or greater degree – with 654 Spanish companies, varying from the large 'national' corporations to the small distributive and commercial firms (Muñoz, Roldán, García Delgado and Serrano, 1976, pp. 331 ff.). The United States stands out among the foreign countries. Of these largest TNCs, 85 are American, 60 of which have interests in 351 Spanish companies altogether. Twelve of these TNCs of United States origin each have ties with 10 or more Spanish companies (Standard Oil of New Jersey, General Electric, Chrysler, Texaco, ITT, Gulf Oil, US Steel, Westinghouse Electric, Firestone Tire and Rubber, Phillips Petroleum, Monsanto and Dow Chemical). Germany has 20 TNCs of the 154, 14 with ties with 78 national Spanish com-panies. The most prominent are Bayer AG, AEG, Telefunken, Volkswagen, Hoechst, Daimler Benz AG, Basf, Krupp, Bosch. France has 13 TNCs in the list, of which 12 have connections with a total of 124 Spanish companies. Of special significance are St Gobain,

Pechiney, Rhône Poulenc, Renault, Citroën, Cie Générale d'Elec-tricité, Peugeot, Michelin. Britain has 15 TNCs in the rankings,[13] eight of which are linked with 64 companies. The most prominent are Royal Dutch Shell, Unilever, Imperial Chemical Industries, British Leyland, Dunlop-Pirelli, General Electric, English Electric. Others are (Holland) Phillips, G Akzo; (Italy) Montecatini Edison, Fiat, ENI; (Switzerland) Nestlé, Ciba-Geigy.[14]

(f) As regards the leading 100 Spanish companies, foreign capital is present – to a noticeable extent – in 28 (see Table 36). Of these companies, 14 are in 'association' with the Spanish private banks; that is to say, with national financial capital (Altos Hornos S.A., Motor Ibérica, Firestone Hispania, La Seda de Barcelona, Explosivos Río Tinto, Fasa-Renault, Aluminio de Galicia, Babcock and Wilcox, SNIACE, Unión y el Fenix, etc.); also in two companies in collabora-tion with the INI – the public industrial holding – of which EM-PETROL is the most important; in another five[15] large companies, foreign capital appears with the private banks and the INI or the State; finally, the TNCs are the major shareholders in a further seven (Citroën, Standard Electrica, ITT, Michelin, Pirelli, Phillips Ibérica, Chrysler and Cristaleria Española-St Gobain).

Banking and financial capital has reserved for itself certain enclaves in which it has not tolerated the slightest hint of external (or internal) competition (see Table 36). It has also known how to re-adapt its role in these new economic activities, where it has had to 'share' them with

Table 35

Cumulative totals of foreign capital investment by country of origin, from 1960 to 1972 and 1975 (majority shareholdings only)[1]
(billion pesetas)

	Total to 1972	Total to 1975
US	22·8	58·0
Switzerland	17·1	23·8
Germany	8·5	15·1
France	5·1	7·8
UK	3·8	14·5
Holland	3·0	6·3
Italy	2·5	3·0
Canada	1·5	2·5
Belgium	1·2	2·0
Sweden	1·1	2·2
Total[2]	71·8	142·8

1 Where foreign capital has provided more than 50 per cent of a company's capital and therefore been authorised by the Presidency.
2 Includes countries not specified.

Source: Presidencia del Gobierno.

Table 36

Links of the largest Spanish companies to banking, foreign capital and public sector,[1] 1974
(billion pesetas)

Links	No. of companies	Own capital	Profits
1. Banks	34	491	52
2. Banks and foreign capital	14	139	12
3. Banks and public sector	7	198	10
4. Banks, foreign capital, public sector	5	24	2
5. Banks and certain family groups	3	22	1[2]
6. Foreign capital	7	33	4
7. Public sector and foreign capital	2	24	2
8. Public sector	5	38	4
9. Certain family groups	2	13	2
10. No links	1	4	—
Total	80	986	92[2]
Links to banks (1 +2 +3 +4 +5)	63	874	77[2]
Links to foreign capital (2 +4 +6 +7)	28	220	20
Links to public sector (3 +4 +7 +8)	19	284	18
Links to family groups (9 +5)	5	35	2[2]

1 Includes INI.
2 Excludes RUMASA.
Source: Compiled from *Actualidad Económica*, April 1975.

those of foreign capital. It has had to cede part of its control and influence over the Spanish economy in return for a strengthening, widening and diversifying of its interest, and improved profitability.

(g) The participation of foreign capital in Spanish capitalism can be better appreciated if one examines the 300 large *industrial* companies. It is basically in this sector that foreign investment is concentrated. Foreign capital directly controls 59; it is also present in another 61 sharing its interests – individually or jointly – with the private Spanish banks, with the INI, and with certain family groups of Spanish capitalism. These 120 companies in the foreign 'sphere of influence' form an integral part of Spanish industrialisation. They account for 47 per cent of the sales, 39 per cent of the workers, 44 per cent of gross profits and 41 per cent of capital.

The Crisis, the Difficulties and the Internationalisation of Financial Capital

In closed economies, external changes have a limited effect, though no economy can be isolated from them. An open economy, on the other hand, tends to follow the cyclical evolution of the world economy in which it is integrated, especially in the dependent economies, like the Spanish since the war, where international economic influences largely determine the economic strategy. In the last few years, the Spanish

G

economy has seen a drastic change in its 'mode of working' precisely when it was in a highly expansionist phase facing a future of continued growth.

The serious difficulties of the Spanish economy and the level of debt have accentuated its dependence. Foreign banks may find shortly a welcome in the Spanish financial market.[16] On the other hand, Spanish financial capital, which continues to be pre-eminent in the economic set-up, is more and more inter-related with foreign capital. Consequently, the specific interests of national financial capital are less and less realisable outside a 'strategy' based on the investment needs of the power centres of world capitalism. The Spanish economy now forms part of what could be called the 'advanced periphery', although with a different type of subordination and dependence from the 'traditional' peripheral countries.

Only in concrete studies will we be able to advance our understanding of this 'dependency'. We have tried to state some of the premises or starting points of such studies. The present problem centres in fact on the different options or possibilities for 'negotiation' facing Spanish capitalism. Room for manoeuvre (or 'possibilities of renegotiation' of the terms of dependence, to use Sunkel's terminology), can give rise to other contradictions. It is in fact this conglomerate of economic and financial interests which is most in need of the political stability that will be provided by the *new democracy*, once the Franco régime has been fully eliminated. Financial capital has emerged with much more strength than the militants forecast. For the big banks, for financial capital, the recent elections justified the slogan *faith and hope*. This has been frequently underlined in shareholders' general meetings. They know that the elections have been also indirectly their own 'legitimisation', even though these required the tacit acceptance of certain reforms. These reforms imply (a) increased competition following the end of economic intervention; (b) the growing influence of foreign capital; and (c) the entry of foreign banks.

The changes in the set-up of economic power may yet be important. But, given the integration of Spanish capitalism with the most developed capitalist economies, financial capital is presented, in any case, with some possible options. These relate firstly to the restructuring of its interests in the home market – involving growing inter-relationship to and dependence on multinational concerns with which they can set up and develop new business and activities. Secondly, it can foresee possibilities of larger participation in foreign markets once it becomes more integrated in the dominant power structures of the 'core economies'. Its prospects are now a logical consequence of the most important trend in economic power since 1939, which, we argue, has been the growing penetration, from 1959 onwards, of foreign capital in the Spanish economy, and its progressive integration as a coherent whole within the field of influence of TNCs. Given these new co-ordinates, possible alternatives are limited. Few 'autonomous miracles' are now possible in a society which is preparing to adapt, obviously late in the day, its peculiar ancestral ways and political and economic institutions to the needs of the international system into which it is already inserted.

Notes

1 Except in 1964, when there was a surplus of 2 billion pesetas, the balance on current account shows high deficits, especially in 1965 (29 billion pesetas) and in 1966 (40 billion pesetas); deficits which foreshadow the devaluation of November 1967.

2 The deficit on current account estimated for 1976 is 40 per cent higher than that of 1975.

3 Our estimates, based on the data of the Balance of Payments and National Accounts of the Bank of Spain, are slightly higher than those of J. B. Donges (Donges, 1976, p. 109).

4 To estimate this figure, we have used the methods in Varela and Rodríguez de Pablo, 1974, p. 14.

5 The analysis of the US Department of Commerce confirms this trend. The low yield of American direct investments in Spain can be due – not considering the existing possibilities for the transferring of 'hidden incomes' etc. – 'to the need for letting some time pass before most of the industrial investment starts to yield profits, especially when we consider the main industries to which this investment has gone' (Gallego Malaga, 1975, p. 38).

6 Note that the outflows due to 'patents' and 'technical assistance' are more than 40 per cent higher than the profits repatriated in the period.

7 There are also concrete analyses by sectors of the clauses in the contracts for technical services, patents, etc., in Muñoz, Roldán and Serrano (1977).

8 Many of the large American TNCs have their headquarters, for tax purposes, in Switzerland.

9 (Rodríguez de Pablo, 1974; 1975.) Both studies were directed and carried out by J. Rodríguez de Pablo under the supervision of F. Varela Parache, the Sub-Director General of Foreign Investment. They each have a dual objective: (a) to measure the degree of penetration of foreign capital and (b) to analyse the economic behaviour of Spanish firms which have foreign participation.

10 Among companies whose capital does not exceed 50 million pesetas, the majority have no foreign participation. For companies with capital of between 50 and 100 million pesetas, there are 93 without, but 166 with, foreign capital. All this seems to reinforce the thesis that foreign capital directs and controls the policy of the Spanish chemical industry, because decisions are taken fundamentally by the larger companies.

11 (Department of Technology and Industrial Promotion, 1973: Economía Industrial, 1973, pp. 7–55.) The sample used for this study were the '600 largest industrial companies in Spain engaged in terms of value of sales, with the exception of the water, gas and electricity sectors, which are principally controlled by Spanish interests.' The classification of companies by sector was on the basis of principal products. The sample chosen

comprises between 50 and 90 per cent of the total production of the sector, with the exception of sectors such as textiles, shoes and leather goods, wood, foodstuffs and sundry industries (where the percentages represented are less than 25 per cent). Only direct foreign investments are taken into consideration.

12   J. Muñoz, 'La concentración de poder económico in España' in (Muñoz et al., 1976).

13   Three of these are not purely British: Royal Dutch Shell (Anglo-Dutch), Unilever (Anglo-Dutch) and Dunlop-Pirelli (Anglo-Italian).

14   Though referring to different spheres, similar results are reached in (Ministry of Industry, 1976) and in (Department of Technology and Industrial Promotion, 1973).

15   The National Telephone Company of Spain has a substantial participation by the State, and the banks (the President and the three Vice-Presidents have been top executives in private banks), but also commercial and technological connections with the important American Company ITT. However, since there is no foreign participation in the share capital nor any foreigners on the board of directors, the Telephone Company has not been treated here as foreign controlled.

16   In the programme of economic measures presented by the Government at the end of February 1977, in the chapter on monetary policy, one can read, for the first time in the last 50 years, official policy with the following characteristics: 'With the aim of stimulating competition in the financial sector and of providing resources for the national economy, the presence of foreign financial bodies in the Spanish market is considered necessary. In the face of this irreversible process, it seems that the battle centres on the determining of areas, functions and requisites to be established for foreign banks: controls on the direct or indirect participation of firms, rules concerning their capital and foreign resources with demands for percentages to be covered by foreign resources, guarantees of permanence, etc. The recent visit of President Suárez to the United States, his interviews with the main representatives of the financial consortia, the "possible" agreements ... officially denied are, in any case, significant enough. Five American banks and some European or Japanese concerns may obtain permission to set up in Spain before the year end. In private conversation held some days ago in New York between the President, Adolfo Suárez, and the president of "Citibank", the subject was apparently touched upon. In the conversation, they also discussed the possibility of a direct credit from the big American banks to concede to Spain a credit of more than 500 million dollars, in addition to the deal under negotiation with the International Monetary Fund which may double its sum.' (El País, 6.5.77.)

References

Acosta, Sánchez J. (1976), *Crisis del franquismo y crisis del imperialismo*, Barcelona.

Alcaide, L. (1976), 'El sector exterior: autarquía y comercio libre', *Información Comercial Española*, 500.

de la Fuente, E. (1975), 'Los cambios en el sector exterior español', *Boletín de Estudios Económicos*, 96.

Dirección General de Promoción Industrial y Tecnologia (1973), Reports presented by the Director General Sr Castañé at Congress organised by Sercobe on the theme of *Multinational Companies and Plant Equipment* (cyclostyled), Madrid; also published as 'The Presence of Multinationals in Spain', *Economía Industrial* (1973), 117 (7–55).

Donges, J. B. (1976), *La industrialización en España. Políticas, logros y perspectivas*, Barcelona.

Fanjul, O., Maravall, F., Pérez, Prim J. M. and Segura, J. (1975), *Cambios en la estructura interindustrial de la economía española 1962–70: una primera aproximación*, Madrid.

Gallego, Malaga M. (1975), 'Las inversiones de las multinacionales USA y el desarrollo industrial español', *Economía Industrial*, 133.

Gasoliba, C. A. (1975), 'Industrias Punta: un renovado intento de determinación', *Banca Catalana*, 38.

Granell, Trias F. (1971), 'El déficit de la balanza de comercio y el subdesarrollo estructural relativo de la economía española', *Moneda y Crédito*, 116.

Ministerio de Comercio (1974), *Inversión extranjera en España 1959–73*, Madrid.

Ministerio de Comercio (1976), *Balanza de Pagos en España 1975*, Madrid.

Ministerio de Industria (1976), *Las 500 grandes empresas industriales españolas*, Madrid.

Muñoz, J., Roldán, S., García, Delgado, J. L. and Serrano, A. (1976), 'El capital extranjero y la formación y desarrollo del capitalismo español. Hacia una economía dependiente. Epílogo y Apéndices Informativos' in Levinson, Ch., *Inflación, capital y multinacionales*, Barcelona.

Muñoz, J., Roldán, S. and Serrano, A. (1977), *¿Qué es el capitalismo español?*, Madrid.

El País, 6.5.77.

Poulantzas, N. (1976), *Las crisis de las dictaduras: Portugal, Grecia, España*, Madrid.

Rodríguez de Pablo, J. (1974), 'Inversiones extranjeras en España' *Información Comercial Española*, 493.

Rodríguez de Pablo, J. (1975), 'Inversiones extranjeras en España: la industria alimenticia', *Información Comercial Española*, 499.

UNCTAD (1974), *Principales cuestiones que plantea la transmisión de tecnología. Estudio monográfico sobre España*, Naciones Unidas, TD/B/AC.

Varela, Parache A. and Rodriguez de Pablo, J. (1974), 'Las inversiones extranjeras en España: 1959–74. Una vía al desarrollo', *Información Comercial Española*, 493.

IO

CORE-PERIPHERY RELATIONS IN THE GREEK CASE
Mary Evangelinides

Greece in the External Arena of the World Economy (the Fifteenth to Nineteenth Centuries)

Greeks lived since the fifteenth century as a subject people in the Ottoman Empire. They were distinguished not by their ethnic singularity but as members of the Eastern Orthodox Church. For 400 years Greece continued as a peripheral province of the Ottoman Empire, subject to its particular forms of decentralised administration and communal self-government. The Ottoman patrimonial system of power was organised in such a way as to prevent the creation of a strong landed aristocracy which might have presented a challenge to the absolute authority of the Sultan. The cultivated land was organised under the timar system of landholding. In contrast to European feudal lords, timar holders (the *spahis*) had no rights of ownership over the land. They had a non-hereditary right to part of the produce in exchange for which they were obliged to provide both administrative and military services to the Sultan and the State (*Porte*). The direct producers, the peasantry, whether Christians or Muslims, had hereditary usage of their land, subject to the obligation to cultivate it regularly. (Mouzelis, forthcoming.)

The relative freedom of the Greek peasant and the relative lack of large agricultural estates or farms accompanied by other factors, such as reforms contributing to further fragmentation of agricultural land, led to the small size of farm holdings and to the non-capitalist exploitation of agricultural land and hence to the marginality and stagnation of the agricultural sector of the economy that in a way still exists in contemporary Greece.

What remain distinctive of that period, features which persist in, and in a way shape contemporary Greek social formation, are the relative importance of the state in the social formation of the country, the absence of an economically dominant class or bourgeoisie to play the role of the technological and scientific innovators, and the presence of a large number of relatively independent peasants working on their own small piece of land or under sharecropping arrangements as well as the minor role of wage remuneration in the agricultural sector and the complete absence of capitalist agriculture.

From the fifteenth century the Ottoman State was omnipotent in occupied Greece. This continued until the middle of the nineteenth century, when with the establishment of a 'free constitutional government' in the country controlled by the Crown,[1] the State apparatus became stronger and nothing could be done in Greece without it necessarily passing through its machinery.

This type of state paternalism still persists today in Greek society and political life. Contrary to the western development of capitalism and rapid industrialisation, due mainly to the emergence and rise of the city-states, of guilds, of manufacturing, of the bourgeoisie and of industry, the Balkans and Greece especially did not follow this path but remained in a state of economic and political dependence on the main world power centres.

All the features present in Greece between the sixteenth and the nineteenth century are typical of the 'Asiatic mode of production' to be found in most countries where the form assumed by a given civilisation was that of tribute-paying: a state-class of a theocratic-bureaucratic type emerged from the communities and asserted itself as organiser of the political and economic life of society (Amin, 1973). The first attempt to understand why the development of these civilisations was blocked was made by Marx in his observations in the *Grundrisse* regarding the Asiatic mode of production.[2]

Greece, then, was a peripheral province of the Ottoman Empire. At that time the centre of the empire was Constantinople. The Ottoman Empire, which in its turn functioned as a semi-peripheral state for the continent in which the core countries (England, France, Spain, Holland, Germany, Italy) were emerging all-powerful, was never organically integrated into the Western European system. When, in the sixteenth century, the Continent experienced a spectacular period of economic expansion marked by technological innovation, trans-atlantic discovery, the development of long-term trade, the influx of precious metals and stones, the growth of populations and urban centres and of the world economy (Wallerstein, 1974), it developed a new international division of labour, and the world was differentiated into core, peripheral and semi-peripheral states. It was during this period that the major European states, in their efforts to improve their economies and secure cheap raw materials and food for their growing populations, started to extract a variety of trading privileges from the declining Ottoman State. The famous capitulatory privileges (trade concessions granted by the Sultan to various foreign powers) were effective in imposing extremely favourable trade terms for the West and in orienting part of the Ottoman economy to the development requirements of Western Europe.

During the sixteenth and seventeenth centuries the Greek territories of the Ottoman Empire felt the impact of rising western capitalism and the creation of a relatively coherent world market. However the impact was chiefly indirect, in that western growth was, to a limited extent, instrumental in shaping the Balkan economies through international trade, by the increasing demand for Balkan agricultural products, and by the imposition of unfavourable terms of trade on the declining Ottoman Empire. Greek territories, as well as the Ottoman Empire, were still not organically integrated into western capitalism, played only a minor role in the economic activities of the world market and were used rather as a sea route or passage for the eastern Mediterranean trade. They were, in fact, rather in the external arena of the European world-economy than in the periphery of it.

Pre-Industrial Greece and its Diaspora Communities in the Periphery of the World Economy (1700–1922)

A major characteristic of that period was the appearance of the Greek merchant. Even though, in the sixteenth century, the Greek merchant class appeared timidly and illegally, it is in the eighteenth century that this class reached the height of its development, growth and consolidation. It was mainly in the eighteenth century, with the assistance and support of the Greek Orthodox Church as well as this of the Phanariote Greeks who were holding key positions in the Ottoman administration and played a crucial role in banking and finance – something like the Mandarins in China – that conditions became favourable for the rise of the Greek Orthodox merchant in the Balkans and the Mediterranean Sea (Mouzelis, 1978).

We can observe an unprecedented growth of Greek diaspora communities in the Balkans, Austria, Italy, South France, Russia, Asia Minor and later in Egypt. With the new expansion of European trade after the long economic crisis of the seventeenth century, Greek merchants were now able to extend their operations beyond Italy to France, Germany, Austria, Hungary and Russia. In the eighteenth and nineteenth centuries we see the growth of Greek diaspora communities in the major urban centres of Vienna, Marseilles, Trieste, Odessa, Budapest, Smyrna and Alexandria. A part of Greece's socio-economic element was starting to be organically articulated within the major European centres. It is from the eighteenth century onwards that Greece, together with its diaspora communities around the Mediterranean sea, became the periphery of the European core countries.

Trade, mercantilism or comprador capital and activities were always the most distinct features of Greek social formation, especially those of the economically dominant class. They emerged timidly in the six-teenth century under illegal practices of Greek seamen and pirates in the Aegean Sea, increasingly developed in the eighteenth century and still remain today the main features and driving force of Greek socio-economic life.

Contrary to the rise of the merchants or artisans, the so-called 'third-class' in Europe, the Greek merchants, bankers or financiers, were agents and protégés of the European economic interests (British, Austro-German, French, Russian) in the Ottoman Empire. They en-joyed special privileges, tax exemptions and legal treatment *vis à vis* the national artisans and productive forces. They became agents of European expansionism in the territories of the Ottoman Empire and, in that way, blocked all efforts for an inward-looking, self-sustained national development. Furthermore, they contributed to the gradual integration of the Ottoman Empire's regions, later to become national independent states, into the periphery of the international capitalist market (Psiroukis, 1975, pp. 52–54).

The growth of the import-export trade over the eighteenth and nineteenth centuries was a very serious source of capital accumulation both for the diaspora and for the indigenous comprador bourgeoisie. The former, during this period, was attracted mainly by a variety of speculative and financial operations which, in a capital-starved econ-omy, ensured enormous profits with minimal risk. Given the inter-national connections and orientation of the diaspora capital entering Greece, there is no doubt that much of the surplus extracted from the peasants was quite systematically transferred abroad. In other words, Greek merchants were promoting foreign interests rather than the interests of their countries of origin (Psiroukis, 1975).

The phenomenon of the Greek diaspora emigrés or cosmopolitan Greek bankers and merchants corroborates the argument of Waller-stein (1974, pp. 351–2) that 'one of the key elements in analysing a class or a status group is not only the state of its self-consciousness but the geographical scope of its self-definition. . . .' Wallerstein comes very close to Psiroukis about the diaspora Greeks, especially the capitalist Greek farmers in Alexandria, Egypt, and in general the role of *pieds-noirs* that the Greeks played in Africa.

Another feature instrumental in shaping the socio-economic struc-ture of modern Greece is the orientation of Greek capital towards the ship-building industry. It was in the eighteenth century that Russia, acting as the protecting power for all Orthodox Christians, was pur-suing a policy of seeking entrance into the Aegean and Adriatic Sea in order to control the passages to Asia and block the sea routes. Most of the Greek islands (Hydra, Spetses, Psara, Chios, etc.) became agents and protégés of Russia, now protecting and supporting the Greek merchant marine capital (Psiroukis, 1975).

From this time, Greece experienced exceptional development and booming activity in its ship-building industry and merchant marine, an activity and tradition which developed such a momentum and dynamism that it made the Greek merchant marine one of the most important merchant fleets in the world today. The Greek shipping houses (*karavokyrei*) of the eighteenth century, as well as the twentieth century Greek shipping companies and ship-owners, located in London, the US and South America, became very prosperous and managed to orient most of the Greek merchant capital, investment and business activity towards the ship-building industry and merchant marine. Even though this activity brought prosperity and profit to the Greek ship-owners (to seamen, as well as to the Greek economy, in the form of seamen's remittances) and always managed to counteract the balance of payments deficit, it contributed very little to the development of a healthy independent economy. It reinforced the cosmopolitan and outward-looking expansion, investment, industriousness and orientation of Greek natural and human resources. Greek diaspora or indigenous capital did not enter agricultural production, neither did it orient itself in industry. It was not used for the technological modernisation of agriculture or for the development of capitalist forms of production.

It is during the period that covers the second half of the nineteenth century to the outbreak of the First World War that Europe experienced a period of expanding industrial capitalism in the countries that now constitute the core of the European sub-system, and of their imperial extension into the now underdeveloped countries of Africa, Asia and Latin America, with the specialisation of the former in manufacturing and of the latter in food and raw materials. During this crucial period the old pre-industrial empires (Portuguese, Spanish, Ottoman, Austrian and Russian) were in a process of relative decline and disintegration (see Sunkel, 1977).

In Greece fundamental changes were taking place which were reflected in the establishment of a new, independent, modern nation state; in the growth of foreign influence, investment and finance; in the emergence of new social groups, ideas, values and culture; in the development of primary export activities and unsuccessful attempts at industrialisation as well as the creation of a transportation and communication network geared mainly to the needs of expanding foreign European trade. Greece was linked mainly to, and controlled by, England, France and Germany.

The picture that emerged from the post-independence period was that of a large state apparatus controlled by the Crown and by a more-

or-less fragmented political oligarchy at the head of extensive clientelistic networks. The greater the range of the state administration
– and it soon acquired enormous dimensions – the higher the patronage
stakes: for if the State lacked any effective policy for the development
of the Greek economy, it indirectly provided employment for many
who were leaving the countryside and could not be absorbed into non-
existent Greek industry. The Greek state administration was and is,
even today, performing the function of absorbing surplus Greek
semi-educated labour (the petite-bourgeoisie of the villages and towns)
that cannot be absorbed into the private sector.

It was a natural corollary that the Greek state bureaucracy achieved
quite early on a size completely out of proportion to the country's
resources and population. This administrative growth was steadily increasing. Its characteristic is germane to an understanding of the basic
structure and dynamics of Greek social formation. It is also at the root
of the corruption and inefficiency of the Greek modern state as it
paralyses all efforts for modernisation as well as for rapid development.
Furthermore, the monstrous administrative expansion, combined with
imported political institutions ill-fitting the pre-capitalist infrastructure of nineteenth century Greece, explains the relative autonomy of
the Greek state in relation to its class structure. For clientelism not
only kept the peasantry, as a class, outside the sphere of activity and
autonomous politics, but also slowed down or actually prevented the
political organisation and the ideological coherence of the economically
dominant classes.

In the productive sector of the economy, most of the foreign and
diaspora capital, in so far as it was not employed in purely speculative
or financial operations, was used for the purchase of *chiflik* lands or
invested in public works projects – mainly railways. But the massive
spending on railway construction hardly helped the manufacturing
sector. There were very few organic links between railway growth and
the rest of Greek industry, since most of the materials used in these
large-scale public works were imported, even those which could
easily have been produced locally. Given this situation, as well as the
usurious rates at which foreign loans were contracted, and the quasi-
colonial behaviour of foreign and diaspora capital, it is not surprising
that Greece went bankrupt towards the end of the century and was
obliged to accept the establishment of an international control commission (manned by the representatives of foreign bond-holders),
which for decades had a very important control in the public finances
of the modern Greek state. On the other hand, the comprador traditions of the indigenous merchant capital left it extremely reluctant to
exchange the certainty of its easy trade profits for the risky and
bothersome business of factory production.

Moreover, despite massive rural unemployment, there was no major source of cheap industrial labour. Peasants preferred to remain in the countryside, or give a minimal high-school education to their children in order that they should find a clerical job in the public administration or, better still, migrate to the US, rather than become proletarians. Thus the number of Greeks who left for the US every year was greater than the total number of workers employed in the Greek industry.

This was the situation and socio-economic spatial structure of the Greek economy and society up to the twentieth century, when it was still a peripheral province of the Ottoman Empire. For five centuries (1453–1922), the socio-economic life of Greece was spread around the Mediterranean sea in Greek diaspora communities distributed around Livorno, Trieste, Vienna, Odessa, Constantinople, Smyrna, and later Alexandria. It is in the towns of Asia Minor, like Constantinople itself, Smyrna and Trapezous, that the bulk of the Greek population, numbering more than two million, was to be found, ranging from farmers, businessmen and artisans to state officials, bankers and financiers, while the Greek mainland (the more or less definite and permanent boundaries of which were finally settled in 1922) was an agricultural economy with non-capitalist modes of production in all sectors. The first Greek population census in 1821 estimated there were 938,765 people living on the Greek mainland. From 1947 onwards Greek land and boundaries became definite and permanent. In 1853 Athens was a small town of 30,000 people. At that time there was little sign of its future development into an international metropolis of 2,850,000 people, who, in 1975, comprised 31 per cent of the national population.

The Greek mainland was connected with the world market only through the activities of the Greek merchants and diaspora communities. It is estimated that more than 600,000 Greek emigrés (merchants, students, bankers, big land-owners, financiers, artisans, clerks, administrators, ship-owners and small-scale industrialists) were living and prospering in the Greek diaspora communities. It is roughly estimated that, in the nineteenth century, the diaspora Greeks in Egypt amounted to 500,000 people while the diaspora Greeks in Southern Europe, the Balkans and Russia, amounted to 100,000 people. (Chouliarakis, forthcoming.)

Even though they were not important in numbers, they have been instrumental in shaping the socio-economic structure of modern Greece and have been the principal architects of the emergence of a modern Greek state run by a large state administration, characterised by clientelism and inefficiency and possessing all the classical characteristics of underdevelopment seen in most formations of peripheral capitalism.

It was not only clientelism that paralysed the state's capacity to implement collective goals, but also the strict limits imposed on internal politics by Greece's political and economic dependence upon the great powers and, to a certain extent, on the big diaspora and Greek cosmopolitan capital, which had, and still has, an outward-looking orientation and interests.

Greek society had no definite or settled boundaries and its socio-economic space as well as its poles or centres of attraction (Constantinople, Smyrna, Alexandria) were located outside the traditional boundaries and territory of what is Greece today. During this period the Greek nation and people were spread around the Mediterranean as there existed no Greek national state.

Post–industrial Greece in the Periphery of the World Economy 1922–77

The year 1922 was a turning-point in the history of modern Greece. In this fateful year the defeat in Asia Minor of the Greek army by Kemal Atatürk's nationalist forces put a stop to Greek irredentism, and set more or less definite and permanent boundaries to the modern Greek state. Moreover, the sudden arrival of more than one million Greek refugees from Asia Minor had fundamental consequences for Greek social structure. This massive influx created severe disruption to a population of only five million.

Not all of the refugees could be accommodated. A sizeable number settled in the big urban centres, especially Salonica, Piraeus and Athens, thus providing an abundant and relatively skilled labour force at the disposal of Greek capital. Moreover, since a number of the refugees had occupied important positions in the industry, trade and finance of the Greek communities in Asia Minor, they brought with them badly needed entrepreneurial skills as well as considerable finance. To this refugee capital should be added the enormous influx of foreign funds, government loans, private investments in public works and international aid to the refugees. This, of course, meant increasing domination of the Greek economy by foreign interests.

In terms of modes of production, capitalism can be said at this point to have become dominant in the Greek social formation. Of course, this dominance did not become markedly visible in the relevant statistics. After all, even today, large capitalist enterprises using wage labour in industry constitute only a small island in the sea of family based artisan units. Also, until the late 1950s, the industrial sector as a whole was less important than the agricultural or the tertiary sector, both in terms of labour employed and of its contribution to the GNP.

The mechanisms through which such a process of distorted capitalist development took place were obvious: enormous state subsidies to big industry, scandalous credit facilities, indiscriminate tariff protection enabling highly inefficient industrial firms to achieve quasi-monopolistic positions, the prevalence of indirect taxation which hit small incomes hard. Inevitably, growing inequalities and the increasing marginalisation of those involved in small commodity production – phenomena closely linked with the dominance of the capitalist mode of production in peripheral social formations – became the two major features of the Greek model of capital accumulation (Sunkel, 1973).

A completely new phenomenon inherited from the Second World War conditioned much of Greece's subsequent history. This was the economic, political, military and ideological influence of the US. After the war, Great Britain lost its predominant presence and influence in Greece.

More recently, and particularly from 1974, the question of the country's entrance into the EEC's integrated economic system, as a full member, became the government's main concern and a highly controversial political and economic issue.

Until the late 1950s, despite the rapid growth of the economy and the clear dominance of the capitalist mode of production in industry, Greece still exemplified the classical characteristics of underdevelopment seen in most formations of peripheral capitalism: a low-productivity agriculture, a highly inflated and parasitic service sector, and an industrial sector unable to absorb the redundant agricultural labour force, which then emigrated to the US, Australia or Germany, or to expand into capital goods production. On this last point, all the development efforts and investment incentives offered by the state and directed towards a rapid industrialisation of the Greek economy failed to direct Greek capital into those key manufacturing sectors of the economy (metallurgy, chemicals) whose growth would have had a great transforming power on the rest of the economy. These key manufacturing sectors were left to foreign capital which, taking advantage of the enormous privileges granted by the Greek State, began to invade the Greek economy and invest in the key dynamic industries as well as penetrate other vital sectors like banking, insurance, construction, engineering and trade. The heterogeneity of the Greek economic structure is very similar to the models suggested by Sunkel (1973) and Holland (1975) who suggest – Sunkel four, and Holland three main categories in the economic structure – which interact in the process of production and accumulation, each sector providing inputs and outputs, the whole process working to the benefit of the foreign sector and to the detriment of the marginalised one.

This last phase of Western imperialism is linked with a new phase of Greek underdevelopment which is no longer that of a weak manufacturing sector. Instead, it takes the form of a technologically advanced, highly dynamic, foreign-controlled manufacturing sector, enjoying enormous privileges granted to it by the Greek State,[3] and not being organically linked with the rest of the economy so that the beneficial effects of its growth are not sufficiently diffused over the small commodity agricultural and artisan sectors but are to a large extent transferred abroad. Greek private capital, following its preference for quick and easy profits, has continued to orient itself towards tourism, shipping, services and other 'comprador' activities. Where it has entered industrial production, it has been in the traditional industrial branches of textiles, food, etc.

Structural Characteristics of Underdevelopment and Dependency in Greece

MARGINALISATION AND FOREIGN CONTROL

Table 37 demonstrates that, in 1974, 45·5 per cent of the total economically active population worked or was employed in the traditional sector of the economy and contributed only 17·3 per cent to the country's GNP. As for the intermediate sector, we see that 24·6 per cent of the economically active population contributed 23·8 per cent to the country's GNP. Thus we have 70 per cent of the country's labour force working or employed in the low-productive and informal sectors of the economy, sometimes as unpaid family members, contributing 41 per cent to the country's GNP.

On the other hand, we see that 13·3 per cent of the economically active population was employed in the national modern sector and produced 29·5 per cent of the country's GNP, while an even smaller percentage of only 4·7 per cent was employed in the foreign sector and produced, as well as 'enjoyed', 12·1 per cent of the country's GNP. We thus have 18 per cent of the country's economically active population employed in the formal modern leading and highly-productive sectors of the economy producing 42 per cent of the country's GNP.

As for the public sector of the economy, we see that 12 per cent of the labour force produce (or more appropriately, receive) 17·3 per cent of the country's GNP. The public sector, as argued above, is in its majority, – with the exception of some cases within the branches of power, transportation, banking, telecommunication, shipbuilding industry, petroleum refineries and the sugar industry, – a highly inefficient and bureaucratic machine that hinders most of the efforts for the country's modernisation and socio-economic development. In no case, however, should we consider these few exceptions and cases of firm or industry nationalisation as a sign of offensive, positive or dynamic state intervention aiming at mobilising investment during a

Table 37
Distribution of output and employment as percentage of national total, by main productive and institutional sectors, 1974

Main productive sectors	Whole economy		Formal organised sectors						Informal sectors				All institutional sectors	
			Foreign		National Modern		Public		Intermediate		Traditional			
	GNP %	Empl. %	GNP %	Empl. %	GNP %	Empl. %	GNP %	Empl. %	GNP %	Empl. %	GNP %	Empl. %	GNP %	Empl. %
PRIMARY	19·6	40·0	—	—	37·0	5·0	—	—	53·0	36·0	10·0	59·0	100·0	100·0
SECONDARY	31·0	26·0	30·0	15·0	27·0	20·0	5·0	3·0	25·0	26·0	13·0	36·0	100·0	100·0
Manufacturing	20·8	16·6	40·0	19·0	26·0	19·0	—	—	17·0	15·0	17·0	47·0	100·0	100·0
Power, Mining, Construction	10·2	9·4	11·0	9·0	27·0	22·0	15·0	9·0	40·0	46·0	7·0	15·0	100·0	100·0
TERTIARY	49·4	34·0	5·0	2·0	29·0	18·0	32·0	33·0	12·0	10·0	22·0	37·0	100·0	100·0
NATIONAL TOTAL	100·0	100·0	12·1	4·7	29·5	13·3	17·3	11·9	23·8	24·6	17·3	45·5	100·0	100·0

Sources: Gross Domestic Product, 1976, General Directorate of National Accounts.
Employment, Results of the Population and Housing Census of 1971, Vol. III.
Annual Industrial Survey, 1973, by National Statistical Service of Greece.
Census of Wholesale and Retail Trade Establishments, NSSG, 1969.
Foreign Capital in Greece, D. Benas, Papazissis Publishing House, 1976.
Statistical Yearbook of Greece, 1976.

period in which private capital hesitates to invest, or as a sign of 'socialisation' of the economy.

The cases of multi-industry state holding companies, like IRI and ENI in Italy, the British National Enterprise Board and the French Planning Agreements (*contrats de programme*) were not replicated in Greece.

AGRICULTURE

Table 37 demonstrates that by 1974 the primary sector was still employing 40 per cent of the country's labour force (1,313,336 persons), who contributed 20 per cent to the country's GNP. The estimate of 40 per cent is highly debatable, as it was based on 1971 Population Census figures. The 1977 estimates give us percentages that range between 25–40 per cent of the total labour force. Nevertheless, as there has been no official National Employment Census since 1971, the amount of 40 per cent will be taken here.

Table 37 demonstrates that within the primary sector 59 per cent of the farmers work in the traditional sector and contribute only 10 per cent to the primary sector's GNP. Furthermore, 36 per cent of the farmers work in the intermediate sector and produce 53 per cent of the primary sector's GNP. Thus, 95 per cent of the farmers work under low-productive and traditional methods of farming and/or as unpaid family members, contributing 63 per cent to the primary sector's GNP. On the other hand, a small proportion (5 per cent) of Greek farmers work under modern and highly productive methods of farming and contribute 37 per cent to this sector's GNP.

SERVICES

Table 37 demonstrates that by 1974 the tertiary sector of the economy had already reached percentages of GNP and employment that resembled those of 'post-industrial' societies (Rostow, 1960). In 1974, 34 per cent of the country's labour force (1,105,016 persons) were employed in the tertiary sector and contributed to, or rather spent, 50 per cent of the country's GNP.

In Table 37 we see that within the tertiary sector almost half its labour force (47 per cent or 520,918 persons) was employed in the informal, traditional and intermediate sectors, working in low-productive, parasitic, backward conditions as unpaid family members. They received 34 per cent of the tertiary sector's GNP. As for the public sector (33 per cent of the tertiary sector's labour force or 362,375 persons), were employed in it and received 32 per cent of the tertiary sector's GNP.

The remaining 20 per cent of the tertiary sector's labour force was employed in the formal sectors: national modern (18 per cent or 199,203 persons) and the foreign sector (2 per cent or 22,520 persons). These contributed 34 per cent to the tertiary sector's GNP (29 per cent by the national modern and 5 per cent by the foreign sector).

Both, but especially the privileged 2 per cent of the foreign sector, were working and controlling modern dynamic branches such as banking, financing, tourism and hotel business, distribution of petroleum products and house electrical equipment, office management and consulting services.

The foreign controlled sector 'is actually a foreign enclave, aimed at the local market, characterised by highly efficient and rational management and organisation procedures, enormous capacity to manipulate consumers and consumption patterns through the utilisation of the mass media, marketing and financial techniques and product design innovations and differentiation.' (Sunkel, 1977.)

INDUSTRY

In the industrial sector the key dynamic industries are controlled by foreign capital leaving the traditional branches of textiles, tobacco and agro-industries to domestic capital and control.

In Table 37 we see that 40 per cent of the manufacturing GNP is generated by 19 per cent of the industrial labour force working in foreign firms and that, together with the national modern firms which invest mainly in textiles, tobacco and agro-industries, these control the market. 38 per cent of the industrial labour force (the labour aristocracy) produce 66 per cent of the manufacturing GNP.

A study made by Roumeliotis and Golemis (1977) showed that most of the foreign investment goes to those sectors of Greek manufacturing that account for 52 per cent of assets of all manufacturing in 1975. These sectors are chemicals, non-metallic minerals, transport equipment, basic metals, metal products, petroleum, paper and rubber.

By looking at the first ten enterprises of each of the above sectors (ranked by sales), a relationship between concentration and foreign investment was found. Table 38 shows the percentage of total assets belonging to 'foreign' firms in the first ten enterprises in each of the eight key sectors. The percentage of 'foreign' participation varies, being 92 per cent out of 99 per cent in basic metals and 30 per cent out of 59 per cent in chemicals.

Another interesting result of the study was that 'foreign' firms were responsible for a high percentage of net profits in the ten biggest enterprises. In the eight key sectors, it was found that the whole of the 64 per cent of the total profits of the ten largest enterprises in chemicals went to foreign firms and that 96 per cent of the 99 per cent of the total profits of the ten largest enterprises in basic metals went to foreign firms.

Furthermore, according to the analysis made (in this volume) by Vaitsos on transnational enterprises and the European periphery it is shown that a large part of existing TNC investment activities, particularly in countries like Spain, Greece, and to an extent Portugal after the revolution, concentrated on import substituting operations which have been induced by high tariff and non-tariff barriers in selected product areas of the periphery. The effects of such investments are not very different from those noted in the Latin American experience: (a) a very small foreign financial contribution, compared to the total funds used by such firms in view of their heavy local borrowing; (b) significant attention paid to non-price competition based on product differentiation and heavy advertising; (c) the direct displacement of several local firms through acquisition or through non-price competition; and (d) the net income and balance of payments effects being in various cases either small or even negative in view of high protection or government subsidies and the ability of firms to remit untaxed effective profits through transfer pricing.

Table 37 shows the lack of participation of the public sector in manufacturing in 1974. Nevertheless, since then there have been a few cases of state take-overs of large groups of companies that belonged to Greek cosmopolitan capital, such as Elefsis Shipyards and some agro-industries of the Andreadis Group of Companies as well as the Petroleum Refineries of Niarchos Group of Companies at Aspropyrgos. The sugar industry is also a state-monopoly industry.

The rest of manufacturing (intermediate and traditional sectors) absorb the majority of artisans and workers. 62 per cent of the manufacturing labour force is working in medium- and small-scale industry and contributes 34 per cent to the manufacturing sector's GNP.

MIGRATION MOVEMENTS

The twentieth century was the century of large transoceanic and intra-European migration of thousands of Greek people to North and South America, Canada, Australia, South Africa and Germany.

The inefficiency and inability of the Greek economy to industrialise and absorb surplus young Greek farmers, a phenomenon further reinforced by the outward-looking orientation of Greek private capital, led to the loss of more than two million people, to core countries of the world system, as well as to the creation of a vast cosmopolitan Greek shipping fleet employing more than 150,000 Greek seamen travelling the world.

Out of a population of 9 million people more than one million emigrated to the American and Australian continents and another million to Central Europe. Table 39 shows that, during the period 1900–30 it was the United States and Canada, in the 1950s, Australia, and in the 1960s and early 1970s, Germany and Belgium that were absorbing surplus Greek workers or farmers as cheap labour for industrialisation.

Table 38

Degree of concentration in Greek industry, 1975

	(I) Percentage of total assets held by first ten enterprises[1]	(II) Assets of foreign enterprises within (I)
Petroleum	A	A
Basic metals	A	B
Transportation equipment	B	D
Paper	B	I
Non-metallic minerals	C	J
Chemicals	E	H
Metal products	E	J
Rubber	F	H

Code: A Over 90
B 80–90
C 70–80
D 60–70
E 50–60
F 40–50
G 30–40
H 20–30
I 10–20
J Under 10

Note
1 Ranked by asset size. In the secondary source, exact figures are not quoted.

Source: *Financial Directory of Greek Companies* (ICAP), 1976, quoted in Roumeliotis and Golemis (1977).

Table 39

(a) Emigration of Greek citizens 1960–75

Year	Total
1960	47,768
1965	117,167
1970	92,681
1975	20,330

(b) Transoceanic emigration from Greece: 1901–75

Years	Number of emigrants[1] Total	To US	To other countries[2]
1901–5	51,479	49,962	1,517
1926–30	40,838	27,352	13,486
1950	4,635	1,890	2,745
1960	17,764	3,561	14,203
1965	29,035	2,782	26,253
1970	24,153	11,484	12,669
1975	8,808	4,567	4,239

Source: *Statistical Yearbook of Greece*, 1976, p. 47.
1 As from 1946, not including tourists in a broader sense and those emigrating for temporary work (less than one year).
2 Until 1924, Canada, Cuba, Brazil, Australia, Union of South Africa; since 1925, all countries regarded as 'countries of emigration' under Greek law, i.e. all except those in Europe and on the Mediterranean.

Another outward-looking manifestation of Greek capital in the years 1975–7 is its recent activity in the Arab and African countries where Greek technical companies are presently building road, harbour and other infrastructural networks, employing 8–10,000 Greek technicians, engineers and architects, and carrying out projects worth 180 billion drachmas (Economic Postman, No. 1235/1978).

TRADE AND BALANCE OF PAYMENTS

In the years 1972–5 Greece imported industrial capital and intermediate goods as well as chemicals and fuels, mainly from EEC countries. 42·5 per cent of its imports came from the EEC. On the whole, Greece is closely dependent on the European Continent as 57·8 per cent of its imports come from Europe. It also imports industrial goods from the US (7·3 per cent) from Japan (8·3 per cent) and crude oil from Saudi Arabia (8·3 per cent).

Greece exports mainly agricultural products (food, beverages and tobacco), other primary un-processed export products (bauxite and cement), crude materials (hides and cotton) and semi-processed or light manufactured goods (textiles, lime, cement, aluminium, shoes, etc.) to EEC countries. 50 per cent of its total exports go to EEC countries and 70 per cent to the whole of Europe. The rest of its exports go to African countries (11·9 per cent), Asian countries (11·3 per cent) and the US (6·1 per cent). (See also Table 57.)

As Greece is heavily dependent on capital and intermediate goods from the European core-countries, its balance of trade deficit is increasing. From $248·7 million in 1958 it was $2,916·1 million in 1975. The financing of this deficit occurs in 'invisible' items of the balance of payments through the import of capital and aid that takes different forms (private capital, i.e. emigrant remittances as well as other private entrepreneurial capital, bank loans, government loans, foreign travel (tourism and transportation receipts). (See Table 40; Balance of Payments Account, 1975.)

Table 40

Balance of Payments
1975

(Million US Dollars)		
Credit	Debit	*Category*
		CURRENT TRANSACTIONS
3,885·1	5,628·6	Goods and services
1,959·6	4,882·3	1. Goods[1]
621·3	455·2	2. Foreign travel
853·8	172·3	3. Transportation
6·7	21·5	4. Insurance premiums
93·7	186·8	5. Investment income[2]
54·3	64·8	6. Government[2]
295·7	145·7	7. Miscellaneous

TABLE 40—*Cont.*

(*Million US Dollars*)		
Credit	Debit	*Category*
		CURRENT TRANSACTIONS
—	1,743·5	Net balance of goods and services
747·2	2·6	Donations
733·6	2·6	8. Private (Emigrant remit.)[3]
13·6	—	9. Official
8·3		9·1 Reparations restitutions
		9·2 Economic and technical
5·3	—	assistance
744·6	—	Net donations
—	998·9	Net balance
		MOVEMENT of CAPITAL and
1,218·6	—	MONETARY GOLD (NET)
790·8	178·9	10. Private
638·9	178·0	10·1 Long-term capital
23·6	37·7	Capital under L.D. 2687/53
77·6	—	Suppliers' credits[4]
177·7	50·7	Other loans by private corp.[4]
13·7	55·7	Other loans by public corp.
346·3	33·9	Other private capital
151·9	0·9	10·2 Short-term capital
151·9	—	Suppliers' credits[4]
—	0·9	Private barter
89·6	83·0	11. Central Government (Long-term)
—	3·3	Loans repayable in local currency
89·6	79·7	Loans repayable in foreign exchange
701·3	326·9	12. Central Monetary Institution
—	—	Participation in intern. organ
606·2	105·8	Loans and credits
89·1	178·2	Other
—	29·9	Payments and clearing agreement
—	13·0	Official foreign exchange reserves
6·0	0·0	Monetary gold
644·9	419·2	13. Other Monetary Institutions
11·9	7·4	Loans and credits
621·3	411·8	Deposits under L.D. 2687/53
11·7	—	Other deposits
		CREATION of OFFICIAL RESERVES
—	—	14. Non monetary gold
—	—	15. Allocation of SDRs
—	219·7	Errors and omissions

Source: *Statistical Yearbook of Greece*, 1976.

1 Imports c.i.f., exports f.o.b. Excluding ships registered under L.D. 2687/53 and franco valuta imports.
2 Including drachmae expenditures of US Government in Greece (government) derived from interest and principal payments in drachmae on US loans, etc.
3 Including workers' earnings from continental Europe.
4 Including capital and credits of public corporations which do not entail the indebtedness of the State.

Conclusion

All the above activities, the so-called invisible receipts, are helping to balance the increasing payments deficit. At the same time they deprive the country of its most dynamic and productive human resources. They contributed to a national socio-economic structure characterised by a combination of underdevelopment phenomena typical of most formations of peripheral capitalism together with particular and exceptional manifestations of parasitic comprador activities. They display an outward-looking orientation of Greek capital and people typical only of 'the Greek nation and people'. And they show acute socio-psychological signs of the 'permanent migrant' syndrome.

Closing this paper on a more optimistic note one would suggest that there is a more constructive way of using the outward-looking orientation of Greek capital and people as well as the vast cosmopolitan Greek shipping marine fleet and the recent activities of Greek capital and people in the Arab and African countries: a lot of effort should be undertaken by Greek people in turning Greece into a centre of international trade, transport and finance, playing a central role and serving as an intermediary reinforcing the presence of European activities in the markets of the Middle East.

Whereas, in the sixteenth and seventeenth centuries, Greece was in the external arena of the world system, owing to the decline of the Eastern Mediterranean trade, Greece is now faced with a challenge: to shift from the periphery of the European core system into the very core by exploiting and turning its own long-held vices into virtues.

Notes

1   The first king of the new independent Greek State came from abroad and was a foreigner. He was the Bavarian prince, *Othon*.
2   See Amin's analysis of the two model centres of tribute-paying civilisations, China, Egypt (Amin, 1976, pp. 53–8).
3   The main body of legislation consists of L. 2687/53 regarding the 'Investment and Protection of Foreign Capital'. Several other laws complete the framework such as Emergency Law 89/67 concerning the 'Establishment in Greece of Foreign Trading and Manufacturing Companies', or Emerg. Law 378/68 re shipping companies. Furthermore, other laws which offer incentives for regional (L. 1078/71 and L. 1312/72) or other development (L. 4171/61 and L. 4458/1965) are used primarily by foreign firms, something that increases their power.

References

Amin, S. (1973), 'Underdevelopment and Dependence in Black Africa – Their Historical Origins and Contemporary Focus', *Social and Economic Studies*, 22, 1.

Amin, S. (1976), *Unequal Development*, Harvester Press, Hassocks.

Chouliarakis, M., 'Studies on Greek Historical Demography', forthcoming.

Friedmann, J. (1973), Urbanisation, Planning & National Development, Sage Publications, Beverly Hills, London.

Holland, S. (1975), 'The Trend to Monopoly' in *Strategy for Socialism*, Spokesman Books, 1975.

Mouzelis, N., 'The Development of Greek Capitalism: An Overall View', Chapter I, *Greece-Facets of Underdevelopment*, Macmillan, London, forthcoming.

Psiroukis, N. (1975), *The Phenomenon of the modern Greek communities abroad*, Epikerotita, Athens.

Rostow, W. W. (1960), *The Stages of Economic Growth*, O.U.P.

Roumeliotis, P., and Golemis, C. (1977), 'Transfer Pricing and the Power of Transnational Enterprises in Greece', paper presented at IDS Conference on Transnational Enterprises.

Sunkel, O. (1973), 'Transnational Capitalism and National Disintegration in Latin America', in *Social and Economic Studies*, 22, 1.

Sunkel, O. (1977), 'Methodological suggestions for the study of the development of the countries of the European periphery', background paper to the Workshop on the European periphery, IDS, November 24–6, 1977.

Wallerstein, I. (1974), *The Modern World System: Capitalist Agriculture and the Origins of the European World Economy in the 16th century*, Academy Press.

II

FAST GROWTH AND SLOW DEVELOPMENT IN SOUTH ITALY[1]

Robert Wade

Dualism and the Southern Development Programme

South Italy was one of the first places to receive the attention of people who called themselves 'development' economists. The self-conscious attempt to 'develop' the South began in 1950, over twenty-five years ago, and has been sustained ever since. In terms of the resources devoted to the purpose, the programme was huge: about one per cent of GNP flowed through the hands of the southern development agency between 1951 and the early 1970s (Saracero, 1974), or 4–5 per cent of regional income during this period. Total investment in the South has exceeded 25 per cent of regional income ever since 1951, much of it coming from the North (Cafiero, 1976).[2] In terms of the resources available, the length of application, the statistical base, the brilliance of the planners, the development programme for the South is rare amongst both developed and underdeveloped countries. What has been the experience of the South in the past twenty-five years or so, with all this development effort?

Let us remember that compared to other parts of the southern European periphery, South Italy is big: almost as big as Greece in area, bigger than Portugal; and bigger than both combined in population (19 million). It accounts for 40 per cent of Italy's area and 34 per cent of the national population (1976).

In 1951 South Italy (or *Mezzogiorno*) showed many of the features of an underdeveloped country: low *per capita* income (just over half the average of the rest of the country), high unemployment and underemployment, over half the work force engaged in agriculture, a small manufacturing sector composed mainly of artisan 'subsistence' units with an average of fewer than three persons in each (Benetti *et al.*, 1975), a small number of social strata, large inequalities in the distribution of wealth, low investment, high fertility, and a history of mass emigration. In rural areas, sharing a dwelling with animals and a mattress with parents, brothers and sisters, was a common necessity (Rogers and Moss, 1977). In these various respects South Italy was

closer to other parts of the southern European periphery than to
North Italy.

Explicitly, the southern development programme was based on the
assumption that the obstacles to southern development were a limited
market and poor infrastructure.[3] Hence additional state funds should
go into improving the infrastructure, particularly that of agriculture,
and to reducing the additional costs that private investors had to face
if they invested in the South rather than in the North. With the expansion of the market and the improvement of infrastructure, the
additional risks of investment in the South would decline, it was
thought, and at a certain point would permit a process of self-generating industrial growth to be launched. Hence when the southern
development agency, the *Cassa per il Mezzogiorno*, was formed in 1950,
it concentrated attention on infrastructure and agriculture. The land
reform was one focus; 500,000 hectares were redistributed in the
South to over 100,000 assignees (Franklin, 1969). And in absolute
terms still more money was spent outside the land reform farms, on
irrigation and land improvement. After 1960, emphasis came to be
placed on stimulating industrialisation by more direct methods, particularly by financial incentives for private companies and locational
controls on public companies. By the late 1960s the financial incentives
were the highest on offer within the EEC.[4] The locational controls on
state holding companies stipulated that 40 per cent of their total investments and 60 per cent of their new investments should be in the
South. The significance of these controls derives from the fact that the
state holding company sector is large in Italy – in 1972, accounting for
31 per cent of gross national investment in industry and 17 per cent of
investment in 'services' (including motorways and telecommunications).

It was clear by the 1970s that a massive transformation of the South
was well under way. The proportion of the labour force in agriculture
declined from 57 per cent in 1951 to 31 per cent in 1971 (27 per cent
by 1974) – a decline of over 2 million workers in twenty-four years.[5]
Employment in 'modern' industry (such as metallurgy, engineering,
chemicals, petrochemicals, textiles) increased by 150,000 between 1961
and 1973 (Graziani, 1976). There was a related switch in the composition of industrial employment: a large fall in self-employment and an
increase in dependent employment (the beginnings of a full-time
industrial proletariate). Illiteracy declined from 24 per cent of the
population over 5 years in 1951 to 11 per cent in 1971 (Sylos Labini,
1976; ISTAT 1976, Vol. X).

Income per head grew by two and a half times between 1951 and
1971 (in real terms). Outside limited parts of Naples one sees little
sign of acute poverty nowadays. Anthropologists report that the

quality of *miseria*, of desperation and resigned fatalism which pervaded southern life is nowadays much attentuated – and to the extent it still exists, is found more in the cities than in towns and villages.[6]

Yet a marked 'dualism' persists between North and South.[7] Despite massive emigration (over 4 million people have left the South since the early 1950s), and despite large absolute increases in income, income per head remains at little more than *half* that in the North,[8] as in 1951. Over half of Italy's agricultural employment is in the South, over 40 per cent of construction employment, and less than 20 per cent of industrial employment in manufacturing and extraction (1975). Manufacturing industry in the South accounts for only 15 per cent of value added in manufacturing in Italy as a whole; compared to 45 per cent for agriculture. The average size of a manufacturing unit in the South was still only just over five persons in 1971; compared to 10 in the North (Benetti *et al.*, 1975).

Unemployment remains high: in 1976 the registered unemployed accounted for 12 per cent of the South's work force (4 per cent of the North's), and 60 per cent of Italy's total registered unemployed.[9] In absolute terms, total employment in South Italy has *declined* by half a million between 1951 and 1975, at the same time as the resident population has *increased* by almost one and a half million.[10]

For those still imbued with the optimistic assumptions of the development theories of the 1950s and 1960s it must be puzzling and disquieting that the results have not been better, given the length of time a development programme has been in operation, the resources devoted to it, and the brilliance of the economists involved in its formulation.

The question of why dualism remains so sharp and what, if anything, can and should be done to reduce it, has almost as many answers as there are southern development experts. There is an important distinction to be made, however, between answers which stress 'internal' reasons for the South's relative backwardness, and those which stress 'external' reasons to do with the relationship between the southern economy and that of the North. Those that stress 'internal' reasons tend to go with an assumption of an underlying harmony of interests between South and North (or more generally, between underdeveloped areas and already industrialised economies); and thus tend to support a prescription of still closer integration of the economy of the South with the North, along similar lines to the past form of integration. Those that stress 'external' reasons tend to go with an assumption of an underlying conflict of interests, and thus tend to support a prescription of a somewhat more autarchic pattern of development, less tightly integrated in the present form with the economy of the North.

Any assessment of the South Italian case which does not start with an *a priori* commitment to either of the two underlying assumptions must conclude, I think, that the evidence about the effects on the South of the South's integration with the North is distinctly mixed. However, the bulk of the development literature on the South, and most of the official Italian literature, does stress the 'internal' reasons, showing South and North as more or less distinct economies, with no important causal connection between the North's progress and the South's underdevelopment – the South, indeed, is commonly seen as the 'stone in the boot', a hindrance to national advance, a drain of modern resources and technology from the North. Hence, the growth of the North is seen as a condition of the development of the South, in order to provide the South with sufficient resources to overcome its various 'internal' disadvantages and to reduce its population by migration (Lutz, 1962; Schachter, 1965; Ministero del Bilancio, 1972; OECD, 1976).

Against this background of development orthodoxy, I shall argue that the *type* of integration between North and South has contributed to the progress of the North (though with important qualifications), and at the same time has resulted in less development in the South than one might reasonably have expected, given the sheer *amount* of the resources involved. I shall therefore concentrate on describing the major features of the relationship between North and South since the Second World War, and their effects on the South during this period.[11] I am not concerned here with the origins of the South's under-development.

Linkages and Their Effects

TRADE

For centuries the South has exported agricultural products (cereals, sheep and cattle products, wine, olive oil), and imported manufactures and services. There has been relatively little trade *within* the South. Today the South is a net exporter of agricultural products and the products of heavy industry (petrochemicals and metals). It is a net importer of almost all other types of product and services. Agricultural products accounted for 34 per cent of total regional exports of goods in 1969, petrochemicals and metals for another 35 per cent. Agricultural exports amounted to 43 per cent of agriculture production in the same year; but imports of agricultural products – frequently the South's exports in more highly processed form – were also large, at 30 per cent of agricultural production (Cafiero, 1976).

Trade between North and South has thus involved an exchange of high value-added products from the North for low value-added products from the South (leaving aside the still small – in terms of employment – 'modern' sector). Southern workers need to work many more hours to obtain the product produced by a northern worker in one hour than northern workers need to work to obtain the product of a southern worker in one hour. In this sense the South may be defined as a 'periphery' of the European economy: as a region having a relatively high concentration of 'peripheral' activities, that is, activities with relatively low labour productivity. Relatively low living levels are the consequence. The South's *growing* specialisation in agriculture (in the specific sense that a rising proportion of national employment and value-added in agriculture comes from the South) tends to reinforce the existing differences.

Transport difficulties prior to the early 1960s helped protect a small-scale manufacturing sector producing for local markets within the South. Since then, the opening up of the South by means of vastly improved road, rail and air networks has had the effect of making the South an open economy. Effectively South Italy has had to industrialise without being able to use tariff barriers, something that North Italy never had to do. Northern manufacturers in search of economies of scale found the cost of exporting to the South had fallen, at the same time as the southern market for consumer goods was beginning to grow. A commercial invasion from the North became worthwhile. And, partly through the media links, southern tastes were changing during the 1950s and 1960s towards northern, mass produced goods. A study of a sample of consumer goods retailers in the region of Campania (excluding Naples, the capital) showed that in 1975 over half their sales of clothing and household furnishings came from outside the South, and in the case of foodstuffs, just under half. Strikingly, over half their fresh and preserved meat, their milk and cheese, and their drinks, came from beyond the South. The proportions have tended to increase over time (Mancinelli, n.d.)[12]

Three important results of this process should be noted. First, cheaper northern goods brought gains in living levels in the South, particularly for those still employed.

Second, the traditional manufacturing sectors in the South (food, clothing, leather, furniture, etc.) lost some 60,000 jobs between 1961 and 1973; while in the North during the same period employment in the same sectors *increased* by 40,000 (Graziani, 1976). Local producers were backwashed out of existence by northern competitors.

Third, the South's imports of goods and services have exceeded exports by a very large margin since the 1950s (at least). Net imports have amounted to 10 to 20 per cent of total available resources since 1951; and have increased proportionately over time. In 1974 net imports amounted to 26 per cent of regional income (Cafiero, 1976).[13] We come to the question of how such a high level of net imports was financed later.

CAPITAL FLOWS

Much evidence suggests that a massive industrialisation is underway. Industrial investment in the South increased from 15 per cent of the national total in 1951 to 44 per cent in 1973, most of it in *heavy* industry (85 per cent in 1962–8). In the 1969–73 period, for the first time, industrial investment in the South *substituted* for investment in the North; it increased while that in the North fell. This flow of investment amounted to 25 per cent of regional income in the period 1951–63, 29 per cent in 1964–74 (compared to 22 per cent and 21 per cent for the North).

Most of the investment has come from outside the South (total consumption in the South is almost equal to its regional income – 94 per cent in 1971). It is often said (I have not found evidence)[14] that a considerable proportion of southern savings are invested via the banking system in the North, from where some part is returned to the South via northern companies. Also, the outflow of profits and dividends on imported capital to the North is high; it has exceeded the volume of migrants' remittances (OECD, 1976).

The state holding companies have been the leaders of this industrial investment, in fulfilment of their locational obligations. They have increased the share of their total investment in the South from 27 per cent in 1959–62 to 56 per cent in 1972, and in 1970–3 accounted for 37 per cent of industrial investment in the South (against only 17 per cent in the North). Private sector firms were slow to move South, despite the incentives – a point of some significance for assessing the potential effect of a regional policy in an enlarged EEC. However, in the great upsurge of industrial investment in the South during 1969–73, the large private companies increased their investment by the same order of magnitude as the public corporations (Giannola, 1977).[15]

The OECD report on South Italy (1976) emphasises the beneficial effects of these massive capital inflows. The South in the post-Second World War period did not have the capacity for endogenous growth, it points out; where else would the capital and know-how needed for development have come from but the North? High rates of growth in the North were a necessary condition for the development of the South. Indeed, the capital *outflow* from the South, in the form of profits and dividends on invested capital, has *benefited* the South, because it made possible higher rates of growth of national production (concentrated in the North), which made possible a higher return flow of capital into the South.

But if one pays attention not only to the size of the capital flow but also to its composition, the OECD assessment looks much too simple. Investment in the South has created very few jobs in relation to the size of the investment. While industrial investment increased seven-fold between 1951 and 1971, industrial employment rose by only 45 per cent. Put differently, industrial investment in the South increased to 44 per cent of the national total in 1973, while employment in industry (excluding construction) fell from 20 per cent to 18 per cent of the national total between 1951 and 1973. The irony is extreme: South Italy, plagued by problems of unemployment and under-employment, has a more capital-intensive, labour-saving set of new heavy industries than the North, alongside 'subsistence' artisans and builders. The second point which the OECD argument ignores is that the new investment has been in production processes linked to local producers neither on the inputs nor the outputs side. Most of the production of the new plants is exported to the North and beyond, their managers are mostly northerners, their R. & D. and marketing work is done back at headquarters in the North.[16] Control of the 'technostructure' resides firmly in the North. Hence their description as 'cathedrals in the desert', or 'outposts of the northern economy': they have had very little stimulating effect on local producers.[17] Indeed, by attracting skilled labourers away from traditional sectors, by promoting a trade union consciousness which spread into the traditional sectors, both of which increased the cost of labour, the big plants, it could be argued, contributed to the backwash effect against local producers.

However, one important qualification needs to be made. The big plants created little employment in relation to the size of the investment, but they did account for most of what industrial employment was created. The new industrial sectors accounted for an increase of 150,000 jobs in 1961–73, while the 'traditional' manufacturing sectors lost jobs.

What of agriculture? As noted, the investment programme has given heavy emphasis to industry since the mid 1960s, on the assumption that agriculture cannot absorb newcomers onto the labour market. The changed allocation of investment helps to explain why, whereas agricultural output in the South increased at just under 6 per cent a year from 1955 to about 1967 (compared to a national average of 4 per cent), the rate subsequently declined sharply to 1 per cent between 1967 and 1975, the same as the national average. Average agricultural productivity per man in the South remains two-thirds that of the North (Cosentino et al., 1977). But there are large differences within the South between plains farms, which tend to be 'capitalistic' (more than 50 per cent of labour input is hired), and farms of the hills and mountains (80 per cent of the South's area), which tend to be family farms. All of the slow rate of growth of production since 1967 has been from the plains farms, and agricultural production from the hills and moun-

H

tains has probably *declined* in the last decade – while Italy's food import bill has equalled between 20 and 25 per cent of total imports between 1965 and 1974, and is now the second biggest item after oil (Fanfani, 1977; Gorgoni, 1977). On the other hand, while state investment policy could undoubtedly have been used to promote higher production from hill and mountain farms, it may plausibly be argued that the best use of much of this land, given its generally poor quality and a climate unfavourable to cereals, is for forestry and livestock production in large-scale units. If so, it makes good sense not to invest heavily in the present type of farming in these areas, but to enable the present, increasingly elderly inhabitants to live out their lives in a modicum of comfort and security before restructuring begins.

MIGRATION

Between 1951 and 1975 just under four and a half million people left the South, leaving an increase of just under one and a half million in the population present.[18]

Throughout the post-war period Italy has remained by far the most important exporter of manpower *within* the EEC (mainly to Germany), though in terms of total EEC immigration Italy now contributes only about 20 per cent, as France and Germany have increasingly recruited their foreign workers from beyond the EEC (King, 1976). In Italy of the 1970s both internal and external immigration have fallen off. Hence the South's population, which grew 1·6 per cent between 1961 and 1971, increased by 4·1 per cent between 1971 and 1975; while for the North, the corresponding figures are dramatically different: 13·5 per cent and 2·8 per cent. 1974 was the first year since at least as far back as the beginning of the 1950s in which there was a *net* return from abroad to the South (Svimez, 1977b). However, by 1973 Italy still had a large number of workers living in other EEC countries (about 900,000), and was the only EEC country to do so (with the exception of the Irish in Britain) (King, 1976). Most (about 80 per cent) of these workers came from the South.[19]

The available data suggests that remittances from abroad to South Italy are a small part of the South's total exports or regional income, in aggregate just over one per cent of regional income in 1974.[20]

However, it has been reported that settlements in Calabria and the interior of Sicily may receive up to half their income through remittances from abroad and from the North (King, 1975).[21]

The OECD report on South Italy emphasises the beneficial effects of the migrations from the South. 'The migrations from the South,' says the OECD, 'while presenting social problems, can also be regarded as a contribution to national economic development, in that labour moved from regions of lower to regions of higher economic potential.

Without such movement it is debatable whether the national economy could have expanded as much as it did, or that the North could have provided the surplus of resources needed for investment in the South' (1976, p. 38). In other words, the migrations benefited the North, along the lines of the Lewis 'surplus labour' model (1954); but also benefited the South, by allowing a greater flow of investment and welfare funds into the South. Indeed, the benefits for southerners go further than the OECD argument suggests: southern migrants got higher incomes in the North; they eased the pressure of employment and welfare in the South; and sent back remittances which were especially important to the income of the relatively poor.

But one should also take account of the effect of higher congestion costs in the North on the competitiveness of Italy's exports, and thereby on the size of the surplus available for the South. One should also allow for the effect of the influx of migrants to the northern cities on basic facilities – though from the migrants' point of view, the conditions they lived in were probably not worse than the conditions they left behind. And as we saw earlier, one must also ask *how* the investment in the South was used, with what effects on its development.

The OECD assessment further ignores the effects of selective migration on agricultural production in the South. At least 30 per cent of Italian migrants to Europe are young males between 20 and 30 years (King, 1976). There is some evidence that the massive movement off the land has been even more selective, so that the southern agricultural labour force is increasingly made up of the weaker members of the family labour force: women, old men, children (Malfatti, 1976, Furnari, 1977). The effect, it has been suggested, is for the contrast between capitalist farming (plains) and family farming (hills and mountains) in the South to grow sharper: increasingly, family farms are becoming oriented to *self-sufficiency* and away from production for the market – goods are increasingly being purchased with migrants' remittances and welfare payments.[22] This helps to explain why what growth there has been in agricultural production in the South since 1967 has come from capitalist farms.[23]

As for the effects of remittances and returned migrants: King concludes, 'Characteristically, emigrant remittances are used to buy land, a house, a shop, or to repair and modernise property – activities which do not generate much permanent new employment' (1976). Signorelli and her co-workers found that in a large sample of South Italian migrants interviewed in 1974–5, 88 per cent said they were saving primarily to buy or improve their house; only 15 per cent said to start an independent business (*including* those who said they wanted to buy a piece of land (Signorelli *et al.*, 1975, Signorelli, n.d.)[24] Hence the main uses to which remittances tend to be put do not change the

conditions which give rise to the emigration in the first place. With capital immobilised in a house, either the migrant remains a permanent or intermittent migrant, sending back remittances, or lives on state subsidies, or both. As one would expect, then, there is little evidence of occupational mobility amongst returned migrants; they tend to go back into their pre-migration occupation (King, 1976, n. 6). They do not act as bearers of development initiatives.[25] The Italian experience thus throws some doubt on the proposition that migration, though painful for the migrants, is a transitory phase which aids the development of the sending country or region. On the other hand, it seems hardly plausible to say that things would now be better in the South if *no* migration had occurred.

TOURISM
The inflow of tourists has been less important a factor in the southern economy than along the Mediterranean coasts of France and Spain, as well as parts of northern Italy. Tourism is still little developed outside a few well-known localities along the coast. Since 1965, however, the *Cassa* has been offering generous incentives for tourist expansion (King, 1975).

INSTITUTIONAL LINKAGES
The South is not an independent state. It shares the same legal framework as the North; the same institutions of public administration and representative government; the same Catholic Church hierarchy; the same trade unions. Nor does the South have a single regional government; rather, it is divided into eight 'regions', since 1972 each with its own administration and elective government, but with very limited revenue-raising powers.

TRADE UNIONS
In the post-war period up to the late 1960s Italian trade unions were relatively weak, and tended in any case to promote the interests of their northern members, or those of the employed as against the unemployed. In the 1940s and 1950s contractual wages in the 'modern' sector were about 30 per cent lower in the South than in the North-west (Lutz, 1962). As the unions became more conscious of their power and of the need to think in wider terms than the narrow interests of their own members, particularly after the 'hot autumn' of 1969, they eliminated the contractual wages gap between North and South and at the same time pressed for more investment in the South. Since the early 1970s more investment and employment in the South has been one of the two or three major objectives of the national trade union confederations, as part of an attempt to champion the interests

of the un- and underemployed as well as those of the employed (though the adverse effects of the migrations on the quality of life for northern workers now reduces the conflict of interests between employed and unemployed). There have been difficulties in maintaining this objective in factory and industry bargaining, and the contradiction between full employment aims and the defence of those already employed is an evident source of dispute within the trade union movement. But some northern-based workers have undertaken industrial action to support more employment in the South. Between 1972 and 1976, for example, five major official strikes took place at the Fiat factory in Turin (many of whose workers are southerners) to press a reluctant management to invest in the South. It is inconceivable that Italian workers in Germany (or Turks) would go on strike to press their management to invest in their respective countries.

REDISTRIBUTION THROUGH THE FISCAL MECHANISM

Earlier I referred to the high level of net imports to the South, and raised the question of how such high levels were financed. There is a close positive correlation between the South's net imports and the volume of transfer payments paid to southerners, and a close inverse correlation for the North-west (the most industrialised part of the North around Milan, Turin and Genova) (Graziani, 1977). Transfers – in the form of production subsidies, pensions, family allowances, etc. – are a means of permitting a constantly increasing level of available resources in the South, in line with the increase in the North.

Social security payments are the major component of transfers. Such payments account for no less than 42 per cent of total public expenditure (including investment expenditure) in Italy, for the administration of which there are, it has been estimated, 41,500 agencies (excluding wholly private or ecclesiastically-controlled institutions)! (Rogers and Moss, 1977). Of the total payments, about 70 per cent is accounted for by pensions alone (mainly for old age, disablement, widowhood). The monetary value of social security payments has grown in the 1970s (1971–5) by five times the growth of GDP (SVIMEZ, 1977).

The number of pensions going to the South increased by 29 per cent between 1971 and 1975 (double the increase in the North).[26] The South receives almost *twice* as much in social security payments as it contributes. Most of the increase in pensions in the South has been of the 'disabled person' type (its share of the national total for this type increased from 36 per cent to 39 per cent between 1971 and 1975), the significance being that this type of pension is especially important in clientele politics: the criteria for its allocation are more flexible than for the other sorts of pensions, it is available to people of younger age, and a pension of disablement is an advantage for getting many jobs in the public sector (since the pension is taken as proof of disablement, and disabled persons have preferential access to certain public jobs).[27]

PUBLIC ADMINISTRATION

The flow of social security payments, industrial incentives, and other transfers into the South is administered by government bureaucrats. From this alone one would expect their power to be strong. But more precise indicators are needed.

The growth in the number of state functionaries in the South has been somewhat greater than in the rest of the country (73 per cent between 1951 and 1973, against a national average of 70 per cent). The South now has the same proportion of state functionaries as its population; but since the 'active' population in the South is lower than its share of population (reflected in lower 'activity rates')[28] the weight of public administration in total employment is substantially greater in the South than in the North. For every employee in public administration in the South (1973) there are 1·5 employees in manufacturing industry; in the North-west, there are 6·4. Furthermore, a job in public administration in the South is worth much more in relation to alternatives than in the North. The average income of state functionaries in the South is about the same as in the North. But the average income in other sectors in the South is much lower and generally more insecure. In 1973, the average income in public administration in the South was *twice* that in industry; in the North, only fractionally higher.

One effect of the very high value of a public post is that, as Ryan suggests, 'much energy and investment which could be channelled into productive enterprise is channelled instead into trying to secure a state post' (1977, p. 76). The consequence is a 'psychological backwash' on attitudes to industry, as strong as the effect of big plant and large northern retailers on their sectors.

The power of the public administration is constantly growing, because uncontested from other sectors. With the decline of traditional industries, the abandonment of an unproductive agriculture, the increasingly limited prospects for emigration, livelihoods in the South are coming to depend increasingly on access to the state Treasury and employment in big plants. This access is controlled (or strongly influenced) by state functionaries. They have a triple control: on the capital market, because subsidies, special credit, all sorts of authorisations go through their hands; on the labour market, because they can influence the choice of who will be employed in the big plants and the public service; and on the distribution of social security payments. Because of the importance of personal relations in southern bureaucracy – resources are relatively free-floating and can be obtained if only the right personal connections are made (Schneider *et al.*, 1972) – an important functionary in one sector (e.g., pensions) is able, to a greater degree than is common in the North, to use his position to secure the personal contacts needed to exert influence in other sectors (e.g., employment in big plants). In this way people in public administration can influence all sectors of southern Italian life, and take a hand in an enormous range of economic initiatives. How then do state functionaries use their power? We must consider the implications of the fact that the South is part of the same political unit as the North.

REPRESENTATIVE GOVERNMENT

The fact that the South is part of the same state as the North in some ways reduces its bargaining power (by removing the tariff instrument, for example). In another way however, its power is greatly enhanced: because the central government has to be supported by southern votes, or risk electoral defeat. (In the 1950s and 1960s the vote for the Christian Democrat and right-wing parties coming from the South accounted for not much less than half their total vote in national elections.) This brings the 'ruling' classes of the North – if ruling is the right word – to enter alliances with those classes of southern Italy which can guarantee election results. The latter *might* use their bargaining power to promote the transformation of the South in line with the needs, in some sense, of southerners, because they see this as a necessary condition for retaining political power.

The reality is different. In the past, the class which could guarantee elections and social order were the landlords, in control of the vital income-earning asset. Now (since the Second World War) the best allies for the dominant classes of the North are the new class of bureaucrats who administer public expendiure, controlling the new vital income-producing asset, access to the state Treasury.[29] They use their control over personal subsidies, the capital and labour markets to secure votes. What La Palombara writes about the *Cassa* illustrates the general tendency: 'Under the Cassa per il Mezzogiorno land is awarded, loans made, credit secured, fertiliser distributed, all on the basis of strict loyalty to the Christian Democrats' (1971, p. 525).

The typical political formation of the South contains a high-level leader of a party faction in Rome, able to influence the spending of one or more government departments, backed up by followers at the regional or provincial level able to guarantee the high-level leader (or leaders) a safe constituency; the followers may be members of the regional or provincial party federation, state bureaucrats who owe their jobs to the faction leader, or members of predatory organisations like the Mafia. The political process in the South is a constant struggle between factions for control of key areas and resources. Party organisation is weak, and voting patterns are unstable compared to the North (Galli and Pradi, 1970), as first one, then another faction comes to prominence in a given area. The extreme consequence of this situation is that development projects and policies which escape the control of leading factions are liable to be sabotaged by them: better no development at all than development which escapes their control. This form of political organisation thus generates pressures in the South for expansion of state posts, expansion of subsidies, investment in big plant and discretionary protection to (often inefficient) small firms of the 'traditional' sector (including family farms of the hills and mountains): all of these are readily tradeable for political support.[30]

The Politics of Fast Growth and Slow Development

We have seen that the South's 'development' pattern has been characterised by: (1) A very high rate of investment over the past 25 years, resulting in the creation of a heavy industry sector which includes a large part of Italy's total heavy industry, (2) a decline in the absolute as well as relative number of jobs, (3) a very high rate of emigration over the whole period (to mid 1970s), (4) a very large deficit on the balance of trade, tending to increase over time, (5) a level of average personal income and consumption which has remained much lower than the North's, but has increased at the same rate – during a period when the North-west had one of the fastest rates of growth of income and consumption in Europe; hence a fast rate of increase in the absolute level of *per capita* income and consumption: fast 'growth'.

The argument I have been elaborating sees state policy in the South as the outcome of an attempt to recruit political support for the ruling parties. The failure of employment to increase in the South, which was only partly offset by heavy emigration (and could not be offset, it was thought, by an attempt to go back to the early post-war solution – investment in agriculture and land reform), created a potentially dangerous threat to the social order. The government strategy consisted of locational controls on the state holding companies, an expansion of the government bureaucracy, a concentration of resources in the hands of state functionaries, and an expansion of aids to industry, grants to agriculturalists and personal subsidies of various kinds. In this way the government could be seen to be doing something on an impressive scale for the South, and resources could be channelled to supporters of the ruling parties and various factions within them. One effect of the transfer payments was to keep income and consumption increasing in line with the rest of the country. But since the South did not, and still does not, have the conditions for flexible supply and ensuing multiplier effects in response to increased demand, much of the increase in incomes was spent on northern-made goods and services; which has destroyed more pre-existing productive capacity in the South. Hence the large balance of trade deficit with the North continues to grow. And hence the need for subsidies continues, despite (indeed, in some respects because of) the huge inflow of investment.

The transfers come via the state apparatus. The power of state functionaries thus continues to grow, as more of the population become dependent in one way or another on transfers. Hence the governing parties are able to continue to get electoral majorities, and hence remain in office. One indication of the success of this mechanism is that the fall of an entrenched 'baron' is very rare; the survivability of leading southern politicians is perhaps greater than in any other European country.

Transfer payments from North to South are thus crucial to the pattern of South Italy's 'development': they are the instrument by which two major objectives can be achieved together: electoral majorities from the South for the ruling parties (and containable discontent); and the growth of some parts of northern industry.

At the same time the transfer instrument has been supplemented by state intervention to ensure the survival of a generally inefficient traditional manufacturing sector, by a flood of laws to give preferential access to credit, reduced liability for social security contributions – able to be implemented in a discretionary manner in return for political support. Little attention has been given to the improvement of commercial and industrial skills, however, which might have been emphasised if there had been more concern for development and less concern for short-term clientelistic gains.

This argument thus answers the question of why the massive amount of (public) investment in the South has done little to promote a vigorous industrialisation, able to increase the demand for labour, in terms of what might be called the 'needs of legitimacy', the need of the ruling parties to get electoral support. However, a rather different argument in terms of the 'needs of capital accumulation', also has some plausibility. In this view the southern development programme and its observed effects have been, in Garofoli's words, 'functional to the process of Italy's capitalist development in its entirety' (1976; my emphasis). The failure to provide employment in the South perpetuated a reserve army of labour for the North; the flow of personal transfers expanded the size of the market for northern producers, helping to maintain the rate of growth of national income; and the concentration on heavy industry in the South came about because

Italian industrialists producing goods for export wanted an enlarged modern heavy industry sector to provide them with cheap basic inputs, and such enlargement was cheaper in the South because of lower land prices, easy access to sea transport, less opposition to industrial pollution, an unsaturated infra-structure (especially housing for workers). And the products of heavy industry were complementary to, not competitive with, the products of northern industry. The incentive policy was a way of subsidising the costs of these big plants, to the benefit of northern buyers of their products. So the explicit objectives of the southern development programme were not the 'real' objectives; and while the programme may have failed against its explicit objectives, it has succeeded in relation to its 'real' objectives.

One sort of evidence which could be used in an assessment of both explanations is the efficiency of the new industry located in the South. The argument based on 'needs of capital' would predict that this industry functions as (or more) efficiently in the South than it would anywhere else in the country – it was put there because northern industrialists thought a southern location optimal in terms of national capital accumulation. The other argument would predict that this industry is highly inefficient, because so vulnerable to manipulation at the hands of rival political factions. Where firms compete mainly to get access to state subsidies and purchasing contracts the results are likely to be different from and more inefficient than market competition – for example plant which is too small and dispersed, in order to get funds to all the various factions in a coalition, agglomerates which are too big, in order to prevent state funds from flowing to rivals. I am not aware of studies which bear directly on this question, except for one still in progress whose preliminary conclusions give support to the conclusion that the new industrial sector in the South is on the whole very inefficient, more inefficient than it would have been if located in the North (Chapman, 1977). If so, this is a case where the effects of state intervention are against the interests of (productive) capital, where the 'needs of capital accumulation' are sacrificed as a by-product of the struggle for political support. On the other hand, the strong increase in private investment in the South after 1969 seems, on the surface, to fit better the 'needs of capital' argument. And if Palloix, amongst others, is right in claiming that there is a tendency for heavy industrial plant to move to the coast of the Mediterranean (1975, pp. 105–6), the flow of capital into South Italy may be seen as part of this more general move; and that would also seem more consistent with the 'needs of capital' than with the 'needs of legitimacy'. And one would need to distinguish different 'fractions' of northern capital, especially those mainly interested in a supply of cheap products from southern heavy industry and those mainly interested in the southern market for their products. And one would have to distinguish between the interests of *private* industrialists and those of the state holding companies, which were mainly responsible, it should be remembered, for the concentration of heavy industry in the South. It might plausibly be argued that the state holding companies chose to concentrate on heavy industry in the South, because (a) such industry needed restructuring, (b) would be more easily expanded in the South than in the North, and (c) would be less enmeshed in the local, non-industrialised society (the 'needs of capital' argument); but that the implementation of the investment programme was heavily conditioned by political manipulation, to which the state holding companies were more vulnerable than the large northern private companies (the 'needs of legitimacy' argument).

As this last point suggests, the two explanations should not be seen as necessarily mutually exclusive: the tendencies highlighted by both may both be operating, and the observed outcome the result of a complex interplay, with the tendencies of the 'needs of capital' argument being refracted through enormously powerful political structures of the kind I have described (more like a double helix than a simple dialectic). The political structures limit the extent to which the tendencies derived from the 'needs of capital' are realised on the ground. And these tendencies set some limits on the extent to which the state can operate against capital accumulation on a national scale in the pursuit of clientelistic political support in the South. In a competitive world, the crisis in national capital accumulation, to which inefficient 'modern' plant in the South is probably a substantial contributor, is expressed in the country's chronic balance of payments' deficit; which in turn prompts other adjustments, such as the deflationary measures wanted by the country's creditors. These in turn prompt reactions from those who feel deprived or threatened, one of which may be a switch in political allegiance, producing a change in the basis of legitimacy, a change in the balance of class forces. It is therefore too simple to see the Italian state as the instrument of capitalist class interests, unable to intervene against the interests of that class; and also too simple to see it as so autonomous from dominant classes that it can sustain intervention to secure political support regardless of the effects on accumulation.

Which powerful groups or categories might react against the South's pattern of development? Not present holders of governmental office, or state functionaries, whose interests are overwhelmingly in ensuring that the need for state subsidies and authorisations of one sort or another continues. It is not just southern politicians and state functionaries *in the South* who have these interests. Southerners, oriented as they are to jobs in public administration and politics, have

come to acquire a grossly disproportionate hand in the public administration and politics of the country at large (Allum, 1973): as
holders of high office in the political parties, the parliament, the trade
unions, the state holding companies, the police. The 'southernisation'
of the state, it has been called. They are able to use their position to
influence decisions about *national* policy so as to protect the people
and the clientele structures on which they depend. At a time when
their rule is under sustained attack, the Christian Democrat party and
its allies are unlikely to abandon the support they get through these
various clientelistic means – even if the peculiar pattern of 'development' we have seen is the by-product.

The state holding companies, which have led the industrialisation in
the South, are more open to political manipulation from Rome than
are the large private companies, particularly on the question of the
location of investment and who gets jobs. Their openness to political
manipulation makes them weak agents of reform. Many private
northern industrialists are unwilling to invest in the South, declaring
that it would be an 'impossible job' – because administration is corrupt
and inefficient, because they cannot recruit the workers *they* wish to
employ. Yet these 'impossible conditions' have been powerfully
strengthened by the political strategy of the Italian governing parties
(within which northern industrialists have considerable influence), as
part of which, as we have seen, there has been an expansion in the
size and power of a stratum of political bureaucrats in the South
whose actions prevent the erosion of these 'impossible conditions'.
Those northerners who do go south to manage the big plants tend to
see their sojourn as just one spiral in their career, and remain un-
involved in local life. They leave local matters to the local elite; 'local'
matters include who gets jobs in their plants. They do not press for
reforms.

Southern businessmen in the South are closely tied to state controls
and state funds. The typical southern 'industrialist' is a man of acute
political, rather than commercial skills, with one or more powerful
patrons able to swing contracts, credits, authorisations his way – in
return for employing people nominated by these patrons. In this
way huge patron-client chains reach right down to the bottom of the
'private' sector labour market, as well as the public sector. Pressures
for reform from southern businessmen are lacking.

Large-scale migration has tended to weaken labour militancy in the
South, by providing an individualistic alternative to concerted action
for reform (MacDonald and MacDonald, 1964). Returned migrants
are also not a force for change, for the reasons discussed earlier.

Trade unions and other forms of 'secondary' associations able to
aggregate the interests of large numbers of people on a non-clientelistic

basis operate with difficulty in this environment. State transfers are a powerful means of 'individuating' the population, keeping people within patronage networks.

The Communist party has been infused by patronage, reducing its effectiveness as a party of reform (Tarrow, 1967). The electoral strength of the Communist party is in any case weaker in poorer parts of Italy, stronger in more developed parts; while the Christian Democrat party, the party of government, is stronger in the poorer parts (McHale and McLaughlin, 1974). (Such evidence, one would expect, would support Christian Democrat politicians in their reluctance to make a serious commitment to the development of the South).

Southern 'nationalism' barely exists, because those in political and administrative control are southerners. Indeed, as noted, southerners have a disproportionately large hand in the public administration and political organisation of the country at large.

Epilogue

It is commonly said, especially on the left, that the southern development programme has failed, and I have given much evidence that would justify such a conclusion: employment has declined absolutely; apart from the insertion of big plants there has been little change in the size and structure of the industrial sector; income per head remains half that of the North despite massive migration. But on the other hand, the fact that income and consumption levels have risen at the same rate as the North can also be taken as partial success, for the North had one of the highest rates of growth in Europe during the 1950–70 period. And I suspect that the improvement in mass living standards in the South has been more rapid than in the rest of the southern European periphery. It is true that these increases in living standards came about because of transfers from the North, not because of an expansion of productive employment in the South, and are in that sense 'dependent' increases. But three points need to be made: (a) It would be misleading to think of the South's growth as simply 'by invitation' of the North, or to think, more broadly, of the South as dependent on and exploited by the North. For the South, or rather, certain strata or classes in the South, does have a strong political muscle in the country at large, thanks to the need of the ruling parties for southern votes. The 'developmental' results observed in the South have, to put it no stronger, not been unwanted by the dominant power holders in the South; it is *not* the case that their interests have been set aside by a dominating, exploiting North (or by a class of dominating, exploiting northern industrialists). (b) Before 1950 the

South was poor and in large part self-sufficient. Now the development mechanism has transformed it into a place which is much less poor and much more dependent on the North. Whether one says that southerners are on the whole better or worse off depends on how much normative weight one gives to consumption on the one hand and 'autonomy' on the other. Some critics go so far as to say that the development programme has failed because the South is now more dependent. I would wish to give more weight to the improvement in consumption, as a goal in itself, whether 'dependent' or 'independent'. However, the point is not only one of the values, but also of whether the North will be able to continue underwriting Southern living standards if the European economy expands more slowly or not at all over the next few decades. If not, then the consequences for consumption standards of having become so dependent on northern transfers will be severe. (c) Can we seriously expect an autonomous self-generating industrialisation in South Italy, under virtually any assumptions about the political order – given its severe physical disadvantages compared to the North (King, 1975) and its distance from the markets of north-west Europe, and given also the deep historical roots of 'dualism' with the North (Procacci, 1968)? Such an expectation lies behind many criticisms of southern development. And even if we can indeed look forward to 'even development' over the whole Italian territory, can we seriously expect 'even development' throughout the whole of the European periphery, again under virtually any assumptions about the political order? I doubt it, for reasons I shall not go into here. If so, then the policy of underwriting living standards by means of state subsidies may have more to recommend it than seems at first sight.

Of course the South Italian case is particular in that the region's political integration with the highly industrialised North enabled a much larger inflow of resources than could have been expected by an independent state.

But the problem to which the transfers are a response is likely to become acute throughout much of the European periphery over the next 20 years: a growing number of educated job-seekers, with 'western' values about work and status, in a situation where because of slower expansion of the European economy and labour-displacing technological change the number of jobs is not increasing proportionately – an imbalance likely to be even more severe in the periphery than in the core. The problem is how in this situation to ensure distribution of income. Everywhere the attempt is likely to be made to expand the state and parastatal bureaucracy, partly to provide jobs for unemployed graduates and thereby reduce their potential for leading mass unrest; and to provide income by means of state transfers. The important question is how the jobs and the transfers are allocated, to whom, by whom, with what criteria. Everywhere they are likely to come dripping with politics. The consequences will be various, but will everywhere include a tendency towards 'individuation' of the population, which will make more difficult concerted action for reform or large-scale political change. The *Mezzogiorno* may in this respect be the image of the future for other parts of the European periphery.

Notes

1. Anyone wishing to understand the development experience of South Italy enters a field in which there is already a large and rapidly growing body of literature to draw on, and to which a large number of scholars, many of them immensely talented, have devoted many years of their lives. A certain modesty is therefore called for about one's own contribution: almost certainly it has been contributed before. This warning is particularly pertinent in the present case, for my own experience of southern problems is limited to two short visits in 1976 and 1977, and to a reading of a number of recent books and papers. In the preparation of this paper I am indebted to many Italian *meridionalisti* who helped me through the complexities of Italian statistics and directed my attention to relevant literature. In particular, to: Dott. Cafiero, Dott'ssa Graziani, Dott'ssa Malfatti, of SVIMEZ; and Dott. Graziani, Fanfani, Gorgoni, Giannola, Pugliese, of the *Centro di Specializzazione e Ricerche Economico-Agrarie per il Mezzogiorno*, Portici, Naples. Discussions with Dott. Graziani were particularly helpful. I am also indebted for critical comment to Anna Ciliberti, Graham Chapman, Mick Dunford, Paul Isenman and Caroline White.

2. Much of the statistical data in the paper comes from Cafiero (1976), Graziani's excellent book (1977), various SVIMEZ and ISTAT publications (see references). When a figure comes from one of these sources I have generally left its source unstated in the interests of brevity.

3. For overviews in English see Wade, 1977, Podbielski, 1974.

4. Holland, 1971. But see Del Monte, 1977, who calculates by a complex method that the effective incentives on offer for the South, Northern Ireland and Scotland after 1967 were greatest in Northern Ireland, least in Scotland with the South in between.

5. Falling from 3,679,000 to 1,606,400, 1951 and 1975. SVIMEZ figures.

6. For an account of the features and causes of the psychological orientation described as *miseria*, see Lopreato, 1967, Banfield, 1958, Silone, 1938. The statement of changes is based on Lopreato, on my own impressions of Banfield's town, on personal communications from Leonard Moss, an anthropologist with experience of the South over many years, and from Dott. Cafiero, of SVIMEZ.

7. There are also important variations within both South and North, which in the interests of simplicity I make only occasional reference to. South Italy is normally defined to include the area south of a line across the peninsula beginning a short way below Rome and running north-eastwards to the other coast. 'North' is used in this paper to refer to the area above this line; I do not use the distinction between North and Central Italy.

8. 47 per cent that of the North-west, 60 per cent that of the North-east. (OECD, 1976, p. 36.)

9   SVIMEZ, 1977a, based on Ministero del Lavoro, 1977. Results from a
    sample survey of persons who declared themselves to be seeking work,
    whether registered or unemployed or not, show a somewhat lower con-
    centration of the national total in the South. Giannola, 1976, Tab. 14.
10 Illiteracy also remains higher: 11 per cent in 1971, compared to 2·5 per
    cent in the North.
11 For a discussion which pays more attention to the weaknesses of the
    policies adopted, see Wade, 1977.
12 At the new University of Calabria the catering is on contract to a northern
    firm, and most of the processed food it serves comes from its suppliers in
    the North (Ryan, 1977).
13 Regional income as distinct from total available resources. Graziani, 1977,
    p. 8, gives the regional balance of payments deficit as a percentage of
    regional income as 19 per cent in 1951 and 36 per cent in 1973.
14 The only study I have seen on the question of the flow of savings back to
    the North dates from 1959. See Occhiuto and Sarcinelli, n.d.
15 The distinction between private sector investment and state holding com-
    pany investment is becoming more difficult to draw, because of joint
    ventures. Little good evidence is available on the significance of non-
    Italian companies in the South. One study (Benetti et al. 1975) suggests a
    growth from 60 foreign firms in 1958 to 360 in 1972, over half of the latter
    figure American. Foreign firms accounted for 19 per cent of manufacturing
    employment in the South in 1972.
16 Aggregate figures are not readily available. But see King, 1977, Ryan, 1977.
17 But see Saraceno, 1974 for a sceptical, but not very convincing view of the
    'cathedrals in the desert' thesis.
18 The scale of the post-war migration exceeds that of the late nineteenth and
    early twentieth centuries; between 1885 and 1915 over 3½ million people
    left the South, mainly for the Americas (King, 1976).
19 Migration statistics, like unemployment statistics, are notoriously un-
    reliable, however.
20 Calculated by assuming that 80 per cent of Italy's remittances go to the
    South (80 per cent of the migrants are from the South). Sources: *Relazione
    Generale* 1976, 1977, Part II, Tab. 179, p. 284; SVIMEZ, 1977b, p. 113.
21 I do not have data on remittances from North Italy to the South.
22 M. Gorgoni, of the *Centro* at Portici, is presently undertaking a detailed
    statistical analysis on this question.
23 There is also the long-term effect of the abandonment of land in many
    parts of the hills and mountains on soil erosion. Erosion by unchecked
    rainwater flows appears to outweigh the reduction in erosion brought
    about by a fall in ploughed area.
24 The sample contained 600 migrants returned permanently or temporarily
    from other EEC countries; 427 said they were saving, and this is the
    figure on which the percentages in the text are based.
25 Part of the reason might have to do with the way migrants cope with the
    stresses of life in the host country. Signorelli (1975) suggests that the
    migration experience strongly reinforces the cognitive distinction between
    the private sphere and the public sphere, and that between the sphere of
    the homeland and the sphere of life abroad: happenings which occur in one
    sphere are kept uninvolved in those of another. In this way the migrant
    stands up to the stress of precarious work and social isolation abroad, by
    relying on the satisfaction to be derived from the 'private' – or at any rate
    strictly local – sphere in the homeland: above all, from a modernised house.

26 SVIMEZ, 1977, p. 453, Tab. 4. These figures, however, refer only to pensions from INPS, by far the biggest parastatal social security agency. In 1975 the South still received slightly less of the total number of pensions than its share of population – 31 per cent of pensions, against 34 per cent of the population.
27 Aids to industry and agriculture should also be considered in this section, but I have no data on their size.
28 The South's 'activity rate' (number of people employed or actively seeking work per 100 residents) is 30·1, the North-west's, 38·5. Barbagallo, 1973.
29 In fact the position of the southern landlords had begun to be eroded during Fascism, and the position of the bureaucracy strengthened.
30 Considering how important the southern political process is for understanding the South's development experience, it has been remarkably little studied in terms of the factors suggested here. A useful case study is Sylos Labini, 1976a; also White, 1977.

References

Allum, P. (1973), *Italy – Republic Without Government*, Weidenfeld & Nicholson, London.
Banfield, E. (1958), *The Moral Basis of a Backward Society*, The Free Press, New York.
Barbagallo, F. (1973), *Lavoro ed Esodo nel Sud, 1861–1971*, Guida.
Benetti, M., M. Ferrara, C. Medori (1975), *Il Capitale Straniero nel Mezzogiorno*, Coines Edizioni, Roma.
Cafiero, S. (1976) *Svillupo Industriale e Questione Urbana nel Mezzogiorno*, SVIMEZ, Giuffre.
Chapman, G. (1977), 'The political aspects of development in Southern Italy', unpublished manuscript, University of Sussex.
Cosentino, V. *et al.*, n.d. (1977), 'Su alcuni aspetti dello svillupo dell'agricoltura meridionale del secondo dopoguerra ad oggi', Manuscript, to be published in forthcoming book edited by A. Graziani.
Del Monte, A. (1977), *Politica Regionale e Sviluppo Economico: Un' analisi teorica ed econometrica degli effetti della politica degli incentivi nel Mezzogiorno, nell'Irlanda del Nord e in Scozia*. Franco Angeli, Milano.
De Marco, C., and M. Talamo (1976), *Lavoro Nero: Decentramento Produttivo e Lavoro a Domicilio*, G. Mazzotta, Milano.
Dunford, M. (1977), 'Regional policy and the restructuring of capital', Working Paper No. 4, Urban and Regional Studies, Sussex University.
Fanfani, R. (1977), 'Crisi e ristrutturazione dell'agricoltura italiana', Inchiesta, Marzo-Aprile, pp. 6–25.
Franklin, S. H. (1969), *The European Peasantry: The Final Phase*, Methuen, London.
Furnari, M. (1977), 'Articolazione sociale e territoriale dell' occupazione agricola in Italia', Rivista di Economia Agraria, no. 3.
Galli, G. and A. Prandi (1970), *Patterns of Political Participation in Italy*, Yale University Press.
Garofoli, G. (1976), 'Un'analisi critica della politica di riequilibrio regionale in Italia: il caso del Mezzogiorno', In F. Indovina (ed.), *Mezzogiorno e Crisi*, Franco Angeli, Milano.
Giannola, A. (1976), 'I dati dello sviluppo economico nel decennio 1967–1974', *Economia Pubblica*, 6, no. 2/3, Feb.-March.

Giannola, A. (1977), 'Imprese a participazione statale e industrializzazione nel Mezzogiorno', in Graziani *et al*.

Gorgoni, M. n.d. (1977), 'Sviluppo del commercio internazionale dei prodotti agricoli e sviluppo dell'agricoltura: per uno studio dell'esperienza italiana dal secondo dopoguerra ad oggi', Manuscript, forthcoming in *Rivista di Economia Agraria*.

Graziani, A. (1976), 'Perche nel sud diminiuisce l'occupazione', Paese Sera, 16 March.

Graziani, A., *et al*. (1977), *Investimenti Autonomi ed Investimenti Indotti nell'- Economia del Mezzogiorno*. Centro di Specializzazione e Ricerche Economico-agraria per il Mezzogiorno, Portici, Manuscript, forthcoming as book.

Holland, S. (1971), 'Regional under-development in a developed economy: the Italian case', *Regional Studies*, 5.

Italy, ISTAT (1975), *Annuario di Contabilita Nazionale*, 1974, Vol. II, Roma.

Italy, ISTAT (1976) 11° Censimento Generale delle Populazione, 24 Ott. (1971) Vol. X, Roma.

Italy, ISTAT (1977), *Annuario di Statistiche del Lavoro*, Roma.

Italy, Ministero del Bilancio (1972), *Programme Economico Nazionale, 1971–1975*.

Italy, Ministero del Lavoro (1977), *Statistiche del Lavoro*, Roma.

Italy, *Relazione Generale sulla Situazione Economica del Paese* (1976, 1977), Roma.

King, R. (1975), 'Italy', in *Regional Development in Western Europe* (ed.), H. Clout, Wiley.

King, R. (1976), 'Long range migration patterns within the EEC: an Italian case study', in R. Lee and P. Ogden (eds.) *Economy and Society in the EEC: Spatial Perspectives*, Saxon House, Farnborough.

King, R. (1977), 'Recent industrialization in Sardinia: rebirth or neocolonialism?', Erdkunde, Band 31, Lfg. 2.

LaPalombara, G. (1971), 'Parentela relations in Italian government', M. Dogan and R. Rose (eds.) *European Politics: A Reader*, Macmillan, London.

Lewis, W. (1954), 'Economic development with unlimited supplies of labour', The Manchester School, May, pp. 139–91.

Lopreato, J. (1967), *Peasants No More: Social Class and Social Change in an Underdeveloped Society*, Chandler, San Francisco.

Lutz, V. (1962), *Italy, A Study in Economic Development*, Oxford University Press.

MacDonald, J. and MacDonald, L. (1964), 'Institutional economics and rural development: two Italian types', *Human Organization*, 23, pp. 113–18.

McHale, V. and McLaughlin, J. (1974), 'Economic development and the transformation of the Italian party system', *Comparative Politics*, Vol. 7, No. 1, pp. 37–60.

Malfatti, E. (1976), *Valutazione dei Bilanci Demografici Annuali della Popolazione Presente nelle Regioni e nelle Province del Mezzogiorno (1951–1975)*, SVIMEZ, Giuffre.

Mancinelli, E., n.d. (1977), 'Produzione locale e concorrenza esterna nell'area delle grande industria', Manuscript at Centro di ... Economico-Agraria, Portici.

Occhuito, A. and M. Sarcinelli, n.d. (c 1960), 'Flussi monetari tra Nord e Sud', reference unknown, paper in hands of A. Graziani, Portici.

OECD (1976), 'Italy', in *Regional Problems and Policies in OECD Countries*, Vol. 1, Paris.

Palloix, C. (1975), *L'internationalisation du capital: Elements critiques*, F. Maspero, Paris.

Podbielski, G. (1974), *Italy: Development and Crisis in the Post-war Economy*, Clarendon Press, Oxford.

Procacci, G. (1968), *History of the Italian People*, Weidenfeld and Nicolson, London.

Rogers, E. and D. Moss (1977), 'Poverty in Italy', unpublished paper.

Ryan, D. (1977), 'Higher education and regional development: the University of Calabria in its regional context', Forthcoming in Paedagogica Europaea.

Saraceno, P. (1974), 'Il vero e il falso sugli aiuti al Sud', *Corriere della Sera*, 14.7.

Saraceno, P. (1974a), 'Le cattedrali nel deserto', *Corriere delle Sera*, 15.9.

Schachter, G. (1965), *The Italian South*, Random House, New York.

Schneider, P., J. Schneider, and E. Hansen, (1972), 'Modernization and development: the role of regional elites and non-corporate groups in the European Mediterranean', *Comparative Studies in Society and History*, 15, pp. 328–350.

Secchi, B. (1975), 'Central and peripheral regions in a process of economic development: the Italian case'. Paper presented to the NWERSA Conference on Centre-Periphery Relations between Regions, London, September.

Signorelli, A. (1975), 'Contadini ed emigrazione: il problema del rientro e l'impiego dei risparmi', Paper given to Instituto di Giornalismo Agricolo, 4 October.

Signorelli, A., *et al.* (1975), *L'Alloggio dei Lavoraori Migranti*, Istituto di Sociologia, Universita degli Studi di Urbino, Urbino. To be published by Offucina Edizioni.

Signorelli, A., n.d. (1977), 'Housing conditions of migrant workers in the European community', to be published by Centre de recherches et de documentation sur la consommation, Paris.

Silone, I. (1938) (1934), *Fontamara*, Penguin.

SVIMEZ (1977), 'Il sistema pensionistico dell'INPS nel Mezzogiorno', Informazioni SVIMEZ, XXX, No. 9.

SVIMEZ (1977a), 'Notiziario economico del Mezzogiorno', II, No. 8/9, 30 Sett.

SVIMEZ (1977b), *Rapporto sul Mezzogiorno 1976*, Fondazione Premio Napoli.

Sylos Labini, P. (1976), *Saggio Sulle Classi Sociali*, Laterza.

Sylos Labini, P. (1976a), 'La questione meridionale: un caso esemplare e quattro punti per la Calabria', *Il Ponte*, XXXII, no. 7–8, July–August.

Tarrow, S. (1967), *Peasant Communism in Southern Italy*, Yale University Press.

Wade, R. (1977), 'Policies and politics of dualism: the Italian case', *Pacific Viewpoint*, September, and IDS Discussion Paper 106.

White, C. (1977), *Patrons and Partisans*, D.Phil thesis in social anthropology, University of Sussex.

IV: THE NORTH-WESTERN PERIPHERY

12(i)

CAPITALIST COLONIALISM AND PERIPHERALISATION: THE IRISH CASE

Raymond Crotty

Modern history may be said to have begun in Ireland, as in large areas of the world, with the impact on it of capitalist colonialism in the sixteenth century. Many of the adventurers who sought their fortunes in the Americas did not overlook the possibilities closer to home in pastoral and hitherto tribal Ireland (Wallerstein, 1974). The Tudor conquest of Ireland was followed, under the early Stuarts, by a remarkable development of Anglo-Irish trade, illustrating the tremendous productive powers of capitalism (Clarke, 1976). But the rapid growth of Irish pastoral exports to Britain that made Irish land profitable threatened to disrupt the course of British economic and political evolution. The exports, by flooding Britain with low-cost pastoral products, reduced the wealth and political power of the emergent landed oligarchy. The trade simultaneously strengthened the monarch, with customs revenues that were outside Parliament's control and with a share in the profits of the trade that the monarchy could more readily exact from its more vulnerable and, therefore, more tractable subjects in Ireland (Edie, 1970). The Restoration Parliament, recognising the economic and political dangers of a competitive trade to British capitals that were still small and far from dominant, lost no time in excluding Irish pastoral produce from Britain under the Cattle Acts of 1663 and 1667. Britain, for the following century, integrated Ireland politically within the imperial system but segregated it economically from its own market.

Irish produce was highly processed, exported to distant markets and exchanged there for specie or tropical and semi-tropical products. These products, the transformed spoils of Irish conquest, were welcomed in Britain in as much as they complemented and did not compete with British products. Because low-cost labour was necessary if the three-cornered trade was to show a profit, the indigenous Irish population was suffered to survive, where the populations of other temperate zone colonies – North America, the pampas of South America, Australia, New Zealand and South Africa – were exterminated. As in other colonies where indigenous populations were suffered to survive, but which – apart from Ireland – were all tropical, an ascendancy class, supported by an occupying army, safeguarded the interests of the metropolitan capitalists. Race demarked ascendancy elsewhere; religion did so in Ireland.

The progression of early, mercantilist, cottage-industry capitalism to factory capitalism made scale of production pre-eminently important. Britain, as the leading practitioner of factory capitalism, had an insatiable need for wider markets and in their pursuit embraced competition and abandoned the protectionism of early, pre-factory capitalism. The barriers to Anglo-Irish trade that had gone up with the Restoration of Charles II in 1660 were demolished during the reign of George III, and the two economies became increasingly integrated after his death.

The sixteen decades from the Restoration of Charles II to the death of George III were a period of sustained, rapid, socio-economic development such as Ireland had not previously, and has not subsequently, experienced. Development in Ireland through this period was more rapid than in Britain, as measured by such indicators as growth of population and of foreign trade per person, and was therefore probably as rapid as in any other European country.

It would be erroneous to suggest that capitalist colonialism had, by 1820, transformed tribal Irish society of the seventeenth century into a modern society. There were grave flaws in the Irish economic structure, especially the accelerated population growth that had occured during George III's reign without a concomitant increase in the stock of capital. But, by comparison with subsequent periods, including the fifty-five years of political independence since 1922, the performance of the Irish economy during this phase of pre-factory capitalism was impressive. Capitalist colonialism, *per se*, did not preclude rapid development; on the contrary, it stimulated growth and development in several important ways.

Economic development at the core, involving the progression from cottage to factory production, gave economies of scale both in production and distribution. These scale economies made it profitable to concentrate labour and capital intensive production at the core, leaving the periphery, to a greater or less extent, dependent on land intensive production. The degree to which this process of peripheralisation occurred was exceptional in the case of England and Ireland. The facts of British/Irish core/periphery dependency are summarised in the tables 41 and 42.

A major demographic crisis in Ireland was heralded by the price collapse that occurred after the end of the Napoleonic wars and by the subsequent change in the pattern of demand for farm produce. Adjustments in marriage, birth and emigration rates, though spectacular, could not immediately halt the growth in the population, which continued until the 1840s but which thereafter declined. Virtually all of the decline in population and workforce occurred in the southern part of Ireland, now known as the Irish Republic.

Table 41

Proportion of Irish foreign trade with Britain

Year	Percentage
1700	50
1760	67
1800	81
1930	85

Sources: L. M. Cullen, *Anglo-Irish Trade: 1660–1800. Statistical Abstract of Ireland, 1939.*

Table 42

Population and Workforce, England and Ireland 1841–1971 (thousands)

	Population		Workforce	
	1841	*1971*	*1841*	*1971*
England	14·999	46·018	6·166	21·583
Southern Ireland	6·529	2·978	2·957	1·120
Northern Ireland	1·646	1·536	814	612

Sources: *Census of Great Britain 1841.*
Occupation Abstract, Census of Ireland 1841.
Census 1971, Great Britain, Economic Activities, Part I.
Census of Population, 1971, Summary Table, Northern Ireland.
Census of Population of Ireland, 1971, Vols. I and V.

The most important single consequence for Ireland of the growth of factory capitalism in Britain has been its effect on Irish cattle prices. Cattle prices in Ireland have risen fourfold relative to grain prices and, to a lesser extent, relative to all other farm product prices, between the death of George III and now (Crotty, 1966; Ireland, 1977). This made the profit from low output cattle production greater than the profit from other, higher output, farm enterprises. It made it profitable to replace people by cattle on land. High cattle prices also caused a diversion of animals from a meat trade to distant markets to a live trade to Britain. They caused cattle exports that, alive and dead, did not change between 1665 and 1805 to increase ninefold by 1875 (Crotty, 1966; BPP, 1890/91). They caused butter exports that had increased from 26,000 cwt. to 827,000 cwt. and pig and pigment exports that had increased from the equivalent of 3,000 pigs to the equivalent of 857,000 pigs between 1665 and 1835, to stagnate thereafter. They caused the grain trade, that had developed from net annual imports of 18,000 tons in the 1750s to net annual exports of 350,000 tons by 1840, to return to an annual deficit of 800,000 tons ninety years later when the population was less than half as large (Crotty, 1966; Ireland, 1936).

Meanwhile, in Denmark and the Netherlands, where climatic, topographical and locational circumstances differ critically from those in Ireland and where, though supplying the same British market, relative product prices also differed, agriculture, in response to British demand, developed through the nineteenth century, much as agriculture had developed in Ireland in the earlier period. Innumerable observers, failing to appreciate the significance of different natural, price and – ultimately – institutional conditions, have ascribed the poorer performance of Irish agriculture in the later period to Celtic myopia in failing to perceive the value variously, of: superphosphate fertilisers, recording cows' milk yields, the use of certified seeds, co-operation, or a host of other practices, popularly associated with 'good husbandry' and used by Danish and Dutch farmers under very different circumstances.[1]

The expanding Irish cattle-exporting industry, by supplanting other agricultural enterprises with a higher output/acre, caused a decline in demand from the land-intensive export sector. Simultaneously, competing imports were depressing non-export industries. The combined effect was greatly to reduce total demand, scale of operations, and hence overall efficiency in labour and capital-intensive industries in Ireland. Unit production costs in industries other than the expanding cattle industry were raised with declining scale and industries not initially threatened by imports or by the diversion of land to cattle became in time vulnerable also. More and more cottage industries were forced out of business and the non-agricultural workforce of Southern Ireland declined even more rapidly than the agricultural workforce (BPP 1824; BPP 1912–13).

Reducing wages did not stem the process. As wages dropped and famine became chronic in Ireland in the decades following George III's death, employment in labour and capital-intensive industry declined, the urban population declined, and more and more people competed with increasing cattle stocks for possession of land (BPP, 1824; BPP, 1833; BPP, 1843). Wage reductions – or, in the latterday phrase 'incomes policy' – had two serious shortcomings. First, beyond a critical level – more quickly and catastrophically reached in temperate zones than in the tropics – they caused a massive rise in the death rate, in Ireland in the 1840s, as in Western Europe in the 1340s. Second, wage reductions by depressing local demand, reduced the scale and so the efficiency of local industry.

Wage reductions, limited initially by the mass starvation of workers and subsequently by their mass emigration, could not normally make labour-intensive products from the periphery competitive with those from the core. The larger proportion of their output which periphery producers were required to export in order to achieve a scale similar to that of core producers offset any possible savings in wages. The four remarkable export successes – linen, whiskey, beer and ships – of the nineteenth-century Irish economy are attributable to special circumstances that simply underline the great structural weaknesses of a peripheral economy closely integrated into a rapidly expanding core. The English core produced no products directly competitive with Irish linen or whiskey; beer, as a result of the steep rise in the 1850s in the Irish excise on whiskey and of the escapist demand of a ruined society for alcohol, was the only commodity the consumption of which increased more rapidly in Ireland than in Britain in the second half of the nineteenth century; and Belfast shipbuilding owed its success to the identity of interests of protestant shipyard workers and employers in the face of a hostile catholic majority competing for jobs in an island, where for 150 years, half of those born have starved or emigrated. The close collaboration and ready innovation that identity of protestant interest generated were crucial in the technologically advanced iron shipbuilding industry of the second half of the nineteenth century.

Capitalist Colonialism and Peripheralisation

Peripheralisation differs from capitalist colonialism. Capitalist colonialism is possible without peripheralisation, as in Ireland from 1660 to 1820. Peripheralisation occurs in the absence of capitalist colonialism, as in Ireland since 1922. But though different, the phenomena are related. Capitalist colonialism expedited Irish peripheralisation.

Much the most important contribution of capitalist colonialism to Irish peripheralisation was the application of externally controlled force to uphold private property in pastoral land. With the qualified exception of Britain, Ireland is the only country where, in the capitalist era, the indigenous population has been suffered to survive *and* where pastoral land is extensively held individually.[2] A British army of occupation in Ireland contained the pressures that have normally precluded the individual tenure of pastoral land elsewhere. It also made possible the substitution of cattle for people when that became profitable.

Ireland's place within a capitalist colonial system facilitated peripheralisation in other ways. It facilitated the development of transport, legal, commercial and cultural links between core and periphery that reduced transaction costs. This furthered trade in labour and capital-intensive commodities from the British core and in land-intensive cattle from the Irish periphery. Both trades, as explained, reduced demand and increased unit production costs for non-exporting Irish industries so that, over time, the range of competing imports from the core widened and the range of exports from the Southern Irish periphery narrowed, ultimately virtually to livestock.

Britain's position as the heart of a capitalist colonial system facilitated growth there and hence reduction in unit cost of production. It also provided opportunities for the profitable redeployment of Irish labour and capital abroad, hence reducing the amount of these employed and the scale of economic activity in Ireland, and thereby reducing productivity of both labour and capital and raising unit production costs in Ireland. The redeployment process gave rise to one of the few 'success' stories of peripheralisation. Reflecting the lucrativeness and safety of transferring savings from the Irish periphery to the British core, Ireland's share of the 100 longest established commercial banks in the world, eight, is third only to that of the US (thirty-eight) and Britain (fifteen) (Orsingher, 1967).

If capitalist colonialism facilitated the peripheralisation of Ireland, extreme peripheralisation in turn ended the capitalist colonial relationship. It was observed above that Anglo-Irish relations from the Restoration of Charles II to the death of George III were characterised by political integration and economic segregation. These relations have subsequently been characterised by economic integration and political segregation.

The movement of labour and capital-intensive goods from the British core to the Irish periphery and of land-intensive goods and of labour and capital from the Irish periphery to the British core transformed the relative class structures of the core and the periphery. The core's growing population became increasingly proletarianised, frequently working with assets created from peripheral savings, while the periphery's declining population became increasingly embourgeoisised (with a share of its assets transferred, via the banking system to the British core and operated on there by the British proletariat). Concern by the increasingly dominant Irish bourgeoisie to protect their increasingly valuable property against the designs of the increasingly powerful British proletariat caused twenty-six Southern Irish, catholic, bourgeois, pastoral counties to secede from the United Kingdom of Britain and Ireland in 1922.

Secession expedited peripheralisation in two important ways. First, by drawing a political boundary between core and periphery, it reduced the increasing backward flows of resources from core to periphery that is everywhere a consequence of the expanding rôle of the modern state and that acts as a counter to the centripetal pull of modern economics. These transfers, if on a similar *per caput* level as core-Britain now makes to the six non-seceding Northern counties of the Irish periphery, would amount approximately to £1,000 millions annually, or about one-third of Southern Irish GNP.

This is about twice as much as is now transferred to Ireland in the form of inflated EEC dairy produce prices and of foreign borrowing. However, the efficacy of core-periphery resource transfers in stemming peripheralisation appears to be slight, judging from the experiences of Southern and Northern Ireland and of Italy's *Mezzogiorno*. The second consequence of secession referred to, which relates to the manner in which the periphery's land is used, is, therefore, deemed to be much the more important consequence of secession in accentuating peripheralisation. Peripheralisation implies a more rapid accumulation of labour and capital at the core than at the periphery. This is both a cause and a consequence of the scale economies that occur at the core, increasing the productivity of both labour and capital and saving capacity. But given fixed land, more rapid labour and capital accumulation at the core changes the relative endowments of those factors with respect to land at the core and at the periphery. A point is reached where labour and capital at the periphery become so richly endowed with land that they are no longer attracted to the core. Firms and industries heavily dependent on land cease to be put out of business by core competition. An extreme example of this is that the number of farmers has been for long stabilised in the Irish Republic so that, with a declining total workforce, it appears to be the only country in the world where farmers account for an increasing proportion of the total workforce.

The efficacy of land use is clearly important in determining the stage at which core/periphery equilibrium is reached. But market mechanisms that induce efficient labour and capital use do not so operate in the case of land.

Prospects of profit induce efficient resource use. Efficient resource use reduces, by competition, returns to inefficiently used resources. Lower returns, at the limit, wipe out the value of obsolete capital or fail to provide a subsistence for labour. But, provided labour and capital accumulation occurs within accessible distance the value of the fixed supply of land must rise; land can neither become obsolete nor starve. The prospect of loss combines with the prospect of gain to compel entrepreneurs to use labour and capital efficiently; the prospect of gain is the sole motivation for the efficient use of land.

Land-owners have traditionally been rentiers. Renting land to tenants, who, through prospect of gain and fear of loss of access, use land efficiently, owners have traditionally consumed their rental incomes. They, unlike wage or profit earners, have not normally been savers or investors. Owner-users of land can exercise preferences for non-monetary rewards, such as leisure, security and adherence to tradition.

Use of land is economically indeterminate. It depends primarily on political decisions governing the ownership of land. The more secure land tenure is, the more likely land use is to reflect the subjective proclivities of the owners and the less likely is it to reflect the objective opportunities of the market.

Three factors in particular have combined to secure the tenure of land in the Irish periphery. First, cattle-rearing, the dominant form of land-use in Ireland, provides a subsistence even for the least competent. Second, the secessionist, bourgeois Irish State has evinced an extraordinarily high regard for the rights of private propery in land; no owner-occupying farmer has been removed from his land by due process since the State's foundation fifty-five years ago. It is, in practice, impossible to distrain for debt on Irish land. Third, reduced mortality has resulted in higher life expectations, for land-owners at least as much as for others in Ireland. Irish farmers, as a consequence, are exceptionally old; a high proportion are elderly females, the widows or sisters of deceased male owners. This pattern of ownership implies that, on inheritance, which is the normal process of property transfer in Ireland, the heir is also old. Heirs to Irish land, as well as old, are also likely to be the least venturesome, the least innovative, the least gifted generally of the owner's potential heirs; careers other than that of heir-apparent with a prospect of inheriting at a late age, will have been chosen by the others.

The market also causes land to go to the least competent. The price of land is the expected future net income from it, discounted to the present at the cost of capital to the buyer. Normally the cost of capital is low for those with land and savings and who are therefore likely to be old and able to make little use of additional land. The cost of capital is high for landless young people, without savings, who can make the best use of land. Those best able to buy land are, therefore, those least likely to make good use of it; those who make best use of it, are least able to buy land.

Rapid inflation, as has obtained for decades in Ireland, accentuates this defect in the land market. Property-owners, with access to credit, buy land in anticipation of future rises in its price. The capital gains as Irish land prices rose from about £25 per acre to £2,500 per acre over the past thirty years justify earlier purchases and feed current speculative buying. Land is kept out of the reach of young people able to work it effectively but without access to credit to buy it. Land, by the laws of inheritance and the working of the market, gravitates into the possession of those least likely to use it efficiently.

The immobilisation of the periphery's land that is inherent in peripheralisation is facilitated and encouraged by the periphery's intellectual dependency on the core. Labour migration from periphery to core, as well as raising at the core and lowering at the periphery, the productivity of labour and capital, creates at the periphery a political vacuum and an intellectual desert. Ireland, drained by emigration of dissent, has generated little creative thought, but instead a decent competence in absorbing and applying locally insights and analytical methods that, like most other commodities consumed at the Irish periphery, are produced at the core. These intellectual products of the core, however relevant to core conditions, are misleading when applied to the different circumstances of the periphery.

The core, with its concentration of labour and capital, is less dependent on land. It readily exchanges labour and capital-intensive commodities for land-intensive commodities produced at the periphery. Its analysts, in so far as they note land, are concerned with the welfare of its users rather than the efficiency of its use. They emphasise secure possession of land and high prices for land-intensive commodities on essentially welfare grounds. They have created a bank of idle land in the USA, and are in process of creating a similar land-bank in the EEC. These ideas and prescriptions, developed at, and appropriate to, the core become, through intellectual dependency, part of peripheral orthodoxy. This they more easily do in that they justify the process of bourgeois enrichment and peripheral impoverishment already in train.

The response of land-owners at the periphery, selected through generations of inheritance and the market to be the least efficient users of land, is likely to be different from that of conventional entrepreneurs. High prices for land-intensive commodities are more likely to encourage old and naturally less gifted land-owners to produce the same, or fewer commodities, and to take the benefit of the improved terms of trade in great leisure, security and stability. Irish agriculture provides ample evidence in support of this hypothesis.

The price of Ireland's principal farm product, cattle, has, for 155 years, been more buoyant than that of any other major traded commodity. Reflecting the nature and actions of the Irish State, the value of land relative to GNP has increased four times since the State's foundation fifty-five years ago. This has been a more rapid increase in land values relative to national product than in any earlier period of Irish history. It has probably been more rapid than in any other country. It has resulted in a land-value/GNP ratio of at least 5:1, which is again probably higher than in any other country. Yet, the volume of Irish agricultural output has hardly changed in 125 years, while world agricultural output has increased manifold (Crotty, 1966).

The political consequences of the embourgeoisement of the periphery and its intellectual dependence on the core combine to immobilise the periphery's principal asset, its land. Inefficient use of land in turn ensures that peripheralisation is carried further than locational and resource endowment considerations alone warrant.

The End of Capitalist Colonialism and the Irish Periphery

The British Empire, that was conducive to the peripheralisation of Ireland in important ways, has been wound up within the past thirty years. The winding up of empire has had two crucially important consequences for Ireland. First, it has meant that military control of Ireland is no longer necessary to secure vital British interests; the British army, that dominated Irish events for four centuries, no longer does so. Second, emigration from the Irish periphery to the British core, where post-imperial employment opportunities are fewer, has ended and an Irish population that declined for 125 years has increased since 1966 and is now one of the most rapidly growing in Europe. Socio-political pressures that formerly escaped through the freely working safety valve of emigration no longer do so; and the British army that contained these pressures, is reduced to a vestigial presence.

Sectarian strife in Northern Ireland is a manifestation of the weakening of customary restraints on a society where for 150 years a livelihood has been available for only half its members. The defeat of the Southern Irish government in June 1977, by the largest majority in the State's existence of an electorate that, for the first time, had increased while the number at work continues to decline as it has done for a century-and-a-half, was a manifestation of the growth of pressures in that society following the closing of the safety valve of emigration. Social pressures are now building up in a manner that has not been experienced in Ireland since the 1840s; and, for the first time in four centuries, these mounting pressures will not be contained by the army of an imperial Britain. A more profound, more widely diffused understanding of the peripheralisation that gives rise to these socio-political pressures is needed if they are to be harnessed constructively, rather than allowed to accumulate to a point of explosion where the havoc created may not be confined to the periphery.

Notes

1 See, for example, (Solow, 1971) for such an interpretation.
2 South America may be another exception. The hunters of the lowlands were exterminated but the crop-growers of the *Altiplano* were suffered to survive. The resulting conflicts are perceived to be the source of the continent's chronic instability. (Crotty, forthcoming, *Cattle, Economics and Development*.)

References

British Parliamentary Papers (1822), (502) XV, *Abstracts of Answers and Returns of the Population of Great Britain in 1821.*

British Parliamentary Papers (1824), (577) XXII, *Abstracts of Answers and Returns from Taking an Account of the Population of Ireland in 1821.*

British Parliamentary Papers (1833), (23) XXXIX, *Census of the Population of Ireland, 1831.*

British Parliamentary Papers (1843), (504) XXIV, *Report of the Commissioners Appointed to Take the Census of Ireland for the Year 1841.*

British Parliamentary Papers (1864), (420) LVIII, *Return showing the official and real value of the exports from and imports into Great Britain for each year in the triennial periods ending 5th January, 1801, 1821, 1861 and 1864 . . . and similar returns for Ireland.*

British Parliamentary Papers (1890/91), (6524) XCI, *Agricultural Returns of Great Britain, 1891.*

British Parliamentary Papers (1912–13), (6663) CXVIII, *Census of Ireland, 1911, General Report.*

Clarke, A. (1976), 'The Irish Economy 1600–1660', Moody, T. W. *et al.* (eds.), *A New History of Ireland,* Oxford University Press, 3.

Crotty, R. (1966), *Irish Agricultural Production: Its Volume and Structure,* University Press, Cork.

Cullen, L. M. (1968), *Anglo-Irish Trade 1660–1800,* University Press, Manchester.

Edie, C. A. (1970), 'The Irish Cattle Bills', *Transactions of the American Philosophical Society,* 60, Pt. 2.

Ireland (1936), *Statistical Abstract 1936,* Dublin.

Ireland (1977), *Trade Statistics of Ireland, December 1976,* Dublin.

Orsingher, Roger (1967), *Banks of the World,* trans. D. S. Ault, Walker & Co., New York.

Solow, Barbara (1971), *The Land Question and the Irish Economy, 1870–1903,* Cambridge, Mass.

Wallerstein, I. (1974), *The Modern World System,* Academic Press, New York and London.

I

12(ii)

REGIONAL DEVELOPMENT AND INSTITUTIONS OF FAVOUR: ASPECTS OF THE IRISH CASE[1]

Bernard Schaffer

Introduction

Ireland can be compared with developing countries in colonial past and contemporary aspects (Kennedy, 1973). Its percentage of employment dependent on agriculture is similar to Greece, Turkey and Portugal in Europe (see tables: official Irish figures at least severely understate part-time and family involvement). As a relatively small, overwhelmingly Catholic, partly Anglophonic republic on an island, with a democratic, electoral, party-competitive and multi-member proportional representation system, it could also be compared with Malta (Bax, 1973. For a humorous version, see Cockburn, 1975). That is expressed in attitudes to Church and history, and land, kith and kin. It enjoys a highly centralised administrative system. At the same time people expect to come face to face with those apparently able to make or intervene in decisions which affect them in politics and administration.

If it is over simple to describe it as an ex-peasant society, there is a culture of subsistence agriculture, a past relation of absentee landlordism to weak patron-client relations, rather than what is called in Ireland the 'gombeen man': the mercantile broker and leader; and then an abolition of landlordism. This is in fact a quasi-peasant society with statistically limited and spatially patchy proletarianisation and successful commercial farming and a highly dispersed minifundia. It is set in a physical environment of grass and stone; a social culture of partiable inheritance and filial subservience; and an historical and political significance for the west and the Shannon. Across it lay Connaught and the mid-west of Munster. On the old bridge at Athlone was the stone with the inscription, 'Here civilisation ends and barbarism begins'. In a stratified land system and a peculiar agricultural economy, 300,000 farmers are owners. Of these, one half have less than 50 acres each and another 130,000 under 100 acres. Fewer than 20,000 have profitable larger holdings. There are a little over 12,000 cattle ranchers owning land worth more than £100 rateable value at the apex. Conacre, part-time farming and wasteful occupation are endemic. The commitment to cattle, dairying and a sort of low level agricultural potential explain the lack of profit on small holdings (see the chapter by Crotty, and Crotty, 1966). This has been maintained by a partnership between quasi-peasant owners, concentrated in parts of the west and the normal majority party, Fianna Fail. The peasants support the party, the party leaves them in possession and appears to give them, as through the dole, what is necessary to maintain their way of life. Politics maintains society by not disturbing the land system and by supporting it through a structure of payments and other benefits.

This association of complex systems of administration with support for political leaderships and machines is another point of comparison, as with European peripheral peasantries (Berger, 1972). The explanation can be pursued through Irish politics and administration, including its delight in administrative discretion, access situations and support for 'messenger' politicians: those who seem to be helping. If people are not actually helped they like to think they are by those who they anyway (for reasons of family, place and memory) approve of. Not all, however, are contained. This is partly spatial: like inter-relations of landholding, family structures, political machines and past migration in still declining areas of the west (Arensberg and Kimball, 1940 and 1968; Brody, 1973). The situation is complex and changing but uncertain too. Some are excluded – more may be, as demography and economy alter.

So the Irish are an ex-colonial people searching for independence. The search continued with sophistication, greater claims for success after 1958 and hopes after EEC membership in 1973, and with the adoption of specific regional development policies and institutions. Amongst all peripheral countries, Ireland had suffered exceptionally and unevenly from population decline and migration. Hence the significance of the symbols of regional development policy: could people be kept at home or brought back? But now the question is about to alter, if too many stay. It is the thesis of this paper that the outcome has been an exacerbation of the role of discretionary access institutions, and notably in Shannon itself. The inter-relation of these factors has been good for some people and places, bad for others. There has been favoured and unfavoured access.

One of the most striking outcomes has been the emergence in the mid-West of the Shannon Free Airport Development Company (SFADCO) and Shannon New Town as archetypal institution and community of favoured and unfavoured access and of regional development policy. They can provide a test of such policies: viz of how such policies could be evaluated, and of how, then, they might now stand, since 1958 and since 1973.

Before and After 1958

Ireland has national aims as Australia has settled policies. Territorial unity and the restoration of language have not been achieved since Independence. The search for economic independence is no less urgent. Up to 1958, dependence was the economic and trading relationship with the UK, the poverty of the rural western and agrarian areas and the politics of De Valera (the dominant Irish political figure from the First World War and the Taoiseach or Prime Minister with only two breaks from 1932 to 1959). The abolition of landlordism did not also ensure the disappearance of the colonial inheritance of migration and population decline, the destruction of the textile industry, or the shaping of Ireland's economy to produce those types of agricultural exports the UK wished to import. The UK had governed Ireland 'by the belief that Irish economic interests should be regulated in a way that would do no harm to England', (Cullen, 1972; cf. the observations of Swift, as in *The Drapier's Letters*). As late as 1960, industry provided only 30 per cent of Irish GNP. Up to 1958, Irish economic policy gave priority to agricultural production for export, with some protection for Irish industries, in response to British post-1931 protectionism, as in shoes, confectionery, soap, furniture: import substitution, in fact. Hence access to state intervention was important, as in dairying, livestock breeding, some areas of protection and taxation and parastatal organisations like electrical supply and distribution.

Post 1922, and particularly 1931–58, policy had evidently been unsuccessful. This was still a poor and dependent society. Despite import substitution industrial employment fell from 228,000 in 1953 to 210,000 in 1958. A new approach was to look to planning, foreign capital, industrialisation and regional development rather than to import substitution. This was how Ireland was to escape from beef, dairying and Britain. The 1932–58 policies created key access relationships between industrialists and authorities who could grant selective protection. They had not created economic to supplement political independence.

The change came around 1958. The new policies were an invitation to foreign capital.[2] They were also a call to new types of access institutions. In the decade 1960–70, 74 per cent of industrial development came from overseas. Of 570 new projects, 401 were foreign owned. Of the 401 foreign projects, 178 were UK and 98 US; 87 per cent of foreign investment in Ireland was UK, US and German. 'Government will welcome foreign participation in the drive for expansion in industry where it is likely to result in a new industrial activity or an increase in our industrial exports' (1958 White Paper, Part 5). But nationally the IDA, in the mid-West region, the Shannon Free Airport Development Company for example, also came into play.

The IDA (Industrial Development Authority) allocated incentives and encouraged applicants. There was an export board, an industrial training institution, an industrial credit company allocating credit, underwriting and advice. Industrial estates were set up in Waterford and Galway as well as Shannon. How did this interrelation of policy, foreign capital and Irish institutions work out?

In the first place, the crucial decisions about industrialisation, employment and location were left to the access applicants, that is to say to the entrepreneurs themselves, rather than the allocating institutions. In the second place, since these institutions granted extremely favourable access to capital, foreign investment was encouraged by the institions themselves to be capital intensive. Over the period 1953–67 there was a rising capital to labour ratio in 42 out of 44 manufacturing industries studied (Long, n.d.; compare Leser, 1967–8). That is, these public interventions did little to correct a worldwide tendency, as Irish policy hoped and claimed. They may have exaggerated it; despite the explicit policy objectives in the 1958 paper, in practice while there was more industrial investment there was actually a lower rate of job creation. Industrial employment rose about 5,000 jobs per annum, 1931–56. In the period 1958–71, favoured applicants to the new access institutions, the new foreign firms, actually created only about 2,500 jobs a year. Furthermore, of the grant-aided projects, which were largely foreign, in for example 1966 of total purchases less than half were domestic (Meenan, p. 132; Long, p. 52, table 6; Central Bank of Ireland Annual Report, 1972). Graduate emigration continued (Lynn, 1968). It can be argued that the net employment effect of the new policies was, in an absolute sense, labour-displacing.

The Outcomes of 1958

The new policies of 1958 claimed to be instruments to fashion economic independence, in a way which political independence and De Valera had not found. The policies had to be expressed through sets of institutions, procedures and incentive packages. Certain consequences followed. The favoured applicants who were successful in the new arenas tended to choose particular sectors, strategies and places for industrial development. Furthermore, grants and licences for mining development were a key area for favoured access (McAleese, 1972; IDA, Regional Industrial Plans, 1973–7, Part I).[3]

That is, the instrumentation of the new policies set up new rules and prizes: successful access to favours of government industrial development institutions. There was then a coincident domination of an 'access game' by foreign enterprise.[4] The game was discretionary and complex. At the same time, it was extraordinarily and demonstrably generous to the winner, the favoured and successful applicant, in what it gave him and in what decisions it left in his hands.

The discretions available were in fact employed. As for the first point, the complexity was comparable with other parts of the Irish administrative culture: the system of medical cards would be one instance; proposals for reform in land tenure would provide another. For example, industrial development policy was inevitably meant to pay respect to regional redistribution of income:

> ... to contribute positively to improving the relative growth rate in incomes in the poor regions and lessening their population decline. (IDA *Annual Report*, 1970–1, p. 24)

The instrument was to distinguish legal maxima for grants between 'designated areas' (60 per cent) and non-designated (45 per cent), and after 1969, 50 per cent and 35 per cent respectively. The administrative discretion available was used: actual rates of grants 1952–70 averaged 53·5 per cent in designated and 40·2 per cent in non-designated areas (McAleese, p. 33). The grants were particularly suitable to the creation of foreign enclave industries, as in Shannon, so that by 1970 foreign company investment was dominant, e.g. 74 per cent total new investment in Ireland by 1970. These were the applicants who were most adept at getting hold of the incentive package. For example, between 1959 and 1971, 50 per cent of all export tax relief and nearly 75 per cent of all grants paid went to foreign enterprises (McAleese; Farley, October 1972).

As for the second point, in total the incentives added up to a considerable package.[5] There is evidence that that was recognised by industry. Foreign firms saw access to government as the largest factor influencing investment in Ireland (Donaldson, 1966). In a survey of foreign firms investing in 1958–64, 85 per cent gave government subsidies, compared with 65 per cent giving market demand or market access, 44 per cent labour factors, as the single most important reason for investment. An IDA survey found export tax relief on profits and grants again as crucial. A comparison with a separate German study tends to show that the Irish system attracted and selected out just those companies who were most responsive to this especially favourable system (Kepschull, 1970). Furthermore, there was a significant increase in the level of grants and export tax reliefs going to these successful applicants round about 1965 and, according to Long (p. 38) the explanatory factors in success were 'size and influence'. The Economic Commission for Europe acknowledged that the Irish package went 'further than those of any other country in Europe in encouraging export industries and in attracting private capital for this purpose'. Other studies have shown, furthermore, that discretionary and complex packaging is particularly beneficial for the most resourceful and best-placed of applicants (Harvey, Jacobs, Lamb, Schaffer, forthcoming).

These policies adopted after the 1958 White Paper went through changes from time to time as in fields like industrial relations and in the regional development and housing sectors. Whatever the changes, though, the 1958 policies were the very symbols of a new search for independence. The outcome however was far from the economic independence and the job expansion which had in the first place been sought. We note the rising capital to labour ratio, increasing dependence on overseas sources for raw materials and intermediate goods, and the types of assembly operation set up. Over the 20 years, 1951–70, total employment actually decreased from 1,272,000 to 1,066,000 (Bank of Ireland Annual Report 1970–1). But public employment increased in the 1960s by about 10,000 (Central Statistics Office, 1971). The policy was associated with a redistribution of Irish trading and investment relationships away from a single dominance by Britain. It did work for some areas, as we shall see for the mid-West and Shannon. Within that sense, it favoured some people and some sectors and not others and other people, even in that sort of region. What did emerge was those new and significant relationships between sharply contrasting categories of applicants, and state institutions of administrative allocation. There was also a continuity with pre-1958. Nothing in the new policies disturbed the continued support in the non-industrial sector for dairy and cattle. Above all, the premise of a declining population continued long after a closing of the gateways to mass migration and a radical change in marriage, fertility, family planning and the population curve. In the end those objective demographic changes came to challenge the viability of the post-1958 policies and these institutional relationships themselves.

Evaluations and Institutions

Inevitably any evaluation of the regional income and employment effects over the last twenty years is complex (an effort at a full study is O'Farrell, 1975, pp. 52–5 esp.). In brief, in population, income and employment increases, the Eastern region and Dublin did best. Elsewhere, and particularly among the designated areas, the mid-West did exceptionally well.

For example, 1961–6, of total net job creation, 34·2 per cent went to the Eastern region compared with 0·4 per cent to the Midlands and

1·0 per cent North-west; Dublin population increased by 9·1 per cent, North-west population declined by 6 per cent, Midland population declined by 2·2 per cent, Donegal by 4·6 per cent; personal income in 1969 was 70 per cent greater in the Eastern region than in Donegal; meanwhile the mid-West gained 22·2 per cent of net job creation and population increased by 1·6 per cent. Hence the ways in which the policy and institutions worked in the mid-West and Shannon need special attention. In general, non-designated areas did better than designated in getting industrial grants. Between 1959 and 1971, for example, £61·3 million went to non-designated compared with £32·3 million to designated areas (IDA Annual Report 1971–2, pp. 31–2).

General studies would have led us to expect this (Sunkel, March 1973). The question came to be examined by Irish authorities (e.g. National Economic and Social Council, January 1975). The problem, however, is not just the complexity of that sort of evaluation.[6] The point is that it is difficult for 'official' examination to concentrate on certain other types of issues. These are just those ways in which for example what is particular about the Irish case is the degree of favour granted to successful applicants and how the complexity and discretion characteristic of Irish administration in the end leave initiative to those entrepreneurs, all this in total contrast with the ways in which workers and tenants are treated. Furthermore, there is the question of how institutionalisation is employed to disguise the growth of conflict in interest and choice. For example, in the words of the 1975 report, there was a conflict between:

1 Concentration of resources on the development of a few growth centres.
2 Dispersal of resources so that a large number of small centres can participate in the industrial development of the regions.

This conflict is the more important because of the exceptionally dispersed pattern of Irish population settlements. That degree of disguise was then markedly exemplified in the range of functions which were in the end allocated to SFADCO itself.

Complex and discretionary administrative allocation systems will be costly, and disadvantageous for some. At the same time they carry a significance in themselves. That is partly because they suit others. In Irish political culture such systems are also held to suit and in part explain such political relationships as the support for one sort of party representative from one sort of voter.

Thus, when changes are proposed in fundamental aspects of Irish society like land tenure, the very proposals tend to assume that complex administrative processes can and should be institutionalised. It follows that, in this sort of society, crucial conflicts like those about regional development tend to be depoliticised by a process of incorporation into institutional programmes and allocations. That is the significance of the access game itself for favoured and unfavoured applicants using these characteristically complex decision-making systems.

The implication is that the outcomes of such regional development policies, as compared with its objectives of independence and employment, are the results of the access game: who wins and who loses. Evaluation must look at that and how far those results are affected by the rules themselves, the institutions and procedures of regional development policy. Irish regional policies have indeed been evaluated. For example, it has been much opened to consultancy advice. The advice has mainly been a debate between growth centres and decentralisation or dispersion. In the event, however, government policy, as judged by authoritative enunciations at least, has been an effort to paper over the cracks, a type of ambiguity. So what policy has meant in practice on that sort of issue has depended on interactions of actual applications with various decisional criteria case by case.

Some observers thought that the government had, by 1972, come down heavily in favour of dispersion and against growth centres. But in 1965 a single government statement coincidentally supported development centres, industrial estates and the dispersal of industrial activity. The chapter on physical planning and regional development in the government's own programme for economic and social development (Stationery Office, 1969) was merely in favour of 'equitable sharing of economic progress, both among individuals and regions'.

It is not just, as O'Farrell said, that:

> ... such statements may be criticised for excessive vagueness. Does an 'equitable sharing of economic progress' imply equal growth rates or regional person *per capita* incomes (in which case the absolute gap in regional *per capita* incomes would still increase) or does it envisage an equalisation of regional personal *per capita* income? It could imply equal regional *per capita* private and public investment. (O'Farrell, 1970)

In the first place, public policy enunciation is bound to be ambiguous. The government is faced with a legacy of emigration and depopulation of the west, an institutional and statutory history of 'congested districts', a political-cultural commitment to the Gaeltacht and the west of Shannon and particular interventions from time to time from investors and entrepreneurs. In the 1970s when a new strategy had just been announced, a major new location in east Donegal was accepted which would in fact have apparently been excluded by just that new strategy itself. That is why actual decisions,

rules, procedures matter so much. Regional development planning is a
sector in which the operation of these rules of access can be seen
clearly. What Paul Samuelson called 'the fallacy of composition' has to
be confronted: some, not all, can succeed in getting grants. Spatial
distribution rules are necessary. What matters to the applicant is also
the distinction, as about percentages and maxima, which follows from
this definition of areas. Hence the definition of congested districts, undeveloped and designated areas. Then there are the problems of
actually using these rules: deciding who will get a grant or a package;
the specific allocation. Hence the significance of the procedures and of
what is contained in the package.

If access is a game, it is a difficult one to play: to know the rules and
to know what the prizes are. The rules become institutional, internal,
ritualistic and complex. For example, grants and packages are given in
part against promises of increased employment. However, even on
government survey figures themselves: 'total employment in 1966 was
66 per cent of the predicted level at full production' (GOI, 1967). Our
own figures for Shannon would suggest that a ratio of 40 per cent of
actual to promised employment would be usual. Sometimes the percentage would be as low as 34 per cent.

Then, some of the participants are the institutions. They are also
amongst the beneficiaries. It is not a bad thing, in the mid-West of
Ireland, to be a well-paid official. The institutionalisation, however, is
as complex as the rules and procedures. It may be an attempt to re-
move conflict; in practice the conflict becomes institutional. That is to
say, conflict is then conducted according to programme rather than
political rules, as between county development teams and a regional
authority like SFADCO, or even within an institution itself, less
openly, as inside SFADCO. This depoliticisation of conflict, as about
differentials between grants for the western and other parts of the
country, becomes expressed in a still greater complication. Hence a
more critical role for the access rules themselves. That is, the development of the policy becomes, inevitably, an increasing complication and
a greater stress on the rules.

Conflict does not actually disappear because institutional programmes occur, not even conflict between and within institutions
themselves (on the general question of the relation between institutional programmes, access procedures and incorporation, see Schaffer,
1978; and on institutional evaluation see Schaffer, 1973–4). If Shannon and the mid-West were taken to be a success by evaluation, we
would have to ask what the success means: success for whom, including
what institutions and who within them; and success for whom within
the region and within Shannon. If this is uneven, what will the grounds
of conflict then become, and how will they be contained? It is the

perhaps inevitable failure to face these questions which led to difficulties for the NESC Regional Policy Committee, under Professor Norman Gibson, which was to advise the government on 'the balanced development for the regions in the country'.

Two conclusions follow. The first is that the problem is not merely to operationalise or quantify the objectives of regional policy: earned income per head; personal income per head; disposable income, or whatever; or even to despair, as the report did, about the existing structure of authorities. It is to detect the degree to which the 'means' (like the rules and institutions) of achieving regional objectives become influential for the outcomes of regional policy. The second conclusion is then to see how far the nature of such authority itself would have to be changed if different outcomes are wanted. These conclusions follow from a study of the mid-West and the Shannon case also (see also Committee on Industrial Organisation, 1963; National Economic Industrial Council, 1968; Arthur D. Little Inc., 1967, (a) and (b)).

The Achievement of Shannon

Mid-West across the Shannon would have been likely in any case to have played a particular role in any Irish search for independence through regional development policy. When it comes to the Shannon area itself, that is the airport, industrial estate and new town, there were particular reasons for that. In the first place, any examination has to begin by acknowledging apparent success. The relatively successful position of the mid-West region through a decade of regional policy like 1961–71 is identified in the NESC Report Tables. The biggest changes, for example in personal income per head, were in the Eastern region. The South-west was also heavily benefitted. The Midlands, West, North-west and Donegal did worst of all. The mid-West is an excellent example of one region which did better than the worst and less well than the existing dominant areas in the east. (See Tables 43(a) and (b).)

But within Clare and the mid-West, the industrial estate, the new town and the authority in Shannon emerged as a response to a particular issue in 1957. It was an understandable objective of the new state and for De Valera policies in the 1930s particularly, that the west should have a transatlantic airport and that it would be sited across the Shannon in De Valera's constituency in the Banner County. Hence the airport developments from 1936. However, despite the building of a jet runway 10,000 feet by 1960, it was clear by 1957 that transatlantic jet air transport demanded long hauls which would overfly Shannon.

A customs-free airport zone had been initiated in 1947. The response to the new crisis for Shannon coincided with the new policies

Table 43(a)

Personal income per head, 1960 and 1969 and actual and percentage change 1960/1969

Region	Personal income per head (£) 1960	1969	1969 at 1960 prices	Change 1960/69 Nominal £	Real £
East	246	517	351	271	105
South-west	195	400	278	214	83
South-east	188	380	258	192	70
North-east	176	380	258	204	82
Mid-west	188	391	265	203	77
Midlands	169	325	221	156	52
West	156	324	220	168	64
North-west	153	316	214	163	61
Donegal	150	305	207	155	57
TOTAL	199	420	285	221	86

Source: National Economic and Social Council Report, 1975, Table A.10.

Table 43(b)

Regional distribution of new industry and small industry grant payments and expenditure on industrial estates (net of expected rent repayments), April 1961–March 1971

Region	Expenditure per head of population 1961/71	Regions ranked by % of total expenditure	% of total expenditure to each region
East	9·8	2	19·4
South-west	22·4	1	20·4
South-east	20·4	4	13·0
North-east	34·8	5	11·7
Mid-west	27·5	3	14·5
Midlands	9·5	8	4·4
West	18·1	6	9·5
North-west	29·6	7	4·8
Donegal	11·6	9	2·5
TOTAL	17·4		100·0

Source: Industrial Development Authority, Regional Industrial Plans, 1973/77 Part 1 (Dublin: Industrial Development Authority, 1972).

of 1958 in Ireland as a whole. The response was simply to extend that customs-free zone to an industrial estate: an enclave indeed. Hence the Shannon Free Airport Development Authority 1957 and 1958.[7]

A new town was then tacked on to that. It seemed cheaper for the state to provide housing near industrial employment than to face the transport costs of bringing in the scattered population of the mid-West to new industries. The coincidence of 1957 and 1958 is striking,[8] the more so still when all these functions were given to one institution and then regional development for the whole mid-West too: an extreme case of institutional incorporation.

Success would indeed be striking. Furthermore, by some standards, success is indubitable (see the figures above). The association with tourism has always been important between Shannon Catering and the Ennis hotel industry, and SFADCO and the Irish Tourist Board. The industrialisation on the estate is obvious.

> This localisation of specialised airfreighting companies is self-explanatory; warehousing thrives on the low rentals of the standard factories, the speed of air services to the rest of Europe and to North America and the exemption from customs duty on the movement of goods. (Soulsby, Sept. 1965)

The industrial estate provides a significant percentage, perhaps a quarter of manufactured exports going through the airport. 80 per cent of the estate's goods were being shipped out by plane. Shannon originated air freight increased by 240 per cent over five years. The stabilisation of passenger traffic at 1955–62 was achieved as terminal passengers increased to replace the fall in transit passengers (see also Dwyer, 1961; Brookfield, 1955; Aalen, July 1963; Nelson, 1963; Vercruijsse, April 1961).

This was a choice in favour of a critical increment to an institutional package. It was not necessarily optimal to Limerick, Ennis and the villages and non-village settlements of Clare. It was bound to lead to an enclave industrial estate. But it did also lead to a new town of a special sort: a tenant community, highly dependent on much less favoured access relationships with this single dominating, depoliticised authority. Cost/benefit and international networks of consultancies were involved in the decision, and there were certainly some beneficiaries in the outcome. The low wage argument against expensive commuting in the grazing, stock-rearing, low tillage, highly dispersed rural settlement pattern of County Clare was especially powerful.[9]

There were, however, two resulting problems. One was that the population created for the Shannon community was peculiarly dependent and vulnerable by any standards of comparison. The second was that both the location of housing and the housing-jobs relationship was essentially a planners' decision, not a community choice. Furthermore, the service provided, the housing, etc. (layout, heating, appearance, shopping centres) was throughout a matter of authoritative planning and consultancy, not of politics or choice.

That does not mean that the conflicts could be submerged indefinitely. They re-emerged at all points. In other words, the very examination of the question for whom Shannon was a success has to become in the first place an examination of the institutional decision-making arrangements at national and local levels and between the institutions and other interests. It then leads to a related question. How far could institutional incorporation in the end depoliticise the conflicts and where did they tend to re-emerge, as in relations between Shannon and County development teams, and between the Shannon tenants and SFADCO? The evaluation becomes a political and institutional drama. We can instance some of the moments.

Shannon is a sort of forced choice. 'If the residents of Limerick, Ennis, etc., have a choice of employment near their homes, they may not be inclined to commute to Shannon in future.'[10] The result is in part an unbalanced, leaderless and dependent population. It is, so to speak, a community which has been selected by the estate's industrialists.

Since the population of the town is so closely tied to employment on the industrial estate and airport in most cases, the core of the population is selected by the industrialists who establish factories on the estate. (SFADCO, 1974)

The resident finds himself in a community unlike anything he would have been used to in Limerick, Dublin, Britain or elsewhere in the Irish mid-West. The problem is worsened by the significance of kin networks for Irish families, by the apparent rapidity with which Shannon families get into financial difficulties and by a lack of the normal sources of leadership: elders, teachers, managers. For example: 'Of the 59 executives . . . who worked in the Company, 1 management . . . live(s) in the town; 2 management and 10 other executives did live but moved from the town.' (SFADCO, 1974.) This is a community created as an offshoot from a different institutional programme. Nor are its members getting what they want from the institution: home ownership (Shannon Company housing 88·6 per cent, private housing 11·4 per cent; nation as a whole, local authority housing 32 per cent, private and grant-aided housing 68 per cent).

Then there is the way in which a Shannon resident has come to get his job and his house. The crucial stages are the job, the housing application, the allocation and then the confrontation between SFADCO and the resident about a level of rent. That is a matter of where his housing is located and whether he will enter the 'graded rent' scheme. The scheme is itself a characteristic example of institutional allocation – distinctive, benevolent and worthwhile from the point of view of the authority; complex, offputting, expensive and barely worthwhile from the point of view of the tenant unless he is already in a degraded or catastrophic situation.

There are grounds for conflict here. Over recent years this has been expressed in a rent strike, which had some success; in participation machinery set up by SFADCO itself, which has largely been un-productive; and by a series of more or less frustrated efforts to create more open political opportunity, as through the redistribution of electoral boundaries (quashed by some County Councillors represent-ing the older politics of the western land system) or a local govern-ment for Shannon itself. These are the potentially crucial challenges. First of all, Shannon does not exist politically as a distinct fact either for the County Council or for the Dail. It is however part of a political and democratic system. Hence central linkages for example between SFADCO, the Department of Local Government and the Depart-ment of Industry and Commerce. The changes coming through those links do have an effect. That was felt particularly strongly in what emerged as the rent crisis of 1971. At the same time what the people in Shannon thought they could do about that was not isolated from what was felt elsewhere. Their weakness as a community and on the political map was also felt.

It was around access arrangements, like the graded rent scheme, that the community mobilisation could at last happen as it had not happened before and scarcely happened again. What looked to SFADCO as a process of incremental change in rents came to be felt by the tenants as something quite different. A crucial challenge to SFADCO itself was presented. It emerged as an actual confrontation, a strike.

The confrontation was one of the rare occasions in which institu-tional relations at Shannon were manipulated somewhat to the benefit of the tenants. It is also a contrast of the actual but temporary success of mobilisation and confrontation around that sort of issue with the constant difficulty of formulating successful long-term relations of tenants and their community organisations on the one hand with the development company. It is of interest to see the types of institutional ideology which SFADCO attempted to deploy. A distinction between two different types of access arrangements, the differential rent schemes of any local authority and the graded scheme of SFADCO is one example.

For the most part, institutional ideologies succeed: the use of state-ments made by ministers; generalised claims about what would be 'out of line with government policy'; the need not to 'create anomalies'; the notion in interpreting and applying hardship clauses that the com-pany must not perform functions like public assistance 'which more properly come from other agencies'; the need for confidentiality; the complexity of actual calculations and particular applications of the access rules.

The limitation of an institution, however, is that it cannot mobilise support for its own participation machinery. The rent strike was effective. The later participation efforts have not been. But as far as Shannon is concerned there cannot be a permanent confrontation between a mobilised tenantry and an institution. There seem to be two directions along which change could be pursued. The first would be an alteration in the property and status of the residents themselves.

The most obvious direction is away from tenancy to home-ownership through a tenant purchase scheme. There are difficulties in moving that way. They are related to the institutional arrangements themselves, the reasons for people being in Shannon, and the status of the service item: a house in Shannon. That is to say, as long as Shannon is run by a single dominating authority, and as long as that operation is felt throughout the housing and employment relationships, tenant purchase by itself will not be perceived as a crucial and worthwhile reform by the residents as a whole.

It follows that a change in property and status has to be associated with changes in employment, in authority and in other institutional relationships. At present, virtually all Shannon residents live in rented houses and feel the weight of SFADCO heavily upon them. It runs the industrial estates, it plans and builds the town. SFADCO are the landlords, they are the people to whom they have applied for their houses, they are the people with whom they communicate intimate household details so as to secure a determination about some of their major expenses. They certainly do not feel they control or participate in SFADCO in any way.

But they happen not to feel that about the County Council either. Hence in practice they will frequently turn to SFADCO, oddly enough, rather than the County Councillor or TD, unlike the practice throughout the rest of Ireland, for example if an approach has to be made to the Mid West Health Board with problems about medical cards.

The second direction for crucial change would be constituted by changes in employment and authority. The housing and planning functions of SFADCO would become a responsible local authority. If the rest of SFADCO is working for the entrepreneurs of the industrial estate it cannot continue to be the centripetal authority, focussing all other institutional and access relationships for everybody living in the community. As it happens, however, the possible arrangements for more effective representation and for local government status for Shannon themselves present other difficulties. Paradoxically, that is partly because they express the continuation of a specifically colonial past. It is also because, as we said at first, the political institutions represent a different sort of settlement or partnership.

In the past the Irish solution has been migration: the option of exit. Indeed, for Shannon, as in other severe access situations, we have to look at the option of exit (Schaffer and Lamb, 1974). It was difficult for people living in Shannon to buy their own houses. They could, and the majority did, choose not to opt for a graded rent scheme. Crucial exit would be to move away from Shannon, the mid-West, even Ireland. Certainly, many people in Shannon would try to move a little, as to Kilkishan. By the mid-1970s, the costs of transport tended to make that exit difficult, just as migration, the traditional Irish exit, has been more difficult still. Yet by the mid-1970s, Shannon was losing enterprises and jobs themselves – the very point of the whole operation. Employment available in Shannon in January 1974 to July 1976 fell by 20 per cent, at least as bad as Ireland as a whole. Some benefits continued. SFADCO continued to be a good employer for its own officials. Unallocated administrative expenditures of SFADCO itself increased from 24 per cent of total to 36 per cent of total between 1970 and 1975.[11]

A regional development policy had since the 1950s been regarded as one of the ways towards independence. We have seen some of the difficulties the policies encountered for the people affected and for such a crucial peripheral area as the mid-West and Shannon in particular. The criticisms we have put forward of what regional development policy came to mean for Ireland as a periphery, and for a periphery within Ireland itself, correspond with points made by others.

> Regional development doctrine ... which is based on the theory of polarised development is fully consistent with the transnational ideology of development; it is a willing instrument in the hands of the managers of unequal development. (Friedman, J., forthcoming)

We have stressed a different point. Irrespective of the relation between doctrines and theories, public statements of regional development tend to ambiguity. The Irish are no exception. However, regional policies rely notably on instrumentation: decision rules, like spatial categorisation (Schaffer, September 1977). Regional policy outcomes express the use of these rules by institutions and applicants, case by case.

Applicants encounter the institutions at points of sensitivity: like getting allocations as nearly as possible on their own terms. Some are better than others: hence the rituals about employment potential in development grant and package applications. The institutions develop their instrumentation to keep things going, equally, on their terms. This suits some more than others. In Ireland, some sort of regional development was inevitable, especially by the 1950s; and complex institutional encounters suited quite a lot of people. As experienced in Ireland, the rules of regional development policy have been changed and complicated over time so as to allocate favours to some (like potential developers), difficulties for others (like Shannon tenants and workers); opportunities and restrictions; and to manage a critically sufficient institutional invention like Shannon itself, as in 1957–8. This can be understood with Irish data in the past by an examination of the roles played by the instruments themselves: institutions, rules and procedures.

That demonstrates a politics which has worked in the past. Migration coincided with these institutional factors of containment. Shannon shows the operation of such an institution of favour and containment set up by regional policy and in the end where points of strain and change could nevertheless now be felt. The point is whether this sort of institutional incorporation can continue. If migration is not available, what other types of voice or exit will be expressed, unless a European regional policy system were supposed to revive the potential for institutional critical adaptations. As Ireland provokes other comparisons, so it could here also.

Notes

1 This paper draws on two chapters of my draft study, provisionally entitled, *The Irish Midwest: The Politics of Favour*. It is in part an application of a theory which attempts to describe and explain what happens in the implementation of policy when government institutions distribute services – such as regional development grants or housing – to applicants – such as potential industrial entrepreneurs or tenants. This is the theory of access. See Schaffer, *Official Providers: Access, Equity and Participation*, Unesco Division for the Study of Development, Reports/Studies Equ. 1, 1977. The revision of the paper has been greatly assisted by my colleague, Percy Selwyn.

2 There were some antecedents in Irish regional development policy before the switch in 1958: the Industrial Development Authority was set up in 1949 and given statutory effect under the Industrial Development Authority Act 1950. Later legislation included: the Undeveloped Areas Act 1952; Industrial Grants Act 1956; Industrial Grants Act 1959; Undeveloped Areas and Industrial Grants (Amendments) Act 1963; Industrial Development Act 1969; Shannon Free Airport Company Development Act 1959; Gaeltacht Industries (Amendment) Act 1965; Local Government (Planning and Development) Act 1963.

3 Resources Study Group, in Ireland, for example in 1958–70, £31 million was invested in natural resource extraction, £23 million in capital equipment and land, £8 million in exploration, the bulk of it after 1965 for the opening of the Tynagh Mine, County Galway. 1960 – 56 prospecting licences for minerals; 1972 – 1,300. R.S.G. 'Navan and Irish Mining', N.B. 'Ireland now possesses the largest zinc lead mines in the world at Navan, the largest underground zinc mine in Europe at Silvermines, the largest producing lead mine in Europe at Tynagh, the fifth largest mercury mine in the world, one of the most important sources of magnesite in Europe, and the most profitable barytes deposit in the world.'

4 Excluding Shannon, IDA figures for 1973–7 showed capital requirements

of foreign-owned companies: £122 million in fixed and working capital, £29 million met by government grants and fixed assets. New industrial enterprises 1960–70 – 74 per cent foreign owned (not foreign included Irish and joint Irish-overseas ventures). Government grants 1952–70 £31 million, £21 million going to non-Irish enterprises.

5   No capital gains tax; the total share of an Irish registered company can be owned by an overseas company; double taxation agreements between Ireland and Austria, Canada, UK, USA, Netherlands, Germany, France, Sweden, Norway and Switzerland, prohibiting corporate taxes of profits of those companies in their parent countries; 15 year complete tax exemption on export and profits; cash grants up to 50 per cent in designated areas, 35 per cent in non-designated areas on total capital costs; industrial re-equipment grants for established industries; grants towards the costs of training workers and managers; grants towards the costs of instructors and consultants engaged to train personnel up to 100 per cent; guarantees of loans; subsidisation of interest on loans; non-repayable cash grants towards the cost of approved company research and development projects, new industrial projects and processes up to 35 per cent; IDA industrial estates with facilities, advance factories, industrial services; grants towards reduction of rentals on factories; industrial housing for workers; aftercare advisory services for newly established industries in early years of production; no restriction on employment of expatriate personnel to managerial and other posts; duty-free access to UK and EEC markets; infrastructure from industrial training centres, electricity projects, new transport networks; credit facilities; duty-free import of capital equipment and materials for export production. Perhaps more important than all of that was the replacement in 1958 of import substitution by the general philosophy of attracting foreign capital. The move towards that philosophy and the type of access structured creates is perhaps typical of one type of LDC policy (MacCarvill, 1971).

6   For a much more favourable comparative study, see Commission of the European Communities, Report of the Study Group on the Role of Public Finance in European Integration, Brussels, April 1977: vols. I and II. Ireland was represented on the group by Professor Martin O'Donoghue, now the Irish Minister of Planning. However, the group did not explicitly look at Irish data, and on 'regional policy narrowly and explicitly defined as such' the inter-regional redistributive effect was found to be (except in Italy) 'relatively minor' (vol. I, p. 37).

7   SFADCO was set up in 1958 to handle regional development, airport operation, customs-free zone, export profits, tax exemption, industrial enclave development and then housing estates development. Customs-free Airport (Amendment) Act; Finance (Miscellaneous Provisions) Act; Shannon Free Airport Development Company Limited Act; all in 1958.

8   The details would be reported in the separate study, The Irish Mid West, forthcoming. The following should be noted: 1959 – 420,000 agricultural employment, 271,000 industrial employment, natural increase 25,000 per annum, emigration 40,000 per annum. As Paul Quigley, General Manager of SFADCO, said 'Ireland's major economic objective to ensure its survival as a nation ... The possibility of increasing employment in agriculture is remote so that the task falls to the industrial sector ... Most Irishmen have friends or relatives abroad. Birmingham and Boston are better known than Dublin to many on Ireland's western seaboard from which emigration is heaviest.'

9   The 1961 Census of Population, Stationery Office, Dublin, 1963, vol. 1,
    makes it possible to calculate the population effects of Shannon on certain
    hypotheses, for example among the thirty district electoral divisions west
    of the Feakle-Shannon bus line, approximately an hour's bus ride, the in-
    creases 1956–61 varied from 10 to 4·5 per cent.
10 Shepperd-Fiddler and Associates (1972), *Outline Development Plan Re-
    appraisal.*
11 By then Ireland as a whole was taking a further crucial step in its search for
    economic independence, namely integration with Britain in the European
    Economic Community, 1973. The European regional and social funds
    were regarded in Ireland as one of the crucial attractions. As far as the
    community is concerned, 'the whole of the (Irish) national territory is
    treated as a single development region' (Commission of European Com-
    munities, June 1977). However, as far as grants from the regional develop-
    ment fund are concerned, the Irish Government still expresses a priority
    to the 'designated areas'. These are the same areas for the same factors
    (agricultural predominance and high levels of unemployment) as before.
    The priority is still for developing the industrial sector. The projects that
    come forward are still justified by uncorrected statements of employment
    potential. But these funds do not merely represent a continuation of the
    past; they are in total minimal.

References

Aalen, F. H. A. (July 1963), 'Review of Recent Irish Population Trends',
    Population Studies.
Arensberg, C. M. and Kimball, S. (1940 and 1968), *Family and Community in
    Ireland*, Cambridge, Mass.
Bax, M. (1973), *Harpstrings and Confessions*, University of Amsterdam.
Berger, Suzanne (1972), *Peasants Against Politics: Rural Organisation in
    Britanny 1911–1967*, Harvard.
Brody, H. (1973), *Inishkillane: Change and Decline in the West of Ireland*,
    Allen Lane.
Brookfield, H. C. (1955), 'Ireland and the Atlantic Ferry', *Irish Geography*, 3, 2.
Cockburn, C. (1975), *Mr. Mintoff Comes to Ireland*, Macmillan.
Commission of European Communities (June 1977), *E.R.D.F. Second Annual
    Report 1976*, Brussels.
Crotty, R. (1966), *Irish Agricultural Production*, Cork University Press.
Cullen, L. M. (1972), *An Economic History of Ireland Since 1960*, Batsford,
    London.
Donaldson, L. (1966), *Development Planning in Ireland*, Praeger, London.
Dwyer, D. J. (1961), 'Shannon Free Airport', *Geographical Review*, 51.
Farley, N. (October 1972), 'Explanatory Hypotheses for Irish Trade in Manu-
    factured Goods in the mid 1960s', *Social and Economic Review*, 4, 1.
Friedman, J., *Territory and Function*, Edward Arnold, London, forthcoming.
Government of Ireland:
(1958) White Paper, *First Programme for Economic Expansion*, Part Five.
(1963) *Industrial Grants*, Committee on Industrial Organisation Fourth Interim
    Report.
(1967) *Survey of Grant-Aided Industry.*
(1968) *Report on Industrial Adaptation and Development*, National Economic
    Industrial Council.

(1969) *Third Programme, Economic and Social Development 1969–72*.

(1971) *Trend of Employment and Unemployment in 1971*, Central Statistics Office.

(1975) *Regional Policy in Ireland: A Review*, National Economic and Social Council (NESC).

Harvey, C., Jacobs, B. L., Lamb, G. B., Schaffer, B. B., *Rural Institutions, Public Services and Employment*, ILO, forthcoming.

Industrial Development Authority (I.D.A.) (1971–2), *Annual Report*, Dublin.

—— (1973–7), *Regional Industrial Plans*, Part I, Dublin.

Kennedy, R. E. Jun. (1973), *The Irish: Emigration, Marriage and Fertility*, Berkeley University Press.

Kepschull, D. (1970), 'Some Aspects of the Treatment of the International Firm in Less Developed Countries', Institute of International Economics, Hamburg, unpublished.

Leser, C. (1967–8), 'Problems of Industrialisation in Developing Countries and Their Implications for Ireland', *Journal of Statistical and Social Inquiry*, Society of Ireland, 21, 6.

Little, Arthur D. Inc. (1967), *Review of the Structure of the I.D.A.*, I.D.A., Dublin.

Long, F., 'Political Economy of Foreign Investment in the Irish Republic 1950–1970', Institute of Social Studies, The Hague, unpublished.

Lynn, R. (1968), *The Irish Brain Drain*, ESRI, Dublin.

McAleese, D. (1972), 'Capital Inflow and Direct Foreign Investment in Ireland 1947–70', *Social and Statistical Inquiry Society*, Dublin.

MacCarvill, P. D. (1971), *A Promotion of Direct Foreign Manufacturing Investment: A Systems Approach*, M.B.A. Thesis, University College, Dublin.

Meenan, J. (1970), *The Irish Economy Since 1922*, Liverpool University Press.

Nelson, J. H. (1963), 'Population Changes in Ireland 1951–61', *Geographical Journal*, 129, 2.

O'Farrell, P. N. (1970), 'Regional Development in Ireland: Problems of Goal Formulation and Objective Specification', *Economic and Social Review*, 2, 1.

—— (1975), *Regional Industrial Development Trends in Ireland 1960–73*, I.D.A., Dublin.

Schaffer, B. B. (1973–4), 'Policy Decisions and Institutional Evaluation', *Development and Change*, 5, 3.

—— (1977), *Official Providers: Access, Equity and Participation*, Unesco Division for the Study of Development Reports/Studies EQU. 1.

—— (1977), *Spatial Dimensions and Institutional Factors*, IDS Discussion Paper 119.

Schaffer, B. B. and Lamb, G. B. (1974), 'Exit, Voice and Access', *Social Science Information*, 13, 6.

Shannon Free Airport Development Company (1974), *A Sociological Evaluation of the New Town*, SFADCO Planning and Research Division.

Shepperd-Fiddler and Associates (1972), *Outline Development Plan Reappraisal*.

Soulsby, J. A. (1965), 'Shannon Free Airport Scheme: A New Approach to Industrial Development', *Scottish Geographical Magazine*, 81, 2.

Sunkel, O. (1973), 'Transnational Capitalism and National Disintegration in Latin America', *Social and Economic Studies*, 22, 1.

Vercruijsse, E. V. W. (April 1961), *Shannon Interland Survey 1961: Preliminary Report*, University of London.

13

CORE–PERIPHERY PROBLEMS – THE SCOTTISH CASE

John Bryden

This paper attempts to examine Scottish problems from a dependency standpoint. This implies a concentration on the factors 'external' to Scotland – trade dependence, technological dependence, capital flows, cultural factors, political and administrative arrangements and the broader decision-making framework – and the extent to which these factors are related to the problems of Scottish development. Such an approach contrasts with the earlier concentration (in both development economics and regional studies) on the internal causes of problems – the 'missing' factors (achievement motivation, entrepreneurial drive, lack of capital etc.) or 'natural' factors such as a restricted – or declining – natural resource base. It argues that there are elements in the dependency approach which either are, or are seen to be, significant in helping to explain Scottish development problems. Indeed, policy initiatives have already taken place in Scotland which to some extent at least recognise this. More are in the pipeline. Whether these initiatives will be sufficient to make real changes in the Scottish situation only time will tell. Dependency theory is still in its infancy and there are in any event difficulties in applying it to a region of Great Britain.

In tackling Scottish problems in this way, the paper takes a broad view. Much material of relevance has been left out, in particular the material (and there is much) on the Union of the Scottish and English Parliaments in 1707 which ended parliamentary independence, created the biggest customs union in Europe and provided access to the empire. Much of the historical analysis of the effects of the Union does seem highly pertinent to the dependency issue, and the Union does of course relate directly to the development of the Scottish economy and society thereafter.[1]

The structure of the paper is as follows. The first section briefly describes the Scottish 'problem', and for the sake of brevity deals with two sub-regions – West Central Scotland and the Highlands. The second section then deals with the manifestation of these problems – Unemployment, overt and disguised, Migration, the Employment Structure, Incomes and Capital Investment. The third section then discusses the relationship between these problems and the elements of dependence which the Scottish 'periphery' exhibits. Finally, the fourth section deals briefly with recent and possible future policy initiatives in the context of the earlier discussion.

The Scottish Problem

The Scottish 'problem' is not one but many, and there are distinct regional differences within Scotland. Thus the Highlands is distinct from Clydeside and the Edinburgh area distinct from both. Whilst the levels of distinction can be almost infinite – even the Highlands being far from homogeneous – this paper concentrates on West Central Scotland (which includes Clydeside) and the Highlands and Islands. These two regions contain roughly two-thirds of the land mass of Scotland and about half of its population. West Central Scotland provides nearly 60 per cent of Scottish manufacturing employment. Both have been the subject of recent policy initiatives which represent an apparent break with past approaches to Regional problems. They define the spectrum of Scottish regional problems although West Central Scotland is much the most significant – politically, economically and socially – of the two.

WEST CENTRAL SCOTLAND

The decline of West Central Scotland's economy has been the subject of numerous studies. One of the most significant, and most recent, of these was the West Central Scotland Plan Report (1974), Supplementary Report 1 of which deals in depth with the Regional Economy and provides much of the basic material for this paper. In its analysis of the history[2] of the region, the report concludes:

    (a)   The growth and decline of the region's industrial policies cannot be seen simply in terms of the advantages of iron ore and coal deposits at the time of the Industrial Revolution and the disadvantages of distance from main markets and decline of the natural resource base faced in the twentieth century.

    (b)   The most notable contrast with earlier years is the absence of 'an ability to adapt to new opportunities and translate industrial invention into commercial innovation' which characterised the period following the collapse of the tobacco trade and later the cotton industry.

    (c)   Lack of regional control and influence on crucial decisions was an important factor in the decline of two important traditional nineteenth century industries in the region – textile finishing and chemicals, whereas mergers 'led to a loss of local control, rationalisation and eventual rundown and decline . . .'.

(d) During the eighteenth and nineteenth centuries the industrial structure of the region was 'heavily geared to worldwide trading opportunities' (tobacco, railway locomotives, ships) and therefore closely integrated with 'worldwide economic growth'. This explained the exceptional severity of the depression in the 1930s and also 'on a more limited scale, the recent recession'. The specific link with the expansion of empire is clear and the loss of colonial trade preferences must also have been important to the region (although the report does not mention it).

In further detailed analysis the report highlights the uncompetitiveness of the region's manufacturing sector in inter-regional and international trade due to an ageing and technologically backward capital-stock and also an inefficient deployment of labour due to managerial inefficiency and restrictive labour practices (West Central Scotland Plan, pp. 66–7). As a result, the region exhibited a decline in manufacturing employment in the 1960s which could not be wholly explained by a poor industrial structure. The report highlighted the failure of indigenous industry – a failure which would have been more evident but for the volume of incoming investment to the region during the decade, particularly from overseas.[3]

HIGHLANDS AND ISLANDS

The Highlands represent a clear contrast with Clydeside. The region never had a significant industrial base. In the latter part of the nineteenth century when Clydeside was heavily dependent on industry, in the Highlands primary sector employment (agriculture, forestry, fisheries and mining) probably accounted for between 45 and 50 per cent of the occupied population. Since that time there has been a severe decline in primary sector employment, both absolutely and relatively. These declines were not compensated by increases in employment in other sectors of the Highland economy, although small relative increases may have occurred in some areas of manufacturing and construction and there has been a relative increase in the share of service sector employment (about 61 per cent in 1971). Throughout the first part of the nineteenth century at least two primary sectors of the Highland economy, agriculture and fishing, had been fairly buoyant. But the expansion of meat and wool production arising from the industrial revolution was checked by technological change in the transport industry (shipping, refrigeration) which, allied to a policy of free trade, exposed the industry to competition from the US, Australia and New Zealand at the end of the century. For other reasons the important fishing industry also declined during this period. The decline of the kelp[4] industry following the Napoleonic Wars is well documented. Although there is no clear evidence on the use made of surpluses generated by the kelp, fishing and sheep farming industries during the nineteenth century, there is considerable fragmentary evidence that they were – on the whole – spent or invested outside the Highlands. As Youngson (1973, p. 138) points out in respect of kelp 'the landlords' gains were not complemented by gains, financial or other, for the rest of the population'. Wages were low, linkages to other sectors of the Highland economy negligible, and profits and rents accruing to landlords used either for luxurious living or for other purposes outwith the Highlands.[5]

This historical experience serves to focus attention on three issues: (a) The vulnerability of the Highlands to *national* policies (such as free trade) which run counter to the interests of the region. (b) The significance of the locus of control over productive assets and the attitudes of the owners of land and capital towards reinvestment – which in turn reflects not only the opportunities elsewhere in the economy but also the extent to which the individuals concerned are (or feel themselves to be) subject to local social control or obligation to reinvest in the region. (c) The fact that it was not *just* a matter of declining employment in primary industry as a result of changing technology, but also a failure of output and incomes in these sectors to *grow* at the same rate as they were in other regions. As productivity growth is often associated with output growth, this had important consequences.

A final point on the Highlands. Evidence suggests that experience in the region varied; it was the gaelic speaking area of the West which suffered most from the declines in primary industry which have been outlined – a point of some later significance. West Central Scotland and the Highlands therefore represent two very different types of problem. The problems of the Highlands are *prima facie* much closer to those of the colonial primary producer.[6] Those of West Central Scotland are of much more recent origin and, because they primarily relate to its industrial base, do not at first sight appear to have much in common with development problems in 'developing' countries. On the other hand, in the analysis of the problems of the two regions there *is* common ground, loss – or lack – of local control over crucial decision-making processes being an important example.

Manifestations of the Problems

The problems described above are manifested in a number of different ways. The main direct indicators are overt unemployment, disguised unemployment, outward migration, a 'poor' employment structure, both in terms of the industrial structure and in terms of socio-economic groupings, differential migration in terms of age and skills or qualifications and relatively low incomes. One might also expect there to be a low level of investment in the region related to low average or marginal rates of return, although this does not appear to have been the case in the 1960s.

UNEMPLOYMENT, OVERT AND DISGUISED[7]

Overt unemployment in Scotland has been generally higher than the national average. In West Central Scotland it has been twice the average rate for Britain for most of the 1960s and particularly severe for males. In the Highlands, it was consistently high prior to the 1970s although the position has improved during this decade with some notable sub-regional exceptions. Although both Scotland and the Highlands have improved relative to Britain since 1974, the level (in 1976 around 8 per cent of the insured workforce) gives no cause for complacency.

In so far as activity (or participation) rates measure disguised un-employment, the indications here are that this is a considerable prob-lem in Scotland, particularly for females. However, in West Central Scotland there has been a relative trend away from male employment towards female employment (related to sectoral changes). While male activity rates there were the lowest of any conurbation in Britain, female rates were about average. This contrasts with the Highlands, where activity rates for females were markedly lower than the Scottish average.

Low productivity may also indicate disguised unemployment. Ac-cording to the West Central Scotland Plan (1974), 'Clydeside produc-tivity is substantially lower than in the UK and slightly lower than in the other conurbations'. Nor can this be entirely explained by different industrial structures (ibid. p. 54). It also seems probable that produc-tivity in the primary and tertiary sectors is somewhat lower in the Highlands than in Scotland as a whole.[8]

NET MIGRATION

A feature of the Scottish situation has been substantial net outward migration. Between 1961 and 1971 net migration from West Central Scotland was 228,000 – a mean annual change of 9·1 per cent, higher than any of the other UK regions. However, whilst net outward migration from West Central Scotland is a relatively recent phe-nomenon, for the Highlands it is one of long standing. The peak population was recorded in 1851 and declines were almost con-tinuous since then until the late 1960s when the population showed signs of stabilising.[9] Since 1971 there has been a consistent and posi-tive inward migration to the region. Again, however, certain areas within the Highlands continued to suffer net outward migration (the Western Isles and Caithness).

EMPLOYMENT STRUCTURE

There is marked regional bias in the employment structure by sector in Scotland. West Central Scotland has a higher proportion of employment (over 40 per cent) in manufacturing, and a lower proportion in primary industry and services.[10] In the Highlands, it is services, construction and the primary sectors which are over-represented and manufacturing which is under-represented (16 per cent).

The class structure of employment is also significant. The evidence of the West Central Scotland Plan (pp. 66–7) is that this region 'tends to have a higher proportion of the unskilled manual workers and a lower proportion of managerial and professional workers than Great Britain'.

EDUCATION, EMPLOYMENT STRUCTURE AND MIGRATION

The bias in the type of employment offered in the Highlands and Islands was shown by Sewel *et al.* (1976). In a survey of school leavers it was found that 'within two years of leaving school, nearly half of these former pupils were no longer resident within their original home districts' and, further, 'overwhelmingly, those who have left for higher or further education do not expect to return. A significant proportion of young skilled, manual workers have already migrated.' The report suggested that:

> ... the lack of professional and non-manual job opportunities in the peripheral area leads to the hypothesis that the higher the social class of the expected job, the greater the expectation of migration ... Those who expect to obtain professional and executive jobs in Class I and II have to a very large extent already left the home district – many of them for courses of full-time education.

The analysis suggested that these expectations were mainly a result of parental attitudes rather than educational experience:

> Where job opportunities are limited, parents expect the educational system to provide pupils with the skills and qualifications necessary for them to compete successfully with other pupils in the wider labour market ... it is not just the case that parents demand that the school system should provide the means of obtaining social mobility and that there is a recognition that social mobility will inevitably mean geographical mobility. Parental rejection of locally orientated vocational courses is indicative of a belief among parents that local job opportunities are limited and unattractive.

Prospects for girls in this respect were seen as being even worse ('almost entirely limited to semi-skilled and unskilled manual work').

This factor is one which proponents of autarkic developmental solutions have to grapple with.

Again there may be regional differences within Scotland. Although there was a fair amount of parental dissatisfaction with educational provision in the Highlands, this seems to be related more to the centralisation of secondary education *per se* than to results. To a large extent, the system otherwise seems to 'deliver the goods' in terms of parental expectations. Of 663 school leavers in the survey, 37 per cent obtained 6 or more 'O' grades and a further $12\frac{1}{2}$ per cent obtained 3 to five 'O' grades. Roughly half of the school leavers therefore obtained 3 or more 'O' grades. This may be contrasted with West Central Scotland where 61·4 per cent of school leavers had no such qualifications and only 19·5 per cent had two or more 'Highers'.[11] To the extent that parental expectations in Clydeside are similar to those in the Highlands, the educational system there does not appear to 'deliver the goods'.[12] Migration from Clydeside is not primarily a means of upward social mobility, but of economic survival.

DIFFERENTIAL MIGRATION

It will be obvious from the above that differential migration is an important factor in the Highlands and elsewhere in Scotland. Differential migration is evident both in skill/qualification categories and in age categories. The greatest relative loss has been of the younger and more skilled and more qualified sections of the labour force.

INCOMES

The evidence on relative incomes in Scotland is rather inadequate. There is little doubt that average *per capita* incomes are lower for Scotland by a factor of 10 to 15 per cent.[13] There is probably a similar difference between incomes in the Highlands and Islands and those for Scotland.[14] These differentials are larger than those reported by inland revenue as shown by data on average weekly earnings, but this is to be expected.[15] Earnings tend to be equalised regionally through the effect of nationally negotiated wage settlements, any differences probably being explained in structural terms. Incomes per head reflect age structure, employment structure, activity rates, self-employment, the significance of unearned incomes. The variations would be much larger but for nationally negotiated wage settlements and 'welfare' payments of one kind or another.

CAPITAL FORMATION

There is no evidence that either average rates of return on capital in Scotland, or rates of investment, have been lower than the rest of the UK in recent years. In fact the evidence for West Central Scotland is that the rate of investment during the 1960s was higher, and over the period 1963–8 grew at a more rapid rate, than the national average. Part of the reason for this seems to have been the intensification of regional policy in 1963 when regionally differentiated investment incentives which applied equally to mobile and indigenous industry were introduced for the first time.[16] Data for other sub-regions are not available, but the general view is that investment rates in the Highlands were lower than the national average at least until the late 1960s.

Scottish Dependence

Scotland thus exhibits some of the 'classic' problems of depressed regions, all of which can be related to relatively poor economic performance, although the origins, nature and extent of this clearly vary as between the different sub-regions of Scotland. In this Section an attempt is made to examine the extent to which these problems are related to the economic and functional relations ('dependency') with the 'centre'.

The distinction between structural and functional dependence has been made – notably by McIntyre (1964) and Demas (1965) in the Caribbean context. McIntyre's definition was perhaps restrictive in attributing an inevitability to structural dependence ('the dependence that arises because of the size and structure of the economy and cannot be helped') and a mutability to functional dependence ('dependence that arises as a result of the particular policies chosen and can therefore be avoided if alternative policies are pursued'). Demas on the other hand imparted a wider meaning to the terms. For present purposes the following distinction is made.[17] Structural dependence can be viewed as primarily related to trade and capital flows – dependence on export markets and imported inputs, on flows of private and public capital. Functional dependence relates to the explicit and implicit links between regions/nations which determine the *rules* of economic behaviour. It may thus be concerned with the location of decision-making entities in the private and public sectors generally, the legal system, the fiscal system, currency and banking, the cultural and social determinants of definitions of 'the good life' and hence the objectives of development itself.

STRUCTURAL DEPENDENCE
Scotland appears to be a relatively 'open' economy, particularly in the manufacturing sectors – about 60 per cent (by value) of all goods produced are exported and two-thirds of these go to the rest of the UK. The proportion of production which goes to the rest of the world – at 21 per cent – is much higher than for the UK as a whole (15 per

cent), and a significantly higher share is exported by the Drink and tobacco, Electrical engineering, Shipbuilding and 'Other manufacturing' sectors (*Quarterly Economic Commentary*, 1977, p. 33). It is true that Scotland is the second most 'closed' economy in the UK, but detailed analysis of trade flows suggests that 'Scotland is a relatively closed economy only in inter-regional trade' (West Central Scotland Plan, 1974, pp. 341–2). Structural dependence becomes of greater significance in the more peripheral areas and, although data are scarce, the Shetland input-output table (McNicoll, 1976) does show this clearly. On average (output weighted) industries purchased 30 per cent of their inputs (8 per cent for UK) through imports and exported an average 23 per cent of their outputs (7 per cent for UK). Export dependence in Scotland is not related in any consistent way to the location of ultimate ownership of Scottish manufacturing employment. Food, drink and tobacco and shipbuilding and marine engineering have a lower than average degree of foreign ownership (7 per cent and 12 per cent respectively) and are roughly 50 per cent Scottish owned. Electrical engineering and 'other manufacturing' on the other hand show the obverse situation (Firn, 1975, Table 5).

Direct subventions from Central Government (mainly through rate support grants) form an important part of the economic system of peripheral areas. In Shetland they ultimately accounted for 28 per cent of employment. In Scotland as a whole MacKay (MacKay, 1975, p. 4) estimates total net regional assistance (after clawbacks on Central and Local Government expenditure and transfer payments and allowing for double counting) of £300 millions or some 5·6 per cent of 1973 GDP in Scotland, although this may be exaggerated. This point relates to both structural and functional dependence.

OWNERSHIP OF PRODUCTIVE ASSETS
Firn's work at Glasgow is the most comprehensive available on the question of ultimate ownership of Scottish manufacturing employment. His results show that in 1973 only 41 per cent of manufacturing employment was controlled internally, this figure varying from 36 per cent in the Glasgow region to 55 per cent in the Highlands and Islands. A further 40 per cent of Scottish manufacturing employment was in plants owned in the rest of the UK. American owned firms accounted for 15 per cent of manufacturing employment, the figure for Glasgow and the Highlands being slightly higher at 17 per cent. Continental European investment was negligible at 2 per cent (Firn, 1975, p. 162).

Little is known about how this situation has developed over time. However, Firn's other detailed findings are disturbing and were clearly recognised as such by the West Central Scotland Plan. These findings are summarised as follows: (1) 'The larger the enterprise, the more likely it is to be controlled externally.' (2) 'Over one quarter of total manufacturing employment is in non-local branch plants.' (3) '110 enterprises account for 46 per cent of total manufacturing employment.' (4) 'The faster growing the sector, the lower is the amount of Scottish participation.' (5) 'The five fastest growing sectors have less than 14 per cent indigenous control.'

The evidence on plant closures during the 1960s does not support the view that employment trends have been directly related to the degree of outside ownership (see West Central Scotland Plan, 1977, p. 88). However, there has been a growing recognition of the wider issues posed by limited local control. Oil employment in Scotland has of course been important in the current decade, and this is substantially 'owned' outside Scotland and indeed outside Britain.[18] By 1976 total direct employment created in all North Sea Oil activities (including construction) amounted to 43,000, and estimates suggest that the total job creation inclusive of indirect and induced effects amounts to around 70,000 or 2·5 per cent of the total employed population in Scotland (MacKay, 1977, p. 140). Net job creation has been less than this however, as many of the firms involved have switched production to North Sea Oil from other markets.[19] Moreover, much of the job creation has been in the East of Scotland, not in the areas with the greatest problems.

Little is known about the ultimate 'ownership' of non-manufacturing employment in Scotland. An estimate of public sector employment in non-manufacturing sectors suggests that this amounts to some 42 per cent of the total.[20] Since the major policy decisions which govern the level and nature of such employment are taken in Westminster (or the Head Offices of the Nationalised Industries), and since the finance to sustain the activities which it represents is allocated by the same sources, a large part of this employment might be regarded as ultimately 'owned' outside Scotland, although the issue is not quite so straightforward as in private sector employment. Differences arise because of Scottish representation (albeit a minority) at Westminster, and because of the existence of a Scottish administration (the Scottish Office)[21] in Edinburgh.[22]

Land is another productive asset with an apparently significant degree of non-Scottish ownership. There are no official figures for Scotland as a whole,[23] but data for the Highlands and Islands indicate that, of a total surface area of some 9 million acres, some 1·6 million are publicly owned and 7·4 million privately owned (Bryden and Houston, 1976, pp. 66–8). Publicly owned land consists mainly of land 'owned' by the Forestry Commission (about 1 million acres) and the Department of Agriculture and Fisheries for Scotland.[24] Most of the latter was acquired under the Land Settlement Acts after the First World War. These Acts were the consequence of many years of conflict on land issues, culminating in political activism (the Land Leaguers) and land raiding (Hunter, 1976, chs. 8–11 *passim*).

Privately owned land in the Highlands is very unevenly distributed, some 35 families with individual holdings of 35,000 acres or more owning about one-third of the total area in private ownership. Many of these larger holdings are owned outside Scotland. However, two points must be made lest too rapid and superficial a view is taken on the implications of this situation. First, about half of all privately-owned land is under crofting or leasehold tenure. Substantial security of tenure is given to both tenants and crofters, and an institution (the Scottish Land Court) exists to administer the legal aspects of landlord-tenant relationships. Landlord control over land use on subjects under crofting or leasehold tenure is therefore extremely limited. Second, most of the larger landholdings which are untenanted are on land with limited production and employment potential. Many of these properties were acquired and built up during the nineteenth century by individuals who had acquired wealth during the industrial revolution and the expansion of empire; Queen Victoria no doubt helped this process by making sporting activities in the Highlands a fashionable pursuit.

The pattern of landowning therefore has more limited (and specialised) implications than the raw data would suggest. The pattern of agriculture in the region is still overwhelmingly one of family units, and some two-thirds of the labour input on farms in the Highlands comes from occupiers and family labour (Bryden and Houston, 1976, p. 76). Although there is a distinct 'dual' structure, large and small units do not generally stand in the same productive or locational relationship to each other as in the Latifundia-Minifundia, or the Plantation-Peasant farm. Taking all employment based on primary land use[25] it seems likely that under one-fifth is subject to non-Scottish control and a major part of this is represented by Forestry Commission employment.

Problems of external control of land use by those whose objectives sometimes differ substantially from those who are trying to make their living from the land in an area like the Highlands do of course exist, and can be a highly significant factor in some areas.[26] Conflicts can also arise where a publicly owned corporation, like the Forestry Commission, with a national remit becomes a significant agent of change in land use.[27]

This discussion has indicated some of the structural strengths of the Scottish economy relative to other UK regions. However, the degree of non-local control over employment implied by the relatively

K

rapid increase in the degree of dependence on outside investment gives
cause for concern even if, by comparison with other peripheral areas,
the size of the indigenous manufacturing base is still substantial and
multi-national corporations are probably less important. The West
Central Scotland Plan and work by Firn suggest that there may be
linkages between this process and the failure of indigenous entrepreneurship, and clues to links of this kind may be found by an
examination of aspects of functional dependence.

FUNCTIONAL DEPENDENCE

The issue of centralisation is one of great significance for any consideration of functional dependence at the regional level. The institutions of State have, with minor exceptions and qualifications, been
highly centralised since the Union, but the increased significance and
complexity of government has made this fact both more apparent and
more important. It has also no doubt reinforced any centralising
tendencies in the private sector suggested by more conventional spatial
theory. But, whilst the direct effects of these trends on the quality and
range of jobs, on the growth of 'branch plant economy' and the like,
are relatively easy to detect, the indirect and dynamic effects are more
elusive.

The absence of higher order decision-making functions and of research and development activities in Scotland are, for example,
thought to be important factors in explaining the failure of indigenous
entrepreneurship, and therefore an important element in any 'cumulative causation' view of Scottish economic problems. Such a view can
be detected in Firn (1975), in the West Central Scotland Plan (1974,
pp. 125–6), and in Johnston et al. (1971, pp. 212–13) among others.
The importance of central government, which provides roughly half
of the total costs of R. & D. work, and the large number of head
offices of major companies in the south-east of England help explain
the heavy concentration of all forms of research activity in that region.

It has also been suggested that the loss of local control may prevent
capital being switched from declining activities to new opportunities
and new industries.[28] Apart from the possibility that outside concerns
are likely to have greater knowledge of alternative investment opportunities and greater flexibility, through other branch plants and subsidiaries, in investment decisions, there is less 'social' control over
such concerns at the regional level, and possibly a greater chance of
conflicting objectives.

Partly as a consequence of this centralisation (and possibly a cause
of its acceleration), Regional policy aimed at the *stimulation* of industrial *movement*; until 1963 (and, more significantly, the 1972
Industry Act) regional incentives applied only to mobile industry, and

indigenous industry was in this sense positively discriminated against.[29] Moreover, incentives were (and still are) biased against office employment, which has become concentrated in south-east England. Even when the inducements for mobile offices and R. & D. units increased in 1973, these still only amounted to about £1,200 per job created compared with £6,000 to £8,000 for manufacturing jobs (West Central Scotland Plan, 1974, p. 286). Again most of the incentive was *removal grant* which: (a) was independent of distance moved; and (b) did not apply to existing indigenous industry or act as a disincentive to further centralisation on their part.

FISCAL AND MONETARY SYSTEM

It will be clear also that the fiscal and monetary system is highly 'dependent', despite the continued issue of Scottish pound notes. Indeed the scope for independent fiscal action in Scotland is almost entirely limited to local authority rates. Moreover, the revenue raising system in the UK is highly centralised and for all practical purposes all revenue can be viewed as accruing to central government in London, which then decides on the allocation of expenditure. This in itself provides a powerful instrument of control and may increase the feeling of dependence on the centre as compared, for example, with the Swiss system where tax revenues (except border taxes) accrue to the cantons and the arguments seem to be about relatively marginal exchanges between the cantons and Central Government. The entrenched belief (at least in Westminster) in the centralised system in the UK is illustrated by the arguments of the past few years over the revenue-raising powers of the proposed Scottish Assembly – powers which it seems will be practically negligible. On the other hand, the scope for independent fiscal and monetary action in Scotland, even as an independent nation, would no doubt be constrained by other aspects of 'dependence' already discussed and the physical difficulties of border controls.

THE LAW AND CULTURE

Scotland's functional dependence on the UK, so far discussed in terms of the economic system, does of course extend into all areas of life, although it has for historical reasons a distinctive character. The legal system, for example, has been traditionally different in Scotland, being based on Roman law, as compared with the Norman-French basis of the English legal system. However, the differences (which are largely in approach)[30] for example in the laws of contract, of property, of matrimony, as well as in criminal law – have been substantially eroded since the Union of 1707, particularly in the laws relating to public and commercial life.

This erosion seems to have come about in part by accommodating changes in English law and in part by amendments to Scots law or over-riding UK statutes. I do not propose to argue whether these changes have been 'good' or 'bad' – arguments still enjoyed in Scots legal circles – but they imply a loss of *de facto* sovereignty.

In a similar but more limited way, entry into the EEC has led to the imposition of obligations on Member States which will lead to British statutory innovations upon Scots law. These innovations will of course be in fields covered by Treaties – especially the Treaty of Rome itself – which cover important areas of commercial life (customs duties, competition, movement of labour and capital, transport, agriculture being the main ones) but leave the vast bulk of Scots domestic law untouched.[31]

Scots law represents an important focus for a broader cultural identity which, despite the Union, is still an important factor of national life which must have a bearing on the 'dependence' issue. Daiches (1964) has explored the 'paradox' of Scottish culture in a way which illustrates the consequences of the Union of 1707. We see familiar signposts on the road; the schizophrenia of the poet Allan Ramsay, who both used the Scots vernacular to considerable effect and yet displayed attitudes elsewhere which suggested that 'the use of Scots is associated with ignorance of the classics and with cultural parochialism'. Increasingly the centre of gravity for the 'literati' was moving southward. Jacobitism and Scottish nationalism, still powerful forces in the eighteenth century, gradually became 'associated with antiquarianism' and it became unfashionable to extol the (probably largely imaginary) virtues of the pre-Union Scotland through the arts. Again, however, regional differences in Scotland are important. The cultural traditions of the gaelic speaking areas lived on among the people during the eighteenth century despite the collapse of the social and economic system which supported it. The popular revivalist theology which was rooted in these social and economic changes and associated anti-landlordism did however have a considerable, but distinctively Highland, effect on the gaelic culture during the nineteenth century enabling people to 'come to terms with the realities of a social and economic system dominated by landlordism rather than by clanship' (Hunter, 1976, p. 101).

Although the gaelic speaking population has declined, and the differences between the outward manifestations of culture as between the Scots and the English and the Gaels and the Scots have diminished during the nineteenth century and twentieth, there is no doubt that they still exist. Indeed one of the features of the post-war period has been a revival of interest in the Scottish cultural tradition – a revival which was preceded by a minor renaissance of Scottish literature at the hands of Neil Gunn, Hugh MacDiarmid and James Leslie Mitchell

('Lewis Grassie Gibbon'), among others. A similar revival appears to be taking place in the gaelic cultural tradition, stimulated no doubt by the changes in local government (particularly the creation of a single Island Authority for the Western Isles) and perhaps also a greater feeling of optimism for the future in some at least of the gaelic speaking areas. Although, in numerical terms, gaelic is the language of a tiny minority in Scotland – much smaller than prior to the Union – the cultural differences which exist are of some significance for the debates about devolution and nationalism.

EEC IMPACT

Such is the nature of Scottish 'dependency' that one is apt to lose sight of the effect of EEC accession. Perhaps this is because the operation of EEC policies has had very little impact to date. The European Social Fund and the Guidance and Guarantee parts of the Agricultural Fund cannot be regarded as instruments of regional policy, with the possible exception of the funds made available under the Less Favoured Areas Directive. Even in this case, however, the only practical effect has been to transfer a part of the burden of financing existing support schemes from the UK Treasury to Brussels, with some minor modifications *on route*. The EEC Regional Development Fund is the main instrument of EEC regional policy, but is small in size (about £210 million per annum), remote, indirect and intangible in its effects.[32] Once again, arguably, assistance from the RDF has simply transferred a part – and a very small part – of the burden of financing existing regional assistance from the UK Treasury to Brussels. Nothing additional in the way of rates of assistance, and no new initiatives as to the form of assistance or its direction, has so far come from the RDF. On the other side of the coin, some policies – such as transport policy – threaten to have serious negative effects on some peripheral areas where road networks are not – and probably will never be – up to central European standards. Fisheries policy is another problem area so far as Scotland is concerned.

SOME INTERIM CONCLUSIONS

It is difficult to escape the conclusion that when one talks about 'dependence' in the Scottish context one is for the most part talking about the problems of Nationhood and Centralism. Even if the problems of centralism can be partly remedied by devolution, many of the features of dependence will remain as an inevitable consequence of Union. And, even if the Union were dissolved, the structural and functional ties with England, within the EEC, would still remain as a substantial limitation on the 'capacity to manipulate the operative elements of the economic system'.

Even the tentative steps towards a form of legislative devolution are fraught with problems. There is undoubtedly a well entrenched lobby in favour of Centralised government in Britain. Thus the Royal Commission on the Constitution reported that:

> Some people consider that in an advanced industrial society, concentrated in a few relatively small islands, government must necessarily be mainly from the centre. They say that the social and economic life of the country is so closely integrated, and that the issues of government are so complex, that there is little scope for the dispersal of government power.... There is a tendency for the procentralist view to be supported also by trade unionists, partly perhaps because they are themselves largely organised on a national basis. Some think too that the interests of ordinary working people and of under-privileged groups will be better protected by strong central government than by relatively weak regional governments. (Kilbrandon, 1973, para. 291)

The Report also pointed out the importance of notions of equity between citizens including uniformity in public service provision. 'The greater the regional discretion, the less guarantee there will be that citizens will be treated alike in all parts of the country in matters which affect their daily lives' (Kilbrandon, 1973, para. 295). It is, however, not always evident that uniform standards *are* always applied, particularly in remote areas. Even if they are, it is not clear that they are desired or appropriate, and the application of uniform standards to widely differing regional conditions can sometimes have curious – and counter-productive – effects. A good example of this is to be found in housing standards, upon which a recent report on the Island of Barra had this to say: 'The effect of raising ceiling heights and enlarging windows to meet the building regulations (will create a house) of a tolerable standard when it is finished, but at a high cost in materials and to great detriment of its appearance. Is it really necessary to build so high?'[33] On the other hand, the evidence cited earlier on education and migration suggests that, at least in the Highlands and Islands, considerable uniformity of standard is desired.

No firm conclusions can be drawn. Suffice to say that a desire for uniform standards (which may itself be related to cultural, political and economic assimilation) in turn must limit the extent to which regional devolution can effect the definition of the 'good life' and hence the objectives of development.

Recent Policy Initiatives

The establishment of the Highlands and Islands Development Board (HIDB) in 1965 and the Scottish Development Agency (SDA) in 1975 both represent policy initiatives which allow for devolved responsibilities over certain aspects of regional development policy. Neither, with small exceptions (mainly the SDA), replaced any major existing institution of regional policy, and neither, again with a few exceptions, had direct powers in relation to the provision of infrastructure, both being intended to provide additional resources of finance and expertise, and additional specialised powers, in attempts to deal with the distinctive problems of the different parts of Scotland. Although the SDA is an all-Scottish agency, it was established mainly as a result of the West Central Scotland Plan, and clearly recognises the problems of that area as its major responsibility. It also recognises that there is a need to 'concentrate on the problems and opportunities of indigenous industry'.[34] As the Chairman of the Agency has recently said, 'We are really concerned with the indigenous companies where boardroom control, management and research and development are all located in Scotland – and we are vitally interested in the small company.'[35] It is a reasonable assumption that the approach of the SDA will relate closely to the analysis in the West Central Scotland Plan reports, and that its establishment marks a significant change in the approach to development problems in Scotland.

The two principal distinctive features of the HIDB relate to (a) its selectivity or discretion, and (b) its comprehensive approach, both sectorally and in the range of inducements which it can offer. Thus it is involved in all the main economic sectors of the Highland economy – agriculture, fishing, tourism, manufacturing and craft industry – and can help by way of grant, loan, equity, provision of land, buildings and plant, training schemes and advice. It can allocate marginal resources between various sectors or activities, and operate businesses itself. The sheer range of powers, and the flexibility with which they could (at least in theory) be used, were quite unique in the UK and reflected the special nature of Highland problems. As the Board's Chairman has recently pointed out ' . . . it is perhaps only where an economic vacuum exists to be filled that such powers are likely to be awarded to a single agency' (Alexander, 1977).

Even so, the role of the HIDB was necessarily limited, especially in its formative years, by the existence of many other government departments and agencies dealing with different industries or parts of industries, and it took time and patient negotiation to establish a role in some areas, such as fishing and agriculture. However, 'more often than not . . . once the rather different objectives of development *per se* and of (say) agricultural development have been grasped by both parties, an effective working relationship can be established which brings more expertise and resources to the problem than either agency could achieve on its own' (Alexander, 1977).

Nor are the powers of the Board free from control by Central Government. Some of its activities require the approval of the Secretary of State for Scotland or the Treasury, while others are subject to detailed arrangements with Government. This partly explains the comment in Bryden and Houston (1976, p. 139) that '. . . the Board does not only have to identify the "right" programme by technical and economic criteria, it must have adequate contacts, understanding and support at the local level and a strong political presence at national government level.' It is perhaps in the nature of control of this kind that it is more its 'style' rather than its form that matters in practice; a negative style on the part of those responsible can stifle new initiatives, a positive style can encourage them. The very existence of control – even if only budgetary – must however limit the extent to which regional institutions such as the HIDB and the SDA are free to fly in the face of conventionally accepted theory and practice.

In their emphasis on locally orientated development, a comprehensive approach, selectivity, and devolved administrative and executive functions, both the SDA and the HIDB represent a distinct break with the tradition of regional policy within the UK. Proposals for a form of legislative devolution for Scotland are also part of the Government's current programme. Even with these changes, it is clear that Scotland will remain – to a considerable extent – structurally and functionally dependent on the UK. Whether these initiatives will be sufficient to alter fundamentally the structure and performance of the Scottish economy must therefore remain an open question.

Notes

1   It is of course important not to exaggerate the effects of the Union *per se*. The Scottish and English crowns had been unified a century earlier and trading and other links were established before 1707. The Union of Parliaments does however provide a convenient bench mark.
2   See the *West Central Scotland Plan* (1974), p. 14 for detail.
3   The report suggests that immigrant industry accounts for 30 per cent of gross employment increases 1959–68. *loc. cit.* p. 190.
4   Kelp is the collective term for the calcined ashes of a collection of seaweeds. It contained low grade vegetable alkalines which were an important input in the growing Chemical Industry in the eighteenth century and the first part of the nineteenth century.
5   It is true that Highland landowners contributed some £250,000 towards Telford's 18 year road building programme (1803–21) in the region, a further £267,000 being contributed by Government. However, this sum is close to that paid for kelp by one agent alone to different proprietors between 1807 and 1817 and, although aggregate figures for kelp revenue are not available, this sum cannot be reckoned to represent a substantial proportion. See Haldane (1962).
6   The recent debate in the Scottish press on whether the Highlands is a

colony of the UK (sparked off by a booklet by Dr. J. I. Prattis of Carleton University, Ottowa) suggests that there is general agreement in Scotland about the historical relevance of the colonial paradigm to the Highlands and Islands (see *The Scotsman*, 31 August 1977 and subsequent debate). Dr. Prattis's policy proposals are however more contentious.

7   The material for this section has been drawn mainly from the *West Central Scotland Plan* (1974) and the Annual Reports of the Highlands and Islands Development Board (HIDB).

8   Some evidence for productivity in Highland Agriculture is given in Bryden and Houston (1976), ch. 3.

9   The net annual migration rate in the 1950s was of the order of 5·6 per cent – in the 1960s this fell to around 4·9 per cent.

10   Individual industries which accounted for a higher proportion of West Central Scotland employment than of British employment in 1959 and 1968 were Food, drink and tobacco; Metal manufacture; Engineering and electrical goods; Shipbuilding and Marine Engineering; Textiles; Clothing and Footwear; Construction; Distribution and Professional and Scientific services. *West Central Scotland Plan* (1974), p. 129 and Table 3.1.

11   A high proportion of those with six 'O' grades may be assumed to have 'highers' or 'A' grades as well. The data for West Central Scotland are from the Plan report, *op. cit.* p. 111, Table 2.17. The comparable Scottish figures indicate that 55·3 per cent of school-leavers had no qualifications and 27·5 per cent had two or more highers.

12   Parental expectation may of course differ markedly, partly due to the class structure and rural/urban differences.

13   Johnston *et al.* (1971, p. 64) suggest that personal incomes per head in Scotland declined from 90 per cent of the UK average in 1954/5 to 86·5 per cent in 1967/8.

14   In 1964/5 the average income per tax paying unit in the Highlands and Islands was some two-thirds of the UK average and 80 per cent of the Scottish average. This is remarkably close to Collier's estimate for 1938 which, on the basis of estimates of income by source, suggested that income per head in the Highlands and Islands was about two-thirds of that of the country as a whole (Collier, 1953). These difficulties were not solely due to the greater relative importance of agriculture in the Highland economy, as the average income per head in agriculture is also around 20–25 per cent below the Scottish average (Bryden and Houston, 1976, p. 10).

15   Average weekly earnings (per man employed) in 1969 were 97 per cent of the UK figure in Scotland and 93 per cent in the Highlands (HIDB Annual Reports).

16   See the *West Central Scotland Plan* (1974, pp. 341–2).

17   Like all analytical devices, this distinction is probably artificial. As Brewster points out, 'Economic dependence may be defined as a lack of capacity to manipulate the operative elements of an economic system. Such a situation is characterised by an absence of inter-dependence between the economic functions of a system. This lack of inter-dependence implies that the system has no internal dynamic which could enable it to function as an independent, autonomous entity.' Brewster (1971), cited in Girvan, N: *Social and Economic Studies*, Vol. 22, No. 1, March 1973.

18   It goes without saying that the North Sea Oil issue is of fundamental importance to the economic, social and political situation in Scotland today. I have not, however, dealt with this aspect of the Scottish scene in any

depth as it has been well covered elsewhere – for example in IDS (Communication 21) (1977), MacKay and MacKay (1975), and MacKay (1977).

19 See also the Scottish Economic Bulletin, No. 7, February 1975. A Department of Industry Survey of non-construction oil-related employment in Scotland concluded that of the total 24,000 job opportunities created by 1973/4 'it would seem unlikely that more than about 18,000 . . . represent net additional employment' (p. 11).

20 Education and Health accounted for some 280,000 jobs in Scotland and National and Local Government administration a further 145,000 in 1974. Total non-manufacturing sector employment was 1,418,000. The bulk of the remaining public sector employment is in the nationalised industries of Gas, Electricity and Water, Railways, Postal Services and Communications, and Coal Mining. Scottish Abstract of Statistics, No. 5/1975, HMSO, Table 99.

21 The Scottish Office is the collective name for the departments of the Secretary of State for Scotland. The office of Secretary of State was created in 1885, the first Scottish Office being established in London! This moved to Edinburgh in 1928. A further reorganisation in 1939 provided the basis of the present departmental structure.

22 Kilbrandon (1973) made the startling discovery that half of those surveyed in Scotland had not heard of the Scottish Office (p. 116).

23 Some data for Scotland have recently been published in McEwen (1977).

24 In the case of both the Forestry Commission (in Scotland) and DAFS, the land is in the titular ownership of the Secretary of State for Scotland.

25 That is, employment in Agriculture, Forestry, and Land and Estate Management (including sporting).

26 Proposals for legislative changes which will enable the HIDB to deal with some of these problems are to be made to the Secretary of State by the end of 1977. See also Occasional Bulletin No. 7: Highland Agriculture and Land Use, Highlands and Islands Development Board, 1977; and Bryden and Houston (1976, p. 70, pp. 124–9).

27 Of a net loss of agricultural land in the Highlands and Islands amounting to 212,293 acres between 1965 and 1974, forestry accounted for 210,523 acres. Bryden and Houston (1976, p. 58).

28 See also the West Central Scotland Plan (1974, p. 14).

29 It is of passing interest that there was a similar de facto bias in respect of tourism investments in the Caribbean during the 1960s. See Bryden (1973, p. 220).

30 The differences in approach are perhaps summarised briefly by stating that Scots lawyers pride themselves on basing decision on a priori principles in precedence to the facts of a particular case, while the English system tends to approach decisions first from the facts of a particular case, and only secondarily from principles.

31 This argument has been put by the Rt. Hon. Lord Emslie (Lord President of the Court of Session in Scotland) in an unpublished address to a Sheriff's Conference, September 1972.

32 See also the evidence of the Highlands and Islands Development Board to the joint parliamentary committee of the Houses of Lords and Commons. House of Lords Select Committee on the European Communities Thirteenth Report 1976–7. EEC Regional Policy pp. 52–63, and House of Commons Paper 41 – xiii and 76 – i – iii pp. 32–43.

33 Housing Improvement Surveys, Barra, 1972. Department of Architecture

and Building Science, University of Strathclyde. HIDB Special Report 12, 1974.

34 The *West Central Scotland Plan* recommended the establishment of a para-government agency, 'accountable to but acting at arms length from Civil Service Departments and their Ministers'. The reasons are given on pp. 263–4 of Supplementary Report 1. *op. cit.*

35 Quoted in *The Scotsman*, Supplement on the SDA, October 28 1977.

References

Alexander, K. J. W. (1977), *The Highlands and Islands Development Board. Characteristics, Aims and Policies*, Paper to a Symposium on the Future of Upland Britain. Centre for Agricultural Strategy, Reading University.

Brown, J. (ed.) (1975), *The Red Paper on Scotland*, EUSPB, Edinburgh.

Bryden, J. (1973), *Tourism and Development*, Cambridge University Press.

Bryden, J., and Houston, G. (1976), *Agrarian Change in the Scottish Highlands*, Martin Robertson, London.

Collier, A. (1953), *The Crofting Problem*, Cambridge University Press.

Daiches, D. (1964), *The Paradox of Scottish Culture*, Oxford University Press.

Demas, W. (1965), *The Economics of Development in Small Countries with Special Reference to the Caribbean.* McGill, Canada.

Firn, J. (1975), *External Control and Regional Policy*, in Brown (1975).

Haldane, A. R. B. (1962), *New Ways Through the Glens*, David and Charles Edition 1973, Newton Abbot.

Hunter, J. (1976), *The Making of the Crofting Community*, John Donald, Edinburgh.

M.Phil Faculty and Students (1977), *North Sea Oil: The Application of Development Theories.* IDS Communication 121, Brighton: University of Sussex.

Johnston, T. L., Buxton, N. K., Mair, D. (1971), *Structure and Growth of the Scottish Economy*, Collins 1971, London.

Kilbrandon (1973), *Royal Commission on the Constitution 1969–1973*, Vol. 1. Report. HMSO.

McEwen, J. (1977), *Who Owns Scotland?* EUSPB.

MacKay, D. I., and Mackay, G. A. (1975), *The Political Economy of North Sea Oil*, Martin Robertson, London.

MacKay, D. I. (1977), in MacKay (ed.) *Scotland 1980*, Q Press (Edinburgh).

McIntyre, A. (1964), *Some Issues in Trade Policy in the West Indies*, University of the West Indies.

McNicoll, I. H. (1976), *The Shetland Economy*, Research Monograph No. 2, University of Strathclyde.

—— *Quarterly Economic Commentary* (1977), Vol. 3, 1. Fraser of Allander Institute, University of Strathclyde.

Sewel, J., Peel, L., Gaskin, M., Nisbet, J. (1976), 'Education and Migration', *Highlands and Islands Development Board.*

West Central Scotland Plan Report (1974), *Supplementary Report 1: The Regional Economy.*

Youngson, A. J. (1973), *After the Forty-Five*, Edinburgh.

14

FINLAND IN THE INTERNATIONAL DIVISION OF LABOUR*

Kimmo Kiljunen

Is Finland a periphery, not only geographically being the northernmost country in the world, but socially and economically? Obviously, dependence on external factors has crucially influenced the forms of evolution of each national economy. That is not least true for Finland, a small society situated at the crossroads of different civilisations and social systems. But the question forced on us is the historical roots of external determination, the roles of each actor in the international system and how external impacts are adapted by certain kinds of internal conditions.

Hence, in order to look at the nature of economic development in Finland in general, and the question of its peripheralisation in particular, it is necessary to illuminate the dual position of the country in the international division of labour, the structural dependence of the economy on the European core and the consequent effects on its internal development. Ultimately the aim is to characterise the specific form of peripheralisation of Finland in European social and economic development.

For almost 700 years, up to the beginning of the nineteenth century, Finland was part of the semi-feudal agrarian periphery of Sweden. Over 80 per cent of the population earned their living from agriculture, fishing or hunting. Productivity was low and the heavy taxes and manpower levies impoverished the rural population; about one tenth of the male population were soldiers. Growth was considerably slower than in the Swedish core areas. Output and unemployment in the manufacturing and handicrafts production was only 5 per cent of the totals for Sweden as a whole. Domestic demand was small, there were few subsidies or army contracts and production had to compete with Swedish manufacturing. In practice there was no external trade, for imports and exports passed primarily through Stockholm. The economic position of Finland was thus conditioned by what we would now

* I am grateful to Professors Dudley Seers and Hans Singer for their valuable comments on an earlier draft.

call asymmetric dependence relations (see Linnamo, 1967, pp. 4–9; Jutikkala 1968, p. 206, and Wuorinen, 1965).

In 1809 Finland became part of Russia, though many traditional commercial and cultural links with Sweden remained for a long time almost unchanged. Finland was not incorporated into the Russian Empire as one of its provinces, but as an autonomous Grand Duchy governed by Finns. The Constitution, including the judiciary and civil administration were not the same as in Russia, but mainly an inheritance from the Swedish period. An independent fiscal system with a separate customs boundary were unique within the Russian Empire.

Finland's altered political status made feasible independent economic development. The network of one-sided dependence relationships with Sweden was broken up. The capital of the Russian Empire was near the Finnish border opening up new markets for Finnish exports. Whereas in relation to Sweden Finland had been peripheral, it was now one of the developed areas of the Russian feudal empire, providing possibilities for growth and diversification of the Finnish economy.

There was little sign of progress, however, in the early years of Russian rule. Years of crop failures caused setbacks to the whole economy. There was a modest beginning of industrialisation – iron, textiles, glass and tobacco factories had emerged. The demand for tar in the international market declined with the passing of sailing ships.[1] Mercantile rules, privileges and monopolies still limited foreign trade and the development of the economy. Moreover, feudal Russia protected her markets against Finnish exports, while Russian commodities enjoyed free access to Finnish markets reflecting the subordinate political status of Finland.

The Start of Industrialisation

From the 1860s up to the end of the century rapid structural changes occurred in the Finnish economy, reflecting the turn in the external relations. A decisive factor was the rapidly increased demand for wood in Western Europe, as a result of deforestation, due to extensive industrialisation and urbanisation. The fall in transport costs after the introduction of steamships, made the utilisation of the abundant wood resources of Finland commercially profitable. A lot of foreign capital (especially German and Swedish) was invested in the first large-scale saw mills, and pulp and paper factories. Apart from Finns, several Swedish, English and Norwegian entrepreneurs helped the new industry (Tandem, 1977, p. 79 and Alho, 1949).

Also during the 1860s and 1870s traditional Finnish textiles, leather, glass and metal industries substantially increased their share of the

Russian markets. Finnish commodities enjoyed a privileged position *vis-à-vis* foreign competitors because of the tariff advantages granted in the 1860s. This offered protected markets for the new vulnerable industrial enterprises, including metal engineering, textile and later paper industries. Raw materials, such as iron ore, base metals, cotton, etc., were imported, processed in Finland and then sold to Russia. Besides domestic capital, considerable amounts of Russian, Swedish and British capital were invested in those branches of the industry (Pihkala, 1969, pp. 32–3, and Alho, 1949).

The Finnish government sponsored in many ways the start of the industrialisation process. A new joint-stock Company Act was enacted. 'Monetary independence' stimulated the development of banking and credit. State loans at low interest rates were also granted to aid new industrial enterprise. New tariff laws reduced the foreign trade restrictions and ended duties on grain and several raw materials, including cotton. Ultimately all the remaining restrictions on economic enterprise were eliminated in 1879. Canals, roads and the first railways were built and postal communications modernised. All these changes paved the way for the structural change of the Finnish economy.

However, from the beginning, Finnish industrialisation has been determined and conditioned by external factors. During the 1870s, 60 per cent of all products produced by the metal and engineering industry were exported to Russia, and over two-thirds of the textile industry products. Practically all forest industry products as well were exported, but to Western Europe. It is estimated that in the mid-1870s some 85 per cent of Finland's total industrial production went abroad (Jutikkala, 1968, pp. 212, 214).

External dependence started, however, decreasing. By 1899 only 50 per cent of the total industrial production was exported: textiles and the metal and engineering industries provided goods mainly for the home market. In 1913 only 10 per cent of the textile industry products and 9 per cent of the metal industry products were exported (Jutikkala, 1967, pp. 86–7). There were obvious reasons for that. First, there was a substantial increase of domestic demand in Finland. Industrialisation itself gradually broke down traditional social relations of the subsistence economy. In particular, the development of the forestry industry generated an extra flow of income into rural areas, especially for landholders.

Secondly, in the middle of the 1880s trade with Russia was restricted again. Finnish products were to be treated in Russian markets like other foreign products. This change decisively influenced the composition of Finland's external trade and industrialisation. During the 1870s Russia had taken one half of Finland's exports whereas thirty years later a little over one quarter of the exports went there. In a similar way imports from Russia decreased though not so rapidly (see Table 44). Instead Finland was increasingly bound to the Western European markets. Great Britain became the most important export market while Germany became by far the most significant source of imports.

Table 44

Finnish foreign trade in 1870–1910 (%)

Exports	1870 World*	1870 Russia	1890 World*	1890 Russia	1910 World*	1910 Russia
Agriculture	37	31	31	27	17	18
Forestry	5	2	6	5	11	7
Sawn timber	47	2	55	2	61	8
Paper industry	0	5	3	21	9	39
Textile industry	0	26	0	13	0	10
Chemical industry (tar)	9	1	4	0	0	0
Metal industry	0	24	1	16	0	5
Others	2	9	0	16	2	13
TOTAL	100	100	100	100	100	100

Imports	1870 World*	1870 Russia	1890 World*	1890 Russia	1910 World*	1910 Russia
Foodstuffs	39	40	35	53	35	59
Raw materials	15	9	15	6	15	4
Fuels and lubricants	4	0	2	3	3	5
Semi-manufactured goods	26	14	23	9	21	16
Investment goods	3	0	9	1	8	1
Consumption goods	13	37	16	28	18	15
TOTAL	100	100	100	100	100	100

Direction	Exports	Imports	Exports	Imports	Exports	Imports
Russia	52	42	39	33	27	29
Great Britain	18	11	18	15	30	22
Germany	8	21	7	32	12	42
Sweden	9	11	8	8	5	5
Others	13	15	28	12	26	2
TOTAL	100	100	100	100	100	100

Sources: Erkki Pihkala (1969), *Finland's Foreign Trade 1860–1917*,
Publications of Bank of Finland, Helsinki.
* Except Russia.

More important than the direction of the trade was the change that occurred in its composition. The range of exports became narrower and the share of processed products decreased as ties with Western Europe increased. The growth of the metal and textile industries stopped. Only the paper industry was capable of expanding its market share and began to dominate the Russian trade (see Table 44). Before the First World War raw timber and sawn goods constituted three-quarters of the total exports. The rest was mainly dairy products (butter). On the imports side there was growing dependence on western manufactured products, especially investment goods, as industrialisation expanded. The Finnish economy had in large part lost the opportunity of diversified, self-reliant industrialisation.

The whole economic development in Finland consequently became vulnerable to the fluctuations of the international economy. Earlier, the only economic cycles were generated by domestic harvests. Since the 1870s, however, cyclical variations have taken place in the foreign trade, causing severe instabilities in economic development. The expansion of trade relations with the European core countries also caused the balance of payments to move into deficit. As long as the Russian trade was dominant, the Finnish trade balance was positive, but after the 1890s it was in chronic deficit, especially with Germany. The current account was balanced by foreign investments (especially from Russia) and by remittances of migrants as well as by foreign loans (Alho, 1949, pp. 61–2, and Pihkala, 1969, p. 54).

The low level of diversification and almost complete export orientation of the Finnish industrialisation led to heavy concentration in the leading industries. International slumps eliminated weak export enterprises. Competitiveness and stable development required large-scale production and common pricing policy. Already by the end of the nineteenth century the most important exports of Finland were in the hands of a few companies, which have continued to dominate the economic development of the country. A few financial groups were developed to finance exports and around them nearly all the largest private enterprises have been grouped.

Spatial concentration has also increased. The beginnings of manufacturing were scattered around the whole country, usually near to the source of raw materials. The use of steam instead of water power made it, however, possible to locate saw-mills, pulp and paper industries on the coast while the lakes and rivers offered efficient low-cost transportation of logs to the mills. Hence the centre of gravity of industrialisation focussed on southern and south-western coastal areas, closer to export markets, causing, in the long run, severe regional disparities.

Though industrial production grew at a rapid rate until the beginning of the First World War, Finland remained predominantly agrarian. The share of the working population making their living from agriculture had decreased from 85 per cent in 1870 to 70 per cent in 1910 (see Table 48), but manufacturing was not able to absorb more than 12 per cent. The landless population had been increasing, and approximately half of the rural population owned no land, one-third were tenants who cultivated land under various lease arrangements and only some 20 per cent were landowners.

The population pressure was relieved by emigration. Before the last decades of the nineteenth century no significant emigration had

taken place. During the 1880s and 1890s some 2,000 people emigrated annually. Thereafter the number grew rapidly. During the years 1900–15 the annual average was about 15,000. Estimates indicated that over 200,000 people had emigrated by 1920 or 6 per cent of the total population, mostly to the US (Wuorinen, 1965, pp. 197–8).

The First World War broke the economic links to the European core. During the years 1915–17 Finnish foreign trade took place almost entirely with Russia. Finnish domestic industry, especially metal and engineering, but also textiles and leather, received from Russia as many army contracts as they could carry out. Also their position in the domestic market strengthened as competition from imports stopped (see Jutikkala, 1968, p. 215, and Pihkala, 1969, pp. 46 and 54). But there was soon a total collapse of economic relations between the two countries, lasting for over a quarter of a century.

Dependent Growth

Finland's political independence was declared in 1917. The result of the civil war in 1918, in which the socialists were defeated, defined the course of economic policy and the pattern of development in the new republic. Agreements on commercial and economic collaboration, that were virtually semi-colonial were made with the Germans, who had occupied the southern parts of Finland during the civil war. The result of the First World War was that instead of becoming a 'colony' of one dominant power, Finland became part of the Western European periphery.

During the interwar period Finland's role in the international division of labour was established. It was conditioned to produce raw and semi-processed wood for export while becoming a market area for central European trading operations. Independence had created formal conditions for a national tariff and foreign exchange policy, but the external transactions of a small open economy became determined by decisions made in the core areas, and international market forces.

Economic growth in Finland was highly dependent on foreign trade. Most investment goods as well as raw materials were imported. Half of the food came from abroad during the 1920s.[2] Trade was predominantly with the western European countries. Finland became part of the sterling area, reflecting its most dominant export relations. In 1933 the Finnish mark was officially tied to sterling and a number of bilateral trade agreements were concluded. For instance free access of wood products into the British markets was gained by offering considerable tariff advantages for British industrial products in Finland (Tuomioja, 1971, pp. 97–8, and Oksanen-Pihkala, 1975).

The export sector was extremely narrow and little diversified.

Wood industry products constituted between 85–95 per cent of total exports. Hence, forestry has been the crucial sector determining the essence of the development in the whole economy. By its nature, it is externally oriented, wholly dependent on foreign markets and has relatively few linkages with other sectors of the economy. In fact the wood-based industry has developed like an external enclave. Its interests in tariff and foreign trade policy and its dominance in national production has rather jeopardised diversification and increased the openness and vulnerability of the Finnish economy in relation to the European core.

The almost complete decline in trade with the Soviet Union (see Table 45) was the main reason why the range of exports narrowed. Manufactured products had previously been sold in the East. The small size of the economy and foreign competition made import substitution difficult. The government sought to promote it for reasons of foreign exchange, employment and defence, but the interests of the export industry frequently carried more weight in short-term policy considerations.

Table 45

Finnish foreign trade in 1920–38 (%)

Exports	1920	1930	1938
Agriculture	3	12	10
Forestry	6	8	9
Sawn timber	50	41	31
Paper industry	37	35	42
Textile industry	0	1	1
Chemical industry	1	1	1
Metal industry	1	1	4
Others	2	1	2
TOTAL	100	100	100

Imports	1920	1930	1938
Foodstuffs	33	27	15
Raw materials and semi-manufactured	41	42	43
Fuels and lubricants	6	9	10
Investment goods	9	9	16
Consumption goods	11	13	16
TOTAL	100	100	100

Direction	Exports	Imports	Exports	Imports	Exports	Imports
Soviet Union	1	0	4	3	1	1
Great Britain	43	27	40	14	45	22
Germany	5	17	12	37	15	20
United States	7	22	8	12	9	9
Sweden	6	6	3	8	6	15
Others	38	28	33	26	24	33
TOTAL	100	100	100	100	100	100

Sources: Heikki, Oksanen and Erkki Pihkala (1975),
　　　　　Finland's Foreign Trade 1917–1949,
　　　　　Bank of Finland Publications, Helsinki.

During the twenty years between the World Wars, economic growth in Finland, based mainly on industrialisation was very rapid. By the end of the 1930s the volume of industrial production was 300 per cent higher than twenty years earlier – one of the highest growth rates in the world. The corresponding figure for Europe, was on average 80 per cent. Reflecting rapid industrialisation the import of investment goods was exceptionally large during the latter half of the 1930s (see Table 45). Capital accumulation was predominantly in Finnish hands, for after independence the strategic mining and forestry sectors were taken into national ownership. But dependence on foreign capital increased during the process of industrialisation. The shortage of domestic capital led to foreign loans from international banks mainly German and British.

Heavy investment in the export sector explains strong economic growth. The demand for forestry products in the European markets was steadily increasing. Though it was sensitive to cyclical changes – the demand for sawn timber is affected by booms in construction – the general price trend was favourable. During the cyclical downswings, import prices usually fell more swiftly than export prices, and hence the terms of trade to Finnish industry tended to improve. This is partly explained by the Scandinavian cartels created by Nordic paper and pulp producers in the 1930s, through which markets have been shared, production quotas defined and price competition eliminated (Oksanen-Pihkala, 1975, p. 19 and Kosonen, 1976, pp. 75–6). Oligopolistic pricing policy has given the forestry industry stable returns to capital and preconditions for further expansion.

Domestic cost factors also favoured expansion of the forestry industry. Raw timber was still relatively cheap. In the rural areas there was always cheap surplus labour. The labour movement was politically and organisationally weak and, consequently the general Finnish wage level remained lower than that of other Scandinavian or west European countries.

As a result of the strong economic growth during the 1920s and 1930s industrial unemployment was quite marginal – except during the Great Depression. On the other hand, there was latent unemployment in the rural areas. The extensive land reform programme during the period 1918–35 eliminated the group of leaseholders and landless population by creating nearly 150,000 new independent smallholdings. This slowed down the rate of urbanisation and structural change in the economy. Agriculture still employed 60 per cent of the population (see Table 48).[3] The structural change of the Finnish economy was slow and painful due to the one-sided, though intensive, growth of the industrial sector.

Finnish - Soviet Economic Relations

The Second World War reorganised Finland's position in the international system both politically and consequently also economically. Twice Finland was at war with the Soviet Union; the second time joining the German invasion of Russia. After the war Finnish security policy was reshaped. Instead of standing as an outmost western bulwark against the East, Finland began to take into consideration the security interests of the Soviet Union in its north-west frontier, culminating in 1948 in the Treaty of Friendship, Co-operation and Mutual Assistance with the Soviet Union. The treaty has since become the basis for improvements in mutual political, cultural and economic intercourse. The general foreign policy of Finland emphasises neutrality and non-alignment, giving the country the role of a bridge-builder between East and West. This has also offered an opportunity for changing Finland's traditional role in the international division of labour.

Finland was obliged to pay war reparations during the 1945–52 period in the form of commodity deliveries; 74 per cent of the reparations goods consisted of the products of shipbuilding, machinery and the metal industries; the rest were paper industry products.[4] Despite the fact that war indemnities were a heavy economic burden during the post-war reconstruction period, in the long run they greatly assisted the diversification of Finnish industry and formed the basis of renewed trade with the Soviet Union.

In 1947 a commercial agreement was signed, under which most-favoured-nation treatment would be applied in Finnish-Soviet trade. Three years later the first Finnish-Soviet five-year trade and payments agreement was signed. Since the mid-1950s intergovernmental scientific, technical and economic agreements and commissions have been established and finally in 1977 a long-term (fifteen-year) framework of trade was agreed. During the 'cold war' Western countries froze their economic relations with the socialist countries with a trade embargo, but Finland did not take part. Consequently Finnish industry faced little competition in the Soviet market and was, up to the end of the 1960s, its main western trade partner; even today it is the third largest, after West Germany and Japan. This pioneering role has provided many advantages (see Hakovirta-Patokallio, 1975).

Firstly, Finnish-Soviet trade takes place through barter agreements planned for a five-year period. The bilateral nature of the trade has meant a balance between imports and exports – a deficit in one year can be adjusted in the next. This saves foreign currency and creates no balance of payment problems, though the trade takes place at world market prices. Thus, the oil crisis did not affect Finland's balance of payments directly. Moreover, the planning of long-term deliveries has made economic development more steady.

Secondly, Soviet trade has alleviated the cyclical fluctuations in Finland's foreign trade and economic development. During upswings, exports to the West have typically increased, matched by decreases to the East: during cyclical downswings when the trade to the European core faces difficulties, Finnish industry has searched for new outlets in the Soviet Union (Hemmilä-Koponen, 1975, p. 58). Consequently during the present recession the Soviet share has substantially increased in Finland's foreign trade.

Thirdly, the composition of trade has been as favourable for Finland as during the nineteenth century (see Table 47). Typically in an infant phase of a production cycle the new industries have been nurtured in the protective environment of bilateral trade, but when the product is competitive enough, export is directed into Western markets. Built up to pay reparations, the expanding Finnish metal and engineering industry has been able to secure export markets in the Soviet Union. Also, paper, textiles and 'new exports' such as furniture, have increasingly penetrated Soviet markets during the past ten years. Moreover, sections of the metal industry, the whole of the textile industry and most of the 'new exports' are labour-intensive in contrast to the traditional capital-intensive character of Finnish exports. Employment considerations have been very apparent in the intergovernmental joint ventures in which the Finns are offering not only knowhow, technical expertise and key equipment, but also labour for building industrial and mining complexes on Soviet soil. These works have mainly taken place in the border areas and relieved the endemic unemployment situation in those undeveloped eastern parts of Finland.

While Finland is exporting highly processed manufactured products, four-fifths of the imports from the Soviet Union have constituted from primary products, mainly fuels (see Table 47). The biggest obstacle to expanding Finnish exports has been the lack of demand in Finland for Soviet manufactures. All in all, Finnish-Soviet economic relations have been highly asymmetric. This has provided Finnish industry, and thus the economy, a sort of core position in this particular section on the international division of labour.

During the 1950s, the share of the Soviet Union in Finland's total trade was on average 20 per cent. Since then, the long-term trend has declined, the share reaching 12 per cent at the beginning of the 1970s. In spite of obvious advantages and efforts by the government to set up institutional frames for economic co-operation with the Soviet Union, the dominant and most dynamic economic relations have been with

Western Europe. The Finnish economy is structurally tied to the European core and the interests of the dominant sectors have demanded that these ties be strengthened.

Integration to the European Core

The main strategy of Finnish post-war foreign trade policy has been to liberalise Western trade and improve the competitiveness of the export industry in European markets. At the same time, there have been obvious limits on commercial integration into the west, because of the fundamental goals of foreign policy to preserve neutrality and national security. In 1947, Finland refused Marshall Aid when it became clear that the plan had generated an interbloc controversy. As a consequence, it was left out of the OEEC and it stayed out of the Council of Europe, both of which were important integrating institutions in Western Europe. But Finland joined IBRD and IMF in 1948 and a year later GATT. Consequently, throughout the 1950s, import tariffs were reduced and finally in 1957 import regulation and licensing were abolished. The abolition of passport control inside Scandinavia and the creation of the Pan Nordic Labour Market in 1954 eliminated barriers to Scandinavian labour mobility. The commercial integration into the west was continued in 1961 by Finland's association with EFTA. The most-favoured-nation status in Finnish-Soviet trade was reaffirmed indicating Finland's aspiration to equality. However, the tariff advantages for EFTA countries were more significant than for the Soviet Union, whose imports consisted mainly of tariff-free primary products.

In 1968, Finland officially joined OECD and started to carry out the recommendations of the organisation to free movements of capital and to make international investments easier. Ultimately, in 1973, Finland signed a free trade agreement with the EEC, though there is no 'development paragraph' in the agreement that would anticipate closer forms of economic or political integration in the future. Soon afterwards, an agreement was made on trade and technical co-operation with the CMEA. These agreements taken together demonstrate Finland's role as a bridge-builder in East–West economic co-operation and its resolute efforts to keep neutral and thus safeguard national security.

However, besides defensive security interests, offensive economic interests have promoted this whole series of institutional frameworks for external economic interactions. It is evident that the driving force in the Finnish trade liberalisation policy has been the dominant forestry-based exporting industry. The country has remained as the leading source of semi-manufactured wood products for the European core[5] and an open market area for multinational trading operations. The economy has performed reasonably well in terms of average growth rate figures and improvements in general welfare. However, the asymmetric commercial, financial and technical dependencies on the European core have generated severe social, structural and regional problems in the development of Finland.

Trade and Financial Dependence

A small developed industrialised country is typically greatly dependent on foreign trade and has a specialised export structure. In the Finnish case, too, foreign trade accounts for about a quarter of GNP and exports have focussed on a few specialised industrial products. However, the structure of Finnish exports differs from those of other small industrialised countries (technically advanced products with a high added value), being mainly concentrated on semi-manufactured product (Western Europe) and on heavy engineering goods (Soviet Union).

Despite the gradual diversification of Finnish exports during the post-war years, still in the 1970s, over half of the exports are from the wood, paper and pulp industry. The forest industry has increased its processing capacity and hence the composition of exports has shifted away from raw and sawn timber towards semi-manufactured pulp, newsprint and paper products (see Table 46). The main markets for the forest industry have traditionally been in Western Europe; the leading one being Great Britain, where over 80 per cent of Finnish exports still constitute processed wood products.

In the reconstruction years after the Second World War the Finnish economy had the opportunity to develop more self-reliant industrialisation and substantial diversification. The reconstruction of the industrial basis took place in the protected framework of a closed economy, and of a new barter-based Soviet trade. For building up new industries, the necessary credits and capital were, however, obtained from the West, predominantly from Sweden and the United States. Even though Finland did not apply for Marshall Aid, the Americans had granted by 1952 over $150 million in credits. The US Export-Import Bank loans were directed especially to setting up the forestry-based export industry. From 1949 up to 1968 Finland received loans of some $220 million through the World Bank, predominantly for the development of the wood processing industry and for infrastructural construction such as power-stations and roads. The apparent aim has been to reinforce the traditional production structure based on exports to the West. During the 1950s the World Bank refused to finance the metal industry on the grounds that it was unprofitable (Wuorinen 1965, p. 468, Maude 1976, p. 110 and Kosonen, 1976, p. 89).

Table 46

Finnish foreign trade in 1950–70 (%)

Exports	1950	1960	1970
Agriculture	4	5	4
Forestry	10	7	1
Sawn timber	35	27	16
Paper industry	42	42	39
Textile industry	1	1	7
Metal industry	5	14	25
Others	3	4	8
TOTAL	100	100	100

Imports			
Foodstuffs	21	11	9
Raw materials and semi-manufactured	42	42	39
Fuels and lubricants	11	10	11
Investment goods	14	27	26
Consumption goods	12	10	15
TOTAL	100	100	100

Direction	Exports	Imports	Exports	Imports	Exports	Imports
Soviet Union	8	6	14	14	13	13
Great Britain	22	16	24	13	17	13
West Germany	6	6	12	20	11	17
US	10	6	5	6	5	5
Sweden	4	6	4	10	15	16
Others	50	60	41	37	39	36
TOTAL	100	100	100	100	100	100

Sources: Oksanen and Pihkala (1975), *Finland's Foreign Trade 1917–1949*, Helsinki.
UN Yearbook of International Trade Statistics 1950–1970.

Table 47

The composition of Finland's trade with the main partners in 1970 (%)

	Soviet Union	Great Britain	West Germany	Sweden
Exports				
Agriculture	7	6	6	7
Forestry	0	1	1	1
Sawn timber	0	34	14	6
Paper industry	34	47	51	5
Textile industry	6	3	1	18
Metal industry	50	4	19	43
Others	3	5	8	20
TOTAL	100	100	100	100
Imports				
Foodstuffs	7	2	1	2
Raw materials	15	5	2	4
Fuels and lubricants	60	2	1	2
Semi-manufactured goods	13	43	38	36
Investment goods	3	27	40	32
Consumption goods	2	21	18	24
TOTAL	100	100	100	100

Sources: OECD, Statistics of Foreign Trade, Trade by Commodities, Series C
Year 1970.

Since the gradual opening of the economy at the end of the 1950s, the composition and direction of the Finnish trade have changed. The export share of the gross production of the industry doubled during the 1960s. Besides the forest industry, the metal and textile industries in particular were able to increase their exports. The diversification of exports has not, however, been the result of restructuring traditional trade relations with Western Europe, but, rather opening up new markets, mainly in the Soviet Union and Scandinavia (see Tables 46 and 47). The exceptionally rapid increase of Finnish exports to Sweden during the 1960s and its diversified composition has partly been the result of the intensive investments of the Swedish textile industry in Finland and increased subcontracting relations between the Finnish and Swedish engineering industries. Hence, though diversified, this type of export has been asymmetric and dependent in its nature.

The increasing openness of the Finnish economy and its participation in the European integration has contributed to the gradual concentration of industrial capital, rationalisation of production and narrowed production structure. Increased and free import of foreign manufactures challenges the position of the domestic small-scale industrial production.[6] Even entire industrial branches, such as textiles, leather, ceramics and glass industries have encountered great problems during the 1970s. Correspondingly the degree of concentration in Finland's industrial production is now very high by international standards.[7]

After the foreign trade liberalisation the deficit of balance of payments has become a chronic problem combined with increasing overseas indebtedness. In the post-war years there were only three years (1958 and 1968–9) when, after big devaluations, the current balance was positive. In 1975 the current account deficit stood at $2·2 billion or some 8 per cent of GNP, which was one of the highest recorded in the OECD area (OECD, 1977, p. 15).[8]

The main unbalancing factor has been the constant trade deficit. Finland's less diversified and undeveloped production structure has not been able to compete in open markets against other European economies. The volume of Finland's exports increased yearly in the period 1960–75 by 4·5 per cent, while the average in the whole OECD area was 7·2 per cent. The weak export performance is a consequence of the concentration of export production on a few, slow growing and cyclically sensitive sectors and its direction into slow-growth countries (UK, Sweden) (Komiteanmietintö, 1976, pp. 3–6).

Imports were controlled up to 1957 but since then have increased rapidly. The relative importance of the balanced Finnish–Soviet trade has declined. The demand for technically advanced investment and consumer goods has been more and more satisfied by imports from the

European core countries (see Tables 46 and 47). The strongest core country, West Germany, has been the biggest exporter to Finland, but also Swedish and Japanese imports have contributed to the severe deterioration in the Finnish trade balance. Some 10 per cent of private consumption is satisfied by importing consumer goods. In investment goods on average 60 per cent are imported. Similarly foreign raw materials and semi-manufactured products constitute some 40 per cent of industrial inputs.[9]

In the short term the deficit in the current account has been filled by importing capital. Hence the trade dependence in terms of the trade deficit results also in financial dependence. At the end of the 1950s Finland's long-term foreign debt was 2 per cent of GDP, in 1965 8 per cent and in 1976 already 22 per cent (Central Statistical Office, 1977, p. 21). Besides the economic burden of increased debt service payments, the economic policy of the country is conditioned by foreign loans. The clearest examples are the loans from the IMF which have imposed restrictions directly on economic policy.

Between 1945 and 1977 there have been nine devaluations in Finland, one of the highest figures in Europe. Frequently, exchange rate changes have taken place in connection with the devaluations of the core currencies (Sterling, Swedish krona). The purpose of the repeated devaluations has been to maintain and restore the competitiveness of the dominant export industries, instead of a consistent policy of import substitution. However, because of the oligopolistic nature of the international market for forest-based products, the Finnish forest industry has not increased its competitiveness by reducing prices, but rather, has acted as a 'price-taker', and thus benefitted in full from the short-term profit potential of a devaluation. This has been one reason why Finnish devaluations have been relatively successful in achieving notable but temporary improvements in the balance of payments (see Bingham, 1976, pp. 66–70).

The long-term consequences of devaluations have been import price increases, multiplying rapidly in terms of general price advances. During the post-war period as a whole, prices rose faster in Finland than in most European countries. Between 1950 and 1974 the average annual increase in consumer prices was 6·6 per cent, compared with 4·0 per cent in the OECD area as a whole (see Central Statistical Office, 1977, p. 22, and Bingham, 1976, p. 11).

Due to the structural weaknesses and lack of autonomous dynamism in the economy, the state has had to participate to an exceptionally large extent in creating preconditions for more balanced development. Besides the usual investments in infrastructure, export promotion, subsidies to private industry etc. the state has taken part in production directly, according to about one-fifth of the total value added in the industry, which is more than the average (10–15 per cent) in other OECD countries. Besides primary production (mining, energy supply) the state takes part also in key sectors of manufacturing such as petroleum refining, chemical, electrical engineering and heavy metal manufacture, as well as the pulp and paper industry. In a dependent, specialised economy the state has had to intervene directly in order to create preconditions for sectoral diversification of industrial production, and to lessen external industrial and trade dependence. The extension of public enterprises has, however, been more a result of *ad hoc* decisions than of a comprehensive and overall programme of structural changes.

Industrial and Technological Dependence

The fastest growing and dominant industries have been capital intensive, such as the pulp and paper, basic metals and chemicals. Capital intensity, especially in forest based industries, is reinforced by the nature of credit allocation in oligopolistic banking conditions and secured profits as well as by exceptionally generous depreciation allowances, and other features of the tax system.

Capital deepening has been one of the reasons for high fixed capital formation in the Finnish economy. The gross fixed investment ratio has been 25 per cent of GNP in 1950–73, the highest in OECD countries apart from Japan and Norway. At the same time the average growth performance has only been moderately good, which suggests that the allocation of investments has been inefficient. There are several reasons for that. Firstly, the investment pattern in Finland has emphasised construction and service industries instead of more productive machinery and equipment. This feature is a reflection of the cold climate, requiring expensive building techniques, of low population density demanding extensive infrastructural investments *per capita*, and of the importance of the public sector (see Bingham, 1976, pp. 50–9). Secondly sectorally unbalanced growth, a consequence of external dependency, has led to excess investments and unusually large stockholdings with consequent price speculation, which together have caused severe underutilisation of industrial capacity, especially in wood processing.

The investment ratio in the forest industry has been especially high. However, the degree of exhaustion of Finland's forest resources has caused serious restrictions on further expansion. Some 10 per cent of the raw timber used by the industry was at the beginning of the 1970s already being imported, mainly from the Soviet Union. In addition, Finnish forestry firms have expanded during the 1960s and 1970s by purchasing and setting up wood-processing plants all over Europe, but also in North and South America, Africa and the Middle East.

Finnish industrial production has focussed on a few sectors with relatively low degrees of processing though high capital intensity. By contrast, in core economies growth has been based on investments in high technology, more labour intensive industries, such as electrical engineering, machinery and appliances and chemicals, turning out products of high added value. Moreover, despite high capital intensity, the productivity of industry in Finland has been low by international standards and its competitiveness had to be maintained by frequent alterations in the foreign exchange rate and by keeping labour costs down.[10] The oligopolistic market position and high profitability of the export industry have not sufficiently encouraged innovations and changes in the pattern of investments (see Hänninen, 1974, and Komiteanmietintö, 1976).

Finnish manufacturing is characterised by non-science based, already standardised and mature production, such as forestry, textiles, and food industries, as well as heavy engineering (shipbuilding, wood processing machinery, agricultural and forestry machinery, cranes, etc.) where technical development is relatively slow. Consequently in 1973 R. & D. expenditures were only 0·9 per cent of GNP compared, for instance, with respective figures in Sweden 1·6 per cent or Great Britain 2·3 per cent. Hence the most dynamic branches of the economy have been dependent on foreign R. & D. inputs. For instance the patents (especially in electronics, electrical engineering and chemical industries) have been mainly owned by TNCs.

Typically, the initiative for expanding knowledge-intensive industries has come, if not from the state sector, then from abroad in forms of joint ventures, sub-contracting and assembling agreements, or direct investments. The foreign investor offers key equipment, and technical knowhow, while the Finnish counterpart supplies basic facilities and a labour force. External technological and industrial dependence is shown when the Finnish electronics industry assembles imported components, or the expanding engineering industry sub-contracts for Swedish machinery production. It is typical of a less diversified and dependent economy that while the mass-producing and standardised forestry industry is exporting capital, the technically most advanced and dynamic sectors of the economy have to rely on foreign technical inputs and investments.

Since the beginning of the 1960s, there has been a steady rise in direct foreign investment in Finland. Governments have been favourable towards importing foreign capital because of short-term employment and balance of payments considerations. However, most strategic raw material resources (forestry, mining) are protected by special legislation.

Direct foreign capital accounted in 1970 for 7 per cent of total industrial turnover in Finland. The share of multinational capital has been, however, higher in the technically most advanced sectors, such as electronic and electrical engineering, the chemical industry, metal engineering, as well as in the labour intensive textile industry. In those branches foreign-owned companies produce 10–25 per cent of the total value added. Half of foreign capital has come from Sweden (Aintila, 1975). Several Swedish textile, metal and electrical engineering companies have moved some of their standardised and most labour intensive production processes into Finland in order to benefit from lower labour costs there. TNCs, instead of investing in industrial enterprises for export purposes, have been mainly interested in widening their market share in Finland. Indeed, two-thirds of the foreign companies operating in Finland have actually been commercial enterprises: they have been responsible for 20 per cent of total imports into Finland.

Structural Changes

Post-war development in Finland has been characterised by relatively strong economic growth and rapid structural change. During the period 1950–74 the average annual growth rate of GNP was 5·2 per cent while the corresponding figure for the OECD as a whole was 4·4 per cent. Although growth has been relatively high it has also been very unstable, fluctuating sharply year after year. In the period 1950–73 no other country has experienced as severe absolute fluctuations as Finland. The average amplitude of the business cycle has been 8·0 per cent (Bingham, 1976, p. 11 and pp. 31–8). For example, whereas in 1974 Finland achieved one of the fastest growth rates of national income among OECD countries, the years 1975–7 as a whole have witnessed zero growth.[12]

In terms of GNP *per capita* (US $5,100 in 1975) Finland ranks today rather near the OECD average, above, for example, the UK, Italy and Japan, but below the European core countries. Moreover, in terms of certain living standard indicators, such as infant mortality, access to higher education, number of telephones or television sets *per capita*, Finland ranks higher than income figures suggest. On the other hand, by using some other living standard indicators such as dwellings with water piped inside, doctors per inhabitants or expectation of life at birth Finland has one of the lowest figures in the OECD area (see Tables 49 and 50).

The shift away from agriculture and forestry towards industrial and service activities has in post-war years been exceptionally intensive (see Table 48). The distribution of GNP and employment over the three major sectors – agriculture, industry and services – is now not far from the European average. However, the share of agriculture in the total labour force in Finland is still higher than the average in OECD countries, being nearer to the respective figures in the European periphery than the European core countries (Table 49).

Furthermore, structural change has been even more intensive during the 1970s (see Table 48). Growth has especially taken place in the tertiary sector (transport and communication, commerce, finance, public administration and other services), which now employ half of the country's total labour force. This indicates on the one hand that the level of public services and general welfare have improved. On the other hand industrialisation has not been intensive and diversified enough to be able to absorb the surplus labour released from agricultural smallholdings. Capital intensive and export oriented industrialisation has not had enough effect on general economic development, so part of the growth of the tertiary sector has been excessive. Severe structural unemployment and finally emigration are further consequences.

Table 48

The employment structure in Finland in 1870–1975 (%)

	1870	1910	1940	1950	1960	1970	1975
Primary (Agriculture, forestry, fishing)	85·0	70·0	60·0	45·8	35·5	20·2	14·0
Secondary (Manufacturing, mining, construction)	6·0	12·0	22·0	29·3	31·8	35·8	36·0
Tertiary (Commerce, transport, banking, services)	9·0	18·0	18·0	24·9	32·7	44·0	50·0
TOTAL	100	100	100	100	100	100	100

The Finnish economy has experienced also spatial concentration of economic activities in the post-war years. Industrialisation has taken place mainly in the southernmost parts of the country, located nearer the export markets. Of the total value added in the industry in 1975 over 70 per cent was produced in the south and south-west regions – which constitute less than one-fifth of the whole land area and 58 per cent of the total population. Consequently, there are wide regional variations in the employment structure. In the four developed southern provinces the proportion of the labour force engaged in primary production is less than 10 per cent and in industry about 40 per cent – quite similar to the corresponding figures of developed core Europe. As opposed to this, the northern and central parts of Finland, i.e. the 'development areas', have remained largely dependent upon traditional, mostly smallholder agriculture which has absorbed almost one-third of the total labour force. Small farms have been unable to offer year-round work. The mechanisation of agriculture as well as forestry – which provided subsidiary earnings for small farmers – has further increased the relative excess labour. Moreover, the structure of secondary industry there has been quite unfavourable, the predominant branches showing slow growth rates and high capital intensity (forestry, mining and energy) (see Kiljunen, 1977, pp. 27–51).

Except for state companies, leading Finnish firms have not been interested in investing in these areas. Consequently, during the 1970s the unemployment rate in the northernmost Lappi province was seven to eight times higher than in the capital province of Uusimaa. The average income level in southern Finland is 40 per cent higher than in the other parts of the country.

Since foreign trade liberalisation, structural unemployment has worsened, especially in the areas where primary activities dominate. Labour intensive, small-scale home market industry has to compete against foreign imports. There has been a surplus of unskilled labour in the Finnish labour market during most of the post-war period. At the same time, especially during the cyclical upswings in the 1970s, there has been a shortage of skilled workers in some industries in southern Finland. Hence, besides the structural imbalances in the labour supply, the unemployment rate has been fluctuating sharply. During the present world recession the annual average has reached 8 per cent of the labour force.

The structural change of the economy, the rapid growth of industry and services in southern Finland, the high level of unemployment in the North and East and generally substantial disparities in regional welfare have generated both 'push' and 'pull' effects for large-scale internal migration and finally emigration. Inter-regional labour movement towards the industrialised and urbanised southern Finland has increased almost continuously every year since the beginning of the 1950s. As a consequence the proportion of urban population in the developed south is twice as high as in the development regions. In Uusimaa province population growth was over 20 per cent during the 1960s, causing severe congestion problems especially in the Helsinki area, with social and environmental effects. On the other hand, each province in Central and Northern Finland has suffered not only from labour outflow, but also from net fall in population during the 1960s and 1970s (Kiljunen, 1977, pp. 43–7).

Internal movement of people in Finland has been coupled with sizeable emigration, which, during the 1960s, increased substantially. Total emigration since the Second World War has amounted to about 455,000 or nearly 10 per cent of the present population. Allowing for return migration the net emigration since the War has been approximately 300,000 (Wiman, 1975, pp. 72–94 and Kiljunen 1977, pp. 47–50).

90 per cent of Finnish emigrants have gone to Sweden. Since the abolition of passport control inside Scandinavia in the mid 1950s there have not been any institutional barriers. The demand for certain types of manpower in Sweden, differences in standards of living and wage differentials (real incomes are 20–30 per cent higher in Sweden) as well as the cultural similarity of the two countries have been factors paving the way for emigration.

Typically, the migration took place in two stages. At the first migrants move into the more prosperous part of Finland. There, however, on the one hand the insecure employment prospects and the housing shortage, and on the other hand the attractions of work in Sweden lead finally to a decision to emigrate. In a free labour market the movement of labour is cyclically very sensitive. The outflow of labour from Finland increases when a cyclical upswing occurs in Sweden. During the peak years of the 1960s emigration reached almost 40,000 people annually, which resulted in the overall population decreasing in Finland. Since then the emigration rate has slowed down, and there was actually a net gain from migration in 1972–4, but since then, once again, emigration has begun to rise.

Two-thirds of emigrants are of working age. They tend to be rather young – 70 per cent between 15 and 35 years of age. They are rather well educated, and are often skilled workers. At the end of the 1960s about 40 per cent of the Finns emigrating to Sweden were industrial workers. Only 15 per cent were from primary production. This is partly explained by the two stage migration flows. Regional impacts of emigration are uneven, socially and structurally. Moreover, Finns living abroad contribute very little to the direct inflow of foreign exchange in the form of remittances since, unlike many other emigrant groups, they take their families with them. In other words, Finland has become an exporter of human capital, which is needed for its own economic development and long-term growth prospects.

To summarise, the essence of Finnish under- or undevelopment is not definable in terms of economic stagnation, social backwardness, archaic technology or lack of industrialisation. On the contrary, the system has embodied structural dynamism. Obvious economic and social developments have taken place in the country in terms of certain quantitative variables, such as some welfare indicators, economic growth or structural diversification. However, by using only quantita-

L

tive methods of measurement we ignore the qualitative aspects of dependent development.

The rapid growth has been unstable and vulnerable. The reasonably high level of welfare is quite unevenly distributed socially and regionally. The structural diversification in terms of industrialisation has been one-sided including high sectoral concentration with little multiplier effect, a low level of processing and productivity and lack of R. & D. efforts. The dependent, one-sided industrialisation has ultimately caused balance of payments problems, increasing foreign indebtedness, high inflation rate and severe imbalances in the labour markets, as well as extensive growth of the tertiary sector.

The position in the international division of labour of semiperipheral Finland has on the one hand paved the way for industrialisation and economic growth, and on the other, caused severe structural imbalances and distortions in the country's economic development.

Notes

1 From the beginning of the seventeenth century up to the mid-nineteenth century tar was the main export product of Finland. It is even estimated that during the seventeenth century Finland was the world's leading producer and exporter of tar. The distilling of tar took place in private domestic production. According to the mercantile trade policy the tar trade was monopolised by few tar companies. In the whole of Finland right to export tar was granted to the Swedish 'Norland-Findland Tar Company' and it defined the prices paid to the producers. As a result of the trade concentration the world market price of tar was steady and high, but the profits accrued to the tar company and the capital of the realm rather than to the Finnish peasant producers. Hence, despite the extent of the trade it was never able to grow beyond the limits of small domestic production, and to act as an impetus for local capital accumulation and large-scale industrial production. (See Alho, 1949, p. 218 and Jutikkala, 1968, pp. 104–5.)

2 During the twenty years between the wars the food self-sufficiency of Finland increased from 50 per cent up to 90 per cent, reducing considerably the share of foodstuffs in imports.

3 In Europe, only in Rumania, Bulgaria and Yugoslavia was the proportion of agricultural population higher than in Finland; in the other Scandinavian countries the corresponding figures were in Sweden 31 per cent, Denmark 30 per cent, Norway 27 per cent (Jutikkala, 1968, p. 218).

4 The war reparations were a substantial stimulus to the Finnish metal and engineering industry and its output doubled. On average about 10 per cent of the State expenditures during 1945–52 were used for the reparations, which constituted on average, 3·7 per cent of GNP. (Oksanen-Pihkala, 1975, pp. 25–7.)

5 Finland's share of total European exports of wood products in 1972 was in sawn timber 23 per cent, plywood 46 per cent, pulp 27 per cent, paperboard 32 per cent, and newsprint 48 per cent (Tandem, 1977, p. 197).

6 Before the trade liberalisation in 1957 the number of enterprises employing less than 10 people was 3,300 i.e. 45 per cent of all industrial enterprises,

but in 1969 respective figures were 2,150 and 28 per cent (Komitean-mietintö, 1972).

7   The largest 30 corporations, while employing 46 per cent of the industrial labour force, account for 60 per cent of total industrial investments and 72 per cent of manufactured exports. The largest 100 corporations account for 82 per cent of investments and 93 per 'cent of manufactured exports (Komiteanmietintö, 1972, pp. 191–2 and 210–11).

8   The balance in the current account in 1977 was mainly the result of the deep recession sharply stopping the imports of investment and inter-mediate goods for the industry.

9   This figure goes over 50 per cent when account is taken of the fact that part of domestic intermediate products have also been produced from foreign raw materials. Since Finnish forest and goods industries have predomin-antly been self-sufficient as far as raw materials are concerned, other sectors of industry have been even more dependent on foreign inputs. The chemical, textile and engineering industries have been importing 75–95 per cent of their needs of raw materials and intermediates (see Komitean-mietintö, 1976, pp. 33 and 46–9, and Kosonen, 1976, pp. 80–82).

10 The labour costs per working hour are for instance in other Scandinavian countries 50–60 per cent higher than in Finland (Komiteanmietintö, 1976, p. 39).

11 The vulnerability of the Finnish economy to international cyclical swings, is not only a result of fluctuations in the export demand. The high import content of investment and industrial production combined with the relatively low level of processing has also meant that the changes in world raw material prices affect the competitiveness of the Finnish industry more directly than elsewhere in Western Europe.

References

Aintila, Heikki (1975), *Ulkomaisessa omistuksessa oleva yritystoiminta Suomessa*, Economic Planning Centre, Helsinki.

Alho, K. O. (1949), *The Rise and Development of Modern Finnish Industry from 1860–1914*, Bank of Finland, Institute for Economic Research Publications, Series B:11, Helsinki.

Bingham, T. R. G. (1976), *Structural Change in the Post-War Finnish Economy*, A Thesis for the Degree of D. Phil. University of Oxford.

Central Statistical Office of Finland (1977), *Living Conditions 1950–1975, Statistical information on the quality of life in Finland and factors influencing it*, Helsinki.

Central Statistical Office of Finland (1976), *Statistical Yearbook of Finland, 1975*, Helsinki.

Dahmen, Erik (1966), *Suomen taloudellinen kehitys ja talouspolitiikka*, Bank of Finland, Institute for Economic Research Publications, Series C: 4, Helsinki.

Hakovirta, Harto-Patokallio, Pasi (1975), 'East-West Economic Cooperation, Is there a Finnish Model?', *Cooperation and Conflict*, 10.

Hemmilä, Pekka-Koponen, Juha (1975), *Suomen ja Neuvostoliiton välisen kaupan vaihtelut* Työväen Taloudellinen Tutkimuslaitos, Tutkimuksia n:o 2, Helsinki.

Hänninen, Sakari (1974), *Suomen tuotantorakenteen erittelyä*, Research Reports, Institute of Political Science, University of Helsinki, Series C, Helsinki.

Jutikkala, Eino (toim) (1967), *Itsenäisen Suomen Taloushistoriaa, 1919–1950*, WSOY, Porvoo.

Jutikkala, Eino (toim) (1968), *Suomen talous-ja sosiaalihistorian kehityslinjoja*, WSOY, Porvoo.

Kiljunen, Kimmo (1977), *Regional Problems and Policy, a Case study of Finland*, M.Phil. Dissertation, Sussex University.

Komiteanmietintö (1972) A6, *Keskittymiskomitean mietintö*, Helsinki.

Komiteanmietintö (1976) 62, *Viennin kilpailukykytoimikunnan mietintö*, Helsinki.

Kosonen, Pekka (1976), *Valuuttakurssimekanismi ja maailmanmarkkinat*, Tandem, tutkimusraportti n:o 10, Helsinki.

Linnamo, Jussi (1967), *Finland a growing economy*, Reference Publications 1, Ministry for Foreign Affairs, Helsinki.

Maude, George (1976), *The Finnish Dilemma, Neutrality in the Shadow of Power*, OUP, London.

OECD (1977), Economic Surveys, *Finland*, Paris, January 1977.

Oksanen, Heikki-Pihkala, Erkki (1975), *Finland's Foreign Trade, 1917–1949*, Bank of Finland Publications, Studies on Economic Growth VI, Helsinki.

Pihkala, Erkki (1969), *Finland's Foreign Trade, 1860–1917*, Bank of Finland Publications, Studies on Economic Growth, II, Helsinki.

Tandem (1977), *Demokratian rajat ja rakenteet*, WSOY, Juva 1977.

Tuomioja, Erkki (1971), *Suomi ja EEC*, Jyväskylä.

Väyrynen, Raimo (1974), 'The position of small powers in the West European network of economic relations', *European Journal of Political Research* 2/1974.

Wiman, Ronald (1975), *The Mechanism of International Labour Migration, A study of the causes of Finnish Emigration to Sweden*, The Research Institute of the Finnish Economy, Series B.9, Helsinki.

Wuorinen, John H. (1965), *A History of Finland*, Columbia University Press, New York.

STATISTICAL APPENDIX

Marja-Liisa Kiljunen

STATISTICS ON TOURISM

When the question is about movements of human beings, a problem arises over the *definition*: deciding in what capacity the person is travelling, and at what point of the person's travel his/her movement should be registered, for statistical purposes, in such a way that the statistics are internationally comparable. There are, of course, numerous purposes for people's visits to a country other than their usual place of residence – some of these purposes can be defined as 'touristic'. Motives for visits vary and often a person entering a country does not know himself exactly the purpose of his visit or for how long he is going to stay in the country. For instance, there is a group of travellers ('working holiday-makers' especially in the UK), who enter a country as tourists, but after some time decide to stay and look for a job.

In the statistical sources used, the definition made by the UN Conference on International Travel and Tourism in 1963 is applied. Any person visiting a country (other than that in which he has his normal residence), for any reason except following an occupation remunerated from within the country visited, is defined as 'visitor'. 'Visitor' covers, therefore, (1) 'tourists', i.e. temporary visitors staying at least twenty-four hours or overnight in the country visited and the purpose of whose journey can be classified under one of the following headings: (a) leisure (recreation, holiday, health, study, religion, and sport); (b) business, family, mission, meeting; (2) 'excursionists', i.e. temporary visitors staying less than twenty-four hours in the country visited (including travellers on cruises).

This definition excludes travellers who, in the legal sense, do not enter the country (e.g. travellers who do not leave an airport's transit area) or passengers in transit, though the transit journey takes more than twenty-four hours.

The definition does not contain any limit to the length of stay of a 'tourist'. Some individual governments define as tourists only those who stay in the country more than twenty-four hours but less than ninety days (Panama, Peru) or twelve months (United Kingdom). The definition of the UN Tourism Conference has been used by most countries in their travel statistics, though differences in definition and coverage exist between individual countries. The definitions used are not always made clear in the travel statistics, and there are ingoing and outgoing movements of people whose statistical category is unclear (e.g. the increasing number of students who stay for purposes of study in another country for a long period of time).

Prior to the definition of 'visitor' and its two categories, an earlier definition of 'tourist' was used. This earlier definition, however, is less precise and makes no difference between 'tourist' and 'excursionist'. Therefore, tourism statistics before and after 1963 are not strictly comparable.

Not only the definition of a tourist but also methods of counting the tourists defined in this way cause problems in practice. Though the definition is broadly uniform, the methods of enumeration vary considerably. In some countries, the number of tourist arrivals (visits) is counted; in others, departures or nights (or tourist stays as in France). Due to the increasing freedom of movement between various European countries (Scandinavia, Benelux, etc.), abolition of visas and passport controls, and development of various supplementary means of accommodation (tent and camping sites, youth hostels, etc.), the accurate counting of tourists either at frontiers (which would cover most arrivals into the country) or at the place of accommodation has become difficult. So has the checking of nationality. The origin of tourists in most countries of arrival is defined by nationality, whereas in some countries, by country of usual residence (Ireland, Finland, Turkey, US, Canada).

In most countries, tourists are recorded at frontiers, but the methods employed are not always known. In many countries, annual sample surveys of foreign visitors at frontiers and/or accommodation are carried out.

Where tourist statistics are based on arrivals at their accommodation, there is often serious non-coverage and multiple registration; while visiting a country, tourists often stay in more than one place of accommodation. Sometimes various types of accommodation, e.g. accommodation in private families, are entirely excluded. (For example, in Norway, arrivals and nights are recorded in classified hotels only, which represent about 25 per cent of the total hotel capacity in the country; in Italy, at all registered tourist accommodation; in Portugal, in hotel accommodation, holiday centres, youth hostels and camping sites; in Spain, in hotels, boarding houses and camping sites, etc.)

The accuracy of statistical methods employed in tourism and travel statistics has improved with the increasing needs of the tourist industry, which has greatly expanded during the past ten years. Despite the differences in definitions, units of measurement and methods employed, the statistics in most cases seem to be sufficiently precise to facilitate their international comparability and to provide an order of magnitude for each country. *International Travel Statistics*, published annually by the World Tourism Organisation, and *Tourism Policy and International Tourism in OECD Member Countries*, published by the OECD Tourism Committee, are the most complete source of information of tourist statistics available. (For the statistics on tourism, see tables 51 and 52).

MIGRATION STATISTICS

Similar differences of definition and methods of calculation are also found in data on migrant workers. The accurate total number of migrant workers (and their families) in Europe is not known. The precise number depends on the definition 'migrant' used, the methods of counting the numbers, and the estimates of the number of illegal migrations and what is legal but 'hidden'. Methods of compiling data vary from country to country and from source to source. The usual practice seems to be either counting the number of frontier arrivals or the work or residence permits issued. The number of illegal migrant workers (estimated at 0·5–0·6 million) is not included in the official statistics.

The question of migration is a problem of larger magnitude than the official statistics suggest, as apart from illegal migrants, one should also allow for the workers' families who, in increasing numbers, arrive in the host countries, legally or illegally, and for the children born in the country.

Very often, several departments of government offices keep statistics on migration on a dissimilar basis (in the Netherlands, three different departments issue slightly different statistics. In the UK, the information comes basically from three sources: (1) The Department of Employment in the Ministry of Labour; (2) Office of Population Censuses and Surveys; (3) Home Office. In Switzerland, foreign workers are divided into four categories ('established', annual, seasonal and frontier workers), and it has not always been made clear which categories are counted in the total number of foreign workers.

Complete, compiled statistics on annual flows and stocks of migrant workers are needed to facilitate research on the impact of migration, both in the exporting and host countries. The existing statistics based on information given either by members of the OECD (published in the SOPEMI *Continuous Reporting System on Migration* annual reports) or the EEC are incomplete and sometimes inconsistent, often without adequate explanation of the methods used, even of the symbols used in the tables. There are also large gaps. New arrivals of Algerian workers are not recorded in France, according to the EEC publication *Foreign Employees in Employment 1975*. Figures by country of origin, e.g. for the UK, are scarce. (The last official figure for the number of foreign workers in the UK is for 1971.) It has not always been made clear whether unemployed foreigners are counted in the total figures or not. Often different estimates for the same year of the number of foreign workers are given in different sources. Very often, analysis has to be based on more or less unreliable basic data.

Those using these statistics should pay careful attention to what has been said about definitions, enumeration and lack of adequate explanation of symbols used in the sources that have been used in compiling these tables. Because of the shortcomings, it is easy to misinterpret the data. (For the statistics on migration, see tables 53, 54 and 55.)

Table 49

Selected countries: structural characteristics (about 1970*)

	Share of labour force in agriculture (%)[†]	% of dwellings with water piped inside[‡]			% of dwellings with electric lighting[‡]		
		Total	Urban	Rural	Total	Urban	Rural
US	4	98	100	91	..	..	..
European core							
Austria	14	88	89	87	..	..	..
Belgium	5	88	..	..	100	..	..
Denmark	11[1]	99	100	96	..	..	..
France	15	91	96	79	99	99	98
Federal Republic of Germany	8	99	..	..	100	..	..
Luxembourg	8	99	..	..	100	..	..
Netherlands	6	90[3]	97	78	98	99	96
Norway	12	98	99	94	..	..	..
Sweden	8[1]	97	99	88	..	..	..
Switzerland	8	96	97	95	..	..	..
European semi-periphery							
Finland	20[1]	72	87	54	96	100	91
Italy	16	86	..	..	99	..	..
UK	3[2]	..	..	..	..	..	..
England and Wales	..	..	..	..	..	..	..
Northern Ireland	..	93	99	84	..	..	..
Scotland	3[4]	94	96	90	..	..	..

Sources: [†] ILO *Yearbook of labour statistics*, 1974.
     [‡] UN *Statistical Yearbook*, 1974.

Notes
  * Data in this table refer to some year since 1960, mostly between 1968–72; for the precise year see the source.
1 Labour force figures relate to persons 15–74 years of age.
2 Inc. Scotland, excl. Northern Ireland.
3 1956.
4 Source: *Scottish Economic Bulletin*, No. 1, 1971.

TABLE 49—*cont.*

Selected countries: structural characteristics (about 1970*)

	Share of labour force in agriculture (%)†	% of dwellings with water piped inside‡			% of dwellings with electric lighting‡		
		Total	Urban	Rural	Total	Urban	Rural
European periphery							
Cyprus	34	77	95	64	43	99	22
Greece	40	65	88	37	88	98	77
Ireland	25	73	96	51	95	100	90
Malta	6	93	..	..	93	..	..
Portugal	30	35	..	..	64	..	..
Spain	25	45	76	24	89	98	84
Turkey	68	36	..	..	41	69	..
Yugoslavia	45	34	63	13	88	98	80
North Africa							
Algeria	50[1]	23	54	6	34	74	12
Morocco	50[2]	..	65	..	76	82	..
Tunisia	41[2]	15	35	2	24	..	..
Other dependent countries							
Brazil	44	27	46	2	48	76	8
Costa Rica	37	81	..	..	69	..	..
Cuba	30	..	..	..	..	..	..
Iran	42	13	38	1	25	67	4
USSR	26	..	..	..	..	..	..
East Europe							
German Democratic Republic	12	82	..	..	..	..	..
Czechoslovakia	16	78	93	57	100	100	99
Hungary	25	36	65	11	92	97	87
Poland	39	47	75	12	96	100	92
Bulgaria	44	28	55	8	95	98	92
Romania	57	12	33	0·4	49	86	27

Sources: † ILO *Yearbook of labour statistics,* 1974.
‡ UN *Statistical Yearbook,* 1974.

Notes
  * Data refer to some years since 1960, mostly between 1970–73; for the precise year see the source.
  1 Excluding nationals abroad. About 1·2 million females mainly occupied in agriculture not included.
  2 Female unreported family helpers in agriculture not included.

Table 50

Selected countries: demographic and economic characteristics (about 1970*)

	Population (million) 1970 or 1971 — A	Average annual population growth rate 1970–3 (%) — A	Birth rate (per 1000) 1970 — B	Infant mortality rate 1970 — B (urban)	Infant mortality rate 1970 — B (rural)	Expectation of life at birth average male and female — B	Population per physician — A	TV sets per 1,000 inhabitants 1970 — A	GNP¹ Total² (bn US$) 1975 — C	GNP¹ Per capita² ('000 US$) 1975 — C	GNP¹ Per capita growth rate 1965–74 (%) — C
US	203	0·9	18	22	19	71	622	412	1,509	7·1	2·4
European core											
Austria	7	0·6	15	26	26	71	510	192	36	4·7	5·0
Belgium	10	0·4	15	16	} 21	71	591	216	59	6·1	4·9
Denmark³	5	0·6	14	16	} 14	73	624	266	35	6·9	3·4
France	51	0·9	17	} 15		72	..	216	305	5·8	4·8
Federal Republic of Germany	61	0·7	13	24	} 25	71	530	272	409	6·6	3·9
Luxembourg	0·3	1·2	13	25		71	933	208	1	6·1	3·2
Netherlands	13	1·0	18	13	} 12	74	695	233	76	5·6	4·1
Norway	4	0·7	17	13	12	74	623	220	26	6·5	3·4
Sweden	8	0·4	14	} 11		75	645	312	65	7·9	2·8
Switzerland	6	1·3	16	15		73	620	203	52	8·1	2·9
European semi-peripheries											
Finland	5	0·4	14	13		70	799	221	24	5·1	5·2
Italy	54	0·8	17	} 30		72	502	181	164	2·9	4·0
UK	55	0·3	16			71	711	293	218⁴	3·9⁵	2·2
England and Wales	49	0·3	16	19	16	72	787	..			..
Northern Ireland	1·5	0·5	21	21	20	71	725	..	19⁴		..
Scotland	5	0·1	17	17	31	70	622	..		3·7⁵	..

Sources: A = *UN Statistical Yearbook, 1974 and 1975*; B = *UN Demographic Yearbook, 1974*; C = *IBRD World Bank Atlas, 1976*.

Notes

* Data in this table refer to some year since 1968, mostly between 1970–4. For the precise year, see the source.

1 These figures are based on average 1973–5 prices and exchange rates.

2 Preliminary information.

3 Demographic figures exclude Faeroe Islands and Greenland.

4 GDP at factor costs } source: Central Statistical Office *Annual Abstract of Statistics*, 1976 (pounds converted into US dollars).

5 GDP *per capita* }

TABLE 50—cont.   Selected countries: demographic and economic characteristics (about 1970*)

	Population (million) 1970 or 1971 — A	Average annual population growth rate 1970–3 (%) — A	Birth rate (per 1000) 1970 — B	Infant mortality rate 1970 urban — B	Infant mortality rate 1970 rural — B	Expectation of life at birth average male and female — B	Population per physician — A	TV sets per 1,000 inhabitants 1970 — A	GNP[1] Total[2] (bn US $) 1975 — C	GNP[1] Per capita[2] ('000 US$) 1975 — C	GNP[1] Per capita growth rate 1965–74 (%) — C
European periphery											
Cyprus	(0·6)	1·4	(19)	28	28	72	1,195	78	1	1·2	5·1
Greece	9	0·7	17	31		69	525	58	22	2·4	6·5
Ireland	3	0·9	22	20		71	836	152	8	2·4	3·6
Malta	(0·3)	—0·4	16	28		71	988	145	0·4[4]	1·2[4]	8·4
Portugal	9	—0·4	20	58		70	939	40	15	1·6	7·6
Spain	30	1·1	20	21		72	673	124	96	2·7	5·4
Turkey	36	2·5	(36)	113	168	54	2,018	1	35	0·9	4·3
Yugoslavia	21	1·0	18	56		68	864	88	32	1·5[5]	5·4[5]
North Africa											
Algeria	14	3·2	(49)	..	..	(51)	8,192	7	12	0·8	4·5
Morocco	15	2·4[3]	(46)	..	..	(51)	13,345	11	8	0·5	2·8
Tunisia	(5)	2·4	(20)	98	46	(52)	5,219	10	4	0·8	5·4
Other dependent countries											
Brazil	92	2·8	(38)	..		59	2,025		108	1·0	6·3
Costa Rica	2	2·7	31	62		63	1,413	57	2	0·9	3·7
Cuba	9	1·7	25	39		(67)	1,153	71	7	0·8[5]	—0·6[5]
Iran	26	3·0	(45)	..		(50)	3,039	19	49	1·4	7·7

Sources: A = UN *Statistical Yearbook*, 1974 and 1975; B = UN *Demographic Yearbook*, 1974; C = IBRD *World Bank Atlas*, 1976.

Notes

* Data in this table refer to some year since 1962, mostly between 1970–5; for the precise year see the source. Estimates in brackets.
1 These figures are based on average 1973–5 prices and exchange rates.
2 Preliminary information.
3 1965–74, source: IBRD *World Bank Atlas*, 1976.
4 1974.
5 Estimates by IBRD. For the method of estimation, see the source.

TABLE 50—cont.

Selected countries: demographic and economic characteristics (about 1970*)

	Population (million) 1970 or 1971 A	Average annual population growth rate 1970–3 (%) A	Birth rate (per 1000) 1970 B	Infant mortality rate 1970 urban B	Infant mortality rate 1970 rural B	Expectation of life at birth average male and female B	Population per physician A	TV sets per 1,000 inhabitants 1970 A	GNP Total² (bn US$) 1975 C	GNP Per capita² ('000 US$) 1975 C	Per capita growth rate 1965–74 (%) C
USSR	242	1·0	17	17	17	69	363	143	666	2·6	3·4
East Europe											
German Democratic Republic	17	−0·2	14	18	19	72	557	..	71	4·2	3·0
Czechoslovakia	14	0·5	16	{ 22 }		70	431	:	55	3·7	2·5
Hungary	10	0·3	15	36	36	69	471	:	26	2·3	2·9
Poland	33	0·9	17	31	35	70	607	:	99	2·9	4·5
Bulgaria	8[3]	0·5	16	23	34	66	489	:	18	2·0	3·5
Romania	20	0·9	21	46	51	69	805	..	28	1·3	8·0

Sources: *A = UN Statistical Yearbook, 1974 and 1975; B = UN Demographic Yearbook, 1974; C = IBRD World Bank Atlas, 1976.*

Notes

* Data in column 'Expectation of life at birth' refer to some year since 1965, mostly between 1970–4. For the precise year, see the source.

1 Estimations by IBRD. For method of estimation, see the source.

2 Preliminary information.

3 1965.

Arrivals of foreign tourists to Southern Periphery, 1965, 1970, 1973, 1975
(thousands)

Country of arrival	Year	Belgium/ Luxemb'g	FRG	France	Netherlands	Sweden	Austria	Denm'k	Finland	Italy	Norway	Switz.	UK	Total countries listed	US	All
Greece[1]	1965	16	100	80	18	40	23	24	5	44	5	22	85	462	173	847
	1970	21	143	116	23	18	30	20	9	76	4	28	167	655	305	1,408
	1973	30	321	177	67	112	70	68	39	125	22	68	336	1,435	616	2,865
	1975	38	234	128	40	57	82	50	45	138	20	67	313	1,212	459	2,840
Malta[2]	1965	—	1	1	—	—	—	—	:	4	—	—	32	38	5	48
	1970	—	4	2	1	5	—	1	:	14	1	1	119	146	12	171
	1973	2	10	7	1	12	2	1	:	26	1	1	118	182	9	211
	1975	2	18	7	3	7	2	2	2	22	1	1	225	293	9	335
Portugal[3]	1965	20	59	178	21	10	5	5	:	49	3	16	220	586	185	1,510
	1970	33	133	204	42	27	11	17	:	79	9	33	406	994	355	3,343
	1973	48	210	249	54	43	16	27	10	80	13	50	512	1,312	346	4,080
	1975	28	144	119	40	27	8	19	11	70	12	30	285	793	71	1,966
Spain[4]	1965	288	1,047	6,441	288	206	46	135	:	311	40	175	1,360	10,337	687	13,072
	1970	616	2,075	8,826	875	439	91	330	76	506	101	423	2,618	16,976	1,030	24,105
	1973	1,102	3,496	12,086	1,290	570	126	434	126	517	170	650	3,895	24,462	1,447	34,558
	1975	1,062	4,226	9,354	1,315	573	144	455	179	413	184	618	3,419	21,942	951	30,123
Turkey[5]	1965	5	50	26	4	5	15	3	1	13	1	7	28	163	78	362
	1970	8	69	48	8	5	13	3	:	24	1	16	32	227	53	446
	1973	11	172	93	22	23	17	17	10	83	4	16	100	561	183	1,342
	1975	10	206	113	16	5	24	7	2	85	1	14	99	582	79	1,541
Yugoslavia[6]	1965	57	561	213	105	47	360	30	7	302	9	59	209	1,959	87	2,658
	1970	93	1,216	315	207	63	558	51	15	787	15	120	263	3,697	206	4,748
	1973	117	1,736	400	323	58	618	55	21	872	23	167	361	4,751	283	6,150
	1975	105	1,686	391	309	62	568	44	27	720	25	158	257	4,352	223	5,835
TOTAL OF ABOVE	1965	386	1,818	6,939	436	311	449	199	13	723	58	279	1,934	13,545	1,215	18,497
	1970	771	3,640	9,511	1,156	557	703	421	94	1,486	130	621	3,605	22,695	1,961	34,221
	1973	1,310	5,945	13,012	1,757	818	849	595	207	1,703	233	952	5,322	32,703	2,884	49,206
	1975	1,246	6,514	10,112	1,723	731	828	577	266	1,448	243	888	4,598	29,174	1,792	42,640

Sources: *Tourism Policy and International Tourism in OECD Member Countries*, 1967, 1972, 1975, 1976, OECD, Paris. UN, *Statistical Yearbook* 1967 and 1972. World Tourism Organisation. *World Travel Statistics* 1974 and 1975.

1 Greece: in addition, the foreign shore excursionists numbered as follows: 1965: 129,178; 1970: 201,754; 1973: 331,133; 1975: 332,864;
2 Malta: in addition, 64,990 cruise passengers in 1970, 57,489 in 1973 and 49,219 in 1975.
3 Portugal: the figures include excursionists and cruise passengers: in 1970 there were 1,756,487 and in 1975 1,046,200. Tourism declined in 1975 because of the 1974 revolution. In 1973, foreign visitor arrivals included 1,393,600 excursionists and cruise passengers.
4 Spain: the figures include excursionists 1,013,035 in 1965, 1,108,641 in 1970, 13,650,325 in 1973 and 10,322,478 in 1975; and Spanish residents abroad numbering 1,448,252 in 1970 and 1,720,644 in 1975.
5 Turkey: in addition, 171,103 excursionists in 1965, and 218,332 in 1970. Their number 534,674 in 1973 and 637,400 in 1975 are included in the respective figures.
6 Yugoslavia: figures represent arrivals at all types of tourist accommodation. The total number of foreign visitor arrivals at frontiers was 6,232,251 (including 3·6 million excursionists) in 1965, 29,392,556 (including 21·4 million excursionists) in 1970, 23,800,000 (including 14·0 million excursionists) in 1973 and 24,149,065 (including 15 million excursionists) in 1975.

Table 52

Receipts from tourism compared with exports of merchandise in core and
periphery, 1960, 1965, 1970, 1973, 1974
(US $ millions)

Country	Year	Exports of merchandise*	Gross receipts from tourism	Net receipts from tourism	†As percentage of*
US	1960	19,488	875	−857	4
	1965	26,242	1,380	−1,058	5
	1970	42,465	2,331	−1,649	5
	1973	71,264	3,411	−2,113	5
	1974	98,217	4,034	−1,950	4
Austria	1960	1,161	232	171	20
	1965	1,579	561	120	36
	1970	2,850	999	676	35
	1973	5,363	2,253	1,557	42
	1974	7,301	2,303	1,415	32
Belgium– Luxembourg	1960[1]	164	6	−1	4
	1965	5,294	200	−82	4
	1970	9,700	348	−144	4
	1973	18,783	646	−428	3
	1974	24,324	717	−462	3
Denmark	1960	1,488	107	33	7
	1965	2,302	190	25	8
	1970	3,317	314	41	9
	1973	6,169	578	79	9
	1974	7,701	642	118	8
France	1960	4,962	511	234	10
	1965	8,565	904	−28	11
	1970	17,810	1,318	210	7
	1973	35,598	2,476	287	7
	1974	45,108	2,666	283	6
FRG	1960	11,462	479	−159	4
	1965	17,929	697	−637	4
	1970	34,076	1,326	−1,469	4
	1973	67,130	2,201	−4,290	3
	1974	90,690	2,323	−4,711	3
Netherlands	1960	4,003	132	5	3
	1965	6,096	276	−33	5
	1970	10,927	429	−177	4
	1973	22,049	970	−218	4
	1974	30,777	1,025	−329	3
Norway	1960[2]	6,334	367	−23	6
	1965[2]	10,379	601	41	6
	1970	2,480	158	−86	6
	1973	4,722	246	−162	5
	1974	6,310	272	−174	4
Sweden	1960	2,573	68	−20	3
	1965	3,963	94	−113	2
	1970	6,748	144	−338	2
	1973	11,445	217	−488	2
	1974	15,790	283	−504	2
Switzerland	1960	2,025	363	217	18
	1965	3,102	633	265	18
	1970	5,386	905	478	17
	1973	9,890	1,674	833	17
	1974	12,262	1,793	850	15

TABLE 52—*cont.*

Country	Year	Exports of merchandise*	Gross receipts from tourism	Net receipts from tourism	†As percentage of*
Finland	1960	990	17	−23	2
	1965	1,420	41	−34	3
	1970	2,294	129	34	6
	1973	3,804	306	91	8
	1974	5,493	315	87	6
Italy	1960	3,572	643	548	18
	1965	7,104	1,288	1,061	18
	1970	13,117	1,639	913	12
	1973	22,002	2,712	1,651	12
	1974	29,813	2,668	1,778	9
UK	1960	10,511	473	−48	5
	1965	13,446	540	−272	4
	1970	19,099	1,037	120	5
	1973	29,025	1,670	−2	6
	1974	37,434	1,948	354	5
Cyprus	1960[3]	17	2	−1	12
	1965	66	6	−1	9
	1970	102	20	8	20
	1973	163	68	45	42
	1974	143	38	10	27
Greece	1960	209	49	31	23
	1965	331	108	66	33
	1970	612	194	139	32
	1973	1,230	515	402	42
	1974	1,774	437	307	25
Ireland	1960	404	111	69	27
	1965	592	190	111	32
	1970	1,092	178	82	16
	1973	2,092	209	61	10
	1974	2,516	239	69	9
Malta	1960[4]	3	1	—	33
	1965	20	5	2	25
	1970	34	24	19	71
	1973	110	44	36	40
	1974	155	58	49	37
Portugal	1960	419	24	11	6
	1965	168	16	16	10
	1970	956	240	142	25
	1973	1,842	550	319	30
	1974	2,288	513	259	22
Spain	1960	746	297	247	40
	1965	1,019	1,105	1,027	108
	1970	2,483	1,681	1,543	68
	1973	5,304	3,227	2,843	61
	1974	7,209	3,209	2,797	45
Turkey	1960	336	6	−2	2
	1965	479	14	−10	3
	1970	588	51	4	9
	1973	1,320	172	79	13
	1974	1,532	194	41	13

TABLE 52—*cont.*

Country	Year	Exports of merchandise*	Gross receipts from tourism	Net receipts from tourism	†As percentage of*
Yugoslavia	1960	575	14	6	2
	1965	1,118	81	63	7
	1970	1,679	276	144	16
	1973	2,853	631	380	22
	1974	4,064	748	688	18
Algeria	1960	..	..	..	..
	1965	..	..	..	..
	1970	1,013	10	−15	1
	1973	1,832	13	−35	1
	1974	3,826	19	−39	0·5
Morocco	1960[5]	1,934	134	14	7
	1965[5]	2,207	332	257	15
	1970	487	135	74	28
	1973	913	246	154	27
	1974	1,692	237	146	14
Tunisia	1960[6]	54	2	6	4
	1965	120	19	6	16
	1970	189	65	42	34
	1973	416	185	144	44
	1974	761	190	143	25

Source: IMF, *Balance of Payments Yearbook*, various volumes.
Notes
1   In billions of Belgian francs.
2   In millions of Norwegian kronor.
3   In millions of Cyprus pounds.
4   In millions of Maltese pounds.
5   In millions of dirhams.
6   In millions of Tunisian dinars.

Table 53

Receipts from migration as percentage of exports of merchandise in peripheral countries, 1970, 1973, 1974

Country	Year	Emigrant workers' earnings and remittances	Percentage of exports of merchandise
Finland	1970	34	1
	1973	66	2
	1974	..	..
Italy	1970	1,017	8
	1973	1,537	7
	1974	1,355	5
Greece	1970	333	54
	1973	715	58
	1974	624	35
Ireland	1970	57	5
	1973	79	4
	1974	87	3
Portugal[1]	1970	525	55
	1973	1,140	62
	1974	1,145	50
Spain	1970	469	20
	1973	974	18
	1974	912	13
Turkey	1970	273	46
	1973	1,191	90
	1974	1,447	94
Yugoslavia	1970	498	30
	1973	1,390	49
	1974	1,718	42
Algeria	1970	234	23
	1973	371	20
	1974	389	10
Morocco	1970	63	13
	1973	250	27
	1974	360	21
Tunisia	1970	29	15
	1973	99	24
	1974	118	16

Source: IMF, *Balance of Payments Yearbook*, 1967–74, vol. 27.
Notes
1 Includes gifts, legacies, pensions and workers' remittances from abroad.

Table 54

Arrivals of migrant workers 1965, 1970, 1973, 1975
(hundreds)

Country of employment	Year	Country of origin Greece	Italy	Portugal	Spain	Turkey	Yugoslavia	Total countries listed	Grand total
Federal Republic of Germany	1965	620	2,031	111	651	598	310	4,321	4,883
	1970	640	1,683	201	488	1,236	2,024	6,272	7,139
	1973	96	1,000[1]	295	304	1,180	815	3,690	4,500[2]
	1975	7	250[1]	3	6	20	30	316	620[2]
France[3]	1965	6	180	473	499	4	67	1,229	1,521
	1970	3	58	886	157	88	106	1,298	1,742
	1973	3	48	321	69	186	90	717	1,321
	1975	1	41	50	11	2	2	107	256
Netherlands	1965	7	23	8	99	43	7	187	305
	1970	5	14	10	71	69	..	169	376
	1973	2	9	6	31	44	14	106	220
	1975	..	6	..	..	..	..	..	180[5]
UK[4]	1973	2	22	10	42	..	9	85	392
	1975	3	18	9	27	2	7	66	348

Source: Commission of the European Communities, Directorate-General for Social Affairs, Directorate of Living and Working Conditions. *Foreign Employees in Employment 1975*; Dec. 1976, Tables 24, 25 and 27.

Notes
1 Starting from 1973, data concerning new arrivals of Community workers are no longer available due to the change in the system of recording information. The 1973 and 1975 figures of arrivals of Italian workers are estimated by the Commission of the European Communities.
2 Estimation made by the European Office of Co-ordination.
3 Arrivals of Algerian workers into France not included in the grand total.
4 Arrivals of Irish workers into the UK are not recorded.
5 Estimation made by the European Office of Co-ordination (1970 and 1975 total figures include new arrivals of seasonal workers and intra-Benelux movements).

Table 55

Number of foreign workers in selected countries 1965, 1970, 1973 and 1975 and breakdown by country of origin, 1975
(thousands)

Country of employment	Grand total				Total countries listed 1975	Breakdown by country of origin 1975									
	1965	1970	1973	1975		Greece	Ireland	Italy	Portugal	Spain	Turkey	Yugoslavia	Algeria	Morocco	Tunisia
Belgium[1]	182†	200	211	230	182	6	–	90	4	34	10	3	3	30	2
Federal Republic of Germany[2]	1,164	1,839	2,519	2,039	1,668	196	1	292	68	125	543	416	1	16	10
France[3]	1,158‡	1,600*	1,900*	1,900*	1,691	5	1	230	475	265	25	50	440	130	70
Netherlands[4]	62	120*	121*	113	65	5	–	9	3	–	23	8	..	12	1
Sweden[5]	151	228	230	204	35	1	–	3	–	2	4	23	–	1	–
Switzerland[6]	..	606	596	553	397	–	..	281	4	72	16	24	–	–	–
UK[7]	..	(1,665)	(1,665)	775	539	3	452§	57	4	16	2	4	1	1	–

Sources: Commission of the European Communities *Foreign Employees in Employment 1975* Dec. 1976, Tables 1 and 2.
OECD, Directorate for Social Affairs, Manpower and Education, SOPEMI *Continuous Reporting System on Migration*, Reports 1973, 1976 and 1977.
Wiman, Ronald, *Työvoiman kansainvälisen muuttoliikkeen mekanismi*, Helsinki, 1975, p. 41.

Notes

* Estimates by Commission of the European Communities.
† 1967.
‡ 1968.
§ 1971.

1 Belgium: Not including unemployed except for 1975 total figure, and frontier workers.
2 Federal Republic of Germany: 1975 figure includes frontier workers but not unemployed who amounted to 132,600 in 1975. Due to new statistics starting from 1974, the total figures are not entirely comparable.
3 France: Not including frontier workers.
4 Netherlands: The total figure for 1975 includes the number of valid working permits for workers from non-EEC member countries employed less than five years. SOPEMI 1976 Report gives the following estimates of foreign workers in 1975: Greeks 2,000, Italians 10,000, Moroccans 28,000, Portuguese 5,000, Spaniards 18,000, Tunisians 1,000, Turks 38,000, Yugoslavs 10,000, total 216,000.
5 Sweden: According to SOPEMI 1976 Report estimate there were 103,000 migrant workers from Finland in 1975.
6 Switzerland: Only annual and 'established' workers are included. In addition, there were 117,900 seasonal workers in 1970, 194,000 in 1973 and 86,000 in 1975, and 72,800 frontier workers in 1970, 98,000 in 1973 and 85,020 in 1975.
7 UK: Figures are estimates reproduced from the table for 1974 by SOPEMI 1976 Report. The latest official figure relating to foreign workers in the UK was established for 1971 (1,665,000).

Table 56

Estimates of net migration and its relation to total population size and natural
increase 1950–70
(*thousands*)

	Net migration[1]			Average annual net migration 1950–70 as percentage of 1960 population	Ratio of net migration to natural increase 1950–70 (percentage)
	Total 1950–70	1950–60	1960–70		
US	+6,896	+2,981[2]	+3,915[2]	+0·2	+15
European core					
Austria	−103	−141	+38	−0·1	−17
Belgium	+211	+59	+152	+0·1	+27
Denmark	−32	−52	+20	−0·03	−5
France	+3,258	+1,080	+2,178[2]	+0·4	+55
FRG	+4,780	+2,723	+2,057	+0·4	+81
Luxembourg	+22	+7	+15	+0·4	+105
Netherlands	−50	−142	+92	−0·02	−2
Norway	−10	−14	+4	−0·01	−2
Sweden	+297	+93	+204	+0·2	+41
Switzerland	+630	+296	+334[2]	+0·6	+72
European semi-periphery					
Finland	−214	−73	−141	−0·2	−26
Italy	−1,958	−1,166	−792	−0·2	−23
UK	−181	−58	−123[2]	−0·02	−5
European periphery					
Greece	−651	−3,475	−3,826	−0·3	−29
Ireland	−558	−397	−161	−1·0	−101
Malta	−81	−43	−38	−1·2	−89
Portugal	−1,952	−662	−1,290	−1·1	−90
Spain	−1,377	−826	−551	−0·2	−19
Yugoslavia	−1,282	−582	−700[2]	−0·3	−26
East Europe					
GDR	−2,488	−1,874	−614	−0·7	−215
Bulgaria	−178	−163	−15	−0·1	−13
Czechoslovakia	−174	—	−174	−0·1	−8
Hungary	−161	−164	+3	−0·1	−14
Poland	−526	−220	−306	−0·1	−6
Romania	−250	−138	−112	−0·1	−6

Source: UN, *The Population Debate: Dimensions and Perspectives*, 1, 1974.
Notes
1 Unless otherwise indicated the estimates of net migration have been derived by
  subtracting natural increase from population growth during the specified periods,
  which run from mid-year to mid-year.
2 Adjusted estimates.

Table 57

Selected countries: composition and direction of trade, 1975
(% of total)

	Turkey with FRG		Greece[2] with FRG		Spain with FRG	
Total (US $ million)	Imports 1,004	Exports 305	Imports 844	Exports 480	Imports 1,667	Exports 822
Foodstuffs (SITC 0, 1, 4)	1·4	44·0[1]	2·2	42·1[3]	1·0	30·9[4]
Raw materials (2, 3)	1·5	19·7	2·6	10·1	6·7	9·2
Semi-manufactures (5, 6)	44·8	15·6	31·1	26·0	34·3	30·3
Manufactures (7, 8, 9)	52·3	20·7	64·1	21·8	58·0	29·6
(Capital goods)	(49·8)	(1·0)	(55·0)	(3·1)	(48·5)	(9·6)
(Consumer goods 725, 732·1, 8, 9)	(2·5)	(19·7)	(9·1)	(18·7)	(9·5)	(20·0)
[Clothing and footwear 84, 85]		[19·3]		[18·1]		[11·4]
TOTAL	100·0	100·0	100·0	100·0	100·0	100·0

Main trade partners
(% of total)

Turkey	Imports	Exports
Total (US $ million)	4,640	1,401
FRG	22	22
US	9	11
Italy	8	6
UK	7	5
Total of above	46	44

Greece	Imports	Exports
Total (US $ million)	5,321	2,278
FRG	16	21
Italy	8	8
US	7	5
France	6	7
Total of above	37	41

Spain	Imports	Exports
Total (US $ million)	16,100	7,675
US	16	11
FRG	10	11
France	8	14
UK	5	8
Total of above	39	44

TABLE 57—cont.

Total (US $ million)	Portugal[5] with FRG		Ireland[7] with UK		Finland with FRG	
	Imports	Exports	Imports	Exports	Imports	Exports
	437	198	1,836	1,723	1,079	438
Foodstuffs (SITC 0, 1, 4)	1·7	13·3	8·6	52·8[8]	1·1	2·0
Raw materials (2, 3)	5·2	9·3	16·3	5·3	2·4	15·3
Semi-manufactures (5, 6)	40·9	29·6	36·3	20·7	36·6	70·1[9]
Manufactures (7, 8, 9)	52·2	47·8[8]	38·8	21·2	59·9	12·6
(Capital goods)	(42·3)	(35·7)	(20·0)	(7·2)	(47·5)	(7·9)
(Consumer goods, 725, 732·1; 8, 9)	(9·9)	(12·0)	(18·8)	(14·0)	(12·4)	(4·7)
[Clothing and footwear 84, 85]		[8·2]		[5·9]		
TOTAL	100·0	100·0	100·0	100·0	100·0	100·0

Main trade partners
(% of total)

Total (US $ million)	Portugal			Ireland			Finland	
	Imports	Exports		Imports	Exports		Imports	Exports
	3,840	1,939		3,769	3,179		7,600	5,489
US	12	7	UK	49	54	USSR	17	21
FRG	11	10	FRG	7	8	Sweden	16	18
UK	9	21	US	7	6	FRG	14	8
France	8	7				UK	9	14
Total of above	40	45	Total of above	63	68	Total of above	56	61

Source: OECD, *Statistics of Foreign Trade. Trade by Commodities*, Series B, 1975.

Notes

1 29·4 per cent of exports were fruits and nuts and 10·1 per cent cotton.
2 Excludes free trade area of Piraeus and Salonika.
3 Fruits and vegetables constituted 32·8 per cent of exports.
4 Fruit and nuts were 20·7 per cent of exports.
5 Escudo area.
6 25·6 per cent of exports were telecommunications apparatus and electric power machinery.
7 Excludes Shannon Free Airport.
8 11·6 per cent of exports were cattle, 9·7 per cent meat and 15·1 per cent dairy products.
9 53·0 per cent of exports were pulp, paper and paperboard.

INDEX